Profiting from the Peak

PROFITING from the PEAK

Landscape and Liberty in Colorado Springs

John Harner

UNIVERSITY PRESS OF COLORADO

Louisville

Published by University Press of Colorado
245 Century Circle, Suite 202
Louisville, Colorado 80027

First paperback edition 2022
Manufactured in the United States of America

The University Press of Colorado is a proud member of the Association of University Presses.

The University Press of Colorado is a cooperative publishing enterprise supported, in part, by Adams State University, Colorado State University, Fort Lewis College, Metropolitan State University of Denver, Regis University, University of Alaska Fairbanks, University of Colorado, University of Denver, University of Northern Colorado, University of Wyoming, Utah State University, and Western Colorado University.

∞ This paper meets the requirements of the ANSI/NISO Z39.48-1992 (Permanence of Paper)

ISBN: 978-1-64642-167-1 (hardcover)
ISBN: 978-1-64642-168-8 (ebook)
ISBN: 978-1-64642-307-1 (paperback)
https://doi.org/10.5876/9781646421688

Library of Congress Cataloging-in-Publication Data

Names: Harner, John, author.
Title: Profiting from the Peak : landscape and liberty in Colorado Springs / John Harner.
Description: Louisville : University Press of Colorado, [2021] | Includes bibliographical references and index.
Identifiers: LCCN 2021015308 (print) | LCCN 2021015309 (ebook) | ISBN 9781646421671 (hardcover) | ISBN 9781646423071 (paperback) | ISBN 9781646421688 (ebook)
Subjects: LCSH: Colorado Springs Pioneers Museum—Archival resources. | Local government and environmental policy—Colorado—Colorado Springs. | Colorado Springs (Colo.)—Historical geography. | Colorado Springs (Colo.)—Economic conditions. | Pikes Peak Region (Colo.)—Historical geography. | Pikes Peak Region (Colo.)—Economic conditions.
Classification: LCC F784.C7 H37 2021 (print) | LCC F784.C7 (ebook) | DDC 911/.78856—dc23
LC record available at https://lccn.loc.gov/2021015308
LC ebook record available at https://lccn.loc.gov/2021015309

COVER ILLUSTRATIONS. *Front, clockwise from top:* Sheepherding, looking south from Templeton Gap toward Colorado Springs, 1885, painting by Charles Craig; promotional brochure from the Manitou and Pikes Peak Railway, circa 1900; postcard of the Broadmoor Hotel; Chamber of Commerce promotional materials, circa 1925. *Back:* Postcard of the second Antlers Hotel. All illustrations from Colorado Springs Pioneers Museum.

In memory of Peirce Lewis,
landscape geographer

Contents

Acknowledgments

Many people and institutions have helped make this book possible since I began working on it in 2012. The University of Colorado Colorado Springs (UCCS) granted two sabbaticals that enabled me to begin and then finish data collection for the project. Many UCCS students in classes have sharpened my skills at reading and interpreting the landscape when we use Colorado Springs as a learning laboratory. Several people read drafts of the manuscript and made helpful suggestions and improvements: Leah Davis-Witherow, Lori Nicholson, Lisa Harner, Tom Huber, and Eric Billmeyer. Thanks to Suzanne Schorsch at the Old Colorado City Historical Society and staff members at the Special Collections in the Carnegie Library of the Pikes Peak Library District, who were always helpful and accommodating, especially photo archivist Erinn Barnes. At Colorado College Tutt Library, special collections staff Amy Brooks and Jessy Randall were gracious in their support and assistance. Mary Rupp in the UCCS Kraemer Family Library archives and Mary Ruwell and Ruth Kindreich in the US Air Force Academy archives all assisted with locating valuable materials. Others provided data for geographic analysis that contributed to both this book and *The Story of Us* museum exhibit: Colorado Springs Utilities, particular thanks to Gary Bostrom; Phil Friesen at the City of Colorado Springs; Stephen Fischer at El Paso County; Kevin Knapp from Tierra Plan, LLC; Eric Swab for tracking relict pipelines on the slopes of Pikes Peak; and Jocelyn Olipane at Saint Mary's Tri-Community Parish. Several people generously gave their time for conversations, feedback and insight about the city, including Judith Rice-Jones, Tyler Hill, Brandon DelGrosso, Jeff Besse, Mike Larkin, Raphael Sassower, Brock Kilgore, Andy Stauffer, Kevin Knapp, and the late Dr. Terry Haverluk—rest in peace my friend.

The vast majority of the research for this book took place at the Colorado Springs Pioneers Museum. I was awarded a privileged status that few others receive, with virtually unrestricted access to archival materials, space, and use of the facilities. I would like to thank Director Matt Mayberry for allowing this to happen, for his valuable comments and advice along the way, and for his assistance acquiring digital GIS data from Colorado Springs Utilities. Matt worked to ensure that my research was integrated in many ways with the mission of the museum, and I have been proud to represent that institution over the years. Throughout the research process, museum staff Meg Poole, Brooke Traylor, Laura Fuller, Kelly O'Hara, Haley Davis, Lance James, Diane Stine, Hillary Mannion, Jim Wahl, Casey Kaza, and many volunteers all helped in so many ways—thank you! Archivist Stephanie Prochaska was especially helpful. She has brought me materials, scanned documents, offered advice, shared her space with me, made special accommodations for me, listened to me whine, and has been an invaluable resource for years, and always with a smile and kind manner. Thank you for your professionalism, competence, and compassion, Stephanie!

The central figure in this research, without whom none of this would have been possible, is Leah Davis-Witherow. Leah is a tour de force. As curator of history at the Colorado Springs Pioneers Museum, she is the go-to source for local history of the Pikes Peak Region. She carefully read and edited the entire manuscript, thankfully identifying the many errors I had made and suggesting innumerable improvements (many I unfortunately could not include). More than that, she is the person who approved and enabled my research position at the museum, granted me the freedom to work without constraint, and enthusiastically supported me throughout the entire project. It was Leah who envisioned, and made happen, *The Story of Us* museum exhibit (see the preface) as I was working on this book, and her repeated support and encouragement kept me going through the long days of slogging through archival materials or writing difficult drafts that I thought would never end. Many conversations and joint presentations with her shaped my thinking and organization of these materials. In many ways, Leah's intellectual prowess is everywhere in the pages of this book (except, of course, for the flaws, for which I take full responsibility). As a major figure in the Colorado Springs community, and great friend, it has been a pleasure to work with her. I have nothing but respect.

Thanks to all staff at the University Press of Colorado, particularly Charlotte Steinhardt for even considering the project, given that the first draft was far too long, and for assisting me throughout the publication process. Two anonymous reviewers provided valuable feedback that greatly strengthened the book, so I appreciate their work.

Of course, I would be nowhere without the love and support of Lisa. She is my greatest fan and, somehow, never loses faith in me. Thank you for the many years we have had together. I remain inspired by Cole, the pride of my life, especially with his recent BA in philosophy—congratulations!

Finally, to all the people who work to make Colorado Springs a better place every day, your contributions are not in vain—thank you!

Preface

When a place speaks to you, you should listen. I have now spent twenty-three years listening to Colorado Springs, trying to hear, decipher, interpret, and understand the clues this city yields to anyone willing to pay attention to its landscape, its history, its daily activities, and its people. Colorado Springs speaks to me; it is now time I try to put that voice to paper.

This book seeks to understand the events and socioeconomic conditions that shape contemporary Colorado Springs and the greater Pikes Peak Region, and then convey that to the reader in a coherent story. It is a historical geography, an exploration into the ways that time and space work together to create a unique place. To understand Colorado Springs as a place, I have organized this book into thematic chapters that address major drivers of change, from development of water infrastructure that was vital to urban growth through other fundamental historical topics that shape the urban landscape and the local culture. I use maps, often with time-enabled data to show snapshots of change, along with historic landscape photos, sketches, advertisements, and other materials to document the evolving landscape. Deciphering clues visible in the contemporary built environment also helps us understand much of the story; then archival research in historical repositories fills in the gaps and orients the context under which change occurred.

What makes this place unique? What creates its sense of place, or the very essence of what Colorado Springs is all about? Capital accumulation has been

DOI: 10.5876/9781646421688.c000

a defining theme of the city from its very beginning, but while its founder and early leaders did generate enormous profits from control of regional industrialization, railroads, land sales, and extraction of coal and gold, wealth generation was founded and sustained by exploiting its environmental and cultural capital—the beauty, use, and shaping of its natural and built landscapes. In short, it has long profited from Pikes Peak and built an urban infrastructure to sustain that relationship. That has led me to focus on three dimensions to place throughout this book: the built landscape, the values of the people, and the nature-society relationships.

First, the creation of the built environment that we know today as Colorado Springs has been in the forefront of my mind as I poured through archival materials and as I go about my daily life. I seek to understand how the urban forms and spatial layout of the city came to be and how their intrinsic qualities help define the city today. Why does this city look the way it does? How do previous land uses affect what we see today? In turn, what do these observations tell us about the city's sense of place? The built environment reflects the prevailing social, economic, and cultural values that existed at the time it was constructed, thereby telling us a story about the conditions that motivated past actors and of those shaping the city today. One conclusion I draw from this research is the vital importance of the historic downtown Colorado Springs. The downtown brings people together. Its architecture and public spaces tell the city's story and project its image to the outside world. It is central to its place identity, and recent revitalizations of the downtown core continue to generate creative place making.

The second dimension I explore is the creation of the cultural values that have come to define the city. How do institutions, political and economic conditions, cultural movements, individual actors, and administrative policy create an urban personality? In turn, how has Colorado Springs influenced and affected other places in the state and nation? Since the material landscape interacts with the cultural environment in such a way that both shapes and informs each other, bringing these two avenues of exploration together seems the best way to distill a sense of place. A core theme that emerged from my research that defines this city is the persistent drive for liberty but specifically the freedom to conduct business and generate profits in a relatively unconstrained setting. This belief manifests itself most pervasively in what Mayor John Suthers calls a "small government" ethic. The city has been the forefront nationally in promoting a government agenda that is anti-regulatory, low tax, and limited. These policies shape the urban sprawl of the built landscape and mold the city's political culture. They also lend support for the military as an expression of freedom. The Rocky Mountain libertarian spirit is very much alive in Colorado Springs and has come to be a basis for the city's identity.

The third dimension to any place is the place setting, the physical geography of the site that shapes the natural world and sets parameters for the human modifications to that world. The importance here is the profound relationship and connections between Pikes Peak, the mountain, and Colorado Springs, the city. Pikes Peak is the lone sentinel, an isolated fourteener abruptly rising from the Great Plains. The city was located at is base because of this proximity between mountain and plain. As each chapter evolved, the integral connections to the mountain became clear: it molds the climate that drove the health seekers; it provided the water for the early city; gold was extracted from its slopes; the trails, canyons, reservoirs, and ski slopes are the basis for tourism and the recreation economy; and its symbolism as America's Mountain provides inspiration for both liberty seekers and spiritualists. Pikes Peak is far more than just a marketing icon, but it has also shaped the city's identity from the start. The two are inseparable, and Colorado Springs continues to profit from the peak.

My hope with this book is to instill curiosity among readers, particularly Colorado Springs residents, so they pay attention to the landscape around them and ask meaningful questions about how this city came to be. As John Stilgoe has advised, "Enjoy the best-kept secret around—the ordinary, everyday landscape that rewards any explorer, that touches any explorer with magic."[1] With an enhanced understanding and appreciation for the unique identity of this place and the many ways that Colorado Springs influenced the state of Colorado and the Rocky Mountain West, I hope that people will feel connected and their sense of place will shine.

Readers should be aware that as this project unfolded, it evolved from just this book into a related, digitally animated museum exhibit and web experience entitled *The Story of Us* at the Colorado Springs Pioneers Museum. Created in collaboration with Tierra Plan, LLC, users can explore a rich variety of digital maps, spatial data layers, georeferenced historical photos, rich textual and graphical content, and physical artifacts. You can also explore online at http://www.cspmstoryofus.com.

The exhibit does not follow the format of this book; nor does it include the same content (though there is overlap). Rather, it provides yet another way to get to know this city at the base of Pikes Peak. Readers may wish to engage with the many avenues for self-paced exploration in *The Story of Us* as they read the chapters of this book.

As with any story of place, the interpretation of historical events that shape it are just that—an interpretation. There is no one truth, no exclusive hold on the "real" meanings of events, nor one way to tell the story. While I strive to remain true to facts, no doubt my personal biases and ways of imposing meaning onto data will show through. Others may disagree, but that is the point of work in the humanities—to raise more questions, open dialogue, and create debate about our human existence. My apologies in advance for any errors I make, and my thanks to you, the reader, for engaging in this narrative.

Profiting from the Peak

1

Grass

> I shall never forget my sudden sense of hopeless disappointment at the moment when I first looked on the town. It was a gray day in November. I had crossed the continent, ill, disheartened, to find a climate that would not kill. There stretched before me, to the east, a bleak, bare, unrelieved, desolate plain. There rose behind me, to the west, a dark range of mountains, snow-topped, rocky-walled, stern, cruel, relentless. Between lay the town—small, straight, new, treeless.
>
> —HELEN HUNT JACKSON, 1873

> A queer embryo-looking place it is, out on the bare Plains . . . To me no place could be more unattractive than Colorado Springs, from its utter treelessness.
>
> —ISABELLA BIRD, 1873[1]

The short grass of the semiarid, treeless, high plains most certainly would have appeared desolate to travelers accustomed to the lush deciduous hardwood forests of the eastern United States or Western Europe.[2] The site that would become Colorado Springs was no exception, as noted by the two prominent visitors quoted above who arrived at the infancy of the city (figure 1.1). To create place—a built environment with meaning to the residents that becomes a very part of their identity—takes time, vision, and commitment—not to mention access to capital, good marketing (even audacious boosterism), and both investors and settlers willing to take great risk. Despite the bleak descriptions from first impressions, Colorado Springs had one great advantage that assisted its founder, General William Jackson Palmer, to envision a great place. Looking east from the relatively flat mesa where the city was founded one would see the endless expanse of short grass plains described above, but one need merely turn around and face west to see the abrupt ascent of the Rocky Mountains, framed by the sheer wall of Cheyenne Mountain to the south, Monument Hill with the Black Forest extending along the northern horizon, and 14,115' Pikes Peak, now dubbed "America's Mountain," centered due west (figure 1.2). Two streams running from the mountains join at

DOI: 10.5876/9781646421688.c001

FIGURE 1.2. Sketch of Cheyenne Mountain, Pikes Peak, and the Rampart Range due west of Colorado Springs, as seen in 1873. The sketch is from Pulpit Rock, about five miles north of the downtown and adjacent to the campus of the University of Colorado Colorado Springs. *Source*: Ferdinand V. Hayden, *Geological and Geographical Atlas of Colorado and Portions of Adjacent Territory* (Department of the Interior: United States Geological and Geographical Surveys of the Territories, 1877).

FIGURE 1.1. Surveyors laying out the original town site of Colorado Springs on the grassy mesa at the foot of Pikes Peak. *Source*: Colorado Springs Pioneers Museum.

the foot of the mesa, eight mineral springs burble from the ground at the base of the mountain in nearby Manitou, and the dramatic sedimentary rock formations of Garden of the Gods protrude upward at the rupture where plains contact mountains. Visualizing a setting for people to play, relax, and enjoy the bountiful splendor can be quite easy for contemporary Americans who have long assimilated the iconic grandeur of the Rocky Mountain West into the fabric of American culture. But to foresee a site of tranquility and comfort amidst the wild and harsh environment in 1871 required a rare vision, one that had to overcome traditional

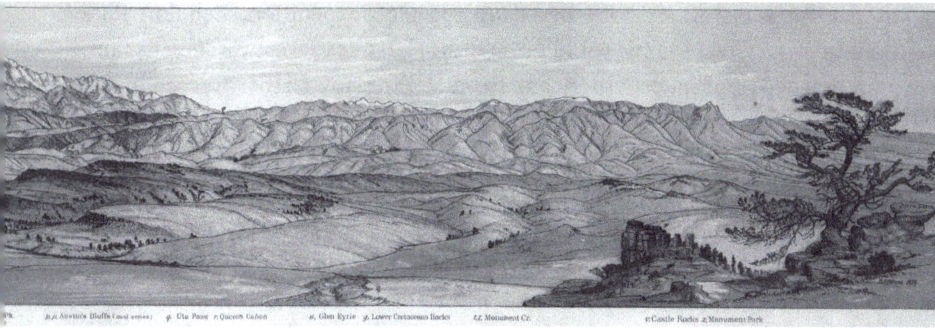

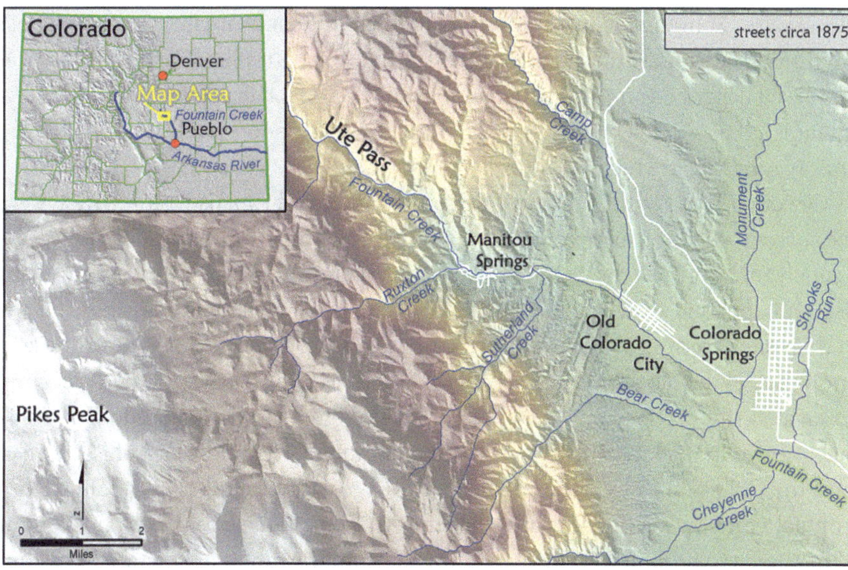

FIGURE 1.3. Colorado Springs, at the junction of Fountain and Monument Creeks, at the base of Pikes Peak. Ute Pass provides access to the mountains. Old Colorado City predated Colorado Springs, and Manitou Springs is nestled at the entrance to Ute Pass where the mineral springs burble from the ground. *Source*: Cartography by author.

views of aesthetics and beauty and one that, fortunately, William Jackson Palmer could see (figure 1.3).[3]

When Palmer first visited the region in the late 1860s and started dreaming of founding a new city, the Rocky Mountain West was still largely unknown—an idea more than a place, a frontier full of potential. Americans were made aware of the dramatic natural environments of the West by early explorer expeditions that included sketches and landscape paintings, and then from reports of gold rush speculators and other adventurers. But getting to the region was still a long and arduous task that required crossing the Great Plains, prohibiting firsthand experience for most Americans. Based on his 1806 expedition, Zebulon Pike reported that the Great Plains would be a natural barrier to westward expansion, a region that would impede Americans from settling any farther west than the Mississippi Valley. From the 1820s through much of the nineteenth century, the Great Plains captured the American imagination as "The Great American Desert."[4] This epithet regularly appeared on maps, and was perhaps first coined in reports from the 1820 Stephen Long expedition by Dr. Edwin James. His report stated, "In regard to this extensive section of the country, I do not hesitate in giving the opinion, that it is almost wholly unfit for cultivation, and of course uninhabitable by a people depending upon agriculture for their subsistence."[5] Like Pike, James also saw the Great Plains as a barrier to prevent westward movement of the restless Americans. Subsequent explorations reaffirmed this conceptualization. Once past the limit of forests while exploring up the Red River in 1852, Captain Randolph B. Marcy described the landscape as "barren and desolate wastes, where but few streams greet the eye of the traveler, and these are soon swallowed up by the thirsty sands over which they flow."[6]

Of course, the Plains were not a barren, uninhabited expanse; rather, they were extensively used for millennia and remained the home for thousands of people. Equally, neither General Palmer nor any other European was the first human to see and appreciate the spectacular setting that is now Colorado Springs. Paleo-Indian sites from the Clovis culture go back as far as 13,000 BCE, and there is mounting evidence that humans lived in the Americas well before that.[7] A recently excavated site on the campus of the University of Colorado Colorado Springs is likely over 9,000 years old.[8] The strip of land immediately to the east of Pikes Peak and the Colorado Rocky Mountain Front Range was particularly appealing. As a contact zone between plains and mountains, inhabitants could exploit different ecosystems to fit their needs. Rivers flowing from the mountains eroded this thin belt to a lower elevation than the plains a few dozen miles east, capturing more runoff and creating a slightly warmer and less windy shelter nestled against the mountains. Use of the region for hunting and habitation has deep roots, and it was the vast expanses of grassland that enabled buffalo and other big game to thrive and hence sustain the Plains Indian lifestyle.

We know that this meeting point of the plains and the mountains was a space used by many groups of people in the centuries prior to European arrival. The Native Americans of the region have a complex history of movement, alliances, intermarriage, trading, contestation, raiding and capture, and cultural exchange that goes far beyond the scope of this book.[9] This history also included a multicultural mix of miscegenation and cohabitation with early European and American explorers, perhaps exemplified by the Bents, traders who established the primary trading post along the Arkansas River in 1833. William Bent married Owl Woman, daughter of a Cheyenne chief, became accepted into the tribe, and raised five children who negotiated both the Indian and Anglo worlds.[10] For the sake of simplification, suffice it to say that at the time of European expansion into the Pikes Peak Region, the Algonquin-speaking Cheyenne and Arapahoe were the most prevalent tribes on the plains in the Pikes Peak Region and north, arriving from the upper Midwest in the mid-to-late 1700s. The Comanches, Shoshone speakers who came from regions north and west of Colorado, had become the dominant force in the southern plains about a century earlier, in what is now Texas, but extending their domain up into southern Colorado and the Arkansas River Valley. They entered into alliances and collaboration with Kiowas, who migrated from the Yellowstone area and occupied the plains in present-day Oklahoma and into Kansas and Colorado. Numerous Apache tribes, Athabaskan speakers who include the Navajo, arrived from Canada by about 1500, and occupied parts of the plains but concentrated in New Mexico to the south.

Immediately prior to European settlement, the group most utilizing the resources of the local site that is now Colorado Springs were the Utes who would trek between mountain park hunting grounds to the west and the plains in regular movements, often wintering near Manitou Springs. Ute Pass is the name now given for the route from the mountains into Manitou Springs, through which now passes US Highway 24 and is also the source for the naming of El Paso County, for which Colorado Springs is the county seat. This corridor between mountains and plains follows a valley that Fountain Creek carved into geologic faults within the granite of the Pikes Peak massif. The mineral springs at Manitou had special significance for the Utes, and migratory settlements were long established among the rocks of Garden of the Gods.[11] Early settler accounts tell of Utes camping along Fountain Creek in 1866, at least 300 Utes camping in Garden of the Gods in 1875, and of Utes returning to camp along creeks and in the foothills long past the establishment of the city.[12]

Despite the long-established use of the region by Indigenous groups, to the early Americans the West was considered wide-open territory ripe for exploitation.[13] Images and descriptions of the region created popular myths for a young nation. George Ruxton spent time at Manitou Springs in 1847, later writing about the natural beauty, his encounters with Native Americans, and the abundance of game and carnivores, particularly wolves.[14] The West became the iconic symbol of freedom from the constraints of culture, class, tradition, government, and religion in the East that inhibited liberty and individual expression. Looming large in the American psyche was a vast open space of opportunity, particularly to claim and own land, and clearly it became the manifest destiny of America to conquer the wilderness and push the frontier all the way across the continent.

The drive to get rich and exploit western resources was nowhere more evident than in the early rushes to gold camps. California, of course, opened the popular imagination in 1849 to the riches of the West, a land reportedly where gold could be simply picked up off the ground. Gold was next discovered in tributaries of the South Platte River by a party led by William Russell in 1858, setting the stage for the founding of Denver and a major gold boom in the Rocky Mountains to the immediate west. The "Pikes Peak or Bust" gold trekkers used the beacon of Pikes Peak as a guide in their movement west across the plains, but the mining activity actually took place some seventy miles north of Pikes Peak. Little activity occurred nearby. The first permanent town in the Pikes Peak Region was Colorado City along Fountain Creek, about two miles west of where Colorado Springs would be founded. A party of explorers from Kansas camped in 1858 near present Glen Eyrie, a cove at the mouth of a canyon where Camp Creek (named for this initial camp) exits from the mountains near the Garden of the Gods.[15] After failed attempts to establish Colorado City as a mining camp in 1858 and 1859, a group of settlers moved down from the Denver area in summer 1859 to establish a trade supply post for mining speculators traveling up Ute Pass into South Park in search of new riches. This group formed the "El Paso Claim Club" and began selling lots.[16] These actions were completely illegal, since the sellers made no efforts to first purchase the land from the public domain or file any land claims, let alone compensate local Native Americans, but their actions lent an air of legitimacy to unknowing buyers.

Although a route over Kenosha Pass into South Park was established from Denver to serve mountain mining camps, Ute Pass provided a competitive alternative. By the winter of 1859–1860, upwards of 100 log cabins had been built and the town reached the peak of its prosperity. In a not-too-uncommon, but nonetheless audacious feat of exaggerated boosterism, a professor Goldrick sent a letter from Colorado City to the *Missouri Democrat* newspaper on March 1, 1860, claiming:

> There are now some two hundred and forty fine, handsome-looking houses erected, and hundreds more in progress and contemplation. Some very large three-story stone houses and some very handsome gothic offices and dwellings are completing. The beautiful red rock quarries and cliffs, within a mile of the city, and also the ridges of beautiful white and brown sandstone and limestone quarries surrounding will furnish the greatest and cheapest opportunities for putting up the finest stores and warehouses, and the handsomest residences this side of Fifth Avenue, New York City.[17]

In reality, Colorado City was a collection of wooden buildings that had brief success up to 1860, then began to decline.

Travelers crossing the plains to Denver or anywhere on the Front Range from the east came via two principal routes, the northerly route along the South Platte or the southerly route along the Arkansas River (figure 1.4). The southern Arkansas River route followed the long-established Santa Fe Trail that connected Kansas City to New Mexico for much of the journey. Travelers would divert from the Santa Fe Trail and continue west on the Arkansas River to the site that would

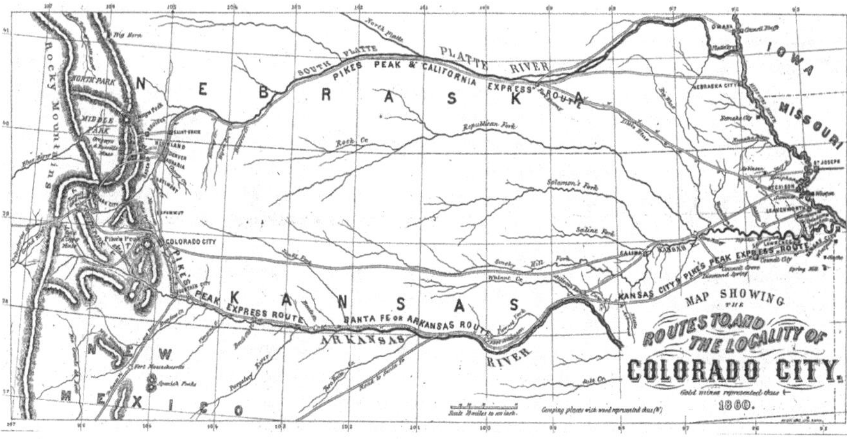

FIGURE 1.4. Two principal routes to Colorado City, 1860: the northern route along the South Platte or the southern route along the Arkansas River. *Source*: Colorado Springs Pioneers Museum.

become the city of Pueblo, then travel up Fountain Creek, past Pikes Peak, and onward over Monument Divide to Denver.[18] This was the route that brought most people to Colorado City and Ute Pass. However, the Civil War slowed all movement west in 1861 and especially inhibited movement along the Arkansas River as Kansas, Missouri, and Arkansas became contested grounds between North and South. More traffic was diverted to the South Platte route, feeding into the growing dominance of Denver and the solidification of routes from there into South Park and other mountain destinations. Although El Paso County was organized in 1861, and Colorado City even vied for recognition as the territorial capital in that year, a census in 1863 recorded only 300 people there. It then continued to dwindle to fewer than 100 houses so that by the official 1870 Census, there were only 81 residents in the city and only 987 in the entire county[19] (figure 1.5).

Into this setting came General William Jackson Palmer, a Civil War cavalry veteran from Philadelphia who worked after the war as secretary and treasurer for the Kansas Pacific Railroad. He worked to survey a route west from Kansas City to San Francisco, via New Mexico, to compete with the Union Pacific's more northerly route.[20] Palmer first came through the area in 1868 while surveying possible corridors. The Kansas Pacific eventually made it only to Denver (and then connected to the Union Pacific running through Wyoming to the West Coast) before funding dried up. Palmer still envisioned a more extensive railroad network, and knew much of the land from his Kansas Pacific surveys. To make this happen, he started his own railroad company to run north-south and connect the interior United States to Mexico, perhaps eventually to connect with Mexico City or Pacific ports such as Mazatlán or Guaymas. The Denver & Rio Grande (D&RG) Railroad was organized in autumn 1870.

FIGURE 1.5. Colorado City looking northeast, 1870 (top), Colorado City looking southwest, 1860 (bottom). *Source*: Courtesy of the Old Colorado City Historical Society; Colorado Colorado College Photo File "Colorado City—Colorado," Colorado College Special Collections.

To run his new company, Palmer needed to live nearby. Plus, this would fulfill his dream of building a home in the West and help assimilate his new wife, Queen, to the rough-and-tumble settlement in an undeveloped frontier. Palmer devised a plan for a new town, one not based on the norms of mining, farming, or other resource exploitation so common in the West. His dream was for a resort, a getaway for eastern friends and investors—a place of refined culture in which to relax amidst the natural splendor of the Rocky Mountains. Palmer sought capital from investors in England, Philadelphia, and New York to create a land company, expecting to sell lots, create a model town, and get rich in the process.

And where to locate his new town? No better place could be found than the contact point between plains and mountains, and no more abrupt transition existed

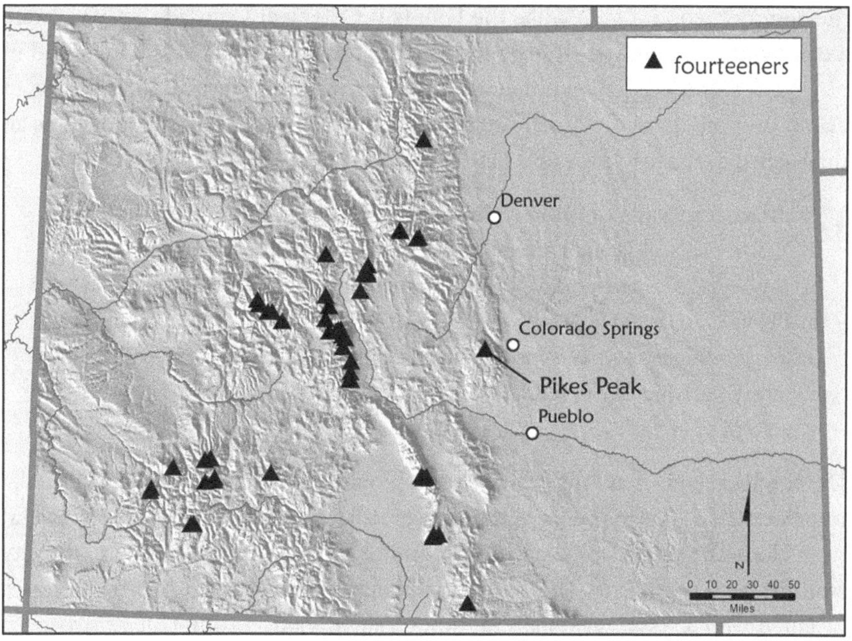

FIGURE 1.6. Mountain peaks in Colorado over 14,000 feet. Note how isolated Pikes Peak is from the rest and how close it is to the Front Range corridor. *Source*: Cartography by author.

than where Pikes Peak jutted up from the piedmont. Called the "Sun Mountain," or *Tava* by the Utes, Pikes Peak is a lone sentinel, an isolated "fourteener" farther east than the other mountains over 14,000 feet in Colorado, and standing above the plains as a clear marker for this new physiographic province, the Rocky Mountains. Its close proximity to the Colorado Front Range provides immediate access to this mountain wonderland (figure 1.6). Pikes Peak is the reason for the location of Colorado Springs. As described by author Helen Hunt Jackson, Colorado Springs would be a town "lying due east of the Great Mountains and west of the sun."[21] Palmer himself described the sensation one feels, after the arduous travel across the Great Plains, of reaching the base of the Rocky Mountains: "It is as though one had crossed the sea and reached the shores of a new country, full of novel attractions and advantages."[22]

Along with other investors, Palmer sought to capitalize on the landscape, to profit from the peak. They started the Colorado Springs Company that sold membership into the Fountain Colony. The colony model was a marketing strategy used in the 1870s to encourage settlers to move west and join in a cooperative endeavor where all would work together in the common cause of building a new town. In Colorado, Fort Collins, Greeley, Longmont, and Colorado Springs were all started as colonies. Some, like the Union Colony at Greeley, organized around the cooperative efforts of irrigated agriculture and settlers did work for the common good. Others, like the Fountain Colony at Colorado Springs, were a colony in name only, a strategy used by the founders to sell lots. Organized in June 1871, Palmer called on influential local, territorial, and eastern friends to put claims and purchase on close to 10,000 acres.[23] The new city was "founded as an unabashed exercise in pure speculative capitalism"[24]

> The Town is a Colony Town, and the whole of the profits derived from the sale of the Colony Lots and Lands, are appropriated to public improvements. The land having been bought in large parcels at low rates, and being sold to colonists in small lots at advanced figures, many thousands of dollars will thus be devoted to the purposes named . . . Persons may become colonists by purchasing certificate of membership, which are of four grades, according to the privileges conveyed: $50, $75; $100, $200.[25]

Despite the claim that "the whole of the profits" would be reinvested in public improvements, the founders certainly expected to profit personally from land sales along the way. Capital accumulation has been a defining theme of the city from its very beginning. The original city plans laid out a two-square-mile area oriented with a classic grid pattern, though slightly offset from true north-south and east-west directions. The town would have broad streets, up to 140 feet wide for the avenues running north-south and 100 feet wide for the east-west streets. Legend has it that the excessive width was to ensure a horse and carriage could easily turn around without backward motion. These wide avenues still exist today in the original town area, though central medians were slowly added onto alternating avenues and streets after 1913.[26] The east-west running streets are generally named after rivers and creeks in the region that flow from the mountains, and the north-south avenues are named after western mountain ranges. The principal thoroughfare, Pikes Peak Avenue, was aligned looking directly at that mountain, and the first surveyor stake was laid on July 31, 1871, at the southeast corner of Pikes Peak and Cascade Avenues. A lot in town was reserved for each church denomination,[27] and Palmer donated much land for parks and schools, including the parcels for what would become Colorado College in 1874. There were strict temperance covenants for Fountain colonists, a business decision Palmer made to protect investment and create a lasting, sustainable urban model. The sale of any intoxicating liquor was considered a breach of contract and resulted in forfeiture of property.[28] Palmer stated,

> I regard the temperance clause at Colorado Springs as doubling the value of property, because people will want to come here for nice houses and they will want to raise families free from the temptation of liquor shops.[29]
>
> The aim was intensely practical—to create a habitable and successful town in the broadest sense of the word.[30]

Palmer was, as he put it,

> desiring to have a different sort of town, and to invite people of gentle breeding to come and make their homes here . . . My theory for this place is that it should be made the most attractive place for homes in the west—a place for schools, colleges, literature, science, first class newspapers, and everything that the above imply.[31]

Despite the arrival of the D&RG railroad from Denver on October 23, 1871, belief in the success of this investment again took vision and dedication; by November 1871, there were only twelve inhabited houses and a number of shacks and tents.[32] Geographer Curt Poulton described the site of the original town plat as "the flattest, driest, least interesting piece of real estate imaginable . . . the setting was beautiful, but the place itself was unremittingly plain and dry."[33] Rose Kingsley, A British friend of the Palmers and sister of Maurice, an initial investor in the town, remembered first arriving to Colorado Springs in November 1871, shortly after its founding:

> "There's the city," said M., pointing eastward; and I will confess that a feeling something like dismay crept over me when I followed his hand with my eyes. All that I could see were a dozen wooden houses of various shapes and sizes, and a large unfinished hotel, standing along the top of a sandy rise. You may imagine Colorado Springs, as I did, to be in a sequestered valley, with bubbling fountains, green grass, and shady trees; but not a bit of it. Picture yourself a level, elevated plateau of greenish brown, without a single tree, sloping down about a quarter of a mile to the railroad track and Monument Creek (the Soda Springs being six miles off), and you have a pretty good idea of the town-site as it appeared in November 1871.[34]

Yet the colony was remarkably successful. After one year, there were 197 settlers invested in land, and by the second year in June 1873, there were about 400[35] (figure 1.7). The company directors did indeed invest much capital from land sales back into the colony. An irrigation canal was dug and provided water by November 1871, only four months after the city was founded. Within the first year 6,000 cottonwood trees were set out along the streets at twenty-five-foot intervals. The newly established newspaper, the *Gazette*, summed up the changes that had occurred within the first two years:

> The progress already made by the Town has been astonishingly rapid. Up to date—that is, writing less than eighteen months from the commencement of the enterprise—there have been 320 certificates of membership taken out, on most of which two locations have been made. The population, according to a recent enumeration taken by order of the town trustees, lacked only about a score of being 1,000, and is now fully that number.[36]

FIGURE 1.7. Colorado Springs Hotel and other first businesses along Cascade Avenue, 1871, looking northeast. *Source*: Colorado Springs Pioneers Museum.

By January 1873, there were two churches, with a third being built; two schools; a public auditorium; a bank; three hotels and numerous boardinghouses; a livery stable; the newspaper; and a telegraph and post office. Nascent industries included a saw mill, brick manufacturer, and a fruit cannery (figure 1.8). In a typical rant of boosterism, the *Gazette* stated, "The springs and the scenery combined are destined, of themselves, to build up a town of considerable size and importance. Here will be a place of resort—of almost unequaled attractions—known the world over"[37] (figure 1.9).

While Palmer's dream for a respite for "people of gentle breeding" came to fruition to some extent, not everybody could sit back and enjoy the good life without actually working. A ranching community grew around the town, taking advantage of the splendid natural grasslands. Since its founding in 1861, El Paso County was known as the largest raiser of sheep in the territory and state and later known for its cattle.[38] Census numbers show this grass-based economy continued to grow. In 1871, the county assessor counted over 5,000 cows and over 10,000 sheep, and by 1872 there were over 6,000 cows and 50,000 sheep[39] (figure 1.10). As the town grew, several dairy farms located nearby (an industry that grew rapidly as tuberculosis patients sought milk for recovery and strength). Over fourteen lumber mills sprouted to supply local construction demands and to export to the Denver market. Even neighboring Colorado City finally grew into its potential as

FIGURE 1.8. 1874 Birds-eye view of Colorado Springs. *Source*: Colorado Springs Pioneers Museum.

a freight supplier; in 1872 county commissioners bonded the county for $15,000 to construct wagon road up Ute Pass (figure 1.11). The result was so successful that by 1873 local outfitters had to subcontract out for more mule teams to keep up with demand from traffic to Fairplay and other mining camps. In one week alone, 45,000 pounds of freight on twenty-two wagons with mule teams were sent to Park, Summit, and Lake Counties.[40] Locally produced beef and mutton were important commodities sent to feed workers in the mountain mining camps. Traffic grew greatly to supply Leadville up until the arrival of railroads to that mining camp in 1880.[41] Colorado Springs was incorporated in September 1872, and became the El Paso County Seat in March 1873. The city was indeed taking shape, as were its two neighbors Colorado City and Manitou Springs (figure 1.12). Even Helen Hunt Jackson, who stated her "hopeless disappointment" at first seeing the city in the quote introducing this chapter, in later years said "To-day that plain and those mountains are to me well-nigh the fairest spot on earth."[42]

However, Palmer envisioned neither a pastoral economy, nor a place for common laborers and teamster services.[43] For his dream resort to come true, he and others immediately recognized the need for a steady and abundant supply of water, the resource most lacking in his little utopian village. With only two small streams and no natural lakes Colorado Springs is one of the few western cities not located adjacent to a reliable and large water source. Generating a sufficient supply of water would preoccupy city leaders from the first years of the city up to the

FIGURE 1.9. Mosaic of the city from the top of the newly built High School, 1874, located on the southeast corner of Bijou Street and Cascade Avenue. Left side of the image is due north, the image panorama sweeps east, to the right side of the image that looks due south, along Cascade Avenue toward Cheyenne Mountain. *Source*: Colorado Springs Pioneers Museum individual images; mosaic by author.

FIGURE 1.10. Sheepherding, looking south from Templeton Gap toward Colorado Springs, 1885. Templeton Gap is a pass through Austin Bluffs north of Colorado Springs, one of the principal routes to Denver. Painting by Charles Craig. *Source*: Colorado Springs Pioneers Museum.

FIGURE 1.11. Mule-drawn wagons traveling up the Ute Pass road, circa 1875. *Source*: Colorado Springs Pioneers Museum.

FIGURE 1.12. Pikes Peak Avenue looking west, 1888. *Source*: *Colorado Springs Gazette* (1888), January 1, courtesy Colorado Springs Pioneers Museum.

present day. The source of that water, of course, could only be the mountains to the west, from which all streams emerged. City leaders wasted little time exploiting the geographical proximity to these water supplies.

2

Water

The American West can best be described as a modern *hydraulic society*, which is to say, a social order based on the intensive, large-scale manipulation of water and its products in an arid setting.

—DONALD WORSTER, 1985[1]

The plains of eastern Colorado receive between ten and twelve inches of annual precipitation. Colorado Springs receives about sixteen inches annually—far too little for rainfed agriculture. The aridity of the West was long known; how to effectively settle in this aridity and establish a sustainable ecological niche for humans has taken longer to learn. America was in the earliest stages of industrialization at the time of initial western expansion. The preindustrial economy meant that most Americans were farmers: 56 percent of the labor force worked in agriculture in 1850 (decreasing to 31% in 1900 and about 2% today).[2] In large part, access to land drove westward expansion, land on which to build the Jeffersonian ideal of a citizenry comprising small, independent yeoman farmers. But Americans had little experience in arid environments; they had to figure out how to farm in this land as they went—land uses and husbandry practices employed in the humid East simply would not work in the arid West. Early visionaries such as John Wesley Powell recognized, and publicized, that traditional homesteads such as those of the Midwest were inappropriate in the arid West.[3] The need was to irrigate, to divert water out of the natural riverbanks and move it over dry land in order to grow crops.

Artificially diverting water from a river to run across a field seems such a simple concept, one almost natural. But the act is fraught with philosophical and economic assumptions and with social and political traps. It is, in fact, a highly complex activity that usually far exceeds the capacity of any individual to undertake

DOI: 10.5876/9781646421688.c002

alone. To be sure, an individual farmer could conceivably build some type of small-scale diversion dam on some small stream, dig a ditch that runs at the correct grade, create plugs to open and close that ditch for runoff onto a field also at a correct gradient, and permit water to flow evenly across seeds planted in that soil. And that certainly happened. But larger rivers require larger-scale infrastructure and a cooperative understanding about how the water will be used. And the West, the region of individual expression and personal liberty, was not known for its cooperative understanding. In the western United States in the nineteenth century, the need for irrigation brought to the forefront one glaring contradiction—the West is the land of the free, where the individual escapes tyranny, yet irrigation requires organization and investment at such a scale that some larger body must finance it, organize and oversee the labor to build and maintain it, and enforce how the water is allocated. The individual must waive some of his or her personal freedoms in order to reach a common good—he or she must acquiesce to some authority, cede autonomy, and ultimately submit to a regulatory power. As water historian Karl Wittfogel famously asserted after studying ancient societies founded on irrigated agriculture, irrigation leads to despotism—a tyrannical leadership or bureaucracy that controls water as a resource, and hence controls people.[4] Perhaps the largest story of the development of the western United States is coming to grips with giving up individual autonomy to succumb to some higher authority in the exchange for water.

How were these issues resolved in western North America? Some were slowly worked out over centuries, others over decades, but none easily or cleanly.

Irrigation was long practiced by the Spanish. One could make the case that they learned the art of water diversion when Iberia was a Roman colony, as seen by the impressive aqueducts for municipal water supply and other water infrastructure in such towns as Segovia, Mérida, Tarragona, Córdoba, Toledo, and elsewhere. But the Spanish certainly perfected the art of irrigated agriculture from the Moors, who had extensive irrigated fields in Andalusia during their 500-year occupation of the Iberian Peninsula. The Spanish brought these technologies to their new-world colonies, and village-based irrigated agriculture became the primary settlement pattern in their far northern outpost in what is now New Mexico. The water ditch, or acequia, was the lifeblood of valleys in the upper Rio Grande; so much so that the ditch administrator, or *mayordomo*, was the most important person in each village. He organized labor brigades for annual ditch cleaning and allocated water for village users. The irrigation lifestyle revolving around communal access to their public works project created a form of civil government, where water access was the basis for organization. In these villages, water is politics.[5] This tradition remains and took hold in southern Colorado as Hispanos expanded out of the upper Rio Grande region. The People's Ditch in the village of San Luis, Colorado, was built in 1852 and remains water priority right Number 1 in the state of Colorado. So for the Hispano villages in New Mexico and southern Colorado, the answer to the conflict between personal gain and communal good was to keep irrigated agriculture at the village scale, where a small community would willingly cede authority to a locally designated mayordomo to the benefit of all.

A similar communal cohesion held among the first Anglo-Americans to develop irrigated agriculture in an arid environment, the Mormons in Utah. The Latter Day Saints had difficulties living among fellow Americans in the Midwest of the 1840s. They were long persecuted, seen as a cult by mainstream Christians in an era when utopian communities and new prophets proliferated on the frontier. After church founder Joseph Smith was lynched in Illinois, the entire body of believers moved to Utah in 1846 under the leadership of Brigham Young to escape persecution and establish a new kingdom of Zion. Mormons firmly believed that their destiny was tied to place; their land ethic was tied to their theology.[6] A group defensive mentality fostered communal cooperation for survival—a rational response from a long-persecuted people. In addition to this defensive bond, church doctrine preached respect for authority with a rigid hierarchy of power. These conditions, experiences, and beliefs created the perfect social arrangement for Mormons to work together under hierarchical leadership. Their goal was to subjugate land by establishing firm ownership and control in order to survive as a people. Their ingenuity was to quickly figure out a system for irrigating arid lands. This system was both communal and theocratic. Authoritarian leadership mandated village design and irrigation patterns, and the believers followed through with the plan. Religious doctrine, therefore, was the bridge between individual expression and acquiescence to authority.

But as the West developed, subsequent settlers belonged neither to small villages practicing folk traditions that evolved over centuries, nor to theocratic communities adhering to religious doctrines. Irrigation initiatives involving many people on large rivers created huge controversies between western individualists and proponents of either industrial capital or government agencies. That story is long and highly contested and well documented elsewhere.[7] By the twentieth century, the water enforcer of the West became the federal government—specifically the Bureau of Reclamation. Enormous federal subsidies went into the development of western agriculture, usually to the benefit of an oligarchy of regional land holding elites rather than of small-scale farmers. The pattern was set for a region living off the federal dole. The libertarian, live-and-let-live West, the mythical self-made land of cowboys and homesteaders who make it on their own, became thoroughly dependent upon federal subsidies—a pattern and paradox that persist.[8]

Colorado Springs was not founded as an agricultural community, even though over fifty ditches were dug in El Paso County by early agricultural settlers.[9] Yet the conflicts and controversies of water appropriation were highly relevant since the city lacked sufficient quantities to survive and because these new American settlers to the West were adherents to a new economic philosophy, with a different understanding about water itself. America was the global experiment for a relatively unfettered capitalism, which creates a culture and mindset that treats water, like land before it, purely as commodity. The basic premise is that land should be divided into private property to grow crops and increase the population and any other resource should also be exploited to its maximum potential. Water, therefore, should be used to maximize economic gain. Any water not being used was seen as wasted, something that was, in fact, irrational in this capitalist mindset.

While the economic philosophy concerning water as just another natural resource was logical, a political system to support this theoretical concept had not yet been created. In this regard, Colorado led the way for the nation. Prior to statehood, territorial legislators recognized that riparian water rights that allocated water to those owning land along the banks of a river might be suitable to the humid East but would not function in the arid West. The Colorado territorial legislature recognized the right to build ditches to divert water in 1861 and approved an early version of water rights in 1864 that gave first priority to those first to claim the water. "First in time, first in right" summarizes the concept—those who first make claim to some amount of water and put it to some beneficial use get first use of that water in times of shortage. No longer would water in a river belong only to those who own land along its banks—water became separated from its source and available to whoever could make the best use for it. This official recognition of what was until then only de facto behavior was highly influential to the entire West and became known in the vernacular as the Colorado Doctrine, but more formally as the Doctrine of Prior Appropriation. It was the product of a new capitalist economic culture and its attitudes toward nature.[10] But at the time there was still no legal system or mechanism to enforce such initiatives: "The laws that applied to the Doctrine of Prior Appropriation were naively written and had no legal nor social institutions to back them. In Colorado it has taken 130 years to build the institutions necessary to make the law work, and these institutions are still developing."[11]

In 1870, one year before the founding of the Fountain Colony in Colorado Springs, another utopian colony was founded, this one based exclusively on irrigated agriculture. Nathan Meeker established the Union Colony and members built their town, Greeley, named after Horace Greeley, the owner of the *New York Tribune* and colony advocate. They undertook an ambitious plan to build four ditches of thirty-five miles in length to tap the Cache la Poudre River just upstream from its confluence with the South Platte. Colonists would work on private lots but in a communal arrangement for the common good, again providing the rationale for both personal gain but tempered with loyalty to colony leadership. Their initial plan proved to be too ambitious, mainly because the expense of building this water infrastructure was severely underestimated.[12] While the colony ultimately succeeded, the importance for Colorado Springs was the outcome from disputes that the Union Colony went through for access to water. The colony built canals to irrigate their farms but rapidly fell into conflict with water users upstream at Fort Collins during the drought of 1873, when those Johnny-come-lately upstarts took most of the water from the river before it reached the Union Colony canal diversion points. Union colonists cried foul—we were here first, this is our water, and those latecomers upstream can't take it before it gets to us! What to do?

First the new state constitution in 1876 adopted the Principle of Prior Appropriation as the law of the land. Article XVI of the Colorado Constitution gave the right to divert public water for beneficial use. Domestic purposes have priority, then agriculture, then manufacturing.[13] Next a convention gathered in 1878 to recommend an irrigation law for the new state of Colorado. A legislative act of February 9, 1879, divided Colorado into water divisions, each with a "water court" that would take testimony about water claims and decide priorities by date of construction. Then in 1881, Colorado further strengthened state authority by setting up a state engineer's office to supervise water claims. The proceedings from the 1879 act were made law in the first General Adjudication of Water Rights of 1882. This was the first official tabulation of water rights and the issuance of decrees that legally stated the parameters of those rights.[14] A subsequent 1897 law recognized the right to exchange water between reservoirs. The result of all this was a system for official enforcement for the Doctrine of Prior Appropriation where claims were documented and made legal based upon the initial date of access.

The shift from riparian rules to the new law released the water from its legal tie to the land and allowed it to be moved from places of plenty to places of want. The appropriation doctrine makes it possible for growth to continue in areas where supplies of water are inadequate. As a consequence, it would now be rational to destroy a river completely, "to send it through canals or tunnels to another watershed altogether, to wherever a man could make money from it."[15] But these laws were also a step toward recognizing that the rivers of the West are in some sense public property and that any private appropriation can only be made under public rules and at public sufferance. So the old tension was still at play: "Wherever economic maximizers and resource scarcity coincided, some kind of external presence, some form of Leviathan, would become inevitable."[16] Just who that Leviathan would be in Colorado is a story of power and might, one fraught with controversy and still being decided. And the city of Colorado Springs would have a play in that evolving legal landscape.

COLORADO SPRINGS WATER: THE IMPERIAL REACH

The water story of Colorado Springs, like that of Denver and other western cities, is not one of diversions for agriculture but water diversions for urban consumption. Water to drink was only part of the need; water also adds value to real estate.[17] Bringing water to land could make people rich, and this speculative aspect of water development has been a key economic driver of growth for the entire history of the city. It is fundamental to the creation of Colorado Springs as a place. Here Colorado Springs became an early leader in creating an appropriate political system to handle the movement of water, particularly when diverting water across natural watersheds—from one drainage basin to an entirely new drainage basin.

THE EL PASO CANAL

The Colorado Springs Company sunk three wells right away for Fountain Colony drinking water. After these municipal sources, individual lot owners began drilling private wells (about fifteen were sunk in the first year).[18] Despite the increasing number of wells, General Palmer and the city founders knew they needed a municipal water supply, primarily to irrigate lawns on individual lots and trees lining the streets but also to provide water for washing, laundry, and livestock consumption. The founders were in the business of selling land, and land with trees, lawns, and a steady supply of water was far more valuable than the dry and bleak mesa the first visitors saw. Irrigation water was a necessary investment for the success of the colony. The El Paso Canal was contracted on August 4, 1871, only four days after the founding of the town, and first delivered water to the city on Nov. 28, 1871. At first about six and one-half miles long, the canal took water from a diversion dam on Fountain Creek two miles above Colorado City. Its path crossed Monument Creek via a quarter-mile-long flume about two miles north of town (figure 2.1). Laterals were dug along margins of the main avenues, with cross-street laterals dug at regular intervals to provide water to the remaining streets.[19]

After water snaked through the city and was diverted to irrigate urban lots, the Boulder Street Reservoir was constructed 1871–1872 for storing extra water at the terminus on the city's east side. The canal was extended south from this reservoir to ultimately irrigate the city's Evergreen Cemetery by 1875. In addition, Prospect Lake was constructed for $15 million in 1890 to store overflow. A lateral connecting ditch extended from the El Paso Canal to fill the lake, which became a popular tourist and weekend picnic recreation center in Memorial Park.[20] The old Boulder Street Reservoir was emptied soon after 1900 and has become today's Boulder Park adjacent to Memorial Hospital.[21] The El Paso Canal was eleven miles long when completed and served the city until 1956.

When the canal was at its full use, lateral ditches could be seen running down most streets, with conduits running under private driveway entrances and under street intersections. Pipes under sidewalks conveyed ditchwater to lawns on

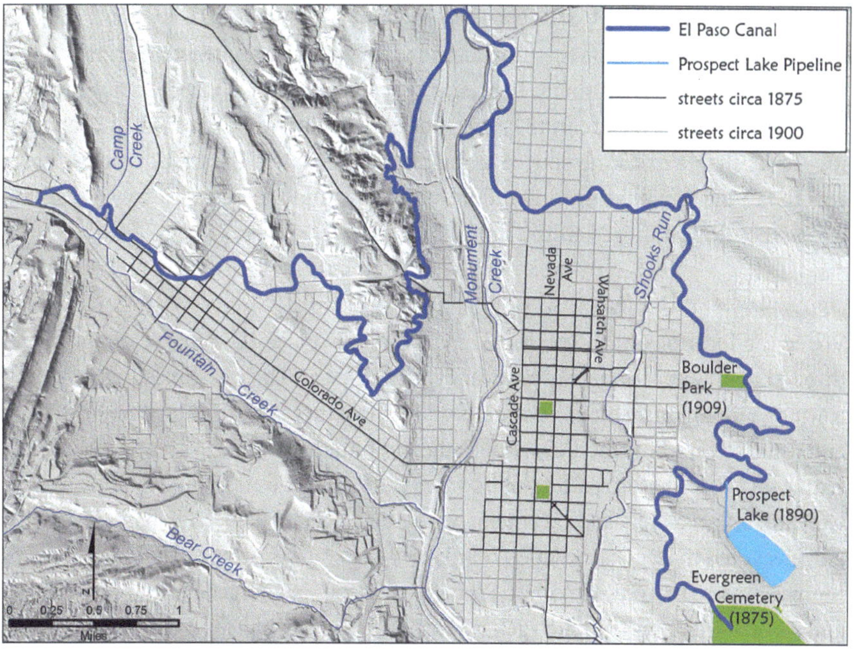

FIGURE 2.1. The El Paso Canal, snaking from Fountain Creek west of Old Colorado City and crossing Monument Creek, brought the city's first irrigation water. Excess water filled Prospect Lake after 1890, and the terminus of the canal irrigates the city's Evergreen Cemetery. *Source*: Cartography by author.

individual lots. For those without easy access to well water, the ditches served water for laundry. But new lots sold to the north and east of the original ditch could not tap into this water since they were higher in elevation. The city therefore tried numerous times to divert Monument Creek as well, upstream of the town, to serve newer growth areas. Although Pikeview Reservoirs No. 1 and 2 were constructed to feed ditches, attempts to bring Monument Creek water into the city repeatedly failed.

The grand El Paso Canal was instrumental to the success of the city. It was the source for urban landscaping that enabled the Colorado Springs Company to sell lots and attract settlers, and it irrigated the urban garden for eighty-five years. Today, its ghostly path is visible winding along the hills of the inner west side and with relict infrastructure such as the pediment for the viaduct over Monument Creek and the remnant lateral ditches (covered with concrete caps in 1954) running down on Wood Ave. This ditch served the city well, but beyond its physical impact, building the ditch drew the city into the legal vortex of water as property. Development of the El Paso Canal required the purchase of privately owned agricultural water rights, a process ongoing to this day, and one that required the legal framework to establish claims to water.[22]

MUNICIPAL DRINKING WATER: LOCAL SOURCES

While the El Paso Canal was not intended for drinking, even for irrigation the water carried much sediment, debris, and seeds of noxious weeds—not to mention a grasshopper plague in 1873 that clogged the ditches. Citizens began appealing for a reliable drinking source to augment well water. The first obvious choice was to tap the streams running off of Pikes Peak, and the best choice was Ruxton Creek that flowed into Manitou Springs.

Initial Infrastructure in an Evolving Legal Framework

While the locations of the physical resources were clear, the organizational structure to bring water to the city was very much unclear. The question of whether the town should organize a public waterworks or whether private enterprise should be entrusted to build the facilities was hotly and bitterly debated.[23] The first bond initiative for $100,000 to create a public waterworks that would bring water from Bear Creek in 1875 was rejected by voters, but by 1878 the public mood changed and the citizens voted to issue an $80,000 bond for a city water system.[24] That decision was momentous: to this day, Colorado Springs Utilities—in charge of water, gas, electric, and sewer—remains a public agency. That is a glaring irony for a city with a majority population that in nearly all dimensions of economy and society, strongly advocates for limited government and privatization of services. Why would the voters in 1878 decide on public ownership? The answer can probably be found from the social context occurring at three scales: national trends, regional comparisons, and local situation. For the first, the economic transition to industrialization created turbulent times that disrupted the lives of everyday, working-class Americans. As the Gilded Age arose, plutocrats who owned banks, steel firms, railroads, and other industries were widely distrusted, and the pseudomonopolies of many industries, particularly railroads, were viewed as gouging the average citizen of their hard-earned pay.[25] Midwestern farmers organized against railroads and corporate monopolies that, in their view, focused on profit at the expense of the small businessman. Growing inequality of wealth led to active labor unions, some quite radical, as well as populist and even anarchist agitators. Added to this was the panic and depression of 1873, in which big financiers such as Jay Cooke went bankrupt through his failed Northern Pacific Railroad, causing the stock market in New York to close for ten days. This event was shortly followed by over fifty more railroad company bankruptcies. Such a precarious situation would eventually shuffle in the Progressive Era, in which people looked to the federal government to solve these problems. Rather than the probusiness sentiments espoused by most politicians today, a populist theme was very strong and protections against the abuse of the general public by private industry had considerable support. While in twenty-first-century Colorado Springs anything publicly administered evokes grumblings of socialism and oppressive governmental interference in the free market, this was not the sentiment in 1878.

City leaders were also likely influenced by national trends specific to municipal water development. Philadelphia built the first public waterworks in 1801, followed by New York in 1842 and Boston in 1848.[26] In the case of Boston, proponents of a private system argued that private companies could provide water more cheaply and warned of crippling public debt and unjust taxes on the wealthy with a public works.[27] But the rapid immigration and urban growth of the nineteenth century had also led to unprecedented levels of poverty, drunkenness, crime, and vice in American cities. Reformers saw public water work as a force for moral good. Indeed, engineers in public works water projects in the American West came to see themselves as agents of social progress.[28]

A second influence, more appropriate to our regional context, was likely that Colorado Springs leaders learned from the experience of its larger neighbor to the north. As many as a dozen water companies vied to serve Denver from as early as 1859. When one company beat out the competition with the twenty-four-mile "Big Ditch" from Platte Canyon to what is now Capitol Hill, citizens complained of monopoly control and overcharging, and friction arose between public administrators and the private company.[29] Colorado Springs officials must have viewed these battles in the territorial capital with foreboding.

Finally, when we look at the local context, the early leaders of the Colorado Springs Company had the clear goal of enriching themselves through land speculation, yet there was no long-established landed gentry such as that found in eastern cities who would oppose a public system. The wealthy elites in Colorado Springs in 1878 were the city founders, and to them private ownership of something so vital as water could jeopardize their investments. Furthermore, public ownership enables projects to be publicly financed, spreading costs among many people, yet concentrating the benefits from increased land values among the few landholders. Dispersing costs while concentrating gains is a compelling strategy for those situated to benefit from such policies. Since there was a genuine need for clean water among the general public, leaders could use the argument that public ownership was a social commitment for the overall good of the community, all the while realizing that a steady water supply under municipal control also ensured future profits. As Gray Brechin eloquently argues concerning the development of water infrastructure in San Francisco, elites "well understood what the ratepayers, then as now, failed to comprehend—that water utilities exist primarily to nourish real estate, not people."[30]

Whatever the motivation to move towards a publicly owned water supply, the initial result was that by 1879, the city's first reservoir, Mesa No. 1, was built on the hill just west of Monument Creek and the downtown. The water source was Ruxton Creek, a tributary to Fountain Creek, which ran through Manitou Springs. The first pipe from the water intake to the Mesa Reservoir was run in 1880 and from there served city lots.[31] This initial system provided vastly better water than that available in the El Paso Canal and came to each lot under pressure due to the 200-foot elevation loss from the Mesa Reservoir to the town. A second Mesa Reservoir was built in 1886, and the pipeline extended twice upstream to capture more pure water.

City Engineer H. I. Reid filed his annual report in 1888 assuring that the Ruxton Creek system would be enough water for more than triple the current population and should "supply the city's want for many years to come."[32] Apparently, city leaders disagreed and tapped another nearby source, Bear Creek.[33] Here city leaders encountered the new Colorado water law—they built this system yet had no water rights to Bear Creek. There were at least four prior claims going back to 1861. The city was sued, lost its case, and slowly learned that purchasing water rights should precede building infrastructure. Colorado Springs repeatedly lost numerous other lawsuits with El Paso County and agricultural irrigators downstream. The net result was that legal rulings against Colorado Springs' brash and arrogant water takings greatly contributed to clarifying the legal framework for Colorado water rights.[34]

South Slope of Pikes Peak

While the legal framework for acquiring water was being fought over, Colorado Springs leaders recognized the need to scale up their water delivery infrastructure. The 1880 intake settler pond on Ruxton Creek, twice moved upstream to ensure water purity, was the first step in their progression up the slopes of Pikes Peak (figure 2.2). Then from 1890 until 1929 the city exploited resources on the South Slope of the mountain, following Ruxton Creek up to its headwaters and, of importance, over a divide and into the adjacent watershed of Beaver Creek that did not even flow to Colorado Springs. Diverting water across watersheds represented a quantum leap in the development of water resources. No longer must people be constrained to the water flowing within their own basin; once this human engineering was accomplished, water from anywhere was conceptually open for the taking. Tapping into Beaver Creek and diverting that water down Ruxton Creek was not the state's first out-of-basin transfer, but it was one of unprecedented scope, an ambitious process of turning waters of streams out of their natural watershed and importing them to areas of demand. In addition to bringing clarity to the legal framework for water, the city was not only tapping into a local watershed but was actively creating new water sources.[35]

At the top of Ruxton Creek sat Mystic Lake, a natural pond formed in a depression with a glacial moraine partially blocking the creek's outflow. Colorado Springs engineers enlarged this moraine to increase capacity, creating Lake Moraine, the first of the city's mountain reservoirs on what was federal land. The federal government had established a military reserve of nearly fifty square miles for the army on most of Pikes Peak, with an atmospheric research station built in 1873 at

FIGURE 2.2. Ruxton Creek intake. *Source*: *Colorado Springs Gazette* (1888), January 1, courtesy Colorado Springs Pioneers Museum.

the summit. The station was closed in 1888, after which the military reserve converted to Pike National Forest in 1905. Over a number of years, Congress granted tracts of this federal land to the city to develop its water facilities. The city now has control over 7,138 acres with limited public recreational uses allowed.[36]

There is just a small rise at the Seven Lakes Divide that separates the Beaver Creek watershed, flowing south to the Arkansas River, from the Ruxton Creek headwaters that flow northeast into Fountain Creek. The city secured water rights to Beaver Creek by purchasing ranches downstream and in 1890 built a ditch, later a pipeline, then the Saint John's Tunnel in 1904 to divert water

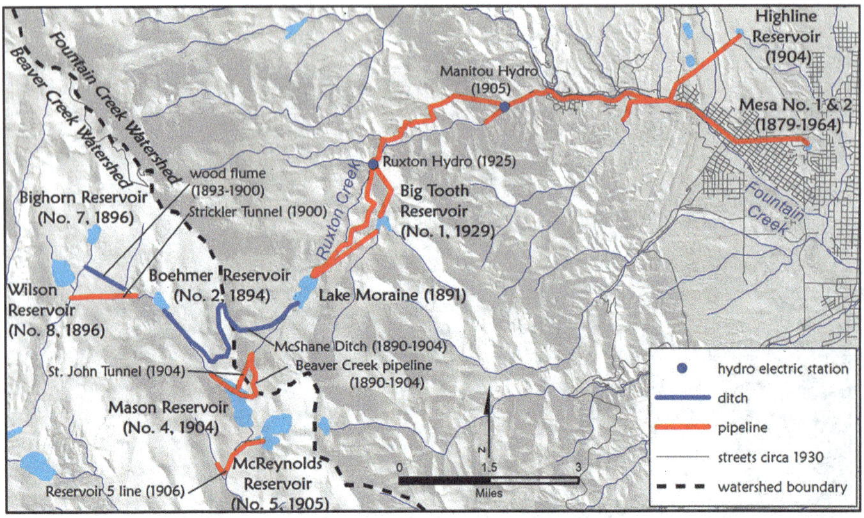

FIGURE 2.3. South Slope water system at full buildout, circa 1930, but with earlier components shown with dates of operation. Note the diversions from the Beaver Creek watershed across to the Fountain Creek watershed divide. *Source*: Cartography by author.

from the Middle Beaver Creek across the divide and into Ruxton Creek (figure 2.3).[37] Tapping the Beaver Creek watershed allowed the city to construct five new reservoirs, all completed between 1893 and 1906.[38] Two of these reservoirs were in the alpine ecosystem above tree line on West Beaver Creek, the highest at 12,099-foot elevation. Water from these reservoirs required a diversion out of the West and Middle Beaver Creek drainage and through the Saint John's Tunnel to Ruxton Creek. The 6,200-foot-long Strickler Tunnel, finished in 1900 was a major piece of the West Beaver Creek diversion, a seven-foot-by-four-foot bore requiring a temporary hydroelectric power station on Ruxton Creek to drill the hole.[39] A lift to haul pipes for this system up Mount Manitou was built in 1907, which later became a tourist cable car and is today the popular Manitou Incline hiking trail—a landmark clearly visible to this day rising above Manitou Springs (figure 2.4).[40] The Manitou hydroelectric plant was installed in 1905 using water flowing from the Ruxton intake; this plant is still generating electricity today.

This South Slope system was, and remains, the core of the city's water infrastructure. It greatly expanded the water supply capacity, but very rapidly concerns for the future supply were afoot. City engineer George Anderson recommended the city seek out new water rights in 1916 because Colorado Springs would undoubtedly continue to grow. This call echoed the earlier summary by engineer Sawyer in 1901: "It seems to me that nothing except a lack of water can stop the growth of a city so desirable for residence as this."[41]

FIGURE 2.4. The Manitou Incline gash cutting up the slopes of Pikes Peak above Manitou Springs, a popular hiking trail and iconic landscape feature today, was built in 1907 to haul pipes up the slope for the Colorado Springs water system. *Source*: Photo by author.

North Slope of Pikes Peak

Even before receiving recommendations to seek new sources for water, the city was moving to buy more water rights. The next logical place to look was on the North Slopes of Pikes Peak. Runoff here ran through a series of small creeks—the Crystal, Catamount, Cascade, and French. These all drop dramatically over a steep precipice into Ute Pass, where Fountain Creek flows down into Manitou Springs and then Colorado Springs. Ute Pass is a graben, a block of land that dropped downward relative to its surroundings between two faults on either side. Fountain Creek exploits this geologic weakness and cuts its path along the southern fault on its journey out of the mountains. The edge of this fault, prior to dropping into Ute Pass, is an ideal place to impound these creeks with a dam and construct storage reservoirs, which is exactly what the city has done (figure 2.5).

The city began building the North Slope system in 1933 with two reservoirs and a pipeline bringing the water into their distribution system on Ruxton Creek at Manitou Springs. In 1933, Congress agreed to pay one-third of the cost for the pipelines and reservoirs as a Depression-era public works project, and the city built a twenty-inch and twenty-four-inch line that dropped into the Manitou hydropower plant.[42] The first diversion of water from French Creek began in 1934, Crystal Reservoir was completed in 1935, and the South Catamount Reservoir was completed in 1937.

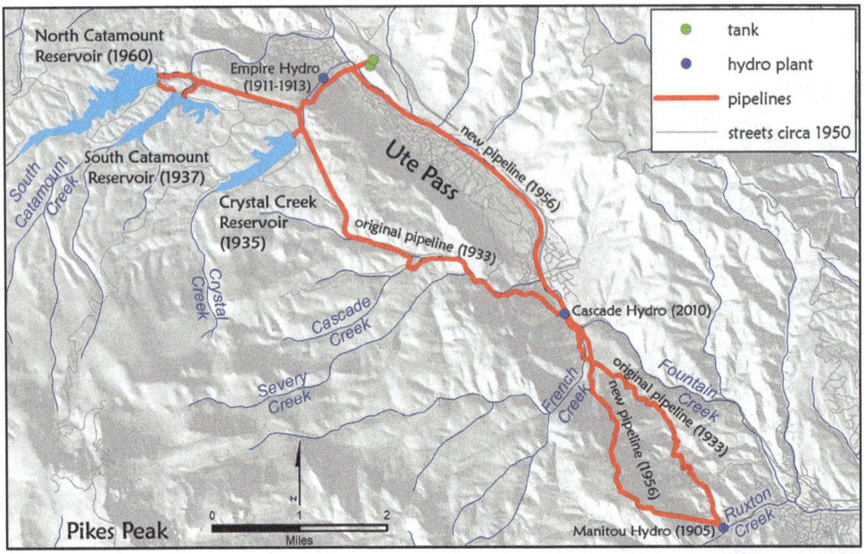

FIGURE 2.5. North Slope water system, with original and newer pipelines shown. *Source*: Cartography by author.

Crystal and South Catamount Reservoirs and associated pipelines constituted the main contribution of the North Slope system. However, local residents know that today there are three reservoirs on the North Slope of Pikes Peak. Subsequent projects that developed water across the Continental Divide required more local storage, so the North Catamount Reservoir was constructed for this purpose in 1960, along with the Rampart Reservoir enlargement in 1970. All told, the North Slope reservoirs store about 2.5 times more water than the South Slope system—though not all water from Pikes Peak, this system created a major increase in capacity for the city.[43]

Competing Water Suppliers

Sandwiched between the agricultural lands surrounding the Broadmoor Dairy and the city of Colorado Springs was the service area for another firm, the Brookside Water and Investment Company. This company was founded in about 1888 and took water from Cheyenne Creek to serve the Ivywild residential area, an unincorporated development south of the city limits. A second rival utility in the southern suburbs came about shortly after influential citizen Winfield Scott Stratton, a local carpenter who became a millionaire from the gold rush at Cripple Creek, passed away in 1902. He deemed that the largest portion of his estate should go toward the creation of the Myron Stratton Home for the Indigent, named for his father. After a long and contentious court proceeding, the executor of the Stratton estate bought large amounts of land to the east and south of the Brookside's Ivywild neighborhood. The estate used their land for farming and ranching to supply the home and to train young residents in agricultural production, but much of the land was used simply as investment. Along with this project came the Myron Stratton Water Department, an agency that built infrastructure, including the Mount Baldy and Mesa Reservoirs, to provide water to the land it owned.[44] While most of the properties were sold off to private residents and the future Broadmoor Land Investment Company over the years, the water company continued to serve them and the Myron Stratton Home. In 1953, the Myron Stratton Water Department and the Brookside Water Company merged to form South Suburban Water, a utility that at the time served about 1,800 customers in this region of south Colorado Springs until bought out by the city and folded into Colorado Springs Utilities in 1966.[45]

The Broadmoor Land and Investment Company gained large tracts of land (most from the Myron Stratton Home) and equally large water rights holdings, plus built several of their own reservoirs, a treatment plant, and a broad-based delivery infrastructure to fulfill wealthy owner Spencer Penrose's vision for grandeur (figure 2.6). The Broadmoor built the Rosemont Reservoir in 1932, giving the resort a dependable supply to become the "polo, golf, and tennis capital of the world."[46] The residential area that grew up around the Broadmoor did not depend on Colorado Springs city water and maintained independence until 1973, when the city purchased the Broadmoor water rights and its water infrastructure. The area was formally annexed to the city in 1980 and is now served by Colorado Springs Utilities.

The legacy today for these three water companies on the south side are a series of reservoirs, pipelines, treatment plants, tanks, and pumps that serve older neighborhoods and new developments in the foothills in southwestern Colorado Springs (figure 2.7). Colorado Springs Utilities has expanded and upgraded these systems greatly, but the foundation was laid by these smaller water and land development companies.

To the north was an equally grand competitor, which was also eventually incorporated into Colorado Springs Utilities in 1949. The Northfield Land and Water Company claimed rights to water on West Monument Creek, which runs through today's US Air Force Academy from the Rampart Range.[47] Northfield was another speculative land company that used water as a means to sell lots to lands not served by Colorado Springs water (refer to figure 2.7). Through the Austin Bluffs Land Company, investors pitched a new suburban development at the southwestern base of what is today Palmer Park, even convincing the Colorado Springs Rapid Transit Company to run a trolley line to this new site in 1889.[48] Lot sales never took off, and the trolley line that was key for development was a perpetual money loser and was shut down in 1892.[49]

Northfield was more successful at serving other, more established residential areas adjacent to Colorado Springs, including Knob Hill, now a city neighborhood

FIGURE 2.6. Much water was needed by the Broadmoor Land and Investment Company for their lakes, golf courses, polo fields, and residential lots. This image shows the Broadmoor Hotel in 1920. Note the apple orchard west of the lake, which gave the name "El Pomar" to owner Julie and Spencer Penrose's house. *Source*: Colorado Springs Pioneers Museum.

on Platte Avenue but at the time outside of the eastern city limits and the entryway to the town from the main east-west highway. This water infrastructure made possible the siting of the Union Printers Home in 1892 (after which Knob Hill's Main Street was renamed Union Boulevard). A pipeline side spur ran west to serve Roswell, a town that provided labor for the Rock Island maintenance yard. Finally, the Northfield system served the Cragmor Sanatorium built in 1905 at the base of Austin Bluffs, now the location of the University of Colorado Colorado Springs, and nearby coal-mining camps. Colorado Springs Utilities took over Northfield in 1949, after which their facilities became crucial elements to the entire Colorado Springs water system. Their reservoir system was expanded so that Rampart Reservoir, first built in 1924 and enlarged in 1970, is now a major storage for Western Slope water.

The story of Colorado Springs water, then, is both direct development of local water resources and infrastructure combined with acquisition of smaller suppliers in the region to profit from Pikes Peak water. These acquisitions continued as the single municipal supplier swallowed smaller providers over subsequent decades.[50] But all of these strategies drew water from the local region only. When

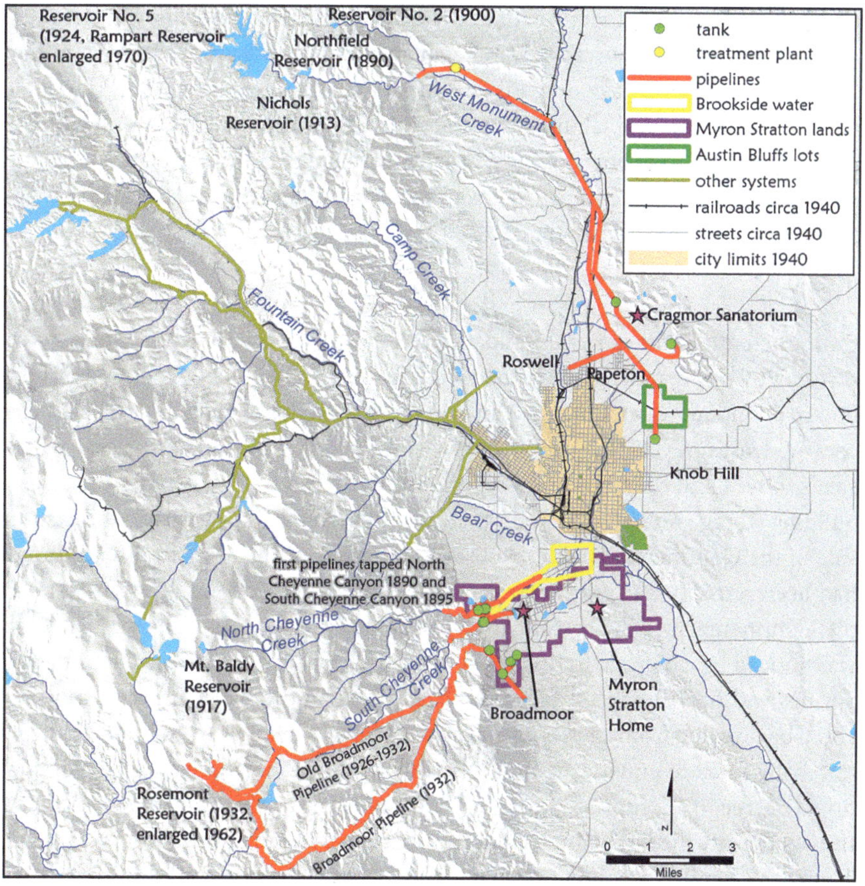

FIGURE 2.7. Broadmoor area ponds and infrastructure, including Rosemont Reservoir, with Myron Stratton Home boundaries and the Brookside service area and its water system tapping Cheyenne Creek. The Northfield water system served settlements north of the city such as the Papeton coal-mining town, the Roswell railroad town, the Cragmor Sanatorium, proposed suburban tracts at Austin Bluffs (Palmer Park), and Knob Hill east of town. *Source*: Cartography by author.

those resources were exploited to their full potential, the time came for the city to extend its tentacles into untapped peripheral regions.

WESTERN SLOPE WATER

The collection system from Pikes Peak was sufficient for the city while its population remained fairly stable at under 40,000 people throughout the 1930s. But while ambitious for its time, this system would not suffice for its ever-growing needs. In particular, World War II led to the establishment of Camp Carson in 1942 (later Fort Carson), a sizeable army post that needed water, and postwar military investments fueled further growth after mid-century. The problem was that there were few other local sources of water available. Engineer Sawyer's 1901 claim that "for water supply we have only Pikes Peak to depend on" was an understandable perception of water availability for the beginnings of the twentieth century, but by the 1940s others were envisioning a broader reach, engineering works that would give the city the capacity to extract water from distant sources at a scale unimaginable to those from earlier eras.[51]

Blue River

From the base of Pikes Peak, builders of the water empire need only look west, across the Continental Divide to the Western Slope of the Rocky Mountains. There flowed abundant water, untapped and unappropriated, not being put to beneficial use—at least not yet. Denver Water first started looking at Western Slope watersheds in 1914 and surveyed areas of interest in the 1920s. The agency was actively building storage reservoirs in their South Platte watershed by 1930 (on the eastern side of the Continental Divide), and by 1934 a bore of the Moffat railroad tunnel had been retrofitted to run water from the Fraser River, on the Western Slope of the Continental Divide, east for use by Denver.[52] Surely this Denver water grab was noticed by Colorado Springs water planners. The closest source for Colorado Springs was near Breckenridge at the headwaters of the Blue River, where water could be diverted from such high elevations that it could flow to Colorado Springs purely by force of gravity (figure 2.8).[53] By law, a user could be granted a conditional decree to appropriate water if that user begins work on a diversion project. In 1949 the city filed its claim for a conditional decree and began work on Hoosier Tunnel, a 1.5 mile bore under Hoosier Pass.[54]

While the Blue River diversion project was new geographical and engineering territory for city developers, it also entered them into new political territories. Right off the bat the utility faced local opposition, and we see the initial signs of the antitax and anti-public-works sentiment that has come to characterize Colorado Springs in subsequent years. A local group, the Organization for Representative Government, was formed, who allied with the El Paso County Taxpayers Association and others to protest the legality and validity of city bonds issued in 1950 to pay for this project. These factions entered a barrage of lawsuits against City Council and the city attorney personally, all of which were subsequently dismissed.[55] They did, however, put the status of the project in limbo while the legal process worked its way through court.

More formidable for city water interests than local anti-tax activists were the "big boys" in Colorado water politics: Denver Water, the US Bureau of Reclamation, and Western Slope water interests aligned through the Colorado River Water Conservation District. Colorado Springs had entered into the game with all of these players when it began vying for Western Slope water.

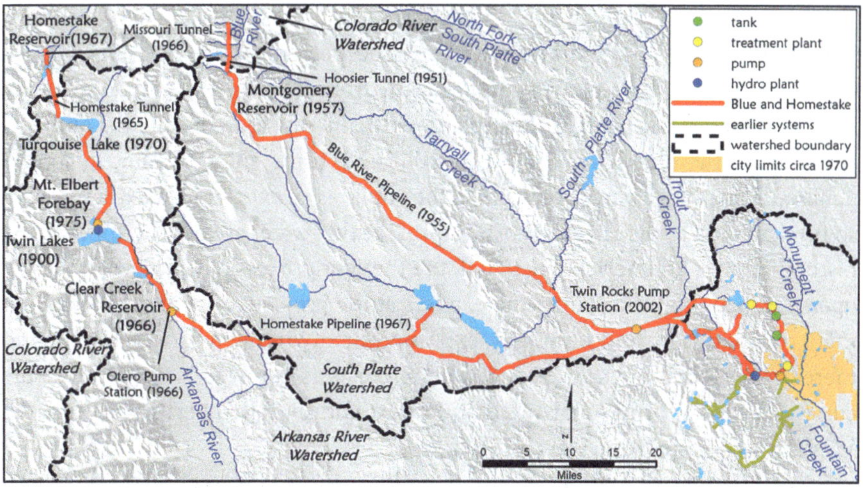

FIGURE 2.8. Blue River water system, crossing through the South Platte River watershed and Denver Water areas. Homestake water system, crossing the Continental Divide into the Arkansas River watershed, then pumped through the Otero Pump Station through the South Platte River watershed and over to storage near Colorado Springs. *Source*: Cartography by author.

The Bureau of Reclamation and Denver Water argued over competing reservoir water rights and Denver's plans to divert Blue River water through the twenty-four-mile-long Roberts Tunnel into the South Platte watershed.[56] The Bureau of Reclamation filed lawsuit against Denver and Colorado Springs, finally settled in the 1955 Blue River Decree, where Denver and Colorado Springs were granted junior rights to the other parties.[57] So Colorado Springs got its water, albeit with some restrictions.[58] The Blue River controversy implemented the initial stages of federal environmental regulation, whereby concerns for watershed ecology would eventually be elevated to a status competing with municipal water needs.

The system was completed in 1961 and produced for Colorado Springs almost as much water as from the entire Pikes Peak watershed. Water from the Blue River Project is stored in the reservoirs on the North Slope of Pikes Peak, hence the North Catamount Reservoir was built in 1960. Blue River water is also stored in the Northfield system of reservoirs, primarily Rampart Reservoir.[59] An interesting geographical oddity is that Colorado Springs water taken from the Western Slope passes through the South Platte watershed, which is almost exclusively Denver water. Because of the course of the South Platte, and the earlier rights to that river by Denver, Colorado Springs must bring water from watersheds beyond the South Platte, through Denver Water territory, until it can be stored in Colorado Springs territory, within the Fountain Creek watershed on the slopes of Pikes Peak.

Homestake

A post–World War II boom saw an over 800 percent population increase for Colorado Springs, from 1950 to 2010, growing from 45,472 people to 416,472. City leaders looked at the near-exponential growth and saw that, despite the audacity and scale of the Blue River Project, it would not bring enough water for future demand. Water has always been sold to the public as an existential need, a resource so fundamental to the city that costs to provide that water are of little concern. As historian Patricia Limerick has stated, the thought process of urban water developers has been to pick a future date, guess at the projected population, consider that growth as right and necessary, express certainty in the future demands, and therefore present proposals for new water projects as nonnegotiable.[60] And so the city of Colorado Springs embarked on its next endeavor to divert water from the Western Slope, the Homestake Project.

Front Range municipalities, from Colorado Springs to Denver and the Northern Colorado Water Conservancy District, obviously diverted the closest sources of water first. Each subsequent project taps water from increasingly farther away, and the expenses (though presented as nonnegotiable) really do become a concern. Colorado Springs looked for partners to develop new water projects and found one in the city of Aurora, Denver's largest suburb. Denver Water, used to asserting its will and getting its way, had alienated surrounding municipalities in 1951 by drawing boundaries around its service area and excluding service, or charging high rates, to those outside this line.[61] Aurora did not wish to be dependent upon this ruthless master and as early as 1949 filed claims to water (along with Colorado Springs) in the Homestake Creek in Eagle County (refer to figure 2.8).

In 1961, Colorado Springs entered into an agreement with the city of Aurora to build the Homestake system. Work began on the Homestake Reservoir in 1963 and was completed in 1967. After collecting water from local streams, water from this reservoir is sent through the 5.5-mile Homestake Tunnel (completed in 1966) under the Continental Divide to Turquoise Lake near Leadville. The remainder of the system was built in stages, so today the water next flows to the Mount Elbert Forebay Reservoir, then down the Mount Elbert power conduit, where hydroelectricity is generated, and into the Twin Lakes Reservoir. From there the water flows via pipeline fourteen miles along the Arkansas River to the Otero Pump Station, built in 1966 and upgraded in 1974, a massive pump that sends 118 million gallons per day of water through the sixty-six-inch Homestake Pipeline up over Trout Creek Pass and into South Park. Aurora took its half of the water to store in Spinney Mountain Reservoir where it flows downstream for its use.[62] Colorado Springs water flows through a pipeline to the Twin Rocks Pump Station, where it is again pumped uphill to store in either the North Slope reservoirs or Rampart Reservoir. The entire system for Colorado Springs is over 130 miles in length and increased its water supply capacity by over 50 percent.[63]

The system is now a main source for both cities' water supply. However, the system as described was only to be Phase I. Phase II was planned to expand the Homestake project to the north, west, and east, but here the project did not go smoothly. By the 1970s, the days of urban utilities or the federal government building large water projects with little opposition were over. The National Environmental Policy Act of 1969 now required any project on federal land, undertaken by a federal agency, or using federal funding to complete an environmental impact statement, for the first time forcing water project planners to consider the environmental consequences and damages their projects would cause. Planning for Homestake II began shortly after Phase I was operational, but the primary impediment was that the proposed eleven miles of tunnels and numerous reservoirs were to be built in the federally designated Holy Cross Wilderness. The project expansion was met by adamant opposition in Eagle County, where the rivers flow toward Vail and other mountain towns.[64] The Colorado Springs Chamber of Commerce Manufacturers' Association defended the city as a "very environmentally oriented community" that simply wanted to exercise the Western Slope water rights it has held for years. Chamber president James Hill, a retired air force general, said that the Homestake II water was vital to continued growth in Colorado Springs and especially to the area's several military bases; any threat to this continued supply would be "disastrous."[65] The US Forest Service approved the environmental impact statement in 1983. This was challenged by the Sierra Club, but an Appeals Court upheld the ruling.[66] In the interim, Colorado enacted House Bill 1041, which gave counties more land use jurisdiction, setting forth another round of lawsuits.[67] After more than two decades of legal wrangling, the project was denied in 1988 by Eagle County, with further appeals running through the mid-1990s before the project finally stopped.[68]

The city's response to the failed Homestake II project was to put further claims to the Eagle River (which have also gone nowhere), then to float ideas of building a reservoir at Elephant Rock in the Arkansas River Valley just above Buena Vista, a project that would drown the premier rapids of the country's most popular whitewater rafting river. Opposition was vehement again, and this project has withered away. But the quest for water did not stop.

Twin Lakes and the Colorado Canal

Lessons learned from the earlier controversial projects led to new strategies to develop water delivery capacity. The first was to limit outright development of new infrastructure and instead make full use of existing waterworks, even those built by someone else. The second was to partner with the federal government to leverage local benefits from larger, regional scale projects. The Twin Lakes project was exactly the former—why build what you need when you can buy?

Twin Lakes are a series of two natural lakes that impound Lake Creek with a terminal moraine before it flows into the Arkansas River, upstream from Buena Vista and south of Leadville. Agriculturalists in the lower Arkansas River Valley east of Pueblo, about 150 miles downriver from Twin Lakes, early on saw the utility of storing water upstream for release when needed for crops. They organized the Twin lakes Water Company in 1890, claimed the water as early as 1896, reinforced and raised the natural dam thirteen feet to add storage capacity, and collected water from Lake Creek that ran into the enlarged reservoir. This water could then be released into the Arkansas River and withdrawn as needed into the Colorado Canal, diverting from the river about seventeen miles east of Pueblo. To increase supply, the company in 1935 built a collection system from the Western Slope streams at the headwaters of the Roaring Fork River, moved the water into a small reservoir at Grizzly Creek, then ran it through a tunnel to divert water under the Continental Divide and down Lake Creek (figure 2.9).[69] In 1972 Colorado Springs purchased shares in the Twin Lakes water rights and again in 1976 purchased more.[70]

The purchase of this irrigation company's water rights saved the city building more infrastructure at the diversion and storage points and simply sent more water out of Twin Lakes through the existing Otero Pump Station. The project resulted in both great efficiencies and a huge increase in capacity—nearly double what the Homestake system provided.

In 1985, Colorado Springs purchased majority shares that expanded water rights, plus added a canal and two reservoirs located in Crowley County east of Pueblo. The city does not extract any water from these reservoirs directly for municipal use, since they are far downstream from Colorado Springs. Rather, the city releases water from these reservoirs for downstream irrigators along the lower Arkansas River (at times leasing water back to the original users) in exchange for extracting more water upstream, from the Twin Lakes system and from Turquoise Lake on the Homestake system. This seemingly devious scheme added more Twin Lakes water alone than the Homestake and Blue systems combined. Water purchases from Arkansas Valley farmers by both Colorado Springs and Aurora brought accusations of political blackmail and excessive use of economic and legal power.[71] Many see urban areas buying out agricultural water rights as an assault on rural America and the farming tradition of this country, raising questions about the social costs and benefits: today only 4 percent of Crowley County's historic cropland is still farmed.[72]

Facing opposition from agriculturalists and rural communities, urban water managers point out that even with increasing urban water use and purchasing of agricultural water rights, over 80 percent of water in Colorado is still used for agriculture.[73] Changing imperatives in a global agricultural system, not lack of water, have shut down the sugar beet industry in this valley and the economics

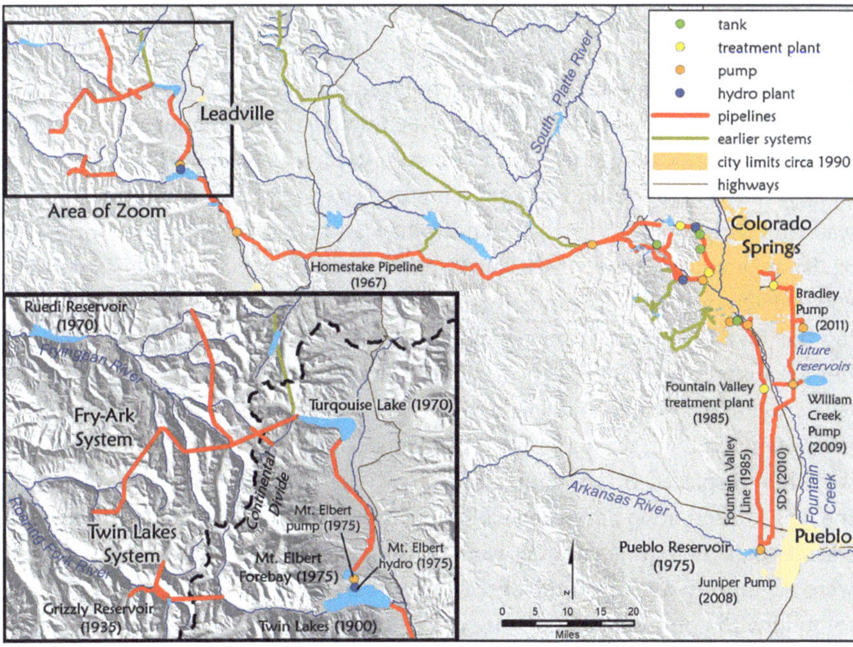

FIGURE 2.9. Twin Lakes and Fry-Ark water systems, including the Western Slope's Ruedi Reservoir. This project built the Pueblo Reservoir, with the Fountain Valley Conduit the first system to pump water from there to Colorado Springs. Also shown is the Southern Delivery System (SDS), the city's newest (and last?) major water infrastructure project. *Source*: Cartography by author.

apply to all crops. Some farmers and ranchers have adapted to focus on niche markets and tap into the growing locavore movement that seeks locally produced food, so we see organic vegetables, raw milk production, and grass-fed beef from the valley now for sale in Colorado Springs and Pueblo. Plus Pueblo chile peppers from the Arkansas Valley now are a product with place-based recognition, renowned for their flavor from the hot sunny days and cool nights (and for their aroma as they are roasted throughout Colorado each fall). The newest niche crop is marijuana, already reaping huge dividends as local greenhouses and fields provide the state medicinal and recreational retailers. But this nascent industry of niche and organic crops, though laudable for numerous reasons, has not replaced the mass-produced, industrial agricultural production of yesteryear, and all the while new economies generate more jobs in urban areas. The nostalgia of the old West confronts modern-day realities of the new. And the Colorado water law is clear—water is intended to be put to its most beneficial use, and in today's economy and society that means larger portions go to cities. As the saying goes, water in the West doesn't flow downhill—it flows toward money.

The Fryingpan-Arkansas (Fry-Ark) Project

Always looking to add to its water supply, the city turned to a second strategy and partnered with the federal government to leverage water from other projects. The big player for water in the West has been the Bureau of Reclamation, renowned for gigantic projects wrought with controversy.[74] As early as 1936, the bureau began to work with Arkansas Valley farmers on methods to provide flood control and more water for irrigation.[75] By 1947 engineers had an audacious draft plan originally envisioned as the Gunnison-Arkansas project, which would take an astounding 800,000 acre feet of water annually from numerous Western Slope rivers, including the Taylor, which is tributary to the Gunnison.[76] This water was to flow into the Arkansas River Valley at various points, with six dams envisioned in that valley between Twin Lakes and Salida to provide hydroelectric power. Western Slope interests were livid, as surely were residents in the Arkansas River Valley who would be displaced by so many reservoirs.[77] The chief engineer and director of the Soil Conservation Service in Colorado, Ralph Parshall, pointed out the unjustifiable costs (he estimated water would cost in excess of 100 times what irrigators were paying). In a letter to the bureau chief, Parshall said, "The Bureau will have to build with common sense or else close up shop. You have reached or possibly exceeded the limit of toleration . . . Your Arkansas scheme is a dead duck."[78]

In response to the criticisms, the bureau scaled back the project to the Fryingpan-Arkansas scheme that would divert 69,200 acre feet annually—less than one-tenth the original plan. A draft was prepared by 1950 and officially drawn up in 1951, the purpose again being irrigation, power, municipal water, and flood control. To pay for the project, the Southeastern Colorado Water Conservancy District was created on April 29, 1958, to administer and help pay for the Fryingpan-Arkansas Project.[79] Upon the advice of city attorney Rick Henry, Colorado Springs joined the district.[80] The district serves cities and counties along the Arkansas River and Fountain Creek, from Lake County to nearly the Kansas border and helps pay for construction, operation, and maintenance costs through a property tax. While a big undertaking, the entire project was intended to supply only supplemental water to existing users. There are no new users for this project, but rather this system provides better and more reliable means to get water for those with existing water rights. The Southeast Water Conservancy District, which is responsible for distributing the water already had on file or anticipated requests by 1967 for close to twice as much water as the project was expected to produce.[81]

After more than a decade of debate, the project was approved by Congress in 1962 and signed by President Kennedy. It takes water from headwaters of both the Fryingpan and the Roaring Fork rivers (refer to figure 2.9). The Boustead Tunnel, under the Continental Divide, was completed in 1972, and work on the collection system on the Western Slope continued until 1979. The project built much new infrastructure and reinforced existing works. Once completed, the project had six storage dams, seventeen diversion dams, two power plants, hundreds of miles of canals, pipelines, and twenty-seven miles of tunnels.[82]

One of the most significant parts of the project for Colorado Springs was building the Pueblo Reservoir, first started in 1970 and completed in 1975. The city—along with the towns of Stratmoor Hills, Widefield, Security, and Fountain to the south—tapped into this new storage works west of Pueblo and completed the Fountain Valley Conduit in 1985, a forty-five-mile long pipeline that delivers about 20,000 acre feet of water annually.[83] The Pueblo Reservoir and Fountain Valley Conduit opened a new distribution system for Colorado Springs. The city could now continue to divert water, including Fry-Ark water, from Twin Lakes and into its existing Otero Pump Station and Homestake Pipeline or let its water allocations run downstream into the Pueblo Reservoir and collect it there.

The Fry-Ark provided water subsidized by US taxpayers. As with most federal western water projects, costs were underestimated and revenue projections were unmet, leaving nearly two-thirds of the costs to the taxpayer. But these are not the concerns of Colorado Springs, the primary beneficiary of this subsidized project. While benefits accrued to Colorado Springs are in one sense fair, seeing that El Paso County pays more than 70 percent of the district's property tax revenue, the project is yet another example of politically conservative population, with a decidedly anti-federal-government, antitax sentiment, drinking from the public trough. As Marc Reisner wrote, "Ideology is the first casualty of water development."[84]

Southern Delivery System

Colorado Springs saw rapid population increases in the late twentieth and early twenty-first centuries with projections for continued growth. The State Demography Office projects over 280,000 new people in El Paso County by 2040, a 42 percent increase from 2015. (Colorado Springs Utilities claims much higher numbers, 350,000 new people by 2030 and a 70 percent increase by 2050.)[85] In anticipation, the city annexed an enormous tract of land in 1988, the Banning Lewis Ranch, which is fourteen miles in length north to south and about four miles wide. The property was adjacent to the eastern city limits and now comprises its entire eastern extent. Developers envisioned at least 75,000 homes at full buildout in this annexation alone. Such a scenario would require more water, and the city already had rights to that water in the Arkansas River through the Colorado Canal purchases. It just needed a way to get the water to the undeveloped plains east of the city, so by 1996 the plan for the Southern Delivery System (SDS) was drawn up and announced to the public by 2000.[86]

This project pulls more water from the Pueblo Reservoir on the Arkansas River and pumps it to eastern Colorado Springs.[87] Intended to fill the city's needs through 2040, construction began for this system in 2008 and Phase I was completed in 2016. The project uses eleven pumps in three pumping stations to send water through a sixty-six-inch pipeline from the Pueblo Reservoir 50 miles and 1,500 feet uphill to two new storage reservoirs (to be built in Phase II) in the Banning Lewis annexation and a new water treatment plant[88] (refer to figure 2.9). It will increase the city's capacity to deliver water by about 30 percent, adding enough water for over 200,000 households.[89] Originally a $740 million deal, Phase I was completed for $829 million in 2016, but including Phase II and interest the ultimate budget could be on the order of $1.6 billion.[90]

Pueblo lawmakers and Bob Rawlings, the editor of the *Pueblo Chieftain*, strongly opposed Colorado Springs taking more water from Pueblo Reservoir. They focused their opposition around stormwater runoff. Fountain Creek flows from Colorado Springs through Pueblo, where it reaches the confluence with the Arkansas River. Historically this had been a muddy little braided stream, even intermittent at times, but growth of Colorado Springs has dramatically affected the stream's hydrology and water quality. After decades of water diversions bringing more water to Colorado Springs from other watersheds, most of that then runs down Fountain Creek after being treated at the municipal wastewater plant. Fountain Creek now runs with about four times the volume of its historical average prior to water diversions. The increase in volume has led to a greater rate of downcutting. The alluvial sands and gravel in the creek bed have been stripped down to the Pierre Shale in certain locations, where the downcutting effect is reduced and the increased flow is largely silt-free, both increasing erosion and carrying capacity.[91] Fountain Creek has changed from a braided stream to a deeper, more concentrated channel. Added to these changes are the vast areas of impervious surface built as the city developed in a classical pattern of urban sprawl with large parking lots near big-box stores and wide arterial roads. In 2009, analysis found that 96 square miles of the city were covered by impervious surfaces, about 49 percent of the entire land cover.[92] These asphalt or concrete surfaces increase the flashy nature of runoff into rapid torrents after a storm, rather than the slow release of groundwater into streams that occurs when rain soaks through natural vegetation. The result has been flooding and erosion along the creek corridor and into Pueblo. As of 1997, federal mandates now require stormwater runoff mitigation, putting pressure on Colorado Springs to fund infrastructure to control runoff.[93]

The real urgency came with SDS, since construction could not begin without a land use permit by Pueblo County commissioners, who demanded stormwater control. So Colorado Springs created a Stormwater Enterprise in 2005, with a fee on landowners based on the percentage of property covered with impervious surface. Activists challenged this fee as a new tax (their campaign called it a "Rain Tax"), not approved by local taxpayers and therefore unconstitutional according to the 1992 Colorado Taxpayer's Bill of Rights, or TABOR law.[94] The court agreed. The city then put to the voters a proposal to fund the Stormwater Enterprise, and again this proposal was rejected in 2009 and the fee was eliminated. In the interim

SDS had begun, and now Pueblo commissioners were waiting for Colorado Springs to create a new funding source.[95] The 2009 land use permit approved by Pueblo County mandated funding for the Fountain Creek Flood Control. A 2012 report found that the Fountain Creek watershed has an $834 million backlog for stormwater infrastructure, with Colorado Springs alone behind by $500 million, yet that report reveals that city residents pay the lowest taxes for stormwater compared to the ten largest Front Range cities: $4.63 per capita annually versus the average of $52.11.[96] The 2012 Infrastructure Report Card by the American Society of Civil Engineers gave the city a D grade in the area of stormwater, citing less than 1 percent of the funding needed to address infrastructure.[97] Mayor Steve Bach did not support a new tax, but the city again put a vote to the public in fall 2014, to fund stormwater infrastructure and again it was rejected, even with the mandate in the SDS approval that a comprehensive funding mechanism would be instituted to deal with this problem.[98] City leaders and citizens in both Pueblo and the Lower Arkansas Valley feel cheated, another case of Colorado Springs getting its water but not following through with its part of the bargain. Mayor Bach, caught in a bind, said he was "searching for efficiencies" to drum up the elusive funding.[99]

The confrontation came to a head in April 2016, as the project was nearing completion. As water was set to begin flowing through the pipeline, Pueblo threatened to suspend the land use permit unless Colorado Springs made a real commitment to stormwater management. With new mayor, John Suthers, in Colorado Springs more amenable to an agreement, the two cities announced a twenty-year, $460 million deal to correct Colorado Springs' neglected flood control infrastructure, and then, on the third try, voters approved a stormwater fee in 2017 that will add to the pot. With these last-minute agreements, the SDS is now a reality, though the Environmental Protection Agency and Colorado Department of Public Health and Environment have an ongoing lawsuit against the city for violating water quality standards from stormwater runoff.[100]

In addition to the legal challenges from Pueblo, local opposition was also strong. The project will likely cost over $1 billion, paid mostly by existing residents and entirely for about 120,000 new water users who do not yet live here in houses not yet built.[101] The bill comes to over $8,000 per existing household. The charge is that the current citizens are unjustly subsidizing both future residents and the housing development industry. The 2008 recession and housing bust brought the big blow—all those projections for 75,000 new homes in the Banning Lewis annexation have not happened and likely won't for a long time, if ever. By 2018 only 600 homes have been built at the northern end of the property.[102] The Banning Lewis property has passed through numerous owners, two that went bankrupt. Despite these trends and historic events, the growth boosters still proclaimed that "hesitating to move forward with SDS would have serious economic consequences to Colorado Springs and El Paso County, with impacts felt among all of its regional neighbors."[103] The SDS Phase I was completed in 2016, "just in time to insure a reliable water supply."[104]

CONTEMPORARY WATER REALITIES

Colorado Springs Utilities, like all water agencies serving western cities, knows it cannot rely solely on grand new diversion projects to meet future needs. Their 1996 Water Resource Plan maps out the strategy to meet future needs and has four components: conservation, nonpotable water development, existing system improvements, and new water delivery systems.[105] Conservation has long been a strategy and includes demand side management programs such as efficient appliances, xeriscaped lawns, and dual-rate metering that rewards lower water usage and penalizes heavy users. Generally popular programs, even these enter the world of politics: a 1998 proposed ordinance that sets standards for drought tolerant plants for Colorado Springs landscaping was said to be "intrusive" by city councilor Jim Null, yet another affront to private property rights and overreach of governmental authority.[106] Regulations (which were really only recommendations) were softened as a result. Substitution of nonpotable water has long been used for large irrigation needs such as golf courses, parks, and cemeteries.[107]

The city has sought addition sources of water, including groundwater rights from regional wells, water exchanges to stretch supplies, and plans for future reservoirs. A rough accounting of the sources for Colorado Springs Utilities water is therefore[108]

Local (Pikes Peak slopes, Rampart Range, groundwater): 13 percent
Blue River: 7 percent
Twin Lakes and the Colorado Canal: 37 percent
Homestake: 11 percent
Fry-Ark (including the Fountain Valley Conduit): 11 percent
Southern Delivery System (bringing water from Fry-Ark and Colorado Canal rights): 21 percent

When we add together water from the Fry-Ark, the Twin Lakes, and the Homestake systems which are all collected into reservoirs in the upper Arkansas Valley, over 50 percent of the city's total water is pumped through the Otero Pump Station and the Homestake Pipeline.

Despite the sometimes ruthless tactics used, the environmental damage accrued, and the costs incurred to build the city's water supply infrastructure, Colorado Springs residents can be thankful for the proactive investments long made by water planners to provide reliable water. We need only see the issues now facing latecomers to the water acquisition game, namely, in the rapidly expanding, previously rural areas between Denver and Colorado Springs. New municipalities

FIGURE 2.10. Photo from the bluffs at Palmer Park in 1903 showing complete lack of trees on the mesa where the city was built (left). The road is Paseo Drive, and the factory is the coal-mining complex near Papeton. Contemporary view but with dense urban forest visible looking toward the downtown, all as a result of irrigation (right). *Source*: Colorado Springs Pioneers Museum, photo by author.

and unincorporated county parcels rely primarily on groundwater, and in affluent Douglas and northern El Paso Counties, new wells are continually approved even while USGS monitors record steady drops in aquifers, but residents oppose "arbitrary" limits on growth.[109]

The net result on the cultural landscape for Colorado Springs from this long history of water infrastructure development is profound. A look at the vegetation land cover shows the transformation from a dry, uninhabited short grass mesa into a city housing over one-half a million people with a dense urban forest canopy (figure 2.10). Dotted throughout the city are pumps, tanks, diversion points, hydro plants, and treatment plants that most people ignore as they pass. In addition to the currently used facilities, relict landscape remnants from decades of projects dot the forest and hills west of the city and throughout the contemporary built environment. The extent of Colorado Springs' impact on landscape and environment reaches far into the Rocky Mountain wilderness and across the Continental Divide. This abundant water has so completely transformed lives that most residents give its availability no thought whatsoever.[110] Being unaware of the enormous costs and complexities that go into water supply, most forget the decades of hard work put forth but also the fragility of the ecosystems that sustain the city and the impacts upon it. The relationship with the natural environment is obscured. Engineering marvels have so thoroughly erased the natural limitations of this place that most forget that, one day, citizens might actually have to confront those limitations.

3

Air

The light, dry air is bracing to the lungs, making the chest expand and the heart throb with vigor.

—*COLORADO SPRINGS GAZETTE TELEGRAPH*, 1905[1]

There is no mud in Colorado Springs.

—LOUIS R. EHRICH, 1887[2]

While the city went to great efforts to manipulate the environment through its water delivery infrastructure, there was one environmental condition that required no human engineering: its climate. Dry air, sunny days, and high altitude are physical dimensions of Colorado Springs that could easily be marketed and exploited, particularly for those seeking relief from the most dreaded disease: tuberculosis. Tuberculosis (TB) has plagued humanity since before recorded history, and until the mid-1940s there was no known cure. By the late nineteenth century, the best option for TB sufferers was to relocate to a place with more favorable climatic conditions. Colorado Springs became a favored destination for those seeking freedom from disease, and caring for those health seekers was the first growth industry of the city.

TUBERCULOSIS

Tuberculosis was a mysterious disease. Unlike epidemics that roared through society, decimating large numbers then going away, TB was a constant reality affecting each of its victims differently. Some died quickly, for many the disease lingered for decades, and others seemed miraculously cured after exhibiting initial symptoms. Despite this inconsistency, TB was a major killer, responsible for up to one out of every five deaths in the first half of the nineteenth century in the United States.[3] It was the most common cause of death among those in their productive years.[4]

DOI: 10.5876/9781646421688.c003

How the disease was viewed changed through the centuries. Called "phthisis" or "wasting disease" in the seventeenth and eighteenth centuries, it was most commonly diagnosed as "consumption" by the nineteenth century in reference to the wasting away of the body; the human body literally seemed to be consumed. In addition to the emaciated frame, symptoms included a hollow cough, night sweats, and regular low fevers. Patients would suffer from loss of breath at the slightest exertion, coughing up—and spitting out—phlegm, blood, and mucous matter from the lungs. Many vernacular phrases were assigned to its victims: "coughers," "hackers," "lungers," "pukers," "wheezers," "invalids," "consumptives," and others even less flattering. Given the range of symptoms and degrees of severity, the diagnosis of consumption was necessarily vague. An affliction of unknown origin, it was at times thought to be genetic, or perhaps brought on by an immoral lifestyle. In nineteenth-century thinking, being poor meant you were immoral, and being poor and immoral meant you were likely diseased. Some placed blame on a "riotous life full of too much sex and folly," masturbation (self-pollution), or even excessive dancing.[5] The disease gained vigor in Europe and the industrial east by the mid-nineteenth century. With increasingly crowded cities, TB slaughtered the poor by the millions, and poverty, malnutrition, overcrowding, and vice made it an ingrained part of the industrial landscape.

In 1882 Dr. Robert Koch identified the cause of the disease, the tubercle bacillus, after which the term "consumption" fell out of favor and the more scientific reference of tuberculosis became the norm. Despite an increased understanding of the cause, and realization that contagion was spread through the cough or sneeze of tuberculars, or through contact with their spit or bodily fluids, there remained no known cure. Treatments were experimental and at times gruesome, seemingly worse than the disease itself: collapsing the lung, forcing patients to inhale sulphuretted hydrogen gas, or drinking concoctions containing strychnine or creosote, and other remedies.

CHASING THE CURE

Because there was no medicinal cure, eventually treatment fell to three considerations: climate, exercise, and diet. Of the three, physicians tended to emphasize climate and, in particular, dry air at high altitude. Climate theory of consumption arose from an antiurban bias prevalent in America and the fascination with the mythical West in American lore. As industrialization took hold of the American economy in the late nineteenth century, cities crowded with immigrant labor in tenement housing were seen to be squalid and unsanitary. Writers such as Ralph Waldo Emerson espoused the pastoral ideal in reaction to the dense and dirty city, and Henry David Thoreau popularized nature as a spiritual respite for city dwellers. Such thinking led to the growth in design and creation of urban parks as places of refuge, and ultimately greater architectural and planning reforms such as the City Beautiful Movement. Certain natural places, particularly mineral water spas, had long traditions as health resorts, and America's newfound embrace of nature extended this therapeutic aspect to the climate itself. Given the prevalence of TB and the difficulties it caused with breathing, the very quality of the air came to be associated with a cure for consumption. This was bolstered by popular theories in the early nineteenth century that disease was spawned by the constitution of the atmosphere. The "putrid-vapor thesis" claimed rotting organic matter, particularly at low elevations and in humid conditions (exhalations arising from swamps and wet soil), was the chief cause of fevers and other ailments.[6] Fevers, malaria, yellow fever, and other diseases were so prevalent in the Mississippi Valley—from Indiana, Illinois, and Missouri down to New Orleans—that the region gained a reputation for unhealthfulness, and a steady number of the "walking dead" left these early frontier regions for higher and drier ground.

The curative power of nature promoted by mid-century writers grew into an interpretation of American wilderness areas as therapeutic in the 1870s and 1880s. Nature and wilderness were no more overt than in the American West. Already romanticized by sketches, paintings, and photographs from early surveys, the grandeur of the landscape came to represent spiritual enlightenment that could manifest physical well-being. There existed deeply held fantasies about the West as Eden, where the air was pure, the atmosphere wholesome, and its climate reinvigorating.[7] The trend of western immigration for cures from fevers from the industrial east and the humid Mississippi Valley was already established as early as 1820.[8] Also, anecdotes from adventurers and health seekers appeared by the 1850s that reinforced these beliefs. The West as a health-giving Eden shaped medical thought, and nineteenth-century physicians saw a strong connection between climate and health. Many recommended that patients go above the "altitude of immunity" line, usually about 5,000 to 6,000 feet above sea level but ranging anywhere from 4,000 to 8,000 feet.[9] In 1888, Dr. Frederick Knight explained to the Boston Society of Medical Observation that the Rocky Mountains were preferred locations because the air is very dry and pure, the number of clear days when an invalid can be outside is high, and the "rarified air" causes "increased respiratory activity."[10] The rationale was that elevation increased heart and lung action so that pure, "aseptic" atmosphere (free from all germ life) got deeper into the lungs and aided healing:[11]

> The effect of the dry rarefied air is to increase the appetite; assimilation is improved, the number and depth of respirations are increased, the chest gains in expansive power, more moisture is exhaled than in humid atmosphere, the effect of which is in time to check secretion from the diseased tissues. The cheeks fill out, the complexion becomes of a ruddy brown, the strength rapidly increases, the spirits revive, and the invalid becomes impressed with the idea that he will recover.[12]

Health seekers were an integral part of westward movement in American history. By 1900 fully one-quarter of the migrants to California and one-third of the newcomers to Colorado had come in search of health. More than half of the residents of Pasadena, California; Colorado Springs and Denver, Colorado; El Paso, Texas; Albuquerque, New Mexico; and Tucson, Arizona, reported to a 1913 public health survey that either they or a parent, grandparent, or sibling had emigrated in search of a cure for consumption.[13] Completion of the transcontinental railroad in the 1870s led to direct promotion of the curative properties of the West by railroad companies that were happy to profit from this narrative, and a plethora of town boosters advocated the benefits of their particular place. Meteorological data and its effects on health regularly appeared in professional health journals, with the central Rocky Mountains of Colorado, or destinations in the Southwest from west Texas through Southern California as preferred destinations.

As was true with much of place boosterism in the West, the conditions that many health chasers found were cruder than the promotional literature suggested: wooden shacks on a remote and barren plot of land, or worse.[14] Most migrating consumptives could not afford to cure at a resort or any type of medical facility. They lived in boardinghouses, private homes run as infirmaries, cheap hotels, small secondary units in private backyards, and tent camps on the edges of towns. Impoverished and weak, many died in places forsaken by those of means and far from health resorts. A harsh reality was that only the wealthy were the chief beneficiaries of the climate cure.[15]

THE RISE OF THE SANATORIUM

To capitalize on the western climate cure, open health resorts began to appear by the 1880s. These consisted of anything from campsites to boardinghouses, hotels, and ranches. The key was the outdoor space, with fresh air, and a regimen of either rest or limited exercise, largely unsupervised and self-directed by the patient. But in Europe, a variation on the climate cure evolved into a new institution: the sanatorium.[16] While fresh air and sunshine were still prescribed, these sites shifted emphasis to the need for a qualified physician, or caregiver, to supervise the recovery process. Chief among the sanatoriums were Nordrach in Germany's Black Forest, and Davos in Switzerland. Building upon the long tradition of health spas in Europe as places to recuperate, these institutions implemented a regulated routine under constant oversight by doctors and nurses. As tourist and health resorts in the United States increasingly refused admittance of consumptives, sanatoriums filled the need, and the European sanatorium model became the norm for half a century.[17]

While the first US sanatorium was at Saranac Lake in the Adirondacks of New York in 1882, western sanatoriums quickly grew: by 1900, thirty-four sanatoriums with 4,485 beds had been opened in the United States. Twenty-five years later there were 536 with 673,338 beds.[18] Koch's discovery of the tubercular bacillus and our understanding of the cause of TB led to the rise of the sanatorium: "A new generation of physicians, social reformers, and philanthropists were convinced that confining the tubercular in these facilities would promote not only societal well-being by isolating those with the disease but also individual well-being by implementing a therapeutic regimen. The sanatorium satisfied both the drive to coerce and cure. Inside it, fear met hope."[19] The intent of the sanatorium was to liberate patients from the disease and restore them to a productive life. The cure would come from the patient's own natural resistance through the recuperative power of nature. Since medicine could do little on its own, the sanatorium could help and promote this power by wholesome rest and graduated exercise. Sanatoriums filled the emotional and psychological needs of the ill through a sense of community, support, and shared experience.

Consumptives were encouraged to live outdoors, breathe fresh air, eat nourishing food, and transition from rest to an active exercise routine once health began to improve. Since the logic of the sanatorium was to allow the patient's own defense mechanisms to assert themselves, physicians explained the value of rest in terms of its ability to regulate the amount of toxin released into the blood circulation; smaller amounts due to rest would activate the immune response and produce a sort of autovaccination and eventually cure.[20] Diet was also prominent in the proscription for cure, specifically an overabundance of food. Following on the standards established at Nordrach in Germany, where patients had to consume several pints of milk daily, physicians and nurses at most sanatoriums overstuffed patients with eggs, meat, juice, and milk to combat the emaciation common for invalids.[21]

COLORADO SPRINGS: CITY OF SUNSHINE

From its founding in 1871, Colorado Springs quickly gained a reputation as a restorative location for tuberculars, partly in response to national trends about the curative power of western air and nature but also due to overt marketing by early city elites and physicians who themselves located here to recover from TB. Consumptive patients were registered in the very first boardinghouses, as early as 1872.[22] The city formed a "Climactic Conditions Committee" to promote healthcare opportunities,[23] and the *Colorado Springs Gazette* jumped on the promotional propaganda bandwagon early on:

> Its scenery is magnificently grand. Its climate is deliciously cheering and healthful. The clear air and the bright sunshine, which continually characterize it, act like a charm upon the system, invigorating the bodily powers and inducing constant

"good spirits." The dryness and purity of the atmosphere render it especially suitable for such as are of consumptive or asthmatic tendencies or suffer from any affection of the throat or lungs; such—unless the disease has obtained too firm a grip—are almost certain to regain health and strength.[24]

Dr. Edwin Solly, a physician who relocated to Colorado Springs in 1874 to recover from TB, published a brochure in 1875 entitled "Manitou, Colorado, U.S.A.: Its Mineral Waters and Climate," followed by another in 1883: "The Health Resorts in Colorado Springs and Manitou."[25] In both he promoted the region as a health resort. Solly was convinced that open-air convalescence was the necessary prescription, and he became a leader in promoting the climate cure. He was an early member, and served as president, for the American Climatological Association, dedicated to the study of climatology and diseases of the respiratory organs. Through its annual transactions, he and others published numerous pseudoscientific research articles correlating climatic conditions with TB recovery. His work was influential in establishing the city's reputation for the cure, a large part of the very reason Colorado Springs saw such rapid and sustained growth from its initial founding.

Within a decade, the city was known as a most desirable destination for consumptives.[26] Coined the "Saratoga of the West" as early as 1876,[27] Colorado Springs was "a veritable Eden for consumptive invalids" said British traveler Iza Duffus Harry in 1884.[28] An 1892 publication confirmed its prominent role:

For fifteen years and more Colorado Springs has been a resort for phthisical patients. Certainly it is fair to say that for the last ten years the proportion of consumptives to the whole population, the year round, is larger than any other city or locality in the country. They are in and out among us constantly. It would be difficult to find a house in town that has not been inhabited at some time in its history by one or more suffering from the disease.[29]

Publications by Dr. Boswell Anderson and Dr. Charles Gardiner in 1898, both leading experts in treating TB, further boosted the reputation of Colorado Springs begun by Dr. Solly. The magazine *Mountain Sunshine* was founded in 1899 to promote Colorado Springs as a haven for consumptives, in which the editor estimated 60 percent of the city's population was diseased exiles.[30] Colorado College president E. P. Tenney invited parents to send their boys to his school for both their education and a cure from TB. And who could argue against the magic of the city, when "health and vigor and the delights of a new existence await all who come within the influence of the tonic air and abundant sunshine of this favored region?"[31]

Yet despite personal recoveries, concerns arose about the conditions many had to face during recuperation in Colorado Springs. Tuberculosis patients typically lived in boardinghouses, but the continual influx of health seekers caused housing shortages. Many impoverished consumptives took to tent colonies that sprouted

FIGURE 3.1. Shepard tent cottage village along Cheyenne Creek. *Source*: Colorado Springs Pioneers Museum.

up around town in parks and in the back of private residential lots. One such place was along Cheyenne Creek, where a Dr. W. A. Shepard established a tent village for "invalids with putrid lungs" (figure 3.1).[32] Other tents of homeless consumptives in Colorado Springs were along the banks of rivers, in city parks, and scattered among private lots through the first decade of the twentieth century.[33] These tent colonies, inexpensive boardinghouses, and private rooms for rent were the typical destination for lungers in Colorado Springs.

In the spirit of the Progressive Era, public health officials sought to intervene in order to prevent the spread of the disease. City ordinances in 1884 and 1886 gave the city health officer full authority to prevent the spread of infectious disease; another ordinance of 1890 gave the health department power to exclude contagious children from schools. In 1897 the City Council enacted ordinances against coughing and spitting and enforced the disinfection of boarding homes where consumptives lived.[34] Other ordinances seemed more draconian, for example, a requirement that names of all infected people be reported to city officials and a card stating their ailment conspicuously placed at the lodgings.[35] While these laws appear to create a hostile environment for invalids, there is little evidence that any of the more strict regulations were enacted. There existed a strong tension in the city between the economic gain for the health-care industries profiting from the mountain climate versus the concerns for public health. The warm welcome many received in the 1870s may have been shifting to suspicion and even open hostility by the 1900s, but health seekers kept arriving, and little was done to stop them.

The tension between economics and public health congealed into a narrative distinguishing between wealthy versus impoverished patients, the latter being a drain on public coffers that harmed the city. Dr. John E. White warned, "We know that it is a mistake to send invalids to Colorado Springs with very limited means, mountain air and sunshine do not clothe, neither do they feed an invalid."[36] While the general public became increasingly resistant to the influx of lungers, those with vested interests in the growth industry sought to reassure residents, and potential new immigrants, that the city was safe, sanitary, and healthy. The same Dr. White who discouraged impoverished health seekers out of concern for the burden placed on the city for housing, sanitation, and public health care, at the same time sought to reassure wealthier victims who could pay for their cure: "I have repeatedly talked with physicians that have been in Colorado Springs for many years, even from its founding and they all say that very few cases contracted here have come under their observation. I believe it would be impossible to hunt up over 10 cases in the whole experience of the profession in the last 20 years."[37] And according to Mr. R. K. Hutchings, "A person in good health runs a minimum amount of risk of contracting tuberculosis here . . . It is amply proved that the tubercle bacilli and spores do not live long in this place."[38] Dr. Charles Gardiner even published an 1898 article in the *New York Sun* with the title: "Is consumption contagious? The extraordinary exemption from the disease in the high altitudes of Colorado," where he reiterated that "our mortality from consumption contracted in Colorado Springs has been ten deaths in twenty years."[39] Those who benefitted from the business of TB knew continual clients were needed to sustain profits, and they sought to reassure the general public and potential new immigrants that Colorado Springs was safe.

After twenty years, the city was going through a crisis of its own success. Catering to consumptive health seekers was the economic engine of the city, yet these same people were increasingly denied access to hotels and boarding houses and discouraged from living in tent colonies. The growth boosting proponents of the climate cure persuaded business and civic leaders that the answer would be more segregated spaces for tuberculars, in controlled environments away from the downtown.[40] The need to deal with the public health problem of a large consumptive population in Colorado Springs correlated with the rise of the sanatorium era, particularly after Saranac Lake was founded in 1882, and gave impetus to their establishment in Colorado Springs. Land donations and incentive packages were initiated that attracted sanatorium investors to preferred locations at the periphery of the populated city. Site selection preferences intentionally shaped the TB landscape.

Early Sanatoriums

The city's first hospital, Saint Francis, opened in 1888 just east of town at Institute Street and Pikes Peak Avenue, and ran a ward for TB patients, though it was a general hospital and not a stand-alone TB sanatorium. Numerous private residences and boardinghouses had been used exclusively for tuberculosis victims, but the first attempt in Colorado Springs to establish an institution exclusively for TB patient care came in 1890, when the Bellevue Sanatorium was built on the east side of Institute Street, across from the two-year-old Saint Francis Hospital. A group of citizens were distressed at the suffering of consumptives in town, so they formed a club with subscription fees that eventually raised money for the sanatorium, on land donated by General Palmer.[41] Bellevue ran as an independent tuberculosis sanatorium but closed in 1894 due to lack of funding. Several attempts to restart the sanatorium were unsuccessful until bought by a Methodist organization and changed to the Deaconess Hospital in 1904. High demand led to tents for invalids erected on the property, and a nearby house served as the nurses' quarters.[42] The Deaconess continued to treat TB invalids until the Methodist Episcopal Church built their new Beth-El Hospital in 1911 on east Boulder Street, which is today Memorial Hospital. The original Bellevue Building on Institute had another brief five-year run as the "Colored Preachers Home," a sanatorium for African American ministers, but that too shut down by 1913.[43]

Around the same time that Bellevue opened, Marie Glockner funded a sanatorium in memory of her husband, Albert, who succumbed to the disease in 1888. This institution, a Catholic alternative to the protestant Bellevue, opened in 1890 on north Cascade Avenue (figure 3.2), but it too ran perpetual debt. It was taken over by the Sisters of Charity in 1892, with the charismatic Dr. Boswell Anderson as the chief medical officer. By 1905 there was a thirty-eight-room sanatorium and eighteen-room general hospital, replete with a sun parlor, a roof parlor, an x-ray room, and a smoking room.[44] The institution was a success (despite the smoking room) and remains today as the Penrose Hospital, one of the city's largest.

After the International Typographical Union received donations from its members and leaders in Philadelphia to establish tuberculosis care for workers in the printing industry, the Colorado Springs Board of Trade offered eighty acres east of downtown to construct a facility.[45] All union members were assessed a fee, and the Union Printers Home was finished in 1892. The institution eventually grew to 300 acres, with many buildings and its own herd of dairy cows. Health care was free for any union member admitted. Dr. Webb, a local medical leader, was the initial chief physician for this institution, which became the largest labor hospital in the world (figure 3.3).[46] The home slowly transitioned to more broadly defined health care, then primarily an assisted living center for the elderly. After the union merged with the Communications Workers of America in 1986, member fees for this institution were eliminated, other residents were admitted to the home, and

FIGURE 3.2. Glockner Sanatorium. *Source*: Colorado Springs Pioneers Museum.

all were required to pay for service. The original building and last remaining property were sold by the union to a health-care firm in 2014, and services today are open to the general public.

Father John Baptiste Francolon invited the Sisters of Mercy to start a sanatorium on his property in Manitou Springs on Ruxton Avenue. The Sisters opened Montcalme Sanitarium (*sic*) on July 31, 1895. As demand grew, they utilized overflow tents on the ground and purchased adjacent cottages to serve more patients. Father Francolon completed his eighteen-room mansion, Miramont Castle, in 1897 adjacent to Montcalme, but left Manitou in 1900, leaving his castle unoccupied. The main sanatorium was destroyed by fire 1907, so the sisters moved into the vacant Miramont, changed the name back to Montcalme, and continued to operate as a sanatorium until 1925 (figure 3.4).[47]

While not a legal requirement, we already see by the spatial arrangement of these four earliest sanatoriums a pattern of locating at the periphery of the urbanized area (figure 3.5). Bellevue and Glockner were at the farthest extent of the 1890 road network, while the Printers Home was outside of the city limits and Montcalme was at the far edge of Manitou Springs. The love-hate relationship played out in the very spatial patterns—sanatoriums and health care were the city's primary economic specialization, yet encouraging infectious patients to live amidst the general population raised health-care concerns and resistance from the nonconsumptive population. A spatial logic began, therefore, to put these institutions close enough to draw on local labor and supplies, and therefore enrich the city, yet remain far enough away to maintain segregation.

FIGURE 3.3. Union Printers Home postcard. *Source*: Colorado Springs Pioneers Museum.

FIGURE 3.4. Montcalme Sanatorium. *Source*: Colorado Springs Pioneers Museum.

Gardiner Huts

As a result of the concentration of health seekers, a supportive business and political leadership, and, most important, an agglomeration of TB physicians, Colorado Springs was a leader in services and innovations designed to serve lungers. Their

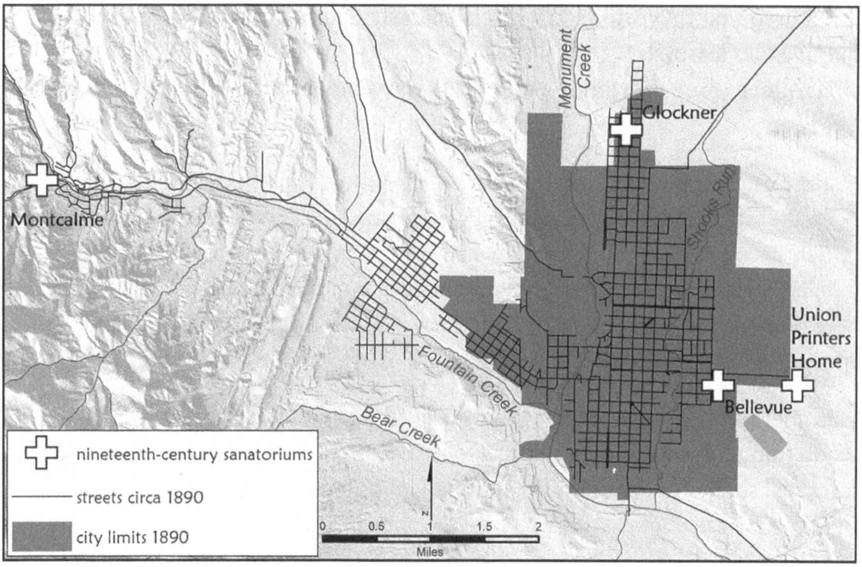

FIGURE 3.5. Locations of nineteenth-century sanatoriums, all at the periphery of the city limits or in neighboring Manitou Springs. *Source*: Cartography by author.

primary marketing pitch was fresh air and sunshine, so all efforts were made to ensure invalids maximized their exposure to both. Windows opened to let in air were an obvious treatment, but contraptions were also built to keep one's head outside while the remainder of the body stayed in the warmth, and sleeping porches became a popular means to immerse oneself in the fresh air. Verandas and sleeping porches became regular architectural elements in many Colorado Springs homes.

Perhaps the most popular innovation was the sleeping hut, originally a tent, designed by Dr. Charles Gardiner and commonly referred to as the Gardiner Hut. Gardiner called his invention the Sanatory Tent, his solution to what he saw as the problem of insufficient access to fresh air through standard treatment methods:

> It seems to be a strong impression in most lay, and some professional minds, that if the windows of an ordinary room are opened wide, all the conditions of ventilation are then sufficient for the pulmonary invalid. This is a great mistake and has undoubtedly caused many unnecessary deaths. Window ventilation of a room does not cause as rapid an air interchange as it should.[48]

In addition to the lack of sufficient ventilation by windows alone, Gardiner recognized that normal care would put patients outdoors only four to six hours per day, wasting the remaining eighteen or more inside. Because he felt that patients should constantly inhale fresh outdoor air, "The only way to achieve this is to arrange so that they will take it unconsciously and not as a task to be performed like a lesson learned."[49]

Gardiner came up with his idea after marveling at the ventilation inherent in Ute tipis:

> The reason for this was, they used a conical tent with a hole in the point of the top for the escape of smoke and plenty of space around the lower edge, where the tent rests upon uneven ground, for air to enter it. In this way the "tepee" acts like an inhabitable chimney or fireplace, and, although in such an Indian home there are, of course, atrocious odors of all kinds, I have noticed that the actual ventilation is much better than in ordinary tents generally used by invalids.[50]

Gardiner's design was an octagonal wood floor with a canvas tent overlaying a wood frame. The walls were vertical for five feet, then the roof sloped inward with a conical shape (figure 3.6). The tent had an opening at the top for air to escape, but the key was that

> the lower edge of the wall is fastened several inches below the floor, and one inch out from it all around; this is to ensure at all times an inflow of air that is gradual and without drafts, since this inch space in a circular tent represents an area of 520 square inches, and the hole in the top for overflowing air has an area of some 177 square inches. In this way the tent cannot be closed, and is ventilated automatically and constantly.[51]
>
> As the heated air can escape at the top, the fresh air can always enter at the bottom of the tent. This is automatic and not under control of the invalid. These facts I wish to emphasize, as they are of very great importance. The average invalid has an aversion to ventilation and will shut windows and in other ways embarrass the inflow of fresh air. In the sanatory tent it is impossible to do this as they are ventilated automatically.[52]

Over the years, canvas was replaced with more durable wooden siding, so the tent became a little house. These Gardiner huts became popular at almost all the sanatoriums, including Glockner, Montcalme, and later institutions, plus they appeared in many backyards throughout the city (figure 3.7). However, it appears that the more permanent structures abandoned the primary design element, that of the open seam along the floorboards. Subsequent design plans and remnant huts visible for inspection today all have sealed foundations and merely rely on windows to circulate air, a seeming violation of the original design intent by Gardiner, but a popular modification nonetheless.

The Sanatorium Golden Era

The open-air craze reached its height when the Nordrach Ranch Sanatorium opened in 1901, run by Dr. J. E. White on land donated by William A. Otis at

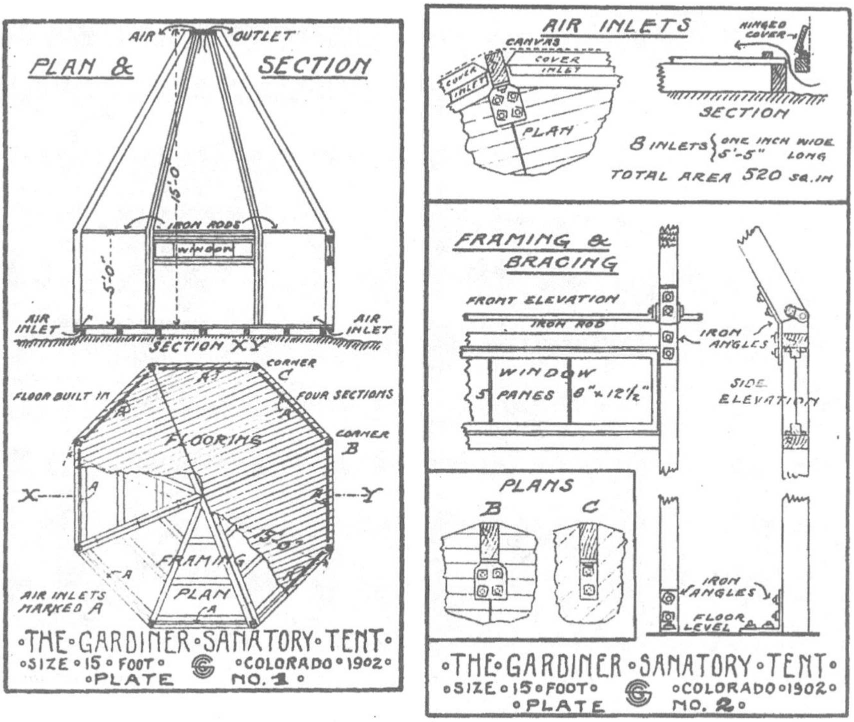

FIGURE 3.6. Sketches of Gardiner's "Sanatory Tent," showing the air inlets for ventilation critical to the design. *Source*: Charles Fox Gardiner, "The Sanatory Tent and Its Use in the Treatment of Pulmonary Tuberculosis," *Transactions of the American Climatological Association* 18 (1902): 216–217.

the base of Austin Bluffs, and named in recognition of the famed TB resort in Germany. Otis leased his sixteen-room mansion as the facility hub, but patients were housed in seventy-two Gardiner huts constructed on a series of nine parallel terraces for continual outdoor living year round: "The inhalation of cold air is a tonic and fever reducer."[53] Many complained of the cold as these were the first use of the Gardiner huts with the original canvas siding (figure 3.8). Yet Dr. White was unflinching in his commitment: "Tubercular patients invariably do better during the colder months of the year, if they only get out into the pure, sharp, bracing air. Cold air is needed by the invalid, because of its stimulating effect on the skin."[54] The institution was known for its firm and undeviating code of discipline, called a "prison" by one resident, with strict adherence to times of mental quietude, an exercise regimen, reading restrictions, bathing hours, and mealtime.[55] But while conditions were strict, at least the residents ate well, in keeping with the standard procedure to stuff the emaciated frame. The treatment at Nordrach was described as a disciplined gluttony, with an intent for each patient to gain between twenty-five and fifty pounds: "it is a question

FIGURE 3.7. Gardiner hut now used as a backyard shed, Colorado Springs. *Source*: photo by author.

of either eating or dying," said Dr. White.[56] In later years the huts were upgraded to shingle roofs with sturdier frames, and even the canvas sides were eventually converted to wood, but designs show again the floor ventilation gone with only two opposing windows used for airflow. Even with the abundant diet (up to three quarts of milk per day), the ranch was an economical choice for money-conscious invalids, and Dr. White ran a small profit until he resigned in 1910. The mansion burnt in 1907, then a December blizzard proved too much for the tent colony in 1913. The remaining patients transferred to Glockner, and the ranch closed down.

The jewel of local sanatoriums offerings was the dream of Dr. Edwin Solly, who originally named his establishment "the Cragmoor" in reference to places in his native England (the name was later shortened to Cragmor). The location was on the south slopes of Austin Bluffs west of Nordrach Ranch, a setting chosen for its capacity to provide mental quiet and fresh air for invalids. Palmer donated 100 acres and a sum of money in 1902 to his friend Solly, who consciously patterned the complex after the most famous and well-established resort at Davos, Switzerland. Solly had grand ideas from the beginning; he intended this to be the biggest and best sanatorium in the world.[57] He hired local architect Thomas MacLaren, who created a design emphasizing sleeping porches and full access to the sun. While Solly had to scale down his design from the original ambitious "sun palace" due to

FIGURE 3.8. Nordrach Ranch, circa 1905. *Source*: Colorado Springs Pioneers Museum.

lack of funds, the health resort nonetheless opened and admitted its first patient June 20, 1905 (figure 3.9). Unfortunately Dr. Solly died shortly after, followed by an interim period when the institution was run by Doctors Gardiner, Hoagland, and Swan, but the dream resurged when Dr. Alexius Forster (who had worked at Saranac Lake) took over in 1910. Renowned for his belief in the need for tranquility, Dr. Forster made the resort famous for free-swinging liberality, a pleasure dome of luxury and ease.[58] Forster emphasized physical comfort, relief from stress, and positive thoughts and was deliberately unconcerned with rules. Cragmor grew and prospered, admitting wealthy, influential consumptives. By 1924 the National Tuberculosis Association called it "the most desirable sanatorium in the world."[59] With cocktail parties and romantic interludes—including excursions along the "High trail to passion" on the bluffs—the patients were a gregarious lot, even publishing their own journal *Ninety-Eight-Six* in reference to the ideal body temperature to which they all strived. After its glory years, Cragmor declined through the Depression and World War II, until a federal government grant arrived in 1952 to serve Navajo patients. The once-proud institution eked along on the federal dole until 1962, when it shut for good. The land and buildings were given as a gift to the University of Colorado in 1964, which opened UCCS in 1965.

At its height, Cragmor showed that those with ample resources found a welcome in Colorado Springs. But as seen by the Union Printers Home, there were other successful models that didn't rely exclusively on wealth. The opulence of Cragmor was perhaps only exceeded by the size of the Modern Woodmen of America

FIGURE 3.9. Cragmor Sanatorium aerial view, 1940. The main facility is the building on the upper left, now Main Hall at UCCS. South Hall, built 1927, is the building on the lower right (demolished in 1980). Between the two are numerous cottages and tents. *Source*: UCCS Archives.

(MWA) Sanatorium, which opened in 1908 and which became the largest of all sanatoriums in Colorado Springs.[60] The MWA is a life insurance organization that had over 1 million members in the early twentieth century. Keeping people alive was cheaper than paying benefits after death, so the firm was motivated to establish a TB sanatorium to reduce expenses. The Chamber of Commerce made generous offers of land and other financial incentives, the lot was purchased, construction began, and the first patients arrived December 17, 1908. The institution could house 245 patients and became famous for the 180 Gardiner huts painted red, white, and green, in the bucolic valley on the city's northwest side (figure 3.10). All patients received free care with a highly regimented daily routine (figure 3.11). Official rules stated that the institution enrolled "white men, believers in a Supreme Being, American citizens, or those in process of being naturalized, and those not engaged in extra hazardous occupations."[61] On site was a farm, orchard, dairy herd, post office, and rail depot. The facility was a success until post–World War II, when it discharged the last nine patients on April 25, 1947, and put the property up for sale. It became home for Sisters of Saint Francis of Perpetual Adoration in 1952.

Theodore Star ran a boardinghouse for invalids he called Star Ranch in the Pines at the foot of Cheyenne Mountain in 1902. He was succeeded by Dr. W. F. Martin in 1904, and then purchased by Maurice Witkind in 1910, a former superintendent at the Cragmor Sanatorium. He set up Gardiner huts, built a central building and cottages, and worked with manufacturers and retailers who would

FIGURE 3.10. Modern Woodmen Sanatorium showing Gardiner huts. *Source*: Colorado Springs Pioneers Museum.

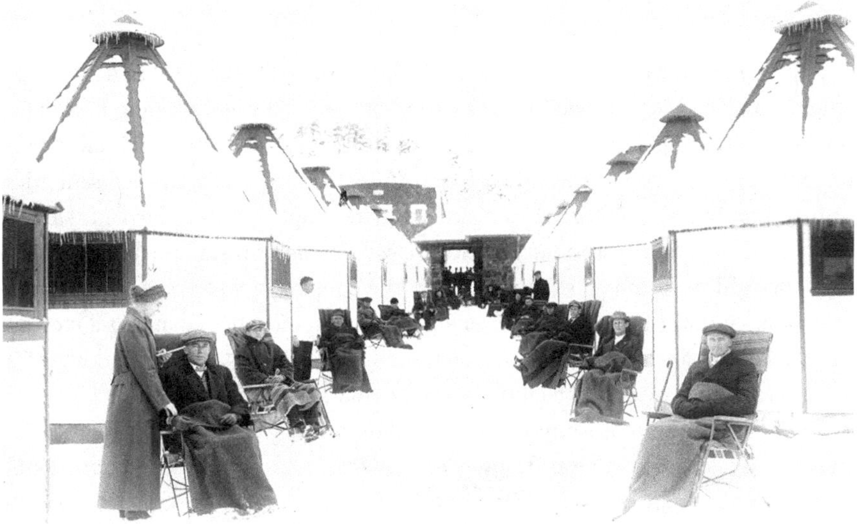

FIGURE 3.11. Patients at Modern Woodmen undergoing the daily regimen, with nurse care in the snow. *Source*: Colorado Springs Pioneers Museum.

send their tubercular employees. The Star Ranch was marketed not simply as a tuberculosis recovery site but also as "A Mountain Resort of the Highest Class" for tourism with cottages, cabins, and tents, providing "all the comforts of a first class hotel."[62] After its remodel in 1918, the federal government contracted with the institution in 1920 for treatment of afflicted soldiers and sailors. After 1922, Fort Lyons, in Bent County, Colorado, increasingly took on a mission of caring for tubercular veterans, and eventually the Star Ranch Sanatorium closed as federal contracts shifted. In 1947 it converted to Christian youth outreach organizations.[63]

Concerned citizens also saw the need for a TB sanatorium for the poor who could not utilize other existing institutions. Associated Charities started 1899, growing out of the Women's Aid Society,[64] and it took on charitable causes in the city (it would eventually become the Community Chest, which continued that mission). Since many low-income invalids continued to dwell in tents and makeshift hovels in parks during winter 1910–1911, a new facility, Sunny Rest, was proposed by the Board of the Associated Charities to take in needy. Intended to rid the city of squatter camps, costs would be subsidized, and even free for those without means to pay. According to Dr. Henry Hoagland,

> A good many people . . . came . . . who did not have much money and sometimes were forced to apply for help to the Associated Charities. They were scattered all over the city in tents in the back yards of many houses and I used to treat them for the Associated Charities. So I organized a campaign and built and operated Sunny Rest Sanatorium.[65]

The timing for this proposal came in part from a 1909 TB exhibit that traveled the country and had just stopped in Colorado Springs. The event was the first major public health campaign that educated citizens about the dangers of TB and means of contagion. So powerful was the program that the city finally enacted sanitation ordinances that were enforced as residents increasingly became alarmed. Despite the need for the Sunny Rest facility, citizens vehemently resisted the proposal with petitions and town meetings, pointing out the dangers of widespread community infection. The city public health officer argued against incentives that might increase tuberculars at City Council.[66] As a result, the City Council passed an ordinance in 1910 against the erection of facilities for tuberculars within the city limits.[67]

The Sunny Rest sanatorium was built and began service in 1911, but its location moved from original site on Boulder Street farther east and north, above Knob Hill, on what today is Cache la Poudre Street. The institution relied on private donors; the Sisters of the Kaiserswerth, a German nursing society, ran it until 1924, when the Community Chest took over. It served as a sanatorium until 1943. Sunny Rest today operates as an assisted living home. The facility expanded across the street in 2013, and the building on the original lot was refurbished into a new facility in 2017.

The local reaction against siting the facility adjacent to established houses codified what had previously been an unwritten rule to locate sanatoriums at the city's edges. This now became law—no sanatoriums within city limits (figure 3.12). The

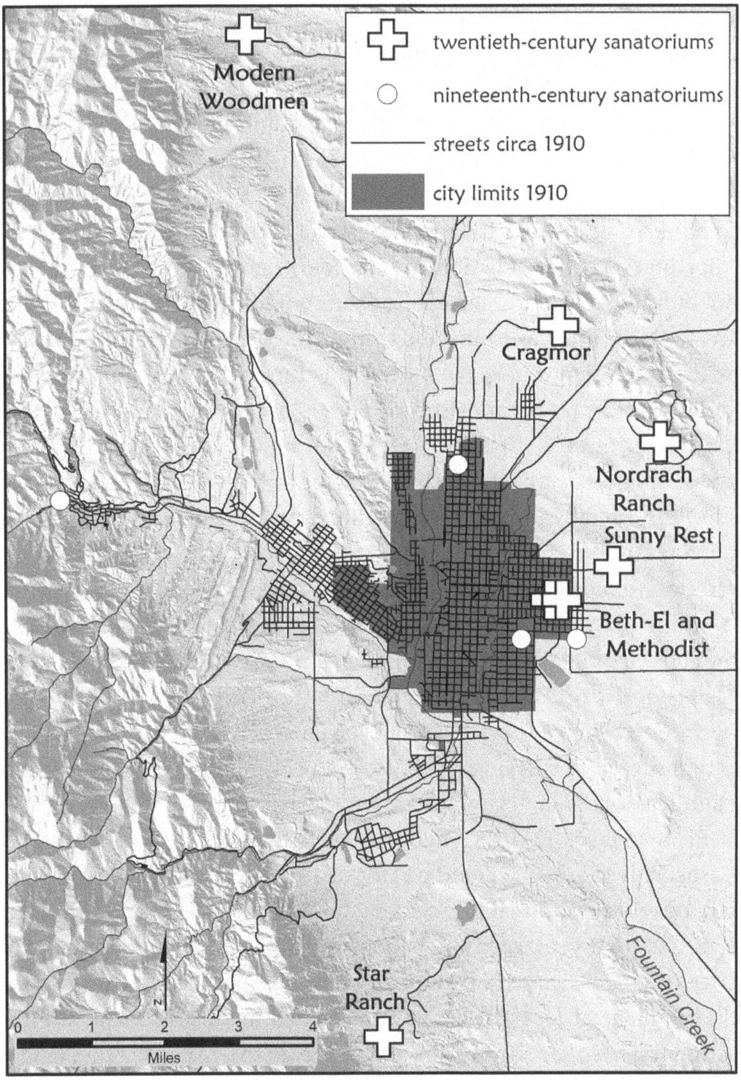

FIGURE 3.12. Location of twentieth-century sanatoriums, again at the periphery or outside of the city limits. Patients remained far enough removed from the downtown to be out of sight. *Source*: Cartography by author.

TB landscape formed a half-ring around the original city, arching from Modern Woodmen of America in the north, across the city's east side, to Star Ranch in the south. This zone of contagion was set aside for the cure of those not wanted in the daily social interactions and business transactions of the city. This segregation affected institutions only, as wealthy immigrants seeking a cure still purchased homes in the city and sought private treatment.

One final organization entered into the sanatorium business and left a lasting impact upon the Colorado Springs landscape: the Methodist Episcopal Church. The Methodist Episcopal Women's Home Missionary Society of the Colorado Conference of Deaconesses purchased land and built the Beth-El Hospital on east Boulder Street in 1911.[68] The nursing school was built one lot to the east, then in 1926 the National Board of Hospitals and Homes of the Methodist Episcopal Church built a stand-alone tuberculosis sanatorium on the next lot to the east, on the northwest corner of Union and Boulder (figure 3.13).[69] A four-story brick, fireproof building had a promenade deck on roof for mandatory fresh air, housed fifty-two patients, and was connected by tunnel to the main hospital. The hospital became city-run Memorial in 1943, while the nursing school (torn down in 1973) and the TB sanatorium became Ent Air Force Base in 1943 and then the Olympic Training Center in 1978.[70] The nursing school moved locations and, in an interesting twist of fate, became the Beth-El College of Nursing and Health Sciences at UCCS in 1997, thereby uniting with the university at the location of the original Cragmor Sanatorium.

In addition to the large institutions discussed, several smaller and less successful operations ran in the city: the Colorado Springs Sanatorium (1901–1905) on W. Kiowa Street, built around small mineral springs; the Battle Creek Sanatorium (1906–1909) on North Cascade Avenue; Bonnie View (1921–1926) on Cheyenne Road; Crestone Heights (begun 1926), a Seventh Day Adventist supported sanatorium that served twenty-five patients on Brookside Avenue; and the Nob Hill Lodge and Idlewold Sanatoriums adjacent to each other on Logan Avenue south of Beth-El Hospital (1912–1925) (figure 3.14). The city truly was a haven for tuberculars, especially those who could pay for treatment. The Chamber of Commerce even published promotional booklets such as *Winning Health in the Pikes Peak Region* in 1923 that promoted the benefits of the local climate and facilities for health seekers.[71] The larger institutions continued as tuberculosis sanatoriums until the big medical breakthrough that relegated the disease to an afterthought, eliminating the need for such places and reducing their sites to relict landscapes.

DEMISE OF THE SANATORIUM

In 1943, Dr. Selman Waksman in the Department of Soil Microbiology at the Agricultural Experimental Station of Rutgers College in New Jersey found that the antibiotic streptomycin completely suppressed the activity of the tuberculosis bacillus.[72] His lab was searching for pesticides to suppress bacterial and fungal diseases for crops and stumbled upon this greater application. Combined with a suite of other antibiotics, the dreaded disease that spawned entire industries quickly disappeared from the public sphere. For nearly a century the sanatorium was the preferred treatment prescription, but after barely a decade the sanatoriums were

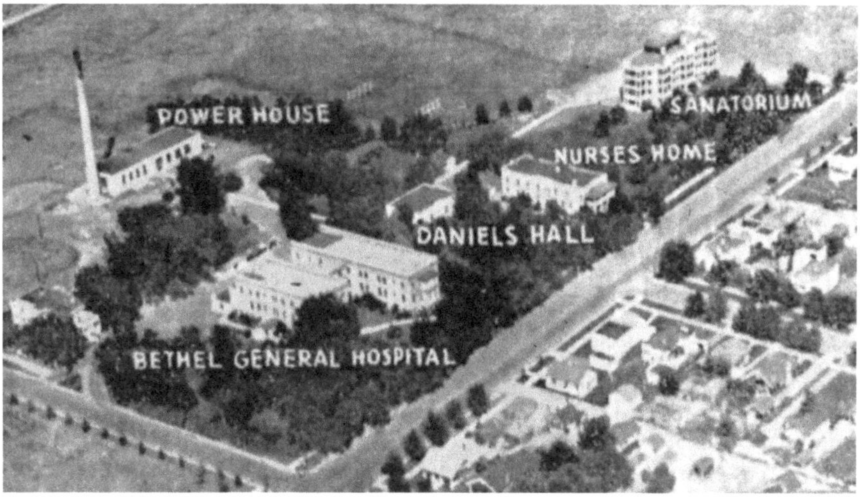

FIGURE 3.13. Aerial shot of Beth-El Hospital and Sanatorium, circa 1938. The buildings face Boulder Street; north is toward the upper left corner. *Source*: Beth-El Historical Collections, UCCS University Archives.

FIGURE 3.14. Nob Hill Lodge, circa 1920. In the background on the hill is the Union Printers Home. *Source*: Courtesy of Special Collections, Pikes Peak Library District, 001-189.

gone, their services no longer needed. Some shut down and sold out (Modern Woodmen, Cragmor, Star Ranch, Nordrach Ranch, Methodist), others converted to assisted living homes (Sunny Rest, Union Printers Home), and others still to hospitals (Glockner, Beth-El). The National Tuberculosis Association itself, in recognition of the new era, changed its name to the American Lung Association,

FIGURE 3.15. Gardiner huts repurposed for food vendor in Manitou Springs. *Source*: photo by author.

but in tribute to its historical founding still kept the double T as its symbol.[73] And the continued use of the symbol may be prescient—in addition to the fact that the disease never fully disappeared in impoverished developing countries, cases globally have increased as drug-resistant strains of TB have now appeared, with a particularly deadly effect on HIV patients.

As local historian Doug McKay stated: "For more than 50 years after its founding, Colorado Springs flourished on a bedrock of bacteria."[74] The first identity of the city popularly associated with Colorado Springs was that of a health resort, and especially one for consumptives. This historical era has had lasting landscape impacts. Many of the most influential citizens of the city originally came chasing the cure. If one looks closely, you can see Gardiner huts repurposed for new uses (figure 3.15) or just used for sheds in backyards. Many houses still have sleeping porches (although now not likely used for that purpose), and many "granny shacks" out back of main houses in the older parts of town were original TB shelters. The two main hospitals, Memorial and Penrose, both began as TB sanatoriums, and UCCS uses the original Cragmor Sanatorium as its Main Hall for administration and student services. The city profited from its mountain climate. The quality of its air and sun, marketed so heavily for consumptives, spilled over onto tourism in general, which remains a major economic engine for the city: the official city motto in the early-to-mid twentieth century was City of Sunshine, a theme still represented on the city flag. As health care becomes a major industry in the twenty-first century, much of the lands once owned by the Printers Union but later sold off remain as private health-care facilities, building a health-care agglomeration economy on the site long serving that industry. But perhaps there is an even larger lasting impact, as suggested this 1892 observation about Colorado Springs: "And above all, the perfection of the Colorado climate, now world-famous, is here attained, and is the loadstone which has drawn from almost every part of the civilized world, but principally from the cities of the East and South, a population of exceptional intelligence."[75] Could it be that Colorado Springs has some of the smartest, most civilized people on earth because of the tuberculosis bacillus?

4

Metal

Colorado without railroads, is comparatively worthless.

—GOVERNOR JOHN EVANS, 1870[1]

While the city profited from health seekers with its mountain climate and land investment opportunities at the foot of Pikes Peak, there remained one nagging geographic constraint—the tyranny of space. Colorado Springs was simply too isolated from the settled East, and it was a long and arduous journey to reach the Rocky Mountains from just about anywhere. But by the 1870s the nation was fully engaged with the Industrial Revolution, a historical era that fundamentally changed the social and economic organization of society. Human ingenuity created new technologies to reduce the barriers to mobility, and the dominant means of transportation became the railroad—steam engines and steel rails.

Much has been written on railroads in the American West and deservedly so. We can hardly underestimate the impact the rails had on the founding and prosperity of settlements throughout the region. Colorado Springs is no exception and, in fact, owes its very existence to railroads. The railroad industry brought General Palmer to the region and became a principal reason why he stayed. He was the founder and president of the D&RG Railroad, the narrow gauge line that connected Colorado Springs to the world and played an integral role in the development of the entire state.

RAILROADS IN THE WEST

Railroads opened the West by providing vital connections to fledgling mining and agricultural towns, even inducing development into areas previously uninhabited

DOI: 10.5876/9781646421688.c004

by settlers. While western town leaders knew connectivity to the settled East was crucial, building rail lines and running a railroad company was expensive. Many early efforts failed, and investment capital was hard to find.[2] By the 1850s, a public-private partnership evolved to solve the need for investment capital: the federal government allowed private rail companies to use the public domain as collateral to generate capital investments. A land grant procedure began, whereby every alternate section (one square mile) in the Public Land Survey System was granted to the company, within a fixed distance from the tracks (originally six sections in width, later ten miles). This typically equated to six to ten sections per mile of track, and if a designated section was already owned, a lieu section was awarded at a farther distance from the track. Title was not granted to the company until the line was completed, and there were set time limits to sell the land (though these limits were challenged and later overturned). This kept railroad companies in the business of promoting town sites and immigration from Europe yet simultaneously prevented land monopolization because alternatives for purchase by the public remained nearby in the sections not granted to the railroads.[3] While some lines held portions of their grants for future speculative profits, most sought to sell as soon as possible to furnish much needed capital and to build up traffic along the line of the road. The traffic gained was usually more valuable than later increases in the value of the land.[4]

Many have argued that this system amounted to an unfair land giveaway that enriched already powerful railroad companies and their robber-baron owners, and, indeed, bribery, corruption and graft were prolific with the system.[5] But this program ultimately proved beneficial to the nation, first because the federal government doubled the price of land on alternate sections it retained to recuperate the value of the acres patented to the companies and also because each recipient rail company was required to transport troops, mail, and government property at rates fixed by Congress. The net result is that the government was paid back many times over for the land granted to the railroads.[6] Western states successfully argued that federal assistance was justified because benefits of railroad lines would accrue to the nation as a whole. Controversies and corruption made the program highly unpopular, so granting land to railroad companies ceased by 1871 but not until 180 million acres had been granted.[7] The ultimate outcome was that transcontinental lines became a reality, and numerous companies opened up the vast expanses of the western United States.

At the outset of the Civil War, six routes were being considered for the national imperative to connect the East with California, under the directorship of Jefferson Davis in the War Department.[8] Sectarian disagreements had stalled all progress; neither the North nor the South would allow a line through the opposing territory that would benefit the other. It wasn't until after secession of the South that the first route was approved, a line that would ultimately connect Chicago with the San Francisco Bay. In the end, it was the Union Pacific line from Omaha going west that connected with the Central Pacific line from Sacramento coming east in Promontory, Utah, in 1869, that completed the country's first transcontinental line. But Omaha was not the preordained origin—the original federal act of July 1, 1862, called for the Central Pacific to meet with four competing eastern lines at a junction around the 100th meridian, somewhere between the Republican and Platte Rivers.[9] The Union Pacific, Eastern Division, was one competitor moving west from Kansas City to this 100th meridian junction, and if it reached that point before the Omaha line it was to continue westward until meeting with the Central Pacific. Alas, the Omaha line won the race, leaving Colorado stranded as the transcontinental route went through Cheyenne, Wyoming, and bypassed Denver. Beaten, directors of the Eastern Division reorganized their company as the Kansas Pacific Railroad in 1869 and changed the route to go straight west from Kansas City up the Smoky Hill River to Denver.[10]

THE DENVER & RIO GRANDE

From 1867 to 1869, progress of the Kansas Pacific line was slow. The Kansas Pacific, low on funds, demanded Denver pay $2 million to finish the line. Denver leaders desperately wanted a rail connection but would not resort to extortion from the Kansas Pacific. In response, Denver residents John Evans and Jerome Chaffee built their own line, the Denver Pacific, to connect the 107 miles to the Union Pacific at Cheyenne. Service began on June 22, 1870. Two months later the Kansas Pacific connected from the East, no longer demanding tribute. In charge of construction was William Jackson Palmer.[11]

Palmer worked as President J. Edgar Thomson's personal secretary for the mighty Pennsylvania Railroad before the Civil War, which gave him the experience needed to direct the surveying and construction of the Kansas Pacific. When the Kansas Pacific reached Denver, it was broke. Traffic from Denver alone could not recoup investments, and even after connecting its own line from Denver to the transcontinental Union Pacific in 1871, little freight from the West Coast was diverted along its route. By 1880, the Kansas Pacific was purchased by the Union Pacific.

Palmer was not about to let the demise of the Kansas Pacific dim his railroading dreams. While the national focus had been, and would remain for quite some time, east-west routes connecting the coasts, Palmer saw the opportunity for a north-south route that could intersect all cross-continental lines and open up trade between Colorado and Mexico. The D&RG was incorporated October 27, 1870, listing its proposed route from Denver, through Colorado Springs to Pueblo, up the Arkansas River and over Poncha Pass, then on to Santa Fe and El Paso, where further opportunities in Mexico would open. Familiar with the unscrupulous dealings in the competition between railroads, Palmer wished to avoid such distasteful business and (naively) envisioned a railroad to share with his investor friends and workers, free from quarrels and jealousies.[12]

Palmer faced daunting odds. His railroad was to be built without federal subsidy or land grant through an unpopulated and undeveloped region, at a time when capitalists were reluctant to invest in new railroads. But the company had a standout marketing angle, namely, a narrow gauge: three feet wide rather than the standard four feet, eight and one-half inches. The narrow gauge reduced construction costs and, it was argued, was preferable for mountainous terrain in that it occupied less land and could pull at steeper grade with tighter turns. Marketed as an entirely new type of transportation, this distinctive feature served to brand the railroad with a unique identity.

Much of the initial route south from Denver was purchased from the United States government for $1.25 per acre, with a right-of-way 200 feet wide through the unoccupied portions of the public domain. The charter privileges allowed for taking timber, stone, and earth from the public lands adjacent to the right of way, and twenty acres of land every ten miles for station purposes. These terms were much less generous than the free land, low interest loans, and other financial incentives and gifts given to earlier American railroad companies. Begun January 1, 1871, the Denver to Colorado Springs route followed a wagon road via Plum Creek, over the Palmer Divide through what is now the town of Palmer Lake, then down Monument Creek to its junction with Fountain Creek. The first passenger train arrived in Colorado Springs from Denver on October 27, 1871, beginning service on the sixty-five-mile route that took five hours at a pace of fifteen miles per hour.[13] In its first year (1872), the D&RG carried 25,168 passengers and over 46,000 tons of freight.[14]

Because of the expense to build railroads in the remote West of the nineteenth century, profits depended on the ability to generate new markets in sparsely populated areas. Dr. William Bell, Palmer's first business partner and longtime friend, stated: "Hand in hand with the railroad came the opening up and development of the country through which it was to pass."[15] Palmer explained, "These lines of railway were rarely built to accommodate existing population or traffic. They were built ahead of both, in order to colonize the country. Their construction was necessary to make it inhabitable."[16] There were two means to generate volume: land speculation that populated sites and created traffic in people, goods and produce; and resource extraction, at times lumber and metal ore, but mostly coal, the primary energy source of the industrial era. The D&RG initial business model was to employ a construction firm, the Union Contract Company based in Pennsylvania (but with board members from the D&RG), to actually build the rail lines. This contractor was funded by associated land and coal companies, organized to aid in the building of the railroad and then provide traffic by encouraging settlement and development. Palmer himself stated, "Our directors have always felt a peculiarly strong responsibility for the associated coal companies. They were formed to create business for the railroad when the country was new and sparsely populated."[17] The Colorado Springs Company's real estate sales were vital to the D&RG, as were other land development schemes run by railroad officials. The many coalfields later established in Fremont, Huerfano, Las Animas, Pitkin, and Gunnison Counties also provided steady freight. The railroad conveyed land to real estate and coal-mining companies, which developed places along the routes to generate traffic for the railway: "Nothing indeed would appear to be more legitimate and business-like than this co-operation of the improvement company with the railway company,"[18] stated General Palmer in 1874.

The little narrow-gauge line became the vital conduit that enabled the founding and growth of Colorado Springs. Despite Palmer's vision for a railroad empire, he knew he needed to accrue capital from his land companies selling lots in order to fund the railroad mile by mile.[19] Palmer and his investors in the Colorado Springs Company avoided more expensive, settled land around Colorado City and instead acquired large uninhabited blocks for eighty cents an acre on the low mesa just east of the Monument Creek–Fountain Creek junction. As would become a regular pattern for the D&RG, when the railroad arrived to a town it bypassed established settlements in order to develop new lands controlled by company investors, where large profits were to be made by selling off lots.

The D&RG worked diligently to expand its rail network, but Palmer's vision of a friendly company isolated from the fierce competition of other lines quickly evaporated. Part of this was brought upon the company by its own actions. The line reached Pueblo on June 15, 1872, yet the company angered city leaders by building the depot not in the existing town but across the Arkansas River in Pueblo South, a new land development enterprise owned by railroad executives.[20] A spur line was next built west to the coalfields near Florence in Fremont County but stopped seven miles short of Cañon City, thereby angering city leaders there.[21] Finally, the line extended south to Trinidad by April 1876 but again stopped five miles short of town, where the railroad established the new settlement of El Moro on the Purgatoire River.[22] With these sleights plus overpriced monopoly rates, residents in southern Colorado gained no allegiance to the D&RG, opening their receptiveness to competing lines, which arrived in the form of the Atchison, Topeka, and Santa Fe (AT&SF).

The AT&SF ran a standard gauge line from Topeka in a southwest direction, ending at Granada, Colorado, in December 1872. This line prospered by tapping into the Texas cattle drives bringing longhorns north and onto the market via railheads such as Dodge City, but the company aim was to reach Santa Fe and then onto California. It ran a spur from La Junta to Pueblo by March 7, 1876, where it agreed to transfer freight and passengers to Denver along the D&RG line.[23] The AT&SF also ran a line to Trinidad to get a coveted route over Raton Pass and into New Mexico to reach Santa Fe. These two connections sparked an epic railroad saga of the West, as the AT&SF and D&RG fought over strategic routes. In both places, locals favored the AT&SF due to perceived mistreatment from the D&RG. In short, the AT&SF won access to Raton Pass by April 1878, then began the "Rio Grande War," a battle for the route up the Arkansas River, through the Royal Gorge, to the booming mines at Leadville. Several long court cases ensued, followed by violent confrontations that included occupation of a D&RG station by AT&SF men on June 11, 1879, and a subsequent siege by Palmer's men to force them out. By 1879 the D&RG finally won the rights to the Royal Gorge route, conceding Santa Fe trade to the AT&SF, which in turn agreed not to build a competing line from Pueblo to Denver.[24] Although shut out of Raton Pass, the D&RG reached Alamosa over La Veta Pass west of Walsenburg—finally earning the "Rio Grande" in its name—in May 1878, and built south to Española, thirty-four miles north of Santa Fe, where it stopped due to its agreement with AT&SF.[25] Abandoning its original strategy to reach Santa Fe and El Paso, the D&RG turned its focus to serving mining and agriculture in the Colorado mountains.

For Colorado Springs, the results of all these battles was that first, the D&RG remained the only line to the city for a few more years. Second, the lucrative mule wagon freight business serving Leadville from Colorado City ceased once the rails connected on July 31, 1880, with the new Leadville rail traffic strengthening connections between these centers. Shipments of people, supplies, and equipment to Leadville were the central piece that kept the D&RG solvent. Finally, these protracted battles and financial woes slowly forced Palmer to relinquish control of his railroad to infamous national magnate Jay Gould. Palmer resigned as D&RG president in 1883, and the company headquarters moved to Denver. However, Palmer was not finished with the railroad business. Along with Dr. William Bell, he had set up a second line in Utah, the D&RG Western in summer, 1881 (changed to just Rio Grande Western in June 1889).[26] The vision was to connect the D&RG with Salt Lake City and the Central Pacific–Union Pacific transcontinental line in Ogden. The two Rio Grande lines connected on March 30, 1883, completing a 735-mile Denver–Salt Lake City route (via Colorado Springs and Pueblo) that took thirty-five hours.[27] Palmer remained president of the profitable Rio Grande Western until 1908. The two lines then merged and consolidated but were ruined by the poor leadership of George Gould (son of Jay), taken over for a time by the federal government, then finally reemerging as the new Denver & Rio Grande Railroad in 1921.

At full buildout, the D&RG reached far into the Colorado mountains, creating the vital market connection for mining towns (many of which today are

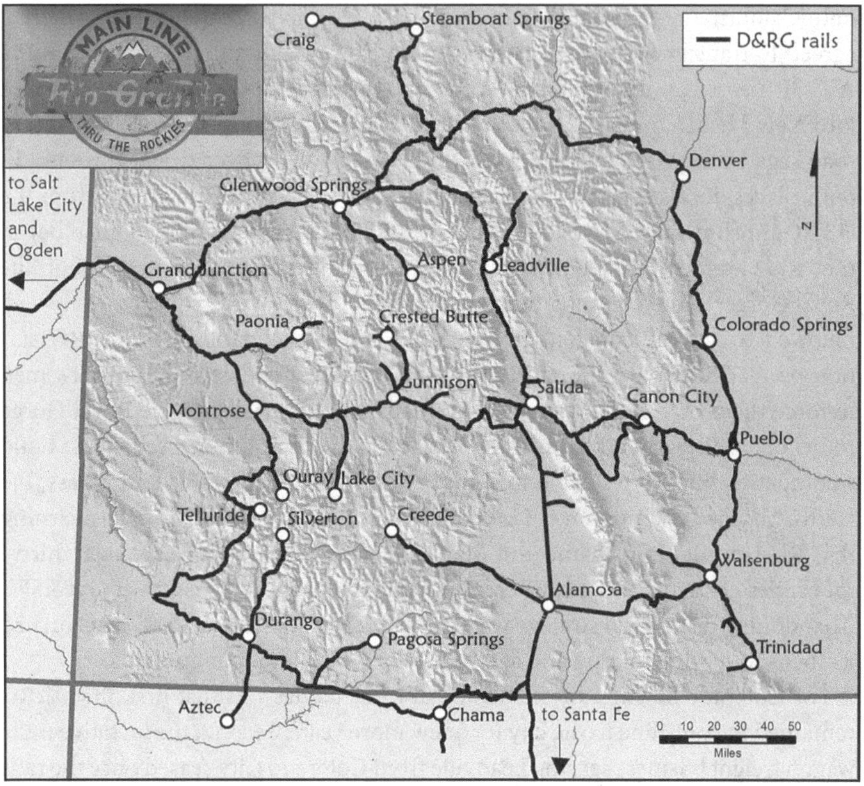

FIGURE 4.1. D&RG lines at maximum extent. Not all of these lines were running at the same time, but this map illustrates the extent of the railroad's service to Colorado mountain towns. *Source*: Cartography by author.

mountain resorts—Crested Butte, Aspen, Telluride, Durango, Salida, Glenwood Springs), while the Rio Grande Western connected Colorado and Denver to Utah and the West Coast (figure 4.1). Nearly all of the lines were converted to standard gauge throughout the 1880s to better connect with a growing national system.[28] The D&RG became a division of the Southern Pacific system in 1988, then was bought by the Union Pacific in 1996. The Moffat Tunnel was bored through the Continental Divide west of Denver in 1928 and tracks connected to the D&RG in 1933 along the Colorado River, after which passenger traffic from Utah and the West Coast took this much shorter route to Denver, greatly reducing volume through Colorado Springs. Passenger traffic through Colorado Springs ceased in April 1971.[29] Today freight trains still rumble through town, primarily carrying coal from Wyoming to power plants across the Great Plains and Southwest, but the little "Rebel of the Rockies" was the first to stamp the railroad imprint on the Colorado Springs landscape (figure 4.2).

FIGURE 4.2. The Denver & Rio Grande Depot in Colorado Springs, in an 1888 sketch (left) and 1974 photo (right), shortly after passenger service ended. *Source*: *Gazette* (1888), January 1 (left), Colorado Springs Pioneers Museum (right).

INDUSTRIAL DEVELOPMENT IN COLORADO RESULTING FROM THE D&RG

From its headquarters in Colorado Springs, the D&RG had a profound impact on the settlement and industrialization of the entire state of Colorado. Palmer and his board of directors were in the business of land development but also needed a steady supply of coal, the energy source that fueled the railroad, and dreamed of a local industrial site to provide steel rails and related metallurgical products needed by the industry. Not long after the D&RG reached Pueblo in 1872, Palmer formed the Central Colorado Improvement Company to develop agricultural and urban plots and possibly spark heavy industry in southern Colorado.[30] Soon coal mining was the Central Colorado Improvement Company's most profitable business activity.[31] The lignite (a soft brown coal) of El Paso County was an inferior quality for steam engines, and supply from the Boulder County mines was fully taken by the Denver market. The D&RG needed to develop sources from southern Colorado, which it did first with mines in Fremont County, south of present-day Florence. Their first initiative, the Cañon Mine, shipped in 1873 almost 13,000 tons of coal, or an average of about 43 tons daily, of which D&RG locomotives consumed about one-third.[32]

Next the D&RG executives organized the Southern Colorado Coal and Town Company to assist in building lines to the extensive coal deposits in Huerfano and Las Animas Counties (figure 4.3). Then they organized the Colorado Coal and Steel Works Company in October 1872, with Palmer was president. In December 1879, all of these offshoot development companies, started as subordinate ventures of the D&RG, were consolidated into the Colorado Coal and Iron Company, based in Colorado Springs, with Palmer as president. The company plan was to focus on four activities: (1) the improvement and sale of town lots and agricultural lands, (2) the production of coal, (3) the manufacture of coke, and (4) a new activity, a plant to manufacture iron and steel products.[33]

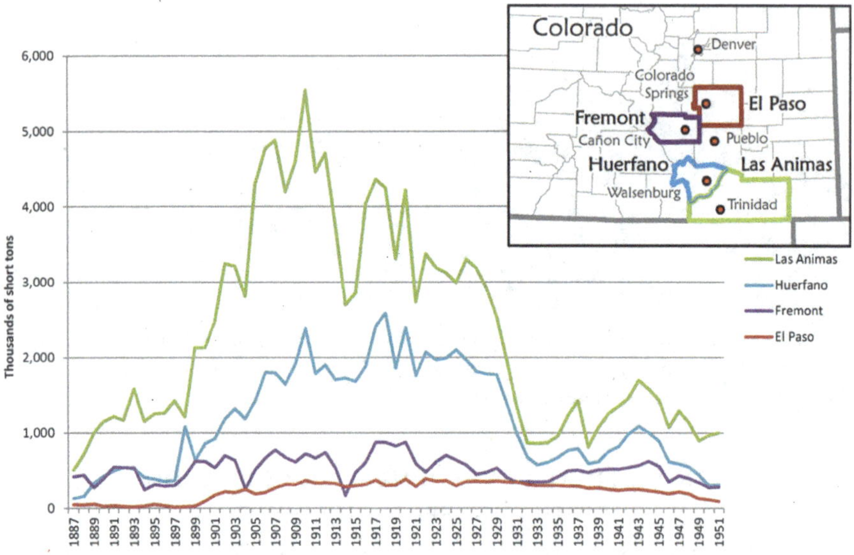

FIGURE 4.3. Coal production in four southern Colorado counties, 1887–1951. *Source*: USGS 1953, graph by author.

The location chosen for their new industrial works was south Pueblo, a site that made sense for multiple reasons. First, they owned the land, and similar to their other land development schemes, the company anticipated great appreciation of land value as they stimulated growth through heavy industry. Therefore, on the mesa south of the river, the company set aside 1,260 acres for the ironworks and steelworks. Second, from an economic geography perspective, the site was a perfectly rational choice that minimized transportation costs associated with steelmaking. The raw material with the most bulk was coke, which was initially made at the El Moro coke ovens using coal from the Las Animas and Huerfano county fields.[34] By 1903 the company was producing over 500,000 tons of coke annually at nine oven sites.[35] Iron ore was brought from two mines the company owned, the Calumet, nineteen miles north of Salida, and the Orient, in the Sangre de Cristo Mountains east of Villa Grove. Limestone was quarried six miles south of Pueblo and easily loaded on the adjacent rails, and water was abundant from the Arkansas River. After the raw materials were processed into iron or steel, Pueblo was amply served with rail lines to take the finished product to market. The location was in many ways a little Pittsburgh, blessed with all the raw inputs and transportation networks to blossom into an industrial powerhouse.

In addition to the optimal location for raw materials and transportation networks, surely Palmer was happy to locate the industrial, gritty, land-extensive production facilities far away from his beloved Colorado Springs. Smoke, noise, immigrant workers, and hulking blast furnaces would not mix well with the

FIGURE 4.4. CF&I steelworks factory in Pueblo, circa 1910. *Source*: Steelworks Center for the West, Pueblo, Colorado.

stunning scenery and more tranquil ambiance of his home. To this day, Pueblo maintains a blue-collar, industrial base and culture, whereas Colorado Springs relies much more on tourism, recreation, and the information economies.

The ground was surveyed in February 1880 at the steelworks site, and work commenced that month on a hot blast furnace, Bessemer converter, rail mill, foundry, and machine shops. Iron was produced by 1881, and the production of steel began in April 1882.[36] Housing for workers was developed immediately west of the factory, in the site named Bessemer. By 1892, with Palmer no longer president of the company, the Colorado Coal and Iron Company merged with the Colorado Fuel Company to form the Colorado Fuel and Iron Company (CF&I). This company would go on to become the industrial behemoth of Colorado (figure 4.4). Once the only steel producer west of the Mississippi, it was a fully vertically integrated company that across many decades owned dozens of coal mines, coke ovens, iron mines, multiple blast furnaces, Bessemer converters, rail and mill plants, and employed tens of thousands of workers in plants across the country. It is also infamously responsible for the Ludlow massacre, the labor strife in 1914 that left dozens killed at the Ludlow coal-mining camp and about seventy-five total deaths in other mining towns throughout the state. Company president

John D. Rockefeller Jr. took a public relations beating as a result of the conflict, leading him to experiment with Employee Representation Plans, or "company unions," and expand extensive sociological and medical initiatives to quell unrest among workers in the isolated mining camps and for the industrial proletariat in Pueblo.[37] In sum, one of the many initiatives of General Palmer and his associates in Colorado Springs led to a profound chapter of Colorado industrial history and a large impact on the Colorado landscape.

COMPETITION IN COLORADO SPRINGS

Despite the temporary treaty keeping the AT&SF lines out of Colorado Springs, other companies were under no such restrictions, and the city attracted competition. The second railroad to connect to Colorado Springs was the Denver and New Orleans, the brainchild of longtime Denver railroad developer John Evans, who incorporated the company in 1881. The intent of this line was to connect Denver to the Gulf Coast through Fort Worth and Galveston. The line—reorganized as the Denver, Texas & Gulf in 1885, the Denver, Texas & Ft. Worth in 1887, then the Colorado & Southern Railway after 1896—was relatively inconsequential for Colorado Springs save for a spur line running into the city from Manitou Junction, about thirteen miles east, near the Franceville coal-mining camp.[38] This connection was completed in early 1883, providing an alternate route to Denver, but the entire connection with Texas and the gulf was not completed until March 14, 1888.[39] The Franceville spur connection came into the southeastern part of Colorado Springs (figure 4.5). The tracks ran along Moreno Avenue and then north on Sahwatch to their depot on Huerfano (now Colorado Avenue) (figure 4.6). The line was in service until 1916, after which tracks were torn out and reused.

Two other lines had a profound impact on life in the city and the landscape. The first of these was the Colorado Midland, incorporated in 1883 by Homer Fisher, who started in railroading with a six-mile narrow-gauge-logging line north of Woodland Park, in what was then called Manitou Park, in 1881. His dream was to build a standard gauge railroad from Colorado Springs up Ute Pass and on to Leadville. Fisher first recruited Irving Howbert, president of the First National Bank of Colorado Springs, then by spring 1885, brought James J. Hagerman on board. Wealthy from investment in iron mines in Michigan, Hagerman moved to Colorado Springs in 1884 from Milwaukee to recover from tuberculosis. After arriving, he began purchasing silver mines in Aspen and coal deposits near Glenwood Springs. Once elected president of the Colorado Midland in June 1885, he steered the company with his vision to connect Colorado Springs to these assets.[40]

The railroad based its roundhouse and repair yards along Fountain Creek near Colorado City, at what today is Highway 24 and 21st Street. This massive investment revived the moribund Colorado City. The west side, as Old Colorado City

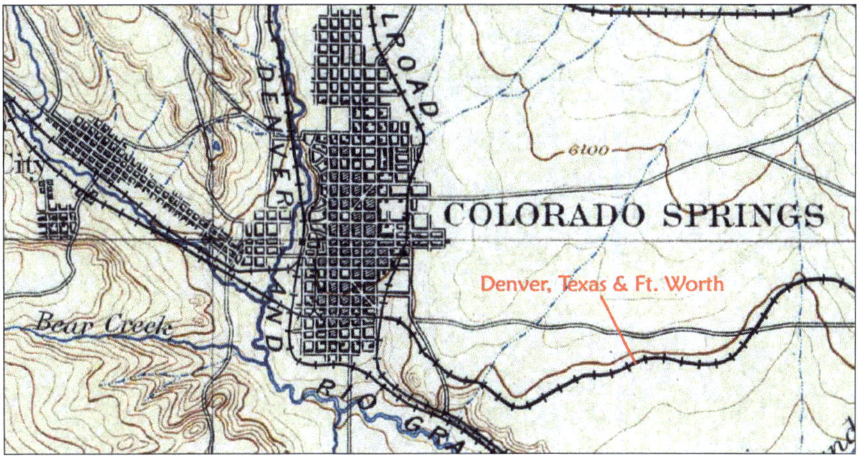

FIGURE 4.5. Denver, Texas & Ft. Worth (later the Colorado & Southern) Railroad route into Colorado Springs from the Franceville coal mines in 1893. *Source*: USGS.

FIGURE 4.6. The tiny depot for the Denver, Texas & Ft. Worth in 1894 at Sahwatch and Colorado (then called Huerfano), now gone. *Source*: Richard C. Overton, *Gulf to Rockies: The Heritage of the Fort Worth and Denver—Colorado and Southern Railways, 1861–1898* (Austin: University of Texas Press, 1953).

is now referred to in the vernacular, had long hosted saloons, honky-tonks, and bordellos as a place of refuge from dry Colorado Springs, but its population was small. The Midland railyards required much labor, leading to growth that solidified Colorado City's reputation as the blue-collar, industrial center of the city. The influx of workers renewed investment in the drinking establishments to support them, all conveniently outside of the Colorado Springs city limits until annexed in 1917 (figure 4.7). The Midland standard gauge tracks extended east to connect with the AT&SF passenger terminal built on the east side of downtown, on

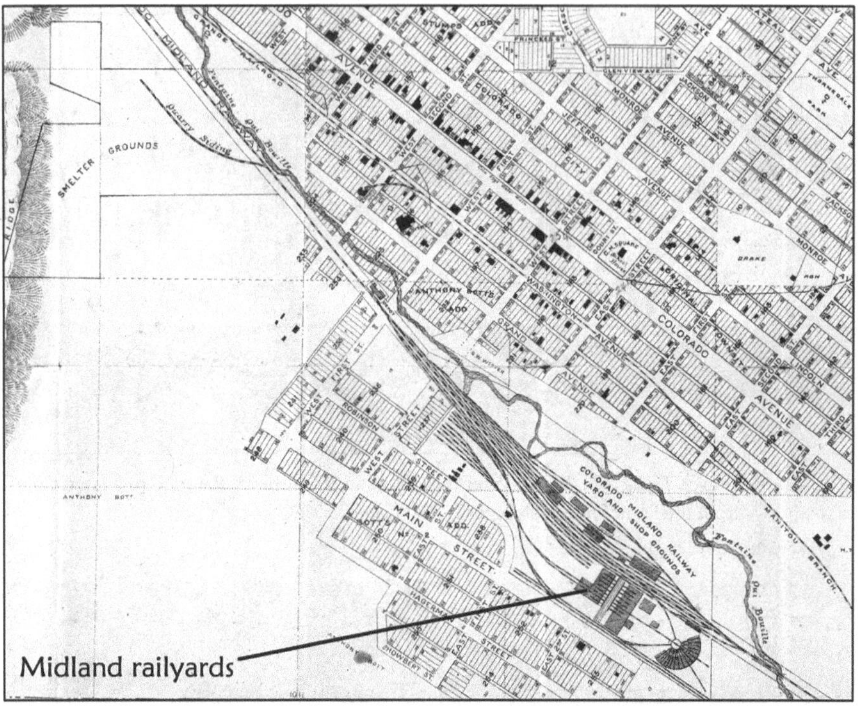

FIGURE 4.7. Midland railyards, including roundhouse, in 1887. Note the few buildings in Colorado City at this time (shown as black squares northwest of the station, mainly along Colorado Ave). The Midland led to a resurgence of population on the west side, but in these early years of the railroad the town was still small. Highway 24 now runs along the path of these tracks. *Source*: Colorado Springs Pioneers Museum.

Pikes Peak Avenue, in 1887. To do so, they built a bridge over the D&RG line near Fountain Creek, then ran parallel tracks along Moreno Avenue since the Denver to Ft. Worth line wouldn't allow them to use their existing tracks.[41] This route through town connected the Colorado Midland to the rest of the country.

The Midland's first passenger train reached Leadville on August 31 1887, then began the difficult work to build a route across the Continental Divide in a race to reach Aspen.[42] The D&RG was building tracks from Leadville across Tennessee Pass to the northwest, down the Eagle and Colorado Rivers to Glenwood Springs (with a line running west to connect with the Rio Grande Western in Utah), and was headed up the Roaring Fork Valley to Aspen. The Midland went west from Leadville, where the 2,100-foot-long Hagerman Tunnel was finished June 14, 1887, 547 feet beneath Hagerman Pass, after which the line continued along the Fryingpan River. The 2.9-mile-long Busk-Ivanhoe Tunnel was built in December 1893, to supersede the Hagerman Tunnel and reduce the long climb over the Continental Divide.[43]

The D&RG reached Aspen November 1, 1887, three months before the Midland in February 1888.[44] But once completed, the Midland could compete with a shorter route to Leadville using its standard gauge line. By 1890 the Midland was competitive, with two daily passenger trains from Colorado Springs and connecting to transcontinental traffic via a spur to Glenwood Springs. The railroad made most money on freight, particularly coal and coke from New Castle and Cardiff in the Crystal River Valley. Coal was delivered to consumers in Aspen, Leadville, Colorado Springs, Denver, and Pueblo, and coke was sent to smelters in Leadville and other smaller locations. The company also moved much timber but relied principally on livestock, with loading points peaking during autumn at Rifle and Hartsel and sheep from Utah brought for summer grazing near Aspen and Hagerman Pass.[45] The Colorado Midland also prospered by tourism out of Colorado Springs, with regular service into the mountains for picnics and wildflower collecting.

The Colorado Midland passed ownership to the AT&SF in September 1890. Poor management by the new owners and the demonetization of silver in late 1893 forced it to foreclose and shut down in 1894. The Colorado Midland Railway Company was newly reincorporated in 1897 but remained unprofitable. It was sold to the Chicago, Burlington & Quincy in 1908 with little success, so on August 15, 1918, a thirty-one-year run of passenger service ended. The Colorado Midland dissolved May 21, 1922.[46]

While this marked the end of the Midland, and rails were torn up for reuse along most of its route, service to Colorado Springs continued with an offshoot company, the Midland Terminal Railway. Incorporated in 1892, this line began as a thirty-one-mile spur connecting the Colorado Midland line at Hayden Divide to the gold-mining camp of Cripple Creek, on the west side of Pikes Peak. The Cripple Creek gold boom of 1891 produced enormous activity and a need to move ore, fuel, supplies, and people up and down the mountain. The district was initially served by a narrow gauge line running through Phantom Canyon to Florence in 1893, but the Midland Terminal connected Colorado Springs to Victor in 1894 and Cripple Creek by 1895. It became the principal transportation route to and from the mining district. The Colorado Midland track from Divide to Colorado Springs was sold to the Midland Terminal, which supplemented diminishing freight from Cripple Creek as the boom wore down with tourism rides along the north side of Pikes Peak.[47] The Midland Terminal continued service between Colorado Springs and Cripple Creek until it too was abandoned and dismantled in 1949.[48] Highway 24—"the Midland Expressway"—is a limited access, four-lane road built in the late 1950s that now runs through the west side along the old train route where the Midland tracks forged the first transit corridor, connecting the city with Ute Pass. The railyards now house an Old West tourism site, but the roundhouse remains, retrofitted into restaurants and shops (figure 4.8).

FIGURE 4.8. Restaurants and shops occupy the retrofitted Midland Roundhouse. *Source*: Photo by author.

The other line of major influence for Colorado Springs was the AT&SF. After the long battle with the D&RG for the Raton Pass and Royal Gorge routes, both companies kept their promises for eight years not to encroach on the other's territory. This changed in 1887, with the Missouri Pacific Railroad nearing completion of tracks from Kansas to Pueblo, which would affect the freight-sharing agreement with the D&RG for traffic to Denver. The AT&SF therefore reneged on their agreement to contract with the D&RG for service north of Pueblo and built their own lines to Denver, through Colorado Springs.[49] The Colorado Springs Station was built on Pikes Peak Avenue, on the east side of town, in 1887, and became the primary competition for the D&RG for travel and freight along the Front Range urban corridor. The two competing companies ran dual north-south tracks through town (figure 4.9). The remodeled 1917 AT&SF depot became the main transit center in the city, complete with a Harvey House restaurant, the innovative chain created by Fred Harvey and associated with AT&SF stations throughout the American Southwest.[50] This new depot enlarged the passenger services and was capable of servicing five trains in front of the station.[51] Like the D&RG, the Santa Fe ended passenger service in April 1971.[52] Whereas the tracks originally skirted the eastern side of town, by 1971 this course ran through the middle of the developed area. Grade-level crossings led to many accidents in the Shooks Run, Patty Jewett, and Old North End neighborhoods.[53] Finally, the tracks in these neighborhoods were ripped up in 1974 and converted to bike paths paralleling Shooks Run, the stream forming the eastern edge of the city (figure 4.10).[54] Today the depot is still there, occupied by offices (figure 4.11).

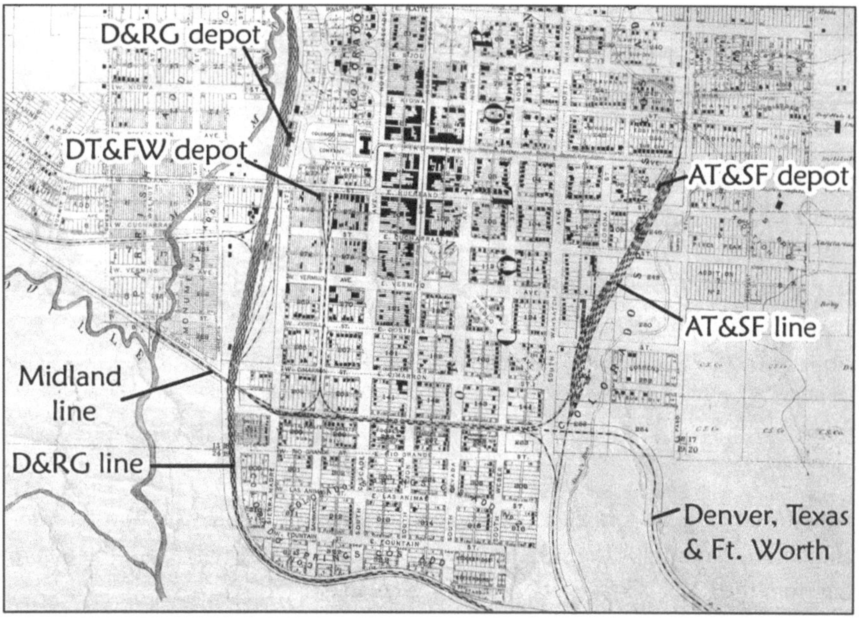

FIGURE 4.9. The AT&SF ran its tracks along the eastern edge of town, paralleling the D&RG. These two lines, and their depots, became the primary passenger service providers. This 1889 map also shows how the Midland extended its line across Monument Creek, over the D&RG tracks, and parallel to the DT&FW lines along Moreno Ave. to connect with the AT&SF Route and Depot. *Source*: Colorado Springs Pioneers Museum.

FIGURE 4.10. Iron trestle crossing Shooks Run and Kiowa Street just north of the AT&SF depot on Pikes Peak Avenue, 1904 (left). The trestle was torn down by 1980; now the line is the Shooks Run bike path, with the old rail berm running adjacent to the path at El Paso and Kiowa Streets (right). *Source*: Colorado Springs Pioneers Museum (left), photo by author (right).

While the AT&SF route through town was a major boost, rail service continued to grow. Even with four lines serving the city, still no direct connection to the populated East existed. All travel went through either Denver or Pueblo before crossing the plains. This changed when the Chicago, Rock Island, and Pacific Railroad

FIGURE 4.11. The original AT&SF Depot in 1888, twice enlarged and renovated, is still used today for offices. *Source*: *Gazette* (1888), January 1 (left) courtesy Colorado Springs Pioneers Museum; photo by author (right).

announced a direct connection to Colorado Springs in 1888. City boosters were enamored, claiming, "The benefit which will accrue to this city from the incoming from the Rock Island is at present incalculable":

> During the last few months the discussion involved in the Rock Island's selection of a western terminal has advertised this city more thoroughly in business circles than it ever was before. Then, the road when completed, may be depended on to secure its share of western passenger business, and we may not only expect a great increase in summer tourists, but also large additions to permanent population from this source alone. Who can safely say that the boom has fairly begun? The advent of the Rock Island is but a long stride in a brilliant career for this city.[55]

The line, completed in 1888, provided a direct route to Chicago, via Rock Island—both a town in Illinois across the Mississippi River from Davenport, Iowa, and an actual island used to shorten and support the railroad bridge crossing the Mississippi River. It is an interesting historical paradox that "Rock Island" lives in railroad lore, even popularized in a Johnny Cash song, when in fact the town was long a steamboat center that saw the rails as a threat. Completing the east-west railroads solidified the Chicago–New York industrial core, and led to the decline of the Saint Louis–New Orleans river traffic running north-south, which was the early raison d'être for towns like Rock Island.[56]

The Rock Island line came into Colorado Springs from the northeast, through Falcon, and along what is now Constitution Avenue. It connected with D&RG lines near Roswell, where a sixteen-stall roundhouse and repair yard were built (figure 4.12). Roswell, like Colorado City also conveniently located outside of the city limits of Colorado Springs (until annexed in 1950), became a railroad worker town, well known for its racetrack and later drinking establishments along the auto route north to Denver.[57] Today the four remaining stalls of the original roundhouse are home to

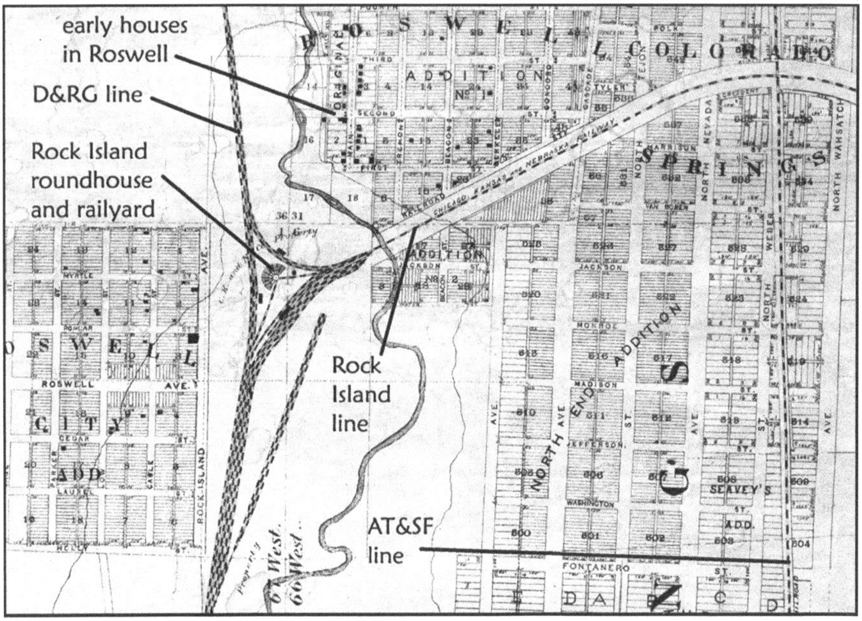

FIGURE 4.12. The Rock Island line entered the northern boundaries of Colorado Springs, where the railroad worker town of Roswell grew around the railyards, as shown in this 1889 map. The tracks connected to the D&RG line to enter into the city. *Source*: Colorado Springs Pioneers Museum.

a local trolley and railroad museum, complete with rusting train remnants parked at the end of a lonesome stretch of abandoned tracks, but the original worker town of Roswell remains as a pleasant neighborhood close to downtown. The last Rock Island train ran in 1979, though a smaller company used the line periodically until 1985, after which most of the tracks were ripped up in stages through 2013.[58]

Two other special purpose rail lines added to the Colorado Springs transportation options. The first was a tourist line to the top of Pikes Peak, the Manitou and Pikes Peak Railway, or more commonly known as the Cog Railway. Begun in 1889, the new line completed its first trip to the summit of Pikes Peak in 1891. It was an engineering marvel, requiring the giant cogs to pull the trains up slope grades reaching of 25 percent, and still runs to the highest altitude of any railway in North America. The line was bought by the Broadmoor in 1925, and internal combustion engines replaced steam in 1938.[59] The line ran until 2018, carrying about 300,000 tourists annually, and hopes are it will reopen after infrastructure repairs are made and a new Summit House is built atop Pikes Peak.

The last line built in Colorado Springs was another route to the Cripple Creek mining district. Prominent mining investors—including Winfield Scott Stratton, Irving Howbert, James Burns, and William S. Jackson—sought to avoid the Midland Terminal Railway monopoly, which also controlled the Phantom

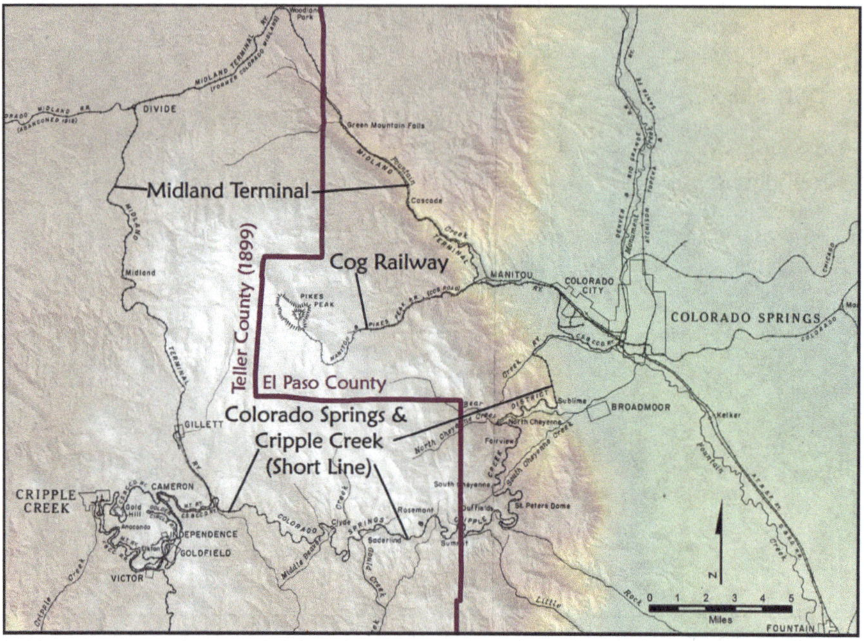

FIGURE 4.13. The Colorado Springs & Cripple Creek District Railway, popularly known as the "Short Line," ran to Cripple Creek from 1901 to 1920. It competed with the Midland Terminal. This map also shows the Cog Railway to the top of Pikes Peak. *Source*: Colorado Springs Pioneers Museum, relief composite by author.

Canyon line to Florence, on traffic between Cripple Creek and Colorado Springs. They created the Colorado Springs & Cripple Creek District Railway in 1901, more popularly known as the "Short Line" because its route cut eleven miles off the trip between the two cities (figure 4.13).[60] Boosters heralded this as a great improvement for Colorado Springs, "the celebrated tourist centre [*sic*] and the great gold camp inseparably joined by a band of steel."[61]

The Short Line initially dominated volume between the two cities and forced rates lower. In addition to carrying supplies up the mountain to Cripple Creek and ore down the mountain to smelters in Colorado Springs, the line was popular for tourists who simply admired the scenery, one of whom was Vice President Teddy Roosevelt in 1901.[62] By 1902, 66,000 tourists traveled the new line during the summer months.[63] It was bought by the Colorado & Southern in 1904, and moved its passenger terminal in 1905 from the D&RG depot across town to the AT&SF depot, where the Colorado & Southern had already been leasing space.[64] Eventually it could not compete with the Midland Terminal, which ended up purchasing the company in 1915. The line was allowed to flounder, repairs went unmet, and operations ceased by 1920. Their railyard hub was dismantled in 1923, and on that site the city built a power plant in 1925, where the Martin Drake power

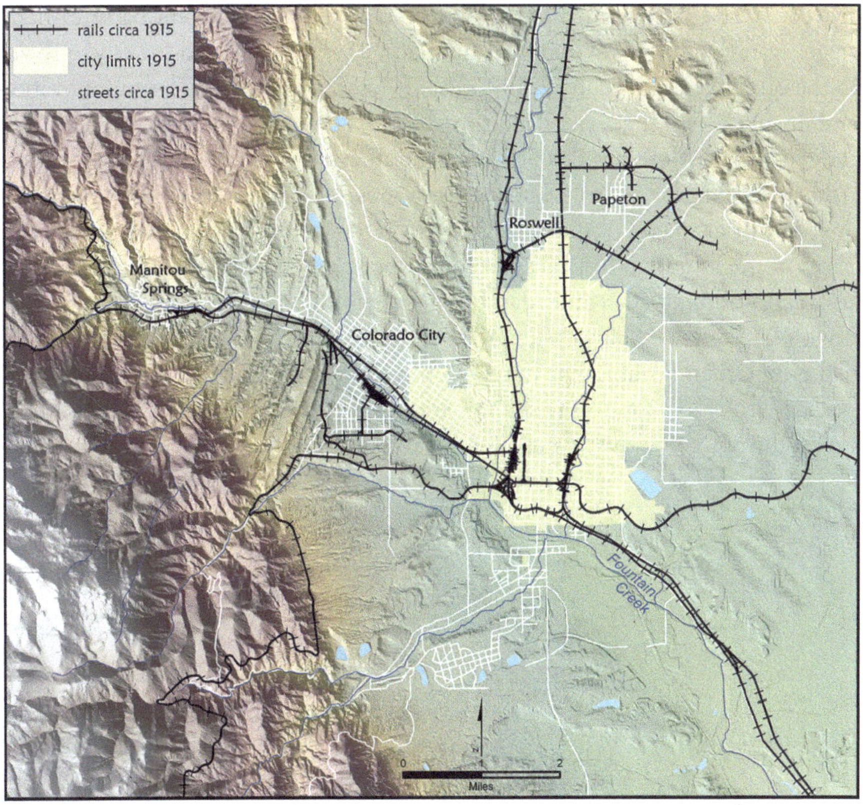

FIGURE 4.14. The height of the rail era, circa 1915, with seven different rail lines serving the city and numerous spurs connecting industrial sites and coal mines. Dense concentration of lines can be seen around all railyard workshops and depots. *Source*: Cartography by author.

plant now sits on the southwest corner of the downtown, illustrating how industrial land use from earlier eras influences contemporary land uses.[65] With all rails removed by 1923, residents today know the lower parts of this route as Gold Camp road, a popular bike and hiking path closed to motorized traffic after one of the train tunnels collapsed in 1988. The upper stretches of the route join the Old Stage road high up on the South Slopes of Pikes Peak, still open for motorized and non-motorized traffic to the Cripple Creek District.

THE RAILROAD LEGACY

By 1915, Colorado Springs had seven railroads serving it, with direct connections to Chicago, north-south routes to Denver and Pueblo, three options to Cripple Creek, connections through Utah to the West Coast, and an extensive collection of lines running throughout towns and mining camps in Colorado (figure 4.14). The railroads, land development, coal, and industrialization all went hand-in-hand to generate profits for investors in this place. The rail era led to the city's growth in the early twentieth century and situated Colorado Springs to be an innovation and finance center that extended its reach across the state. Today only tracks from the old D&RG route run through town, but they are still in use to transport coal from Wyoming for power plants on the plains, with spurs to serve Fort Carson and industrial spaces throughout the city. In the city today remain ghostly remnants of tracks and industrial spaces, transportation corridors that now serve as bike and walking paths, and adaptive reuses of old buildings such as the roundhouses and depots. Many dream of a renewed, high-speed rail passenger service along the urban Front Range to relieve perpetual congestion on Interstate 25, so perhaps it is too soon to say the rail era has ended. No matter what the future holds, the railroad industry has already profoundly shaped Colorado Springs.

5

Rock

> Cripple conferred its greatest blessings on Colorado Springs. Every foot of that pleasant place bears Cripple's stamp.
>
> —MARSHALL SPRAGUE, 1953[1]

GOLD

The initial goals of the railroad era were to connect Colorado Springs to the outside world. The first D&RG link to Denver illustrates this, as do the plans to build to Santa Fe and Mexico stated in the articles of incorporation. We also see this external connection logic in the link with the Rio Grande Western to Ogden and the Union Pacific transcontinental line, and through connections with other lines coming to Colorado from the east. After completing these linkages, the subsequent strategy of the rail era was to use railroads to generate profits through land sales and consolidate control over resources among the business leaders in Colorado Springs: to extend the city's imperial reach throughout the state. Capital raised or owned by Colorado Springs leaders played a major role in developing far-flung regions of Colorado and enriching the city. Palmer himself created both the D&RG and what became the CF&I steelworks, tying the important mining districts such as Leadville and the many coal-mining camps to the city, while Hagerman and friends linked silver mines at Aspen to Colorado Springs. But nothing created a regional control center, generated profits, constructed the built landscape, and fueled business-friendly politics like the bonanza from the Cripple Creek gold mines. While true that the steel of the mighty railroads first brought industry to the region, the more precious shiny metal injected wealth into Colorado Springs at unprecedented levels (figure 5.1).

DOI: 10.5876/9781646421688.c005

FIGURE 5.1. On New Year's Day, 1900, the golden explosion of Cripple Creek was sending rivers of wealth down to Colorado Springs, engaging the entire population and forever changing the city. *Source*: *Colorado Springs Gazette* (1899), December 31, cover art for New Year's Eve supplement courtesy Colorado Springs Pioneers Museum.

CRIPPLE CREEK

The Colorado gold rush of 1859 created mining towns such as Central City, Idaho Springs, and Georgetown; consolidated Denver as the central place along the Front Range for supplies and later processing of ore, made it the western transportation hub, and established a stable and growing population in the territory.

This boom started with prospectors finding gold flakes and nuggets in the streams draining the mountains, which led to hard rock mining at the sources of that gold, followed by the expansion of mining for silver and gold across the state, to places such as Leadville, Aspen, and the San Juan Mountains. Despite the "Pikes Peak or Bust" motto of Argonauts crossing the plains, none of this mining boom directly affected the Pikes Peak Region, other than help Colorado City become a freight supply center and later provide justification for Palmer's railroad to build lines to the camps.

By 1890 many of the smaller boom sites had worn out and hard rock mining became consolidated into larger operations funded with external capital. The era of the lone prospector on his burro striking a vein at some remote mountain spot was rapidly fading, and most of the state had been thoroughly explored and picked over. The thought that gold would be discovered some twenty miles from Colorado Springs was lunacy. Cripple Creek, on the west side of Pikes Peak, had been prospected for some time with little success. Panning for gold, or placer mining, turned up virtually nothing, and the few exploratory shafts that were sunk returned the same. Furthermore, at the urging of local merchants looking to drum up business, two miners "salted" a pit in the area in 1884 by spreading gold ore from Leadville, claiming to have found a new bonanza at Mount Pisgah.[2] The flurry of activity associated with this scam, and the subsequent lack of any precious metal, gave the region a bad reputation for mining. So when "Crazy Bob" Womack, a local cowboy, came to town from Cripple Creek in October 1890 with gold-bearing ore, few gave him credence.

In addition to the 1884 Mount Pisgah hoax and the poor reputation Womack had in town, the delayed recognition of Cripple Creek gold was due to its geology. The Cripple Creek District is an ancient volcanic caldera, the core of which is fine-grained andesite breccia surrounded by granite outside of the plug. Into this breccia, or "porphyry," hot telluride solutions of gold salts precipitated along cracks and fissures. These fissures are very narrow, and the materials in the mineralized solutions were small, so there are no massive veins of gold in the districts. Furthermore, the color and composition of the mother materials make ore identification very difficult.[3] There are no nuggets of gold lying on the ground, and to the untrained eye, ore-bearing rock is indistinguishable from waste material. Nevertheless, Womack's persistence paid off, his ore assays generated renewed interest, and by spring of 1891 the excitement spread among an initial surge of prospectors.

Most of 1891 saw many small sites prospected but little gold. Due to the nature of these ore types, Cripple Creek requires capital-intensive operations. One-man glory holes are not found here; discovering a vein means first removing much overburden, sinking considerable shafts, and on-site assaying of ore to determine the quality. The initial surge of dreamers floundered until somebody with deep pockets was willing to invest. That occurred in November 1891, when Count

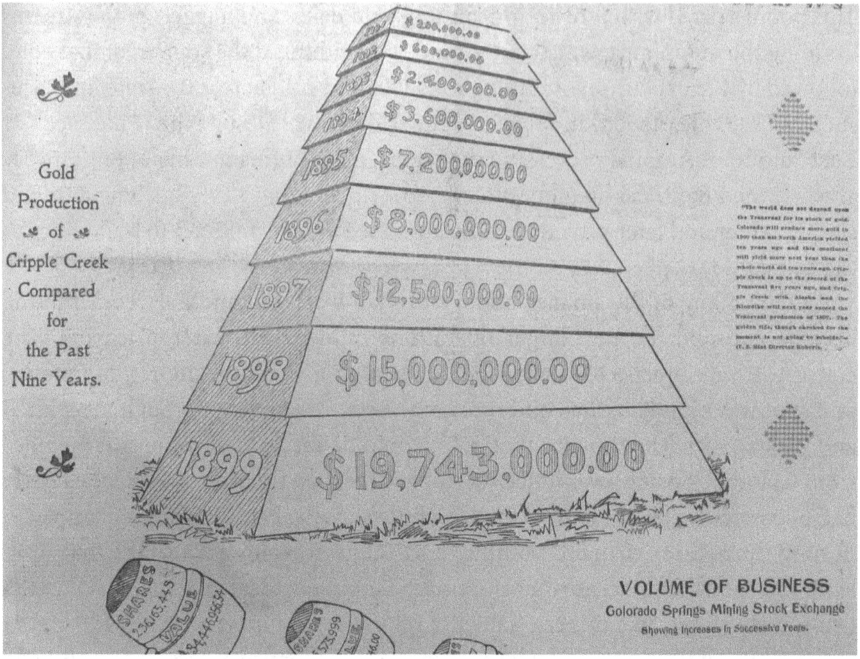

FIGURE 5.2. The volume of business, and wealth generated, was ever increasing throughout the 1890s. *Source*: *Colorado Springs Gazette* (1899), December 31, courtesy Colorado Springs Pioneers Museum.

James Pourtales, a German aristocrat who opened the first casino at what is now the Broadmoor in Colorado Springs, invested $80,000 in the Buena Vista Mine.[4] His faith in the prospects of the region led to a surge of investors and quickly produced gold in abundance. The boom was on.

Cripple Creek gold production increased each year throughout the 1890s, peaking in 1900–1901, then saw gradual decline through the mid-twentieth century, by which time it had produced over 20 million ounces of gold worth over $450 million (figure 5.2).[5] Cripple Creek produced the most gold of any mining district in North America, far surpassing the California, Black Hills, or Alaska strikes. It was the undisputed king of gold camps in the United States and even the world. The population of the district went from a dozen or so in 1890 to about 30,000 by 1900, when the town of Cripple Creek was the sixth largest in Colorado.[6]

WEALTH IN COLORADO SPRINGS

The Cripple Creek mining district has a rich history full of Wild West lore, and impacts of this gold craze on Colorado Springs were profound. Much of the investment came from Colorado Springs, and most of the wealth generated went there. According to Marshall Sprague, author of the Cripple Creek history *Money Mountain*, by 1908 at least twenty-eight Colorado Springs residents had become millionaires due to Cripple Creek gold. The local Western League professional baseball team that played from 1901 to 1905 was named "the millionaires," reflecting the new reputation of the city.[7] One of those who struck it rich was Winfield Scott Stratton, a local carpenter and part-time prospector. He was the first to strike big returns with his Independence Mine, which he tried to sell in 1891 for $500, did sell for a $5,000 down payment in 1892, then reclaimed it in 1893, when the buyer was disillusioned. In July 1893, he hit a major vein and eventually sold the mine in 1899 for $11 million. He believed that any man who derived his wealth from the natural resources of a region was obliged to use that wealth to further develop the place from which it came. Stratton remained loyal to his blue-collar roots, giving away most of his money, buying the moribund Colorado Springs trolley car network, and investing $2 million to create top-class service, constructing the Mining Exchange Building, donating land for City Hall and the US Post Office, and buying the El Paso County Courthouse so a new one could be built (today's Pioneers Museum) (figure 5.3). Stratton also insisted on paying good wages and providing life insurance to his trolley line workers (the first corporation in Colorado to do so), financed a home-buying plan for his trolley workers and bought homes outright for other employees, and built the popular park at Cheyenne Canyon, at the end of his trolley line, for residents to enjoy weekend outings.[8] Even after selling his Independence Mine, he continued to invest in Cripple Creek, believing he could find the root source of all the gold deep underground in "An undertaking which for boldness of conception and magnitude of execution surpasses any mining enterprise ever conceived by the minds of men during all the ages of history."[9] Despite his vast wealth, Stratton continued to live in his humble house on Weber Street, but became increasingly morose and removed from society. He bemoaned the constant pleas for charity from nearly everybody and scammers vying for his wealth. He turned hard to whiskey, eventually fell into a coma, and died at age fifty-four. Upon his death in 1902, Stratton willed his wealth to create the Myron Stratton Home for the poor without means of support or unable to earn a livelihood. The Myron Stratton Home opened in 1913, funded by the Stratton estate that included numerous mining companies still operating in the Cripple Creek District. From the time of Stratton's death in 1902 to the mid-twentieth century, his estate operations produced gold worth over $10 million, all for the benefit of the residents at the Myron Stratton Home.[10] This one person, in the end an unhappy loner, left a deep and lasting impact on the landscape of Colorado Springs.

Another to strike it rich was Spencer Penrose, perhaps the mirror opposite personality of Stratton. From a wealthy Philadelphia family, he arrived in the city nearly broke and worked his way to fabulous riches. A hard-drinking playboy, he and partner Charles Tutt struck gold at Cripple Creek, then went on to

FIGURE 5.3. Previously the El Paso County Courthouse, today's Pioneers Museum is the city's architectural jewel and a by-product of Cripple Creek wealth. W. S. Stratton's purchase of the old courthouse building enabled the county to build this new structure in 1903. *Source*: photo by author.

develop the Bingham Canyon copper mine in Utah; build two ore-processing mills in Colorado City; control the railroad interests to Cripple Creek; and, in his crowning achievement, build and develop the Broadmoor, today a world-class resort that has through the years owned affiliated projects such as the zoo, the Cog Railway, golf courses, and a skating palace. He later funded conversion of the Glockner Sanatorium into the Penrose Hospital, and his wife, Julie, donated her house on West Dale Street to the Broadmoor Art Academy in 1919, which was converted to the Colorado Springs Fine Arts Center in 1935 with the new art deco building constructed by 1936.[11] In 1937, just prior to his death, he and his wife established the El Pomar Foundation, one of the largest philanthropic foundations serving the state of Colorado.

The wealth generated by Stratton and Penrose from Cripple Creek, along with that of many other successful miners and investors, fundamentally changed the built environment of Colorado Springs. A level of opulence shaped the architecture of civic and private buildings downtown and of houses in the nearby neighborhoods. The economic activity also drove new jobs as investors congregated in Colorado Springs to reap the rewards of the gold bonanza.

With little exception, mining in Cripple Creek was corporate driven. In 1900, there were 256 mining stockbrokers listed in the Colorado Springs Business Directory, plus 572 mining companies, twenty-two mining engineers, seven assayers,

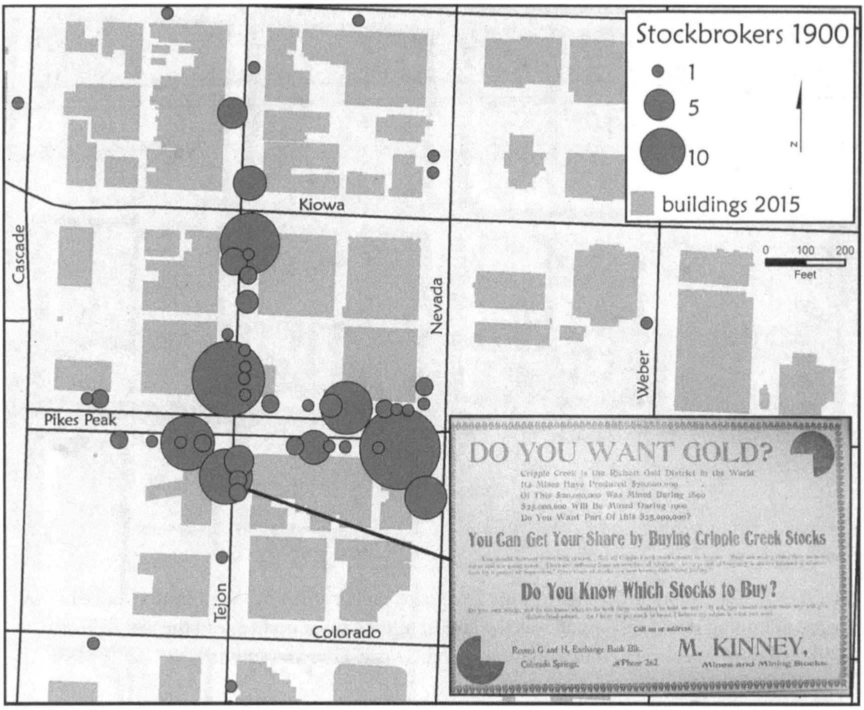

FIGURE 5.4. Downtown Mining Stockbroker offices. *Source*: City Directory 1900 (data); *Colorado Springs Gazette* (1899), December 31, 1899 (advertisement image), courtesy Colorado Springs Pioneers Museum, cartography by author.

and three mining exchange offices (figure 5.4).[12] The mining exchange, today a boutique hotel, became, for a time, the largest mining stock exchange in the world (figure 5.5).[13] The Exchange National Bank, Giddings Building, Carlton Building, and Lennox Building—all still located on Tejon Street—were built with Cripple Creek money. The Burns Theater was built by James Burns, another Cripple Creek millionaire. It was a landmark theater for live shows, then later movies, but sadly was torn down in 1974 (figure 5.6). The many stately homes in the Old North End, a historic residential district north of Colorado College, were mostly built with Cripple Creek money, with Wood Avenue garnering the moniker "millionaires row."[14] Gold seemed to be on the mind of everybody in Colorado Springs in the early twentieth century (figure 5.7).

COLORADO CITY INDUSTRY

In addition to residential houses and the built landscape downtown and at the Broadmoor, Cripple Creek fundamentally changed the economic character of Colorado Springs. The Colorado Midland Railroad first brought heavy industry

FIGURE 5.5. The Colorado Springs Mining Exchange, built in 1901 by W. S. Stratton, once housed dozens of mining stockbrokers and was the largest mining stock exchange in the world. Today the building has been renovated into a boutique hotel. *Source*: Photo by author.

FIGURE 5.6. The Burns Theater, 23 East Pikes Peak Avenue, was built in 1912 with James Burns's Cripple Creek fortune. It was converted from live theater to the Chief Movie Theater in the 1950s, then torn down in 1974. Photo is circa 1930. Today the site is a surface parking lot. *Source*: Colorado Springs Pioneers Museum.

FIGURE 5.7. The all-consuming Star of the West: Cripple Creek Gold. *Source: Colorado Springs Gazette* (1900), January 4, courtesy Colorado Springs Pioneers Museum.

to the west side in 1887, but even then a proposal to build a smelter in Colorado City to process ore from Leadville and other mining camps met resistance from residents "not in favor of permitting a change in the character of the place as a health resort."[15] The Cripple Creek boom altered that attitude drastically and exacerbated the transition to industrialization. Because of the low-grade quality of the gold ore in the district, processing to extract the metal was crucial to the profits of the mines. In the initial years of mining, the ancient routine of stamp mills and amalgamation using mercury processed ore on site in the Cripple Creek District. Ore was crushed to granular size, and passed over mercury that bonded with the gold, then the mercury was entrapped on different types of surface materials and heated to separate the gold. This process was very inefficient, leaving over half the gold remaining in the ore after processing.[16] By 1893, a chlorination process developed in the Transvaal of South Africa successfully functioned at a mill in the town of Lawrence, Colorado, adjacent to Victor in the mining district. The chlorination process replaced the old amalgamation stamp mills. Here ore was first crushed and the pulp mixed with water and concentrated. This slime was roasted to remove volatile materials, mixed with water again, and put into gravel-bottomed vats with lime. Chlorine gas was then introduced into the base of these vats, and twelve to twenty-four hours of leaching produced a chloride of gold solution that was filtered and treated with a reagent to precipitate out the gold. Residue tailings were thrown away on piles, and the gold precipitate was melted down into bullion.[17] The successful Lawrence Mill ran for two years but burned down in 1895.

Even though the mill was a success, there were great problems with the Lawrence chlorination mill: economies of scale require large volumes of ore, coal, and water, of which the latter two were unavailable near Cripple Creek. Industrialists recognized the need for two changes: first, the district needed railroad service. Most people and supplies—including the heavy, bulky ore shipped out—were transported via a three-hour stage or freighter ride from the connection with the Colorado Midland Railroad at Florissant to the north, some eighteen miles distant. David Moffat, in collaboration with D&RG officials, exploited the opportunity to eliminate the inefficient freighter wagons by building a narrow gauge railroad from Florence, south of the district, up Phantom Canyon to Victor to connect with the entire mining district. His Florence & Cripple Creek line arrived in July 1894 and could link directly to the D&RG narrow gauge at Florence without the slow and costly transfer of cargo to standard gauge cars, referred to as a break-of-bulk point by transportation geographers. The rail connection, plus the availability of water from the Arkansas River and both coal and oil nearby, led to an early concentration of mills and smelters in Florence. This turn of events led to the second revelation: The economics of transportation favored mills nearby to coal and water, not nearby to the ore. It is cheaper to move ore downhill to process than to move coal and water uphill. The Florence and Cripple Creek, and all subsequent lines, profited by taking people and supplies uphill, then bringing ore downhill. The Florence line quickly made profits and provided a vital service to the district, connecting with what would become two interurban electric trolley lines by 1897.

Colorado Springs investors sought to link the mining district to their city via rail connection with the Colorado Midland Railroad, which skirted the district to the north. The Midland Terminal Railroad incorporated in August 1892, with the original intent to run a narrow gauge line from the Colorado Midland Station at Hayden Divide to Cripple Creek. However, this would require break-of-bulk transfer, manually moving cargo from narrow gauge cars to those on the standard gauge Midland. After laying some six miles of narrow gauge track, Midland Terminal owners halted construction because of concerns with the transfer from narrow to standard gauge. A group of Colorado Springs investors reinvigorated the project and built a standard gauge line that entered the district just in time for big gold discoveries to the east of Cripple Creek, in a region not directly served by the Florence line. The Midland Terminal quickly became profitable, completed the connection to Cripple Creek in December 1895, and opened a direct route to

Colorado Springs, gaining a strategic advantage over the Florence line. Susceptible to repeated washouts in Phantom Canyon and connecting to a smaller and more remote location in Florence, service on the Florence & Cripple Creek diminished such that Moffat turned over all stock to the Midland Terminal in 1899; all services on the Florence line ended in 1912.[18]

With the new rail connection to Colorado Springs and the chlorination mill near Victor destroyed by fire, Spencer Penrose and partners Charles MacNeill, Charles Tutt and others jumped on the opportunity to build their own mill in Colorado City, the Colorado-Philadelphia plant in 1896, at the time the largest reduction mill in the world.[19] Located near what is today 31st Street and Highway 24, this plant dominated ore processing in the region (figure 5.8). The partners were so successful that they bought out most of the Florence mills to create the "mill trust," later formalized as the United States Reduction and Refining Company in 1901. This conglomerate came to dominate both mill processing and rail transport in the region, consolidating operations in Colorado City and making the Florence operations inconsequential. By 1906, one of only two mills still operating in Florence burned down, further diminishing the town's industrial capacity.[20] The Colorado-Philadelphia Mill was expanded with the Standard Mill, built in 1901 immediately adjacent to the older plant: "The very fact of its building will be an attraction to outside capital and with the smoke rolling from additional stacks to give a metropolitan air to the surroundings, El Paso may well congratulate herself on the material evidence of the steady growth of her industries."[21] These mills were sold to the Guggenheims 1906, owners of the American Smelting and Refining Company (ASARCO) with smelters in Globeville (Denver) and Pueblo, among others.[22]

The Colorado-Philadelphia and Standard Mills solidified Colorado City as a gold-processing center. As prominent citizen Irving Howbert stated in 1902, "The growing prominence of this city as a center for the reduction of mill ores is doing much to establish the prosperity of the city on a permanent basis."[23] Other miners, particularly James Burns, who owned the Portland Mine, resented the monopoly of the Midland Terminal on transportation and the dominance of the mill trust owners on processing plants. He and other investors built the Colorado Springs & Cripple Creek "Short Line" in 1901, and Burns opened the Portland Mill in the same year, shipping ore directly from his mine at Cripple Creek to his mill in Colorado Springs. This mill was located on the east end of what is today Bear Creek Park, now the Penrose Equestrian Center (figure 5.9). It provided competition for the mill trust operations until closing in 1918.[24]

Demand was such that the General Metals Company opened a third mill in the city, the Telluride Reduction Works, in 1902. Lacking their own mines for supply, this plant was bought and renovated in 1906 into the Golden Cycle Mill.[25] The Golden Cycle Mill was formed originally to process ore from the Golden Cycle Mine in Cripple Creek, then owner John Milliken bought a conglomerate

FIGURE 5.8. The first west-side mill, the Colorado-Philadelphia, built 1896. *Source*: *Colorado Springs Gazette* (1899), December 31 (top); Colorado Springs Pioneers Museum (bottom).

FIGURE 5.9. The Portland Mill, 1907, built 1901. *Source*: Colorado Springs Pioneers Museum.

of mines in 1908, expanding production to increase ore deliveries. The mill was a new cyanide plant, based on a much more efficient process. Chlorination was certainly an improvement over the old mercury amalgamation but still wasted

FIGURE 5.10. Golden Cycle Mill. Undated photo on left shows the enormity of the facility, looking southwest from a worker neighborhood near Colorado City. Aerial view from the 1940s photo on the right shows the gigantic tailings piles, including impounded reservoir of wastewater. The road cutting diagonally across the image is 21st Street; a rail line crosses that road and terminates at the tailings dam adjacent to the smokestack. View is looking towards the southeast. *Source*: Stewarts Commercial Photographers, © Pikes Peak Library District 013-394 (left), image 001-2066 (right).

much gold into the tailings. The cyanide process involved first grinding and roasting the ore, then wet-grinding again in a cyanide solution. Next are a series of filtering, thickening and agitation steps for the chemical reduction of gold tellurides by potassium cyanide, then the precipitation of gold using zinc dust. Finally the precipitate is refined in furnaces into gold bullion.[26] This new technology was desperately needed as gold content of ore continually decreased after the richest veins were depleted. The Golden Cycle enabled Cripple Creek to continue in the gold-mining business through the mid-twentieth century. It was by far the largest reduction works in the area, with daily capacity of 1,500 tons by 1909—more than all other Colorado City plants combined (figure 5.10).[27] By 1909, up to 85 percent of all Cripple Creek ore was processed at the Golden Cycle.[28] The Golden Cycle Mill became the world's largest plant dedicated to processing gold ore.[29] As a consequence, the Colorado-Philadelphia and Standard Mills shut down in 1911, with the Portland closing by 1918, even though it too had converted to a cyanide process in 1906.[30] As became the case with most things Cripple Creek related, Spencer Penrose, along with Albert Carlton, bought out the company in 1915. The Golden Cycle Corporation formed in July 1929, consolidating most of the remaining mines in the Cripple Creek District. By the 1930s it essentially controlled all Cripple Creek gold activities, even taking control of the Midland Terminal Railroad by 1934.[31] The Golden Cycle Mill shut down in 1949, but this organization operated using the newly constructed Carlton Mill in the Cripple Creek District through 1962.

The landscape of the city was forever changed (figure 5.11). For many years, these industrial plants belted out smoke and noise that disrupted the genteel

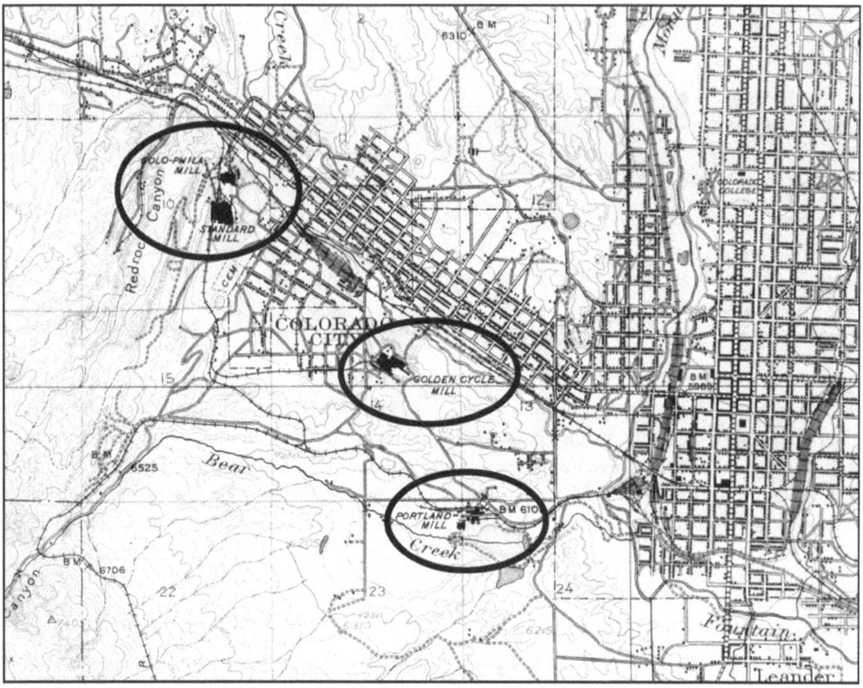

FIGURE 5.11. Four mills and smelters are outlined in this 1909 map. Also note the rail lines shown on the map, plus all buildings. *Source*: USGS.

ambiance of Palmer's little village, a change Palmer noted with regret when commenting on the "odors of sulphur [*sic*] and arsenic."[32] Although the mills have all been torn down, foundations and old railroad track grades remain on the land. The lone remnant of the Golden Cycle plant is the smokestack, kept intact as an iconic symbol to create a very postmodern place identity for a new housing development called Gold Hill Mesa. This residential infill project sits on top of the enormous tailings piles that were long an eyesore and environmental nightmare as dusts full of heavy metals blew into neighboring housing areas and eroded into Fountain Creek (figure 5.12). The Gold Hill Mesa developers graded the heavily eroded tailings pile and laid several feet of topsoil over the remnant waste before constructing houses. At full buildout, plans call for a thriving urban infill project complete with shops and restaurants at the old industrial site that few will know as previously an industrial wasteland.

POLITICAL ENVIRONMENT

The Cripple Creek gold rush also fundamentally affected labor relations and set the tone for the probusiness and antiregulatory political culture that remains

FIGURE 5.12. The Gold Hill Mesa infill development project will be built on top of the enormous tailings hill created from the Golden Cycle Mill waste. Note the original smokestack remnant preserved on the right side of the mesa used as a place-making identity icon. *Source*: photo by author.

prevalent in Colorado Springs today. The industrial nature of the Cripple Creek mining operations required many wage laborers. In the early days of industrialization, relations between capitalists and labor led to numerous struggles, with large pools of industrial workers attracting unions. In Cripple Creek, the Western Federation of Miners (WFM), one of the more powerful and militant trade unions to arise in the nineteenth century, gained a stronghold.

Governor Davis Waite, a Populist, was elected in 1892 partially due to statewide discontent for both Republicans and Democrats about pending and potentially radical reversal of federal purchase of silver for coinage. The US government had switched from a silver and gold bimetallism in 1873, after which it stopped silver coinage and based US currency solely on the gold standard. Pressure from western silver mining interests led to the Sherman Act in 1890, which reinstated federal purchase of silver for US currency. Opposition to this dual standard led to the repeal of the Sherman Act in 1893, which again converted federal currency solely to the gold standard. With the sudden decline in demand for silver, many unemployed miners migrated to Cripple Creek to mine for gold. In 1894 several large mine owners, recognizing the surplus of labor could be exploited to their advantage, demanded increase in the work day from eight to ten hours with no increase in pay.[33] The WFM organized workers against this change and went on strike. Mine owners hired nonunion strikebreakers, protected by privately subsidized deputies under the El Paso County sheriff, and refused to negotiate, with two exceptions: Stratton remained sympathetic to labor and, to the dismay of other mine owners, negotiated a deal with the union. Portland Mine owner James "Jimmy" Burns also sympathized with labor from his Irish heritage and working-class roots, aligning with the many Irish (and other Catholic) miners in the district. Burns had long disdained the wealthy Protestant industrialists meeting at the El Paso Club in Colorado Springs since his days as a plumber in the city and continually played the role of maverick among mine and mill operators in the region.[34]

Most mine owners refused to negotiate with the WFM and continued to employ strikebreakers. Armed conflict followed with near autonomous control of parts of the mining district by union labor; violence was prevalent on both sides. Opinion pieces fomented fear in Colorado Springs that radical miners would march on the city, and the *Gazette* issued a call to arms, asking volunteers to serve as deputies.[35] A Home Guard formed, patrolling the outskirts of the city on the lookout for radical infiltrators.[36] The El Paso County sheriff deputized a force of 1,300 mercenaries to march on the WFM camps. The state militia had to intervene in the Cripple Creek District between deputies and miners. With the intervention of Governor Waite and Adjutant General Thomas Tarsney, the WFM won recognition of their demands. Cripple Creek gained a reputation as a labor stronghold friendly to the workforce, which Colorado Springs mine owners did not take lightly. In retribution, Tarsney—the man in charge of the state militia—while staying overnight in Colorado Springs, was abducted from the Alamo Hotel, taken nearby to the Otis house at Austin Bluffs, and tarred and feathered. He was abandoned along the D&RG railroad tracks, where he made his way to Palmer Lake before the governor sent a train to rescue him. Nobody was convicted of the affair, even though the perpetrators were known, and El Paso County solidified its reputation for antiunion, probusiness Republican politics. Colorado Springs mine owners and operators subsequently gained great power in state government, most immediately with the election of Colorado City resident Irving Howbert as chairmen of the state Republican Party, who managed the campaign to elect Governor Albert McIntire in 1894.[37]

As population rose in the Cripple Creek District throughout the 1890s and political outlooks between mine owners in Colorado Springs and wage laborers in Cripple Creek increasingly differed, administration of these two centers under one county became unwieldy. The differences were exacerbated by the influence of the American Protective Association, a one-issue organization opposed to Catholic immigrants in the mining labor force that allied with the dominant Republican Party of El Paso County.[38] Miners and district leaders petitioned and successfully lopped off the western end of El Paso County to establish Teller County in March 1899, with Cripple Creek as the county seat. Colorado Springs would continue to wield great influence over the mining district through corporate control of operations, but civic control moved to the new county.

Labor relations again flared up in 1903, this time beginning at the three mills operating in Colorado City: the Portland, Telluride, and Standard. The Standard was the largest, owned by the United States Reduction and Refining Company, run by Spencer Penrose, with Charles MacNeill in charge of day-to-day operations at the mill. Workers demanded $3 per day in wages, but MacNeill adamantly refused union representation. In February 1903, WFM called millworkers out on strike. This time the governor, James Peabody, was firmly aligned with mine and mill owners' interests and sent in the state militia to Colorado City, against the wishes of the Colorado city mayor, chief of police, and city attorney. Three hundred soldiers occupied the city for seventeen days, again with corporate-subsidized private deputies, including MacNeill himself. Officials at the Telluride and Portland Mills came to terms of agreement with the WFM—an eight-hour workday and nondiscrimination against union workers—but the Standard held out. After a period of truce, a larger general strike began in July. The governor appointed both Penrose and MacNeill, along with other company officials and the county sheriff, as aides-de-camp with ranks of colonel in the National Guard. The strike spread to Cripple Creek to target mines providing ore to the Standard Mill. A Mine Owners Association formed, which viewed the WFM leaders as criminals and, along with the governor, sought its total elimination. The governor sent in the state militia, which was once again financed by mine owners, against the wishes of local officials, including the Teller County Sheriff and town officials. Declaring martial law, Adjutant General Sherman Bell systematically arrested and detained men for merely belonging to a union. Courts routinely ordered these defendants released because they could not be charged with any legitimate offense. Those arrested included a justice of the peace and the chairman of the Board of County Commissioners. This blatant disregard for civil rights raised important constitutional questions about the authority of a military occupying force over the civil affairs of local government. The governor declared that Teller County was in a state of insurrection and rebellion. The armed occupation and strike continued into 1904 in an uneasy impasse until a train bringing strikebreakers to the Independence Depot near Victor was dynamited on June 6, killing thirteen nonunion workers and wounding six more. Outrage ensued, followed by armed conflict, a shoot-out in Victor, and the sacking of union halls throughout the district. In the end, Governor Peabody justified rounding up WFM workers and deporting them, ignoring all due process in a wholesale violation of civil rights. In all, 225 workers were put on trains and dropped off the side of the tracks in Kansas and New Mexico.[39] With the WFM broken, Cripple Creek was firmly under the control of the Association of Mine Owners in Colorado Springs, from that point on run with nonunion labor.[40]

As a result of this labor violence, the statewide alliance of business owners skillfully presented their message of the labor disputes as one of American individualism against "outsider" tyrant union bosses. More important, the business interests of Colorado Springs, backed by the power of the state, were able to define labor relations for the region and wield influence on state politics. This activity has left a lasting imprint on the political culture of the city.

POPULATION

Another lasting impact of this early industrial era came through immigrant workers who moved to Colorado City to work in the railroads and mills. The era from the mid-1800s through the Great Depression in the 1930s has been dubbed "the immigrant century," when waves of dispossessed left persecution and lack of opportunity in Europe to seek a new life in America. Since colonial times, initial immigrants to the Americas were from the predominantly Protestant, Anglo-Saxon countries of northwestern Europe: Great Britain, Germany, the Netherlands, and Scandinavia. The Irish were the first Catholic immigrant group to arrive in large numbers, as they fled the infamous potato famine of the 1840s that led to a million deaths from starvation, up to 2 million emigrants to flee, and the consolidation of untold smallholder farms into the hands of wealthy landlords. Arriving in abject poverty, Irish immigrants were demonized, caricatured as subhuman, and heavily persecuted. Their struggle to gain a foothold into American society earned them their reputation as the "Fighting Irish." By the twentieth century, the source of immigrants shifted to the Catholic and Orthodox regions of southern and eastern Europe: Greeks, Italians, Poles, and people from all of the Slavic countries, often simply referred to as "Austrians" due to the political control of southeastern Europe by the Austro-Hungarian Empire. These workers filled the demand for labor in the factories of the growing twentieth-century industrial cities, but like the Irish, they also faced persistent discrimination—a different tone of skin color, a different religion, and different language and traditions fueled worries that Protestant, Anglo-Saxon, "American" values were threatened. Our nation's first immigration law banned Chinese immigrants in 1882 (extended to all Asians in 1917), but the first immigration law to affect European immigrants passed in 1921 (and amended in 1924 to become more restrictive) that privileged quotas of immigrants from northwestern Europe and restricted immigrants from southern and eastern Europe. The perceived threat to national identity drove nativist opposition against unfamiliar people, a fear that continues to this day, only with a new caste of immigrants from other regions of the world to scapegoat.

In Colorado, many of these immigrants worked in the coal camps of Las Animas and Huerfano Counties. To avoid a unified labor movement, the CF&I mine owners at times encouraged animosities between the immigrant groups, and generally held their workers in disdain, referring to them as un-American foreigners who "live like rats."[41] After the 1914 Ludlow massacre, the company sought to ease assimilation of the many different immigrant groups and avoid

TABLE 5.1. Foreign-born population sources in El Paso County, 1900–1930

El Paso County	*1900*	*1910*	*1920*	*1930*
Total population	31,602	43,321	44,027	49,570
Total foreign born	3,601	4,820	3,972	4,041
Percent foreign born	11.4	11.1	9.0	8.2
Of the foreign born, percent from				
NW Europe, excluding Ireland	64.0	55.8	55.6	43.9
SE Europe and Ireland	19.8	26.5	27.8	24.3
Mexico or Latin America	0.3	4.2	5.8	18.8
Total non-Anglo (not NW Europe or Canada)	22.0	33.5	33.8	46.4

Source: U.S. Census 1900, 1910, 1920, 1930; compiled by author.

further conflict, restarting a socialization program that had previously been suspended by Director Lamont Bowers as an unnecessary employee benefit. Its purpose was to "Americanize" these workers, focusing particularly on teaching housewives to adopt mainstream customs, including cooking and eating habits.[42] Their business model depended upon these social experiments to create conformity around "American" lifestyles and work ethic.

These immigrants also filled the mills and railyards in Colorado City and, to a lesser extent, the mines in Teller County. Census data for the first four decades of the century show the rise in "non-Anglo" immigrants (meaning anybody not from northwestern Europe, excluding Ireland) in El Paso County (table 5.1). By 1930 nearly 50 percent of the foreign born were from the more recent immigrants sources, including a rapid rise in Mexicans. These percentages were likely higher in Colorado City, where industrial workers were concentrated in the county. While we don't have census data for immigrant source regions for Colorado City alone, the census does record that the percent foreign born in Colorado City in 1910 was over 13 percent, higher than the county percentage.[43] Furthermore, the 1900 business directory lists 1,569 residents in Colorado City, of which 1,361 (87%) listed their place of employment. Of those, 18 percent worked in the Colorado–Philadelphia Reduction works and 33 percent worked for the Colorado Midland Railroad. Just over 50 percent of all workers in the city (n = 691) were employed at these two industrial powerhouses, certainly raising the rates of immigrant labor.[44] By 1905, Colorado City industrial employment grew (table 5.2).

The Colorado City total population grew to 4,333 people by 1910, and by 1920 (annexed by Colorado Springs in 1917) it had approximately 6,330. The west side grew rapidly with this industrial workforce, much of it immigrant labor. The Colorado Springs Chamber of Commerce lists 150 industrial plants employing 3,500 wage earners in 1919, a far cry from the early days in Colorado Springs.[45]

FIGURE 5.13. Sacred Heart Catholic Church constructed in 1921. The parish served the many immigrant laborers in the Colorado City mills and railroads. *Source*: Photo by author.

This changing demographic of the immigrant industrial workforce is reflected in the built environment on the west side. Colorado City's Parish of Saint Mary's split from the Manitou Springs congregation in 1891, with the beautiful Sacred Heart mission style church constructed 1921 to serve the growing Catholic population (figure 5.13). Throughout the neighborhoods surrounding the smelters and railyards are a mixed collection of bungalows, shotgun shacks, and self-built box houses serving the working class, many of which today have become gentrified as the charm of the older neighborhoods becomes increasingly attractive to urban dwellers.

Parish records, though incomplete, help tell the story of the immigrant population the church served. Marriage records from 1891–1916 list places of birth for 43 of the 92 entries (46.7%). Of these, eight (18.6%) were from northwestern Europe, and 14 (32.6%) were from either Ireland or southern and eastern European countries. Marriage records from 1917 through 1931 list the place of baptism for the couples in 70 of 110 records (63.6%), of which 3 (4.2%) were from northwestern Europe, 8 (11.4%) were from southeastern Europe or Ireland, and 3 (4.2%) were from Mexico. Finally, burial records from 1891 through 1904 list place of birth for 37 out of 56 entries (66.0%), where 4 (10.8%) were from northwestern Europe, 8 (21.6%) were from Ireland or southeastern Europe, and 2 (5.4%) were from

TABLE 5.2. Approximate numbers of employees in Colorado City Industries, January 1, 1905

Company	*Number of Employees*
U.S. Reduction and Refining Company	350
Portland Mill	150
Midland Railroad shops	150
Other branches of the Midland Railroad	200
General Metals Company	125
Schlesinger Brick Plant	25
Pikes Peak Brick Company	15
Total	1015
Total monthly payroll	$71,600

Source: "Colorado City," *Sunday Gazette and Telegraph*, January 1, 1905, 25–26.

TABLE 5.3. Saint Mary's Catholic Church marriage and burial records, 1891–1931

	Number	*Percentage*
Marriage or burial records that list migrant origin	150	100
Foreign origins	50	33
Of foreign entries, records from		
NW Europe, excluding Ireland	15	30
SE Europe and Ireland	30	60
Mexico	3	6
Canada	2	4

Source: Saint Mary's records, Tri-Community Parish. Compiled by author.

Canada. A summary of these records shows that of 150 records listing origin locations for parishioners, 50 (33%) were foreigners, and of that foreign born, fully 60 percent came from Ireland or southeastern European countries (table 5.3). These numbers are also probably undercounts, as many surnames in the entries that lack birth or baptismal places appear to be Slavic, Irish, or Hispanic.[46]

COAL

Gold ore was not the only rock, or the first, to be extracted from the ground in the Pikes Peak Region. El Paso County had a thriving coal-mining industry, albeit one comprising a softer, brownish lignite, rather than the richer bituminous coal in southern Colorado or the very hard, metamorphic anthracite deposits from Crested Butte. The earliest mines opened in 1883 thirteen miles east of the city at Franceville, along the rail lines of what was originally the Denver and New Orleans Railroad, and by 1888 these mines had already produced over 15,000 tons.[47] The larger deposits in Las Animas, Huerfano, and Fremont Counties served railroads and the steelworks in Pueblo, hence had higher outputs than El Paso County mines, but the mines in the Colorado Springs region produced about 350,000 short tons per year during the second and third decades of the twentieth century.

The El Paso County mines primarily served the Colorado Springs market, including large amounts of coal for the gold smelters, and for the earliest utility companies. In the early industrial era, engineers developed a process to convert coal to gas for use as fuel in urban markets. The coal was heated to extract volatile gasses, a very dirty process that left toxic waste sites in many cities. Prior to the arrival of natural gas pipelines from west Texas in the late 1920s, this process was employed in early Colorado Springs to provide fuel for heat and light in the city. As early as 1879, the Colorado Springs Gas and Coke Company began converting coal to gas at a plant on west Cucharras Street, extending lines into the heart of the city and burning two street lamps.[48] The El Paso Electric Company formed in 1886 and burned coal to generate electricity. By 1900 the plant at Sahwatch and Cucharras employed 75 workers and burned 150 tons of coal per day.[49] Coal-generated electricity quickly competed with coal gas as a source for lighting and energy, but the two continued to operate simultaneously. Under new ownership in 1890, Colorado Springs Gas and Coke extended their network of gas-burning streetlights throughout the city and by 1894 was also serving Colorado City.[50] A coal-fired power plant near the Curtis Mine at Austin Bluffs in 1900 sent steam to downtown buildings for heat, then by 1910 the Colorado Springs Light, Heat, and Power Company had acquired all earlier companies' assets, moved the gas production plant to south Conejos Street in 1921, and served 4,800 gas meters with over sixty miles of pipes.[51] City voters approved the purchase of this company into a public municipal utility in 1925, despite vehement disapproval from the *Gazette*.[52] Throughout all of these corporate and public utility changes, the local sources of coal were fundamental to develop the city's heating and lighting modernization.

Up to ninety-eight coal mines ran in an arc from the northwest part of the city along the base of Austin Bluffs, extending southeast all the way past the current airport to the Franceville Mines (figure 5.14).[53] The main coal beds dip at about a five degree angle to the northeast, so most shafts drove downward from the exposed coal seams on the cliffs' southern faces, well underneath the capstone at the top of the bluffs. Population nodes—suburbs to the city—developed at the larger of these sites, along with rail spurs extending from the main tracks to service the production facilities. During peak exploitation, all of these mining camps were well outside of the city limits. One of these was the Pikeview Mine, the largest in the region. The mine started production in 1897, and Pikeview opened as a stop on the D&RG rail line (figure 5.15). The mining company built housing units for workers and constructed seventy-five miles of underground rail up to

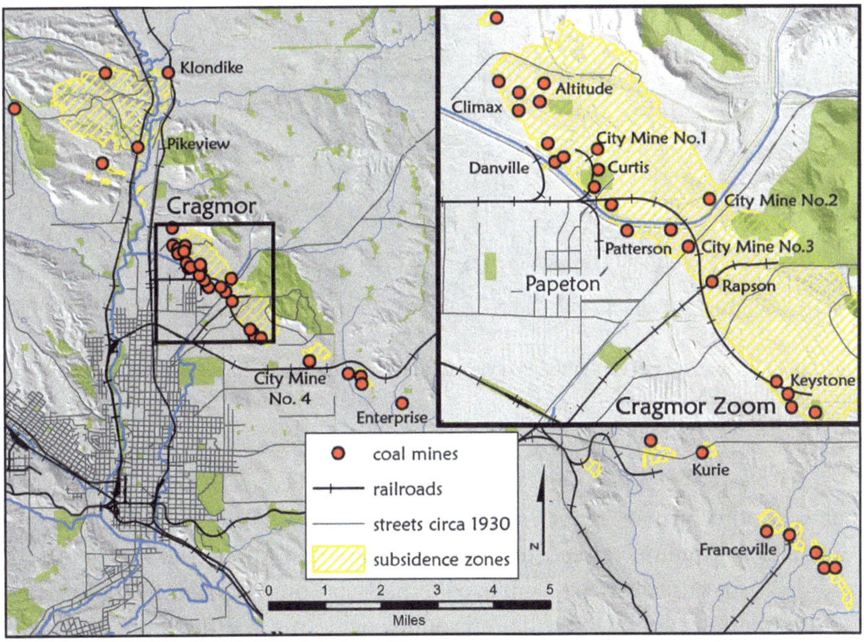

FIGURE 5.14. Coal mines in El Paso County. Some mine locations were never recorded, others consolidated over time. *Source*: Data compiled by author from City of Colorado Springs, *Mining Report: Colorado Springs Coal Field, A Guide for Future Land Use* (Colorado Springs: Planning Department, Geology Section, 1967); Dames & Moore, *Colorado Springs Subsidence Investigation*, vol. 1, *Executive Summary* (Denver: Colorado Division of Mined Land Reclamation, 1985); cartography by author.

480 feet deep to extract as much as 1,000 tons of coal daily from their deposits.[54] The Pikeview Mine alone extracted over half of the total coal production in El Paso County.[55] The mine was bought by the Golden Cycle corporation in 1910 to provide energy for their gold-processing mill in Colorado City, which consumed about one-third of the coal output, but the mine also maintained a fleet of 30 trucks throughout the 1940s to deliver coal to city consumers.[56] The mine closed in 1957, and few would know this thriving center existed adjacent to Interstate 25.

Pikeview was the largest regional producer because it sat over the thickest coal bed, but numerous mines existed in the adjacent Cragmor neighborhood, including Danville, Curtis, City Mine No. 1, Altitude, and Climax. During the regionwide 1903 labor unrest, workers established the community of Papeton, an Italian mining community, which also gained a reputation for producing bootleg spirits during prohibition and serving the clientele of wealthy TB patients at the Cragmor Sanatorium (figure 5.16).[57] From the Cragmor District, several large operations extended east to today's Palmer Park with the Rapson and Keystone Mines in the Country Club neighborhood, and others beyond in today's Rustic Hills neighborhood.

FIGURE 5.15. Loading rail cars at the Pikeview Mine along the D&RG line. *Source*: Colorado Springs Pioneers Museum.

A 1902 report claimed 400–500 coal miners worked in El Paso County coalfields, another in 1905 reported up to 600 miners working in local mines, the Chamber of Commerce reported 600 men employed in the coal mines in 1919, and the 1930 census lists 425 employed in El Paso County coal mines.[58] The standard extraction method in the underground coal seams was the "room and pillar," in which "rooms" typically twenty feet wide and between 100 to 300 feet long were excavated, with 22 to 25 foot pillars left between rooms to support the rock strata above the excavated void.[59] Mines also used retreat mining, where roofs were shored up with timbers as all of the coal was extracted. These rooms remained until the timbers failed and the roof collapsed.[60]

The voids left underground create a hazard zone of subsidence, or collapsing ground at the surface. The peak years of subsidence over room and pillar areas is typically thirty to forty years after mining.[61] In the 1960s residents were quite aware of past industrial activity as peak years for subsidence corresponded with suburban expansion into the mining districts. The Cragmor neighborhood saw a rash of events in 1963, including cave-ins over the old Keystone Mine on today's Circle Drive.[62] Unsuspecting residents today live in houses constructed directly over old mine shafts (figure 5.17).

Few today know the legacy of this mining history, but across eight decades El Paso County produced over 15 million tons of coal.[63] Increased access to oil and natural gas caused production to taper off by the 1950s, and low-sulfur coal strip mined in enormous quantities in Wyoming and western Colorado became a much cheaper and higher quality alternative for coal-fired power plants. Most mines closed in the 1940s, extending to the 1957 Pikeview closure, and the last coal mine near Franceville shutting down in 1965.[64] Apart from the lasting hazard of subsidence, toponyms also remind us of these past activities. For instance, Portal Park, with the city pool that required concrete reinforcement in the 1980s, is named for its location near the entrance portal to the Curtis Mine. Streets in

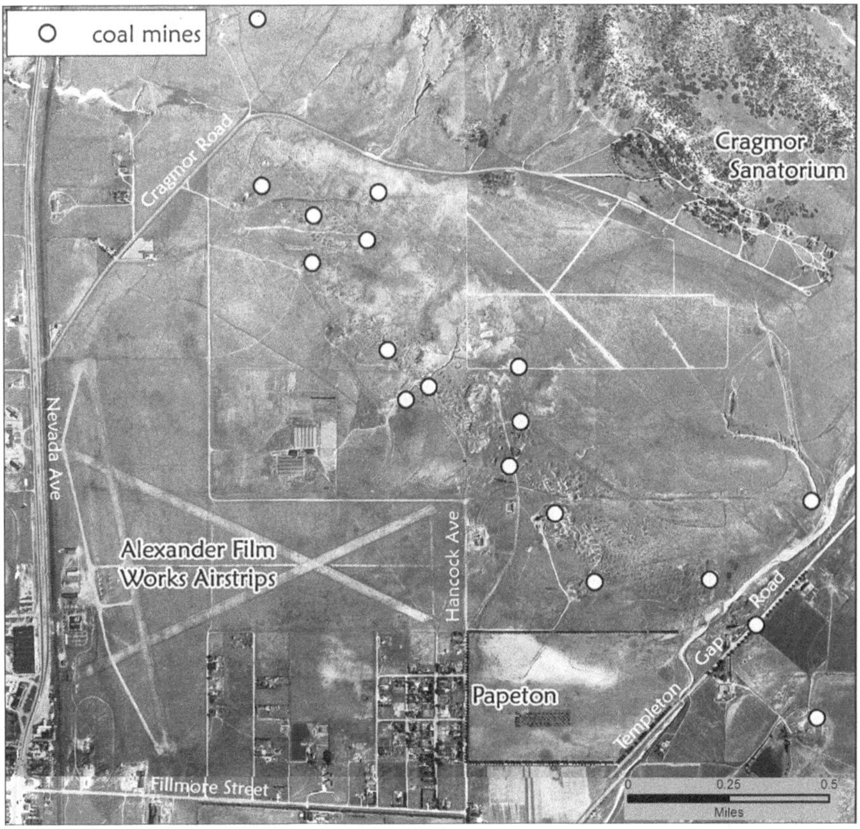

FIGURE 5.16. 1947 aerial photo mosaic showing Papeton as a suburb north of the city, with major mine shafts also shown. Note the pock-marked surfaces of pits and subsidence in the vicinity of the mines. *Source*: USGS (imagery), processed by author.

the nearby Cragmor neighborhood reflect a mining identity, with names such as Westmoreland, Cumberland, and Newcastle referencing British and Appalachian mining districts. Despite a defunct industry, the coal-mining history has not been completely erased from the landscape.[65]

LASTING LEGACY OF MINING

The railroads, the Cripple Creek gold boom, and the coal mining that fueled them all injected an industrial presence into the tourist town of Colorado Springs. While never an industrial powerhouse such as Pueblo, the character of the city was affected by the heavy industry, noise, smoke, and immigrant labor that established a new west-side identity, centered today on the gentrified downtown of Old Colorado City (figure 5.18). This industrial base facilitated related industries, such as the Hassell Iron Works located on Sahwatch Street. Founded in 1887, this

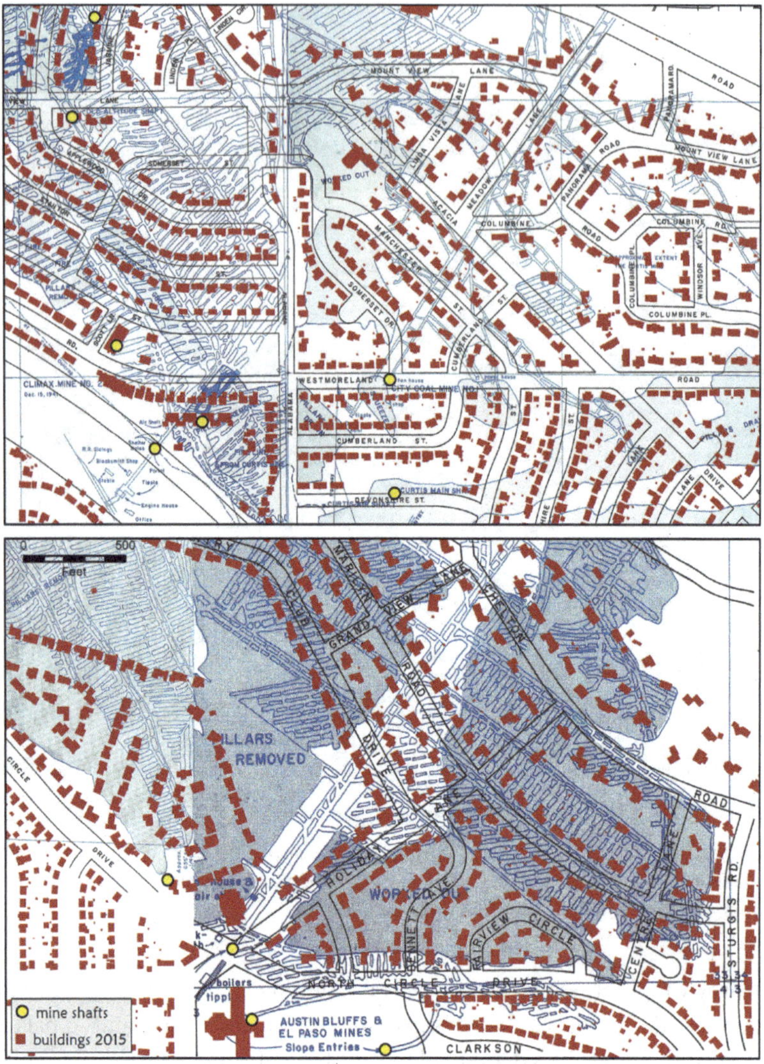

FIGURE 5.17. Light-blue engineering background maps show detailed mine shafts, tunnels, room and pillar excavation, and entire voids that have been worked out with pillars removed. Contemporary houses and buildings are overlain in dark red, with previous mine shaft openings shown in yellow. Cragmor neighborhood (top), Country Club neighborhood (bottom). *Source*: City of Colorado Springs, *Mining Report: Colorado Springs Coal Field, A Guide for Future Land Use* (Colorado Springs: Planning Department, Geology Section, 1967); cartography by author.

company produced ore cars and castings for the mining and refining industries, many products for the railroads, but also consumer items such as wrought iron fencing, many of which are still visible throughout older neighborhoods in the city.[66] Adolphus Busch started an early brewery in Colorado City, and he and

FIGURE 5.18. Old Colorado City, almost torn down for urban renewal in the 1970s, is now a gentrified entertainment district in what was the commercial center of the industrial town. Note the magazine rack representing an old ore cart, complete with gold-tinted rocks atop. *Source*: photo by author.

Jerome Wheeler established the Colorado City Glass Company in 1889 near the Golden Cycle Mill, providing bottles for their beer and for commercial sales of Manitou Mineral Water (figure 5.19). A vibrant brick and tile industry reached its height in 1904, when the city was one of the chief brick manufacturing centers of the West. There were seven companies, each able to make 20,000 bricks per day.[67] You could argue that those early initiatives paved the way for twentieth-century industry, such as Western Forge, the Alexander Film Works (which, in addition to films, manufactured airplanes and ran an airstrip off of North Nevada Avenue), and later silicon chip producers Atmel and Intel. The industrial past has left a large footprint in the city and shaped the urban form.

Four public art statues in downtown Colorado Springs memorialize its most influential citizens. One, of course, is of town founder General Palmer, mounted on his horse in the Nevada Avenue intersection in front of Palmer High School. A second, on the west side of the Colorado Springs Pioneers Museum facing Pikes Peak, honors Katherine Lee Bates for writing "America the Beautiful" after being inspired by the view atop that mountain. The other two are memorials to two residents who struck it rich in Cripple Creek and used their wealth to build lasting landscapes and greatly benefit the city: Winfield Scott Stratton, located directly in front of his Mining Exchange Building, and Spencer Penrose, gazing from the intersection of Tejon Street and Pikes Peak Avenue at the mountain and Cripple

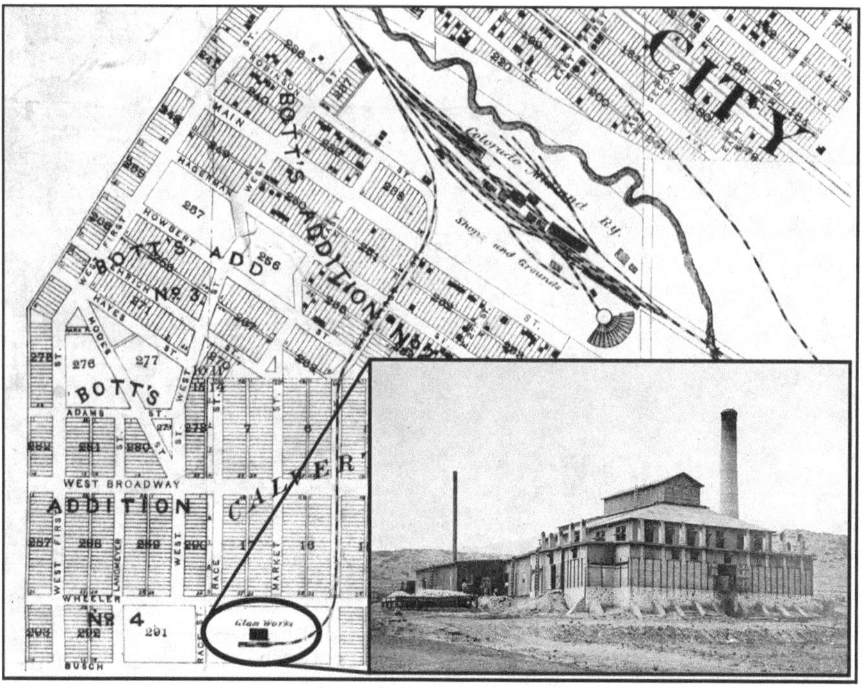

FIGURE 5.19. 1889 map, with 1884 photo, showing the Colorado City Glass Company, with rail connection to Colorado Midland Railroad. *Source*: Colorado Springs Pioneers Museum.

Creek beyond. The Broadmoor, the Mining Exchange, the Post Office Building, the Fine Arts Center, Penrose Hospital, the Myron Stratton Home, and the lasting legacy of the El Pomar Foundation all result from the actions of these two individuals, who hit it big in the nation's largest gold camp. Colorado Springs benefitted enormously from Cripple Creek gold as the city expanded from a small, quaint tourist and health spot to a financial, transportation, and industrial center exerting strong regional influence with probusiness politics.

Cripple Creek itself had a less fortunate fate, one that required drastic action. The inevitable bust that follows the boom led to a long, slow decline as gold production decreased. From over 1 million short tons of gold produced in 1917, by 1950 there were less than 2,000 short tons, and in 1962 all operations ceased. Population slowly declined to 1,240 in the entire mining district by 1960 as gold production dropped, and Cripple Creek itself had only 614 people.[68] Cripple Creek was nearly a ghost town until Colorado voters elected to allow limited stakes gambling in 1991 there, along with Central City and Black Hawk, two ex-mining towns west of Denver. Sold to voters as a means for historic preservation that would also inject life in moribund mining towns, the businesses quickly transformed from the promised locally owned, mom-and-pop small casinos to Las Vegas–dominated corporate players. Urban facades along the principal streets are preserved to conform with historic preservation regulations, but the interiors of these small stores are gutted and opened up to connect entire blocks of buildings into slot machine meccas. Buses cart willing gamers from Colorado Springs to Cripple Creek to spend their incomes in a "Disneyesque" environment of false-front western facades and cliché references to the mining past.[69] In 2006, voters gave up on the false hopes that small, local businesses would thrive with the limited stakes gambling and approved full-blown, Las Vegas–style casinos and betting. Because, as we all know, the house always wins, today a steady flow of money goes uphill from Colorado Springs to Cripple Creek, making up in some small way perhaps for the great wealth extracted from that town that enriched Colorado Springs.

While Cripple Creek itself morphed into a gambling, tourist-oriented town, new technologies renewed interest in the original source of wealth in the district. After a postwar lull in mining lasting several decades, gold production resumed through a South African company, Anglo Gold, in 1995. Today massive open-pit operations blast the mountain away, load 600-ton dump trucks with ore, spread the crushed rock onto enormous leaching pads, and trickle a cyanide solution through to an impervious liner to leach out the metal. Gold is then extracted from the saturated solution and shipped away for final purification. Gold mining is again very much alive and well in the Cripple Creek District to this day, albeit even more highly mechanized and capital intensive, and completely detached from any investment connections to Colorado Springs. Massive amounts of low-grade ore produce about 200,000 ounces of gold annually through open-pit, capital-intensive production that employs about 600 people. The legacy of the past lives on as the topography on the Western Slopes of Pikes Peak is reshaped daily with each new detonation and dump truck load of ore carted off.

6

Fun

> Take away the mountains and Colorado Springs would have but the slenderest foundation for building even a village.
>
> —NATHAN MEEKER, CIRCA 1875[1]

While the city has seen the waxing and waning of economic activities that shaped the landscape—the rise and demise of TB sanatoriums, the railroad era, the Cripple Creek mining boom and bust, and sporadic bursts of activity around water infrastructure projects—there has been one profitable sector shaping the city that began with its founding and continues to this day: tourism. People have long been attracted to the Pikes Peak Region for enlightenment, pleasure, entertainment, and recreation. There is fun to be had in Colorado Springs and its nearby environs.

The transcontinental railroad opened the West to travelers in 1869, but initially most traveled only along a narrow corridor that bypassed the heart of the Rocky Mountains.[2] The Union Pacific and later lines began to market imagery for tours at sites they alone could access, leaving the spaces between (much of the West) as a void. After 1872, Colorado Springs became accessible to travelers through the D&RG and its connector lines. But even as railroad routes expanded in the late nineteenth century, the general public was largely excluded from rail travel for tourism. Travel remained a significant time commitment and expense, particularly with any extended stay. Those partaking tended to be wealthy, especially in the earliest days of the city. Furthermore, tourism in the late nineteenth century was not seen as a recreational experience for personal pleasure but more for cultural and philosophical enrichment. Travelers sought contact with the wonders of nature to encounter the sublime, the awesome majesty of God's work seen

DOI: 10.5876/9781646421688.c006

through the natural landscape. Regions untouched by humans were valued as a way "to discover eternal truths about the world."[3] Such places and experiences served as a foil to the tumult of industrial and urbanizing social change, a conduit for humanity to find meaning and purpose.[4]

Tourism was also seen as an educational experience—a form of cultural literacy. The relatively unknown expanses of the Rocky Mountain West helped address insecurities and uncertainties about national identity in a quest to understand America and its place in the world. The dramatic landscapes of the West were uniquely American, and their representations through paintings, photography, and travel writing became a foundation of American identity. With the discoveries of cliff dwellings and other Ancestral Puebloan sites, romantic constructions of past civilizations furthered western lore as central to the American story. Cultural tourism to experience our national heritage could draw upon a mythic and noble past. These experiences and tales helped construct a vision for the essence of American society and generated enormous curiosity about the region that attracted more and more people.[5] As the rail network grew with competing companies and a newly emerging middle class arose, rail travel became more affordable and western places became more accessible to greater numbers of Americans.

MANITOU SPRINGS: SPA RESORT

In the nineteenth century, Manitou Springs provided the direct access to the Rocky Mountains. Most of the Colorado mountain resorts we think of today—Aspen, Breckenridge, Telluride, Crested Butte—were at best rough-and-tumble mining towns with a highly skewed male gender imbalance, largely devastated landscapes with tailings piles, acidic water runoff, headframes and noisy industrial machinery, and smoke belching from smelters. Worse, many were decaying landscapes suffering from long abandonment and decline. They were ill suited for family recreation and, furthermore, largely inaccessible to pleasure travelers. Places with easier access to eastern travelers, such as Estes Park and Manitou Springs, were the entrée into the Rockies.

From the founding days of the city, General Palmer recognized the economic potential of tourism in the Pikes Peak Region. Well aware of the 100,000 or so wealthy Americans who annually traveled to Europe, particularly to its resorts and spas, Palmer advised would-be entrepreneurial settlers that "the annual swarming of wealthy tourists to the Spas and Parks of Colorado and New Mexico, seeking pleasure and health, means the free expenditure of large sums of money, a good market, of itself, for many of the articles of luxury and necessity which he may raise."[6]

Prior to the consolidation of the West into an essential element of American identity, and therefore as a popular landscape in and of itself, Palmer thought that replicating the European spa experience in the Pikes Peak Region would provide the primary tourist attraction.[7] Because of Palmer's many British connections, Colorado Springs gained the nickname of "Little London," along with a reputation as a haven for wealthy easterners and foreign noblemen that catered to wealthy travelers.[8] Visitors loved the English flavor of Colorado Springs that set it apart from other towns in the American West. The initial imagery constructed for Colorado Springs was in some ways a detachment from place, an attempt to re-create a "European" experience insulated from the more typical shoddily constructed Wild Western towns.[9]

Manitou Springs was the natural spa setting. Its eight mineral pools at the base of Pikes Peak—with proximity to canyons, waterfalls, and Garden of the Gods—provided the perfect conditions (save for the unfortunate fact that the mineral springs were not hot). Ferdinand Hayden stated in his geological survey of 1873 that the scenery was "grand beyond any I have ever seen" in proximity to other mineral springs. Early observer Fitz Hugh Ludlow prophesized that "when Colorado becomes a state, the springs of the Fountaine will constitute its spa. In air and scenery no more glorious summer residence could be imagined."[10] Palmer's partner Dr. William Bell set out to develop the townsite in 1872. The town, five miles west of Colorado Springs, quickly grew into a tourist destination "peopled by a well-to-do and intelligent class of citizens."[11] The D&RG built a connection spur between Manitou Springs and Colorado Springs in 1880 to increase accessibility for tourists.

A series of hotels, some up to three stories tall and quite opulent, were quickly built to serve visitors, with the spa environment dovetailing nicely with tuberculosis sanatoriums to foster a health resort image for the region. In 1872 the Manitou House Hotel was built, followed by the Mansions in 1873, the Cliff House in 1876, then the Barker and Iron Springs Hotels by 1885 (figure 6.1). As summarized by the *Gazette* in 1888:

> Manitou is essentially a town of hotels, and there are hostelries of every degree from the cheap boarding house to establishments that rival anything in the large cities of the east. It is estimated that two thousand visitors can be entertained at one time in the various places. The five large houses can accommodate about one thousand and as many more can be provided for in the small hotels and boarding places.[12]

The Manitou Bath House was built in 1883, an upgrade from an earlier facility, with thirty-two changing rooms, hot and cold soda baths in twenty different rooms, vapor therapy, and a thirty-two-foot-by-thirty-two-foot freshwater plunge tank. The building was torn down in the early twentieth century, but just west of the bath house the Soda Springs Pavilion was also built in 1883 for mineral water bathing.[13] Centrally located amidst the many resort hotels, the pavilion was fully enclosed by 1903 and became the primary bathing facility in town. This

FIGURE 6.1. Manitou Springs hotels and Soda Springs Pavilion, circa 1900. *Source*: Colorado Springs Pioneers Museum.

facility was torn down in 1920 when a newer bath house opened with separate health-related treatment rooms for men and women, hot baths and steam rooms "combining all the best features of the leading bath houses in the world."[14] This building still exists today, but the expense of heating water tore into profits and led to numerous ownership changes over the years with only intermittent profitability. Nonetheless, Manitou secured its reputation as a tourist destination by the early twentieth century: "Its permanent population numbers about 2,000 which is multiplied many times during the summer season by the tourists, making it a scene of gayety and pleasure" (figure 6.2).[15]

FIGURE 6.2. Soda Springs Pavilion, circa 1915, with the Navajo Spring in the lower right foreground, the Cliff House in the background, and trolley car that began service in 1896. *Source:* Colorado Springs Pioneers Museum.

Before the 1890s, most travelers showed little interest in foraying much beyond the comfort of the spa and hotel settings to truly immerse themselves in the outdoors. Wealthy Victorian travelers preferred to spend their days on the verandas, carriage paths, pavilions, and ballrooms of Manitou Springs—enclaves of comfort and sophistication, sheltered from the harshness of the elements.[16] Such places provided an exposure to wildness and danger, the mystical, yet all within the confines of civilization. This was a delicate balance for tourism boosters, constructing images simultaneously wild and interesting yet safe and comfortable enough to entice travelers.[17] Yet while vacationers came for therapeutic treatment in the Manitou mineral baths, over time they were increasingly drawn by the easy access to hikes, rides, or excursions to nearby scenic spots. Tourism started to veer towards nature and personal recreation:

> Perhaps no other resort under the sun presents such a diversity of amusements as does Manitou. Every hour in the day can be filled with some new pleasure for weeks at a time . . . There is probably no place in the world that so well combines the pleasures of out-door life in the mountains with all the luxuries known as "modern improvements."[18]

FIGURE 6.3. The Narrows in Williams Canyon, a popular burro trek. *Source*: Colorado Springs Pioneers Museum.

Horseback and burro adventures traversed trails on Pikes Peak and the foothills. Rainbow Falls and Williams Canyon (the "Baby Grand Canyon of Colorado"), both directly accessible from Manitou Springs, were favorite excursions (figure 6.3). At the top of Williams Canyon, the Cave of the Winds became a popular destination when opened to visitors in 1885 and continues as a tourist adventure to this day. Of course, tours to the Garden of the Gods were an early attraction. As if the spectacular scenery of the park were not enough, tourism embellishments at entrances to the garden promoted a giant viewer ("the world's largest camera"), where a 360-degree view was magnified and projected onto a table, along with, at one time, a mummy dubbed Moonbeam, an "Indian Princess" said to be 300 years old.[19] Trips to Cheyenne Canyon and Seven Falls were also regular outings on the tourist circuit. Commodifying nature became a key component of tourism.

FIGURE 6.4. Promotional brochures from the Manitou and Pikes Peak Railway, circa 1900. *Source*: Colorado Springs Pioneers Museum.

Railroads entered into the tourism business as well. After a grueling trek by mule to the summit of Pikes Peak, Zalmon Simmons, of the Simmons Beautyrest Mattress Company, partnered with local residents to organize the Manitou and Pike's Peak Railway Company. They constructed the Cog Railway in 1889, with the first passenger train running to the summit of Pikes Peak on June 30, 1891 (figure 6.4).[20] The *Gazette* called the new train "the greatest achievement of the ages."[21] The Short Line to Cripple Creek also marketed to tourists for its spectacular scenery "that bankrupts the English language," and the Midland Railroad ran popular wildflower excursions up Ute Pass to high meadows.[22]

To facilitate construction of Colorado Springs' water infrastructure, a cable lift was cut straight up the side of Mount Manitou in 1907. After pipelines, hydroelectric plants, and reservoirs were built, this gash in the mountain was converted by 1908 into the Mount Manitou Incline, the "world's longest scenic cable railway" (figure 6.5). Supplemented for a short time with a second cable railway just to

FIGURE 6.5. Image and promotional brochure for the Manitou Incline. *Source*: Colorado Tourist Brochure Collection, Colorado College Special Collections.

the east, the Red Mountain Incline (which ran 1919–1925), the Manitou funicular provided thrills and scenic vistas for tourists until 1989. After rails and machinery were removed, social hikers slowly converted the ascent into today's popular hiking trail known as the Manitou Incline. Climbing 2,000 feet in less than one mile, the incline was formally recognized as part of the regional trails system in 2013. The top of the incline connects with the famous Barr Trail, the thirteen-mile hiking trail to the Pikes Peak summit, originating in Manitou Springs, that was completed in 1921.[23]

Perhaps the greatest coup for tourism promotion became the Manitou Cliff dwellings, which opened in 1906. Growing interest in the Native American past increasingly fed into legends of a unique American identity, generating the popularity of heritage tourism.[24] But the Ancestral Puebloans who built the cliff dwellings found in the American Southwest never lived near Colorado Springs. To compensate for this geographic omission, local entrepreneurs purchased and/or sacked materials from sites near Mesa Verde and rebuilt a replica, using

FIGURE 6.6. The reconstructed cliff dwellings, circa 1910. *Source*: Colorado Tourist Brochure Collection, Colorado College Special Collections.

original stones, under the sandstone overhangs high above Manitou Springs (figure 6.6). The entire site is a facade, a reference to authentic places farther away but now easily accessible to tourists. Early promotions neglected to mention that the dwellings were only recently constructed by Anglo boosters, and while later pamphlets acknowledge that they were moved from sites throughout the Southwest, they all the while maintained that this was "a major archaeological preserve" with "*exact* and *scientific* reproduction."[25] The site was embellished with the Tewa House, another replica, this one of a New Mexican pueblo that contained pottery and other artifacts, at one time even "bodies of the Cliff Dwellers," along with a tipi, regularly scheduled Indian dancer Chief Little Deer, who lived on site with his family during summers, and Navajo weavers. Like all tourist sites to some degree, everything here is marketing of images, a manufactured authenticity.[26] In today's postmodern world, where the imagineering of places such as Disneyland and Las Vegas infiltrate all dimensions of society and "authenticity" consists of overtly constructed imagery for economic gain, the Manitou Cliff dwellings replica may seem simplistic. But such a construction in 1906 set the stage for our contemporary use of romanticized images to construct a sense of place. While an offense by contemporary archaeological standards, there are advantages with a site that is fake—lack of concern for preservation, unexcavated archaeological digs, or spiritually significant spaces allow visitors to freely wander through and touch all features, with a simplified and easily understood narrative of Ancestral Puebloans constructed by guides and informational materials. Plus, visitors seem to enjoy the entertainment spectacle as they seek an "enhanced" archaeological experience.[27]

The increasing list of attractions shows that the nature of tourism had changed from the quest to replicate the European spa experience to a search for the soul of America, to find the essence of our national identity. The West contributed mightily in that role, as tourists sought to see the dramatic landscapes, national parks, and experience the land of the mythic "cowboy and Indian."[28] By the twentieth century, the brutal Indian wars were over, and the threat to Anglo travelers and settlers from Indigenous peoples was removed. Americans became increasingly fascinated with Indians, once subjugated, and Colorado Springs tapped into this national curiosity to generate tourist revenue by promoting images and events to situate the city as a true representation of the West. Promoters of the annual Flower Carnival arranged for twenty-three Utes from the Southern Ute Reservation to present a series of highly choreographed events in 1894—carnival-like shows for visitors to enjoy the spectacle of real Indians, all in a safe setting.[29] The high tourist demand for these events ensured that they continued for many years, leading to the Shan Kive festival first launched in 1911. This popular Wild West festival attempted to present a more romantic interpretation of the Utes as a disappearing race, celebrating their historic contribution to the region, but again showcased the Indigenous people in a tourist setting more resembling theater. Promotional brochures offered "an opportunity to see nearly the last of them now living in tribal conditions."[30] The Shan Kive continued as an annual event until 1930, after which tourist numbers plunged due to the Great Depression. The spirit of these western-themed tourism events continued, however, through the promotion of the Pikes Peak or Bust Rodeo, an event that began in 1937 and continues to this day, including an annual parade and march of longhorns down Tejon Street. The success of the rodeo helped establish the Pro Rodeo Hall of Fame and Museum of the American Cowboy in Colorado Springs in 1979.

FIGURE 6.7. The original Antlers Hotel, 1892. *Source*: Colorado Springs Pioneers Museum.

COMPETING HOTELS: ANTLERS AND BROADMOOR

Manitou and the Colorado Springs region gained the reputation as the oldest and most socially exclusive western resort. However, ten years after its founding, the city still had few lodgings apart from the spas and some smaller hotels in Colorado Springs.[31] Local promoters recognized the city needed a posh hotel to maintain its growing reputation, so General Palmer rose to the challenge. The Colorado Springs Company donated land and subsidized construction of the new Antlers Hotel, completed and opened on June 1, 1883. The hotel was strategically located due east, and up the small hill, from the D&RG station, so visitors arriving in town walked from the depot, across Antlers Park, and up a grand staircase to the impressive hotel foyer. Replete with turrets and bay windows in Queen Anne architecture, the seventy-five-room hotel boasted central heating, an elevator, an elegant restaurant, and two shared bathrooms per floor.[32] It quickly gained the reputation as one of the best in the West and served to solidify the resort aura of the city (figure 6.7).[33]

The original Antlers Hotel burned down, along with much of the business district southwest of Cascade Avenue, on October 1, 1898, from a fire in the railyard freight cars. Palmer quickly pledged to rebuild, and the second Antlers was completed with a new Italianate style building on July 2, 1901 (figure 6.8). The second rendition was even more opulent, with modern amenities of plumbing, heating, water, and electricity serving 230 guest rooms. The lobby boasted a fireplace and central stairway of Italian marble, a balcony for the orchestra, ivory and gold decorations throughout, oriental rugs, dining rooms with chandeliers, and a sun parlor with potted palms. The grand ballroom could host 650 people.

FIGURE 6.8. Postcard of the second Antlers Hotel, embellished with an exaggerated Pikes Peak immediately behind. *Source*: Colorado Springs Pioneers Museum.

Promotional ads played up the elitist romance of the city, claiming that "its inhabitants are essentially cosmopolitan, recruited as they are from among the most cultivated people in the United States and Europe" (figure 6.9).[34] Who could resist coming to Colorado Springs, where "the poet finds his paradise, the philosopher his Arcanum, the artist his theme, the dramatist his climax, in this mighty vista. Sun-kissed and snow capped, it is the beginning and the end of Seasons. One may run the whole gamut of feeling and strike never a discord, so perfect is the harmony of Nature."[35] Railroads willingly promoted the resort image of the city to generate more traffic, particularly to escape the humid subtropical heat of the gulf states to visit "the American Alps." The Rock Island Railroad, being the only direct line between Colorado Springs and eastern cites, published brochures on the "Colorado Hotels, Lodges, and Guest Ranches" so visitors could "Ride the Rocket to the Rockies": "A place to play, a place to rest . . . where world-weariness is joyfully exchanged for the health-giving body weariness of an outdoor life which renews appetite and induces sound refreshing sleep—always under blankets. Colorado, the land of clear eyes, ruddy cheeks, and laughter."[36]

The success of the Antlers Hotel generated increased tourism, and numerous other hotels—such as the Alta Vista, Alamo, Plaza, Spaulding, and Elk—were established to serve the demand. Despite these options, an even grander scheme for a resort developed on the piedmont below the dramatic and abrupt ascent of Cheyenne Mountain, just south of town along Cheyenne Creek, in the area known as the Broadmoor. Here the Broadmoor Dairy had long provided milk and cream

FIGURE 6.9. Promotional brochure for the Antlers Hotel, date unknown. *Source*: Colorado Tourist Brochure Collection, Colorado College Special Collections.

to the city and owned water rights in Cheyenne Creek, but owner Count James Pourtales, a Prussian diplomat who arrived in 1885, saw a higher potential for this setting. He formed the Cheyenne Lake, Land, and Improvement Company; built a reservoir using Cheyenne Creek; and divided the land into large lots. In 1889, several wealthy residents built a country club on one of these lots, with tennis, golf, and horses as amenities, but the polo field became its most famous diversion. This club formally organized as the Cheyenne Mountain Country Club in 1891, with membership from the Colorado Springs socialites. Count Pourtales built a casino that opened also in 1891, beyond the city limits and its restrictive ordinances (figure 6.10). Offering live music, cocktails, and gambling, he intended "a beautiful palace of refined pleasure" to complement the nearby country club: "It is a veritable temple of pleasure delighting the eye and the aesthetic sense,

FIGURE 6.10. The first Broadmoor Casino, circa 1894. *Source*: Colorado Springs Pioneers Museum.

and fascinating by the perfection of its every appointment."[37] The casino burned down in 1897, and though Pourtales's first attempt was never profitable, he built a second, slightly smaller version, in 1898. His vision for the casino and land speculation never came to fruition, so Pourtales sold his Broadmoor landholdings to the estate of Winfield Scott Stratton, whose wishes were to use this property for the Myron Stratton Home for the indigent. The Stratton estate eventually built the Myron Stratton home at the eastern extent of the land, selling off the remaining parcels for profit. The prime real estate, 450 acres that included the lake and casino, was sold to Spencer Penrose in 1916.[38]

By the second decade of the twentieth century, Spencer Penrose was already a wealthy man. He earned his first fortune at Cripple Creek, added a milling and refining empire to process Cripple Creek ore in Colorado Springs, then grew that significantly through his investments and development of the Bingham Canyon copper mine in Utah. Married in 1906 to Julie Villiers Lewis McMillan, a Detroit native and recent widow, he settled down from his more raucous days as a bachelor in the mining camps to focus on new projects in Colorado Springs. After the death of town founder and chief philanthropist William Jackson Palmer in 1909, Penrose set his sights on transforming the city into a premier resort location and filling the role Palmer had played as chief proponent, developer, and investor in the city. He first tried to purchase the Antlers from the Palmer estate but could not agree to a price. After the couple moved to El Pomar, a Mission Revival villa west of the country club, Penrose purchased the neighboring Broadmoor properties and announced he would build a new Broadmoor resort. The Mediterranean-themed, pink stucco building with red tile roofs opened June 29, 1918, exquisitely decorated throughout and hosting 350 guest rooms (figure 6.11). The Penroses spared no expense, with full-service shops, fine art, and a front entrance and grounds designed by the famous Olmsted landscape architectural firm; it also hosted the best golf course in the West. It was Penrose's crowning achievement, a

FIGURE 6.11. Postcard of the Broadmoor, built 1918, showing the front entrance. *Source*: Colorado Springs Pioneers Museum.

playground for the wealthy and the hub from which he built complementary companies. Throughout the years he added a rodeo and racetrack, more polo fields to expand on those of the Cheyenne Mountain Country Club, a world-famous ice arena, and increasingly more golf courses. The entire complex was largely self-contained, with its own power plant and water system served by the Rosemont Reservoir on Pikes Peak. Penrose also developed events and programs to serve as a sports hub, contributing to the reputation for Colorado Springs as an amateur athletics node.[39]

Penrose became the king of regional tourist activities. Even before building the Broadmoor, he was fascinated with the invention of automobiles and saw the opportunity for auto-related tourism. He created the Pikes Peak Automobile Company in 1912, one of many auto-tour companies competing for tourist dollars in the city. Penrose created the Pikes Peak Auto Highway Company and leased the old wagon road from the Department of Agriculture. He began upgrades in 1915 and opened the Pikes Peak Highway in 1916 with the first of what would become the annual Pikes Peak International Hillclimb. This race captured the imagination of the nation, and the "Race to the Clouds" remains the second-oldest auto race in the country, after the Indianapolis 500. The race wonderfully supplemented business at the Broadmoor in subsequent years, including revenue from the many tourists who paid the toll to drive up Pikes Peak.[40] This event served to promote

FIGURE 6.12. Pikes Peak by Auto, with stylized drawing of the Pikes Peak Highway ascending the mountain. *Source*: Colorado Springs Pioneers Museum.

auto excursions up the peak and throughout the region that proved a powerful attractor (figure 6.12).

Penrose bought the Manitou Incline funicular in 1915, then the Cog Railway in 1925. That same year he built the Cheyenne Mountain Road to Cheyenne Mountain Lodge, a rustic resort at the summit of Cheyenne Mountain.[41] He had long collected exotic animals that roamed the Broadmoor grounds, including a monkey, camel, elephant, and peacocks, but when their presence grew distracting to guests he relocated his collection to what would become the Cheyenne Mountain Zoo at the road's entrance in 1926.[42] On this road he built the Will Rogers Shrine of the Sun, which would house his own mausoleum, and the Broadmoor later purchased

Seven Falls in South Cheyenne Canyon as an added attraction for guests. He tried to revamp sales of mineral water through the Manitou Mineral Water Company in 1926, then built the Will Rogers–Penrose stadium 1937 to revive rodeo in the city. The stamp of tourism and recreation Penrose made on the city's landscape is profound and continues to this day. After his death in 1939 and Julie's in 1956, the El Pomar Foundation converted their assets into one of the state's largest philanthropic organizations, supporting many local institutions. The West Towers, across the lake from the main Broadmoor Hotel, replaced the old arena and ice rink, so today the resort hosts conventions and conferences and its five-star status ranks it among the best in the West. It still attracts an elite clientele.

By the early twentieth century, Colorado Springs had solidified its reputation as the premier resort in the Rocky Mountain West and became a model for other locations to emulate.

AUTOMOBILES

Spencer Penrose was certainly prescient in seeing the potential for automobile-related tourism, but even he could not have fully gauged the profound impact private cars would have on tourism and the American landscape. Whereas travel up to the 1920s was primarily by train and difficult for middle-class families, Henry Ford's assembly line production brought the price of a motor carriage down to the realm of affordability for many Americans. This development, coupled with increasing prosperity, led to the rise of the family vacation, and the Rocky Mountain West loomed large in the American imagination as a prime destination.

By 1905 there were more than 80,000 automobiles and trucks registered in America, and their popularity grew rapidly. In 1910, the numbers reached 458,000, and by 1920 8 million; they rose again to 23 million by 1930.[43] In El Paso County, there were three automobiles registered in 1903, increasing to 4,859 by 1918 then 10,891 by 1924.[44] Despite the rapid increase in automobile ownership, adequate roads did not keep pace, particularly highways crossing the vast distances in the West. Boosters such as Penrose joined the Good Roads Movement, a national group advocating increased investment from state and federal governments in road infrastructure.

The Automobile Association of America (AAA) was founded in 1902 and began pushing for transcontinental auto routes.[45] Colorado Springs missed out on the first transcontinental route, dubbed the Lincoln Highway, but did connect with another network of roads to market the Pikes Peak segment of the Ocean-to-Ocean Highway (figure 6.13).[46] To induce visitors to travel the route, the Merchants Association, affiliated with the Chamber of Commerce, created envelopes with regional facts printed on them in 1906 to promote tourism.[47] They also encouraged all residents to use the City of Sunshine slogan and sunburst logo on stationery and letterheads. The Chamber of Commerce included

FIGURE 6.13. The Pikes Peak segment of the Ocean-to-Ocean Highway, "The Appian Way of American," marketing the region for auto-oriented tourism. *Source*: Colorado Tourist Brochure Collection, Colorado College Special Collections.

an Advertising Committee that became the greatest promoter of the region for tourism in the auto era, supporting the Good Roads Movement, running ads in newspapers across the Midwest and Great Plains, buying ads in trade journals and on radio, and mailing glossy pamphlets around the country.[48] In 1911 it distributed 20,000 postcards each Saturday in July with images of the Garden of the Gods, Pikes Peak, and other attractions, with text on the back promoting the city's parks and cool summer temperatures. Locals were asked to mail these cards to friends and family and encourage them to visit, with the chamber paying the postage if the sender personally signed the card.[49] In 1915 the Advertising Committee urged all residents to write friends in the East to again encourage them to travel here and provided a postage stamp and card with a Pikes Peak image to include with their letters.[50] The chamber and other civic boosters then organized "Automobile Sociability Tours" beginning in 1914. One intent of these tours was to promote good roads to Texas, Kansas, and Oklahoma, in particular the Colorado-to-Gulf Highway that connected to Galveston, but the main purpose was to advertise the Pikes Peak Region.[51] Traveling by convoy, members of these tours were typically local businessmen who acted as regional ambassadors. On a 1915 tour, several cars had big banners with a picture of Pikes Peak and text stating, "See America now. The Pikes Peak Region—the Playground of America."[52] They were quite successful, for these tours created much press coverage and continued into the 1930s.[53]

Tourism as recreation was not new, but the freedom the automobile offered made it a tradition in American society, travel as a rite of passage toward self-fulfillment.[54] Existing tourist sites that previously required horses, mules, or donkeys could now be accessed directly by automobile. A vibrant industry of auto tours taking visitors on regional scenic routes competed for customers throughout town—the Broadmoor alone had sixty tour vehicles in 1926.[55] Pamphlets advertised "Pikes Peak Region: The Motorists Mecca."

In the railroad era, travelers disembarked from the train station and walked or paid for a ride to downtown hotels. Especially in resort-oriented sites such as Colorado Springs, these hotels offered a full suite of services, they were rather formal, and, of importance, they were expensive—not the ideal place for penny-pinching families to stay with young children. Towns quickly adapted to the new type of tourist—the young family—and the new mode of travel—the automobile. Increasingly flexible forms of accommodation arose in new locations that reflected a different spatial logic.

In response to the growth of car-oriented vacationing and travel, American cities developed totally new landscapes to deal with the automobile, and Colorado Springs was no exception. Brand-new functions arose: gas stations, car sales lots, and other auto services; drive-up lodgings with restaurants and tea rooms, diners, then fast food joints, plus other types of drive-in conveniences. Often complementary functions evolved together in one business location (figure 6.14).

FIGURE 6.14. Postcard for the Rodeo Court, a full service center with cottages, gas pump, and café. *Source*: Colorado Springs Pioneers Museum.

Buildings became set back from the street to allow for parking lots, and standalone signs grew increasingly large to attract the attention of people speeding past at over thirty miles per hour. By the late 1920s, signature architecture developed, where the buildings themselves became the sign: giant chickens, hot dogs, or, in Colorado Springs, a giant sombrero and a Navajo Hogan (figure 6.15). Exaggerated regional architecture in the form of tipis, cacti, mountain chalets, or Spanish forts became prevalent in the West.[56]

All of these building forms were designed for easy accessibility to cars. The classic commercial strip was the result, an incubator of new building types, a new frontier beyond the established urban core.[57] The commercial strip was usually characterized by small, privately owned businesses with local financing. The personal relationship between small businesses and their local banker enabled more experimentation than with nationally financed franchises that expected "proven" returns on investment through a standard product. The emerging strip became the place to get business started with reduced barriers to entry. In many ways, the strip represents economic democracy.[58]

In Denver, mid-century Colfax Avenue exemplified the classic strip.[59] Where did we see these strips develop in Colorado Springs? Along the four entryways to town, conveniently beyond city limits with its more restrictive rules and regulations about liquor laws, zoning, and architectural conformity (figure 6.16). North and South Nevada Avenue were on the main highway to Denver and Pueblo, the

FIGURE 6.15. Signature architecture on North Nevada: the Navajo Hogan and Sombreros Mexican food, 2003. *Source*: photo by author.

Knob Hill neighborhood on East Platte Avenue evolved around the highway coming from Kansas, and West Colorado Avenue was the entrance to tourist-oriented Manitou Springs and the mountains.

For families of tourists arriving in cars, the main land use they increasingly sought was affordable lodging for the entire family. To snag consumer income from these travelers, Colorado Springs, like many other towns, set aside free camping zones (figure 6.17). In March 1924, mayors of most Colorado cities voted to abolish the free municipal campground to inhibit transients living free for long term at city expense.[60] Campgrounds became largely commercialized, with entrance fees, as private businesses grew to serve the tourist market. Tourists directories in 1932 list 19 auto tourist camps: 10 at the eastern entrance to Manitou Springs, 2 on North Nevada Avenue, 2 on East Platte Avenue, and 1 on South Nevada Avenue, the rest dispersed at other locations. Prospect Lake in Memorial Park had a popular campground, with thousands camping there each year.[61] Remnants of these RV parks are still found on west Highway 24; tourist campgrounds were also located on both South and North Nevada Avenues into the twenty-first century. The early auto camps evolved to cabins and eventually to the new creation, "motels," a hybrid of "motor-hotel," first coined in 1926 after competing terms, such as "autel," "motor court," "tourist court," "auto court," "Tour-o-tel," and "Motor inn" vied for supremacy. Lodging forms evolved from auto camps, to cabin camps by the 1930s, cottage courts with more permanent structures, motor courts that joined

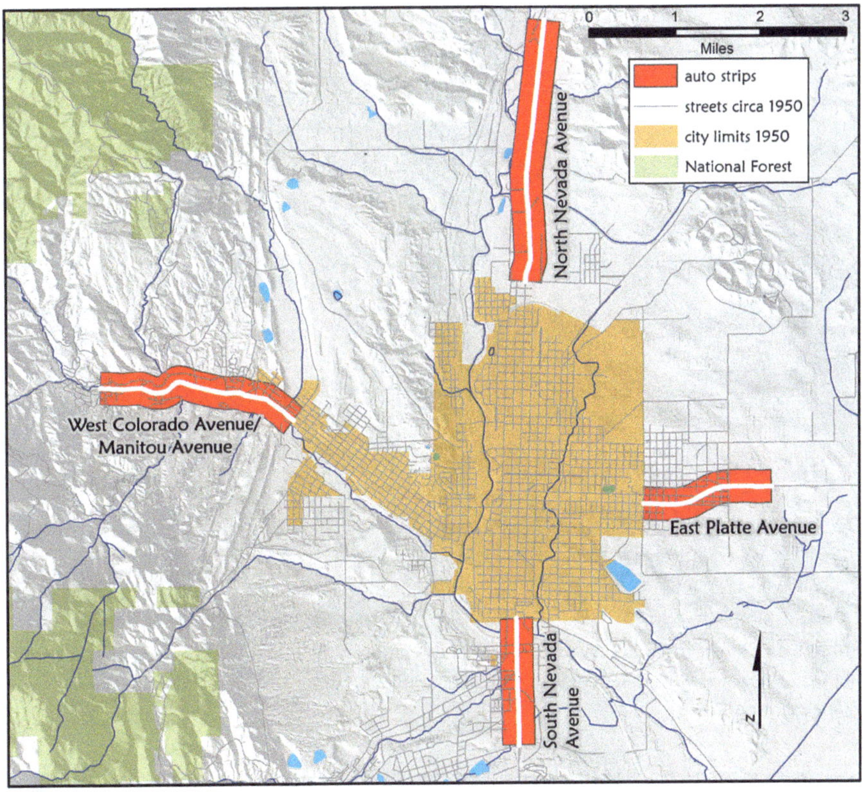

FIGURE 6.16. The four commercial and tourist auto strips, on the main highways entering town and conveniently outside of the city limits. *Source*: Cartography by author.

TABLE 6.1. Evolution of naming, Colorado Springs and Manitou Springs Strips (percent of total)

Year	*"Camp" Names*	*"Cottage" and "Cabin" Names*	*"Court" Names*	*Motel*	*Lodge*	*Inn*	*Other*
1929 (*n* = 25)	72.0	12.0	0.0	0.0	4.0	0.0	12.0
1939 (*n* = 56)	30.4	46.4	5.4	1.8	12.5	0.0	3.6
1951 (*n* = 120)	9.2	7.5	39.2	19.2	15.8	5.0	4.2
1965 (*n* = 145)	0.0	1.4	11.2	72.7	13.3	1.4	1.4
2003 (*n* = 65)	1.5	3.1	1.5	63.1	15.4	7.7	7.8

Source: Polk's Colorado Springs City Directory, author survey.

the cabins under a single roofline by mid-century, motor inns with multiple stories, and eventually to highway hotels, usually national chains near interstates (table 6.1).[62] One classic cabin camp still in operation is the El Colorado Lodge, where the Pueblo Revival architecture evoked comforting notions of place-based tradition as respite from the uncertainty and hypermobility of the new auto age

FIGURE 6.17. Postcard for a very early tourist auto-camp, off the highway to Denver, in the north of the city near today's Vindicator Drive and Centennial Boulevard. *Source*: Colorado Springs Pioneers Museum.

FIGURE 6.18. El Colorado, still a popular cottage court lodging with a comforting, southwestern Pueblo style. *Source*: photo by author.

(figure 6.18). Such masking of contemporary retail service in revival architecture and historical reference was common in 1920s and 1930s to ease the transition to modernity.

Often motor-lodges, or motels, appealed to a sense of place using regional place imagery, and simple naming schemes served a similar function. Colorado

TABLE 6.2. Number of motels or camp lodging

Strip	*1929*	*1939*	*1951*	*1965*	*2003*
North Nevada	1	3	16	35	14
East Platte	1	5	11	7	6
South Nevada	2	7	26	27	10
West Colorado / Manitou	21	41	67	76	35

Source: *Polk's Colorado Springs City Directory*, author survey.

Springs had the Buffalo Lodge, the High Country Lodge, Apache Court, the Trails End Motel, the Hacienda Motel, the Silver Saddle Court, Log Cabin Camp, Sky-Hi Lodge, and the Frontier Motel. Some targeted a specific clientele, such as the Kansas Court, Okla-Texas Courts, Oklahoma Cottages, and Illinois Lodge. Because financing and depreciation credits encouraged rapid turnover, these motels often became very transient places, rapidly evolving with new innovations. Hence they were not without controversy, as seen through concerns for "Hot Pillow" trade in 1920s and 1930s, when motels were attacked by the established hotel industry for promoting loose morals.[63] In response, national sponsorship through groups such as Duncan Hines, Best Western, and the AAA gave a stamp of legitimacy to reassure customers (though this appears to not be of concern to the Lucky Nite Motel advertised on east Platte Avenue in 1951).

The motels on the four Colorado Springs strips evolved at somewhat different timelines (table 6.2). Clearly, West Colorado Avenue was the early and sustained leader due to the popularity of Manitou Springs, whereas North and South Nevada Avenues peaked in the early 1960s. Shortly after Interstate 25 was completed in 1960, the number of motels on North Nevada Avenue declined as the strip was bypassed. As traffic engineers built increasingly large interstate highways and multilane arterial corridors designed for high volumes and speeds, the early auto strips became too congested, lacking the carrying capacity and not being fast enough. Overbuilding during boom years led to abandonment, and by the 1960s interstate exit interchanges lured the large franchises away from the strip and suburban malls internalized the business that once occurred on the street.

SKIING

Tourism itself changed in response to automobile travel, allowing people to experience nature firsthand, engage in active recreation, and escape the daily routine and problems of their increasingly mechanized and industrialized lives guided by the clock. Beginning in the 1920s, nationally marketed recreational tourism involved physical experience in the outdoors.[64] Promotions for skiing used the slogan "Colorado's Climate—The Magic Ingredient" as the industry developed.[65]

FIGURE 6.19. Advertisement for Ski Pikes Peak, affiliated with Ski Country USA, circa 1970. *Source*: Colorado Springs Pioneers Museum.

The first ever ski meet on Pikes Peak took place April 6, 1924, at a location called Cascade Hill on the Pikes Peak Highway, two miles from the toll gate. It was an amateur ski jump contest on a 100-foot course, open to the public, which led to enthusiasts organizing the Pikes Peak Ski Club on April 10, 1924.[66] Local advocates later cleared two downhill trails at mile marker 11 on the Pikes Peak Highway, at a site known as Glen Cove, and then another called Elk Park, later "Ski Pikes Peak," about a mile downhill (figure 6.19). Ski Pikes Peak remained open until 1984, and the runs are still visible on the North Slope.

Lack of reliable snow on Pikes Peak, the giant massif standing in isolation to the east of Colorado's other fourteeners, which captured most of the snow from the prevailing westerlies, was a prime reason why Colorado Springs' local ski runs were eventually doomed. But other regional forces within the state played an equally dominant role. By the early 1950s state and local tourism interests were busily constructing the image of Colorado's high country as a vacationland. Promoters learned from Aspen, the early and highly successful ski town, that there was money to be made off the unique qualities of place, and increasingly sophisticated marketing could manipulate these qualities to appeal to the people's yearnings for personal fulfillment and respite from the daily grind.[67] Towns adopted the ski industry and tourism as mainstays of the local economy, along the way branding images that consumers could attach to place, perhaps best exemplified by Vail.[68] Built entirely from scratch and opened in 1962, Vail's Bavarian village landscape theme constructed a fantasy escape, a physical setting and environment naturally suited for leisure. Tourists responded to this replica of European ski culture. Vail was a smashing success, particularly after Interstate 70 reached the valley in 1966. Colorado high country became a product for consumption and magnet for tourism.[69] In addition, the corporate ski industry made huge profits as land developers, with the new ski resorts hosting lodges, condos, hotels, restaurants, and all sorts of entertainment that created a new type of vacation experience. Large, corporate ski resorts today dominate the industry and attract thousands from around the world each year. Small, local runs could not compete.

Three other small sites ran mon-and-pop local operations on the west side of Pikes Peak, but by the 1960s skiing was no longer just a local community activity. Colorado Ski Country USA began a marketing campaign, so by the mid-1960s skiing had become Colorado's marquee attraction.[70] In an attempt to compete in this new industry, Ski Broadmoor officially opened 1959 with two runs cut along the base of Cheyenne Mountain, just southwest of the Broadmoor Hotel and on the edge of the city of Colorado Springs. The site remained open until 1991.

Although Colorado Springs is not a player in the contemporary ski economy, the creative destruction of capitalism leads to perpetual change as new logics impose themselves, and one day skiing on Pikes Peak might make a comeback, not as competition to the giant ski resorts in the high country but as a local theme park and training site. There have been several efforts to market small-terrain parks and night skiing to Denver residents in the foothills along Interstate 70, and there has been repeated rumor of entrepreneurs considering new sites for similar parks on the slopes of Pikes Peak. The mountain has continually served the city well in all other endeavors, so perhaps one day it will again serve the local ski demand.

THE RECREATION ECONOMY

The local ski hills that existed on Pikes Peak were as much, or more, for local residents as for tourists, which points out the obvious—outdoor recreational activities attract not only visitors, but also locals, and greatly contribute to a quality of life for Colorado Springs' citizens. This recognition goes back to the founding of the city, when General Palmer initially set aside land for parks and donated more throughout the years, perhaps inspired by his time in New York, when Frederick Law Olmsted and Calvert Vaux were designing and building Central Park.[71] After initial donations at the founding of the city for three parks—Antlers, Acacia, and Alamo—Palmer later donated 700 acres for Austin's Bluffs (now Palmer Park), 480 acres for North Cheyenne Canyon and for his crowning jewel, Monument Valley Park, the city's main artery along Monument Creek from the Antlers Hotel to what was the north end of the city.[72] This park was planned by 1903, landscaped over several years, and opened in 1907 (figure 6.20). In addition to Palmer's donations, the generous contribution of Garden of the Gods from the Charles Perkins estate was deeded to the city in 1909 under the condition that it remain free

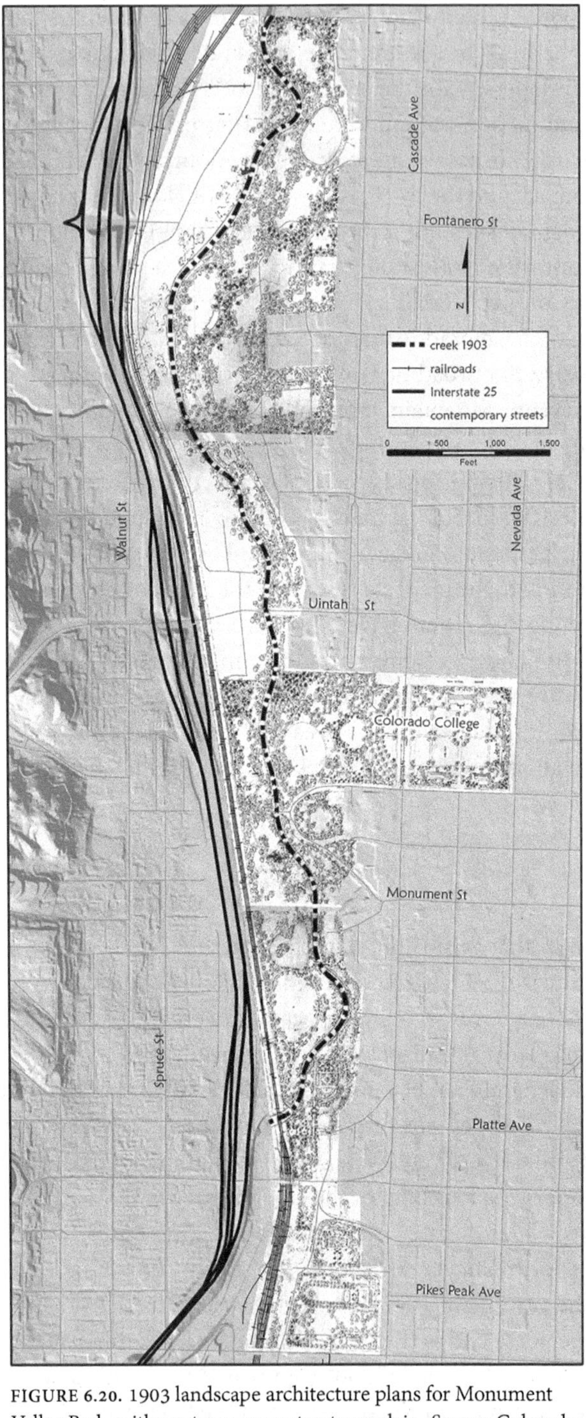

FIGURE 6.20. 1903 landscape architecture plans for Monument Valley Park, with contemporary streets overlain. *Source*: Colorado Springs Pioneers Museum; cartography by author.

and open to the public forever. Renowned landscape architect Charles Mulford Robinson, an advocate of the City Beautiful Movement, was impressed by the total acreage of parkland when he visited the city in 1912 but called for a more accessible ring of parks around the downtown, "like jewels on a necklace."[73] The city intends to fulfill this recommendation when it finally completes two small missing links and creates the "Legacy Loop," a bike path amidst parks that spans Monument Valley on the west and Shooks Run on the east of the downtown, following old railroad tracks.

Parks became a key element to the city's appeal by the early twentieth century: the "city park system is spacious and beautiful and famous the world over," said the *Gazette* in 1918.[74] The city kept up park acquisition as it grew, despite setbacks from Monument Valley Park flooding in 1935 and severe underfunding in recent decades.[75] The state has pitched in to help with open space acquisition through the Greater Outdoors Colorado lottery fund (GOCO), and nonprofits and city volunteers have tried to pick up the burden for park maintenance and new land acquisition. For instance, the Trails and Open Space Coalition formed the mid-1990s, and in a tax-averse city that regularly denies ballot initiatives to raise taxes for public works, voters approved a Trails and Open Space (TOPS) sales tax in 1997, then extended the tax in 2003 to run through 2025. By the twenty-first century, the Parks Department managed nearly 12,000 acres of open space and parkland, 160 miles of park trails, and 105 miles of urban trails.[76]

The city is fortunate that Pike National Forest borders its entire western edge, designated as protected public land since 1905. The numerous reservoirs built by Colorado Springs Utilities attract regional anglers, and the trail network for hiking, mountain biking, and equestrian activities provides a playground for all levels of enthusiasts. Events such as the Pikes Peak Marathon, a grueling ascent and descent of Barr Trail on Pikes Peak, and the increasingly recognized mountain bike opportunities put the city on the map with outdoor activity enthusiasts and organizations. The legacy of recreational tourism, combined with an early and sustained effort to protect open spaces from development, today pays increasing dividends.

Recreation is increasingly recognized as an economic powerhouse, not just a diversion from "real" work. Statewide, the 2018 Outdoor Industry Association reports that Colorado saw $28 billion in outdoor recreation industry consumer spending, generating 229,000 jobs—more than double that of the oil, gas, and mining industries.[77] Residents in the Pikes Peak Region spend $2.14 billion every year on trails, open space, and water-related activities.[78] Spending on the outdoor recreational economy in the Colorado Springs Congressional District is one of the strongest in the entire country. Companies such as Borealis Fat Bikes, MBS Mountain Boards, Angler's Covey, and Koobi started here; others such as Fox Shox have moved here—all at least in part to build on the outdoor activity attributes of this place. Despite repeated efforts by conservative voices throughout the Rocky Mountain West to turn federal land over to state control for private development and resource exploitation, Pike National Forest is yet another example of the importance of federal public lands for the recreation economy and for Colorado Springs, the very identity of the city.

In addition to the powerful recreation economy, Colorado Springs is also banking big on the related sports economy. Building once again upon an earlier focus, this time the amateur sports established at the Broadmoor, local leaders convinced the US Olympic Committee, fiscally strapped and cramped in its New York City headquarters, to relocate to Colorado Springs in 1977. Enticed by generous donations from the city, land and facilities donated by the US Air Force, and a grant from the El Pomar Foundation, plus the 6,000-foot elevation beneficial to athletic endurance, the committee converted a thirty-six-acre site that was at one time the Methodist Beth-El tuberculosis sanatorium and later the Ent Air Force Base into their campus.[79] The city built the Olympic Training Center (OTC) in 1978, a complex with residence halls and a multitude of gyms, rinks, pools, tracks, and other sporting facilities. Today about 15,000 athletes live for short durations each year at the OTC, with facilities such as the Velodrome bike track hosting regional competitions and meets. About 130,000 tourists visit the OTC annually. This has spawned a host of related businesses—fifty-nine national and international sports organizations, plus twenty-three national governing bodies for Olympic sports—that generate an agglomeration economy around amateur sports. The Olympics and Paralympics alone employ 2,100 people.[80] The University of Colorado Colorado Springs has a growing focus on exercise science, sport nutrition, and biochemistry, among other fields, with a new Sports Medicine and Performance Center opening in 2020 to further develop regional expertise in the sport industries.

Not only does the city host the flagship center, renamed the Olympic & Paralympic Training Center, it is the home for the US Olympic and Paralympic Committee (USOPC) Headquarters. Also established in 1978 at the OTC site, the USOPC considered relocating in 2008 after it outgrew its facilities. The city gambled on the cultural and economic capital it could exploit by subsidizing the USOPC, offering $53 million in taxpayer money (paid across thirty years) for a new downtown location, upgrades to the OTC, and other site improvements to entice the organization to stay. In exchange, the USOPC agreed to stay for twenty-five years and, more important, allowed Colorado Springs exclusive marketing as "Olympic City USA" (figure 6.21). The city started using the coveted theme in 2016 for its new brand identity. The Olympic brand is widely recognized, is respected, and is unique to Colorado Springs—a coup for urban identity construction. Despite criticism over the public subsidy, dividends are already paying off—Colorado Springs was awarded a state tourism grant for their "City of Champions" proposal to help build the first ever Olympic Museum, to open in 2020 in an industrial quarter of the downtown. Expected to bring 350,000 tourists annually, the

FIGURE 6.21. The "Olympic City USA" brand is prominently displayed throughout the city. The Olympic rings are adapted to form slope faces of Pikes Peak in the city's logo, as seen on this sign for the Center for Sustainability. *Source*: Photo by author.

project has also sparked major redevelopment plans around the future museum for housing and commercial facilities, including a pedestrian bridge to span the barrier created by railroad tracks and connect America the Beautiful Park along Monument Creek with the central urban core.

A RECREATION IDENTITY

The early city growth industries of health retreat and spa resort evolved into today's recreation and sports economies that drive the tourism sector. Recent years brought record-setting tourism numbers: 2016 saw over 23 million overall visits, nearly 500,000 drove the Pikes Peak Highway, and over 4 million people visited Garden of the Gods. Tourism is the city's third-largest industry, supporting over 17,000 jobs.[81]

There is a danger to becoming overly reliant upon tourism, and many scholars have pointed out the negative effects of the tourist industry: environmental degradation, expensive housing, low wages, economic gain only for a few, revenue exported to distant corporate entities, and a loss of authenticity or place-based traditions as legends and landscapes become commodified.[82] As historian Hal Rothman has said, "the embrace of tourism triggers a contest for the soul of a place."[83] Meanings and authenticity are regularly contested by various stakeholders, and Colorado Springs has seen its share of constructed and appropriated identities through such offerings as the spectacle of American Indian dancers, reconstructed cliff dwellings, display of human remains, Wild West "ghost town" fabrications, European-themed spas, the North Pole (Home of "Santa's Workshop") amusement park, and a performative rodeo culture. Manitou Springs both benefits and suffers from crowds of summertime tourists playing in the arcades and purchasing American Indian–themed souvenirs. The crowds hiking the incline have forced the city to provide off-site parking with shuttle buses, and a similar plan is set to go into effect for Cheyenne Canyon. But Colorado Springs is a large-enough city, with a sufficiently diversified economy, to enjoy many of the benefits of tourism without the overt drawbacks, especially when we see the more traditional forms of tourism evolve to active participation in recreation and sport-based events. Whereas small mountain towns such as Vail and Breckenridge have fabricated identities for tourists to escape in a theme-park-like landscape, the tourism industry in Colorado Springs has not been so dominant as to overwhelm all other sectors or generate a kitschy cultural landscape. Residents benefit from the many trails, reservoirs, streams, parks, and sports facilities and events just as much, or more, than do tourists. Local citizens can participate in the Pikes Peak Marathon or Velodrome races like anybody else. There remain ample opportunities to get away from crowds and find solitude on Pikes Peak, ride along urban trails, or catch cutthroat trout in mountain streams. The proliferation of breweries, restaurants, and coffee shops are positive changes in the urban environment for all to enjoy. And even Manitou Springs, crowded with tourists, has a very strong and tight-knit community loyal to its local pubs, cafés, and music venues, proud of an identity that sets it apart from greater Colorado Springs.

Historian William Philpott has said, "Tourism is about the interaction between people and place. It is an utterly landscape-specific phenomenon."[84] The dominant regional landscape element for this city has always been Pikes Peak, "Colorado Springs' greatest marketing asset from its founding to present."[85] Tourism and recreation solidified the bond between the city and the mountain, generating an enduring sense of place for Colorado Springs residents (figure 6.22). It is near impossible to think of the city without images of Pikes Peak coming to mind.

Colorado Springs, from its very founding, charted a path different from most western cities, banking on recreational pleasure seekers and the beauty of its environment. It has successfully marketed its landscape to create a place identity before this became a standard strategy among the many western amenity-based towns of today. From today's perspective, this focus may seem "natural" or obvious, but considering that the main economic driver of the late nineteenth century

FIGURE 6.22. Pikes Peak has always been the dominant icon to serve the recreation and tourism industries but also to create the sense of place for Colorado Springs. *Source*: Colorado Springs Pioneers Museum.

was agriculture—with commerce, industry, and mining close behind—then to gamble on the success of a real estate venture based on tourism and relaxation was risky. During the same era that Colorado Springs was starting this new experiment, the competing Union Colony, now the town of Greeley, was founded to the north based on a communal commitment to irrigated agriculture. Asked to compare the likelihood for success between the two, Nathan Meeker of the Union Colony said, "The people of Greeley are engaged in creating wealth, those of Colorado Springs, in spending it, and we all know which fountain is the deepest." To this, Palmer responded,

> This attractiveness of the locality, then, has been the dominant fact, and it is not unlikely that men may always continue to succumb to its "subtle and indescribable beauty." If so, our "fountain" may be deeper than Meeker was willing to admit . . . Men may even be willing to sacrifice the chance of "producing" more wealth, for the sake of enjoying better what they already have. Here is a resource less exhaustible perhaps than a garden soil, large streams of irrigating water, iron and coal mines, or the other usual elements of industrial growth.[86]

Few were likely to have believed William Jackson Palmer when he stated this in 1896. Agriculture and industry were the wealth generators at the time, the foundations upon which the economy revolved and the reason people moved west and new towns were founded. Tourism was certainly not a common economic driver, and disposable incomes for travel and leisure were not widespread. And yet, perhaps this is one of the most visionary statements that Palmer ever made. From the perspective of the twenty-first century, in a postindustrial economy, it seems clear that this was the right choice. How could he foresee the profound impact tourism and the recreational economy would have, how they would persistently contribute to jobs, revenue, and quality of life for the Pikes Peak Region? Palmer was correct about the draw of the scenic beauty and the outdoor recreational activities the land provided. His gamble paid off, and the city benefits from it today.

7

War

Space Capital of the Free World

—COLORADO SPRINGS BOOSTERS, MID-1980S[1]

While Colorado Springs lived on tourism to a large degree, that economic sector alone could not sustain the city as the twentieth century progressed. This was particularly true as the Great Depression lengthened, tourism dropped due to economic hardships, and fewer people traveled west. By the late 1930s, Colorado Springs was stagnating: "It had none of the traits considered essential for a prosperous future: no highly trained labor force, no local companies of any note, no research university, no hub airport."[2] A survey of housing undertaken by the city found 1,500 vacant homes in 1940, close to 20 percent of the entire housing stock.[3]

The onset of World War II shook the country out of the doldrums. The war economy fundamentally changed cities and entire regions, and such changes were even more pronounced in Colorado Springs than most other places in the country.

FORT CARSON

When the United States entered into the war after the attack on Pearl Harbor in 1941, industrial production of war machinery and the inscription and training of troops ramped up rapidly. Even before we entered the war, with an ominous future seeming inevitable, local boosters in Colorado Springs saw an opportunity "to lead their beautiful resort town from oblivion into economic stability."[4] Putting together a tightly knit campaign lasting more than a year, beginning in 1940 a determined group of city businessmen traveled to Washington, D.C., and

DOI: 10.5876/9781646421688.c007

promoted Colorado Springs to politicians and military brass for a new military installation. Leaders included local banker H. Chase Stone and Charles L. Tutt, Jr., director of the Broadmoor. With the rise of gilded-age capitalists such as Spencer Penrose in the early industrial era, Colorado Springs had developed a highly unequal distribution of income and a concentration of wealth in the hands of a few. These business elites worked collaboratively to attract investment in the city, the Broadmoor was the social hub of this clique, and the Tutt family that ran it had powerful connections to national leaders. Over the years, the Broadmoor came to play a key role in military boosterism for the city.[5]

The city had purchased the 5,533-acre Cheyenne Valley Ranch among others that had gone bankrupt during the Great Depression. As a result, the city could offer 35,000 acres of contiguous land at the base of Cheyenne Mountain to the army for a new facility. The prairie and low-rising mesas of the site were ideal for training, with plenty of sunshine to undertake yearlong maneuvers. These incentives and the efforts of the boosters' early campaign were successful—the US Army announced on January 6, 1942, that it would establish an army training camp just south of the city. Although the Corp of Engineers crew sent to survey the site encountered so many rattlesnakes they almost backed out, the deal went through.[6]

The magnitude of the army's decision was grandiose and audacious: a $30 million contract to house 30,000 soldiers, to be built within six months. This investment was about the same as the total assessed property value for the existing city and would nearly double the local population. Utilities promised access to sufficient water and power, and a team of designers and builders set to work right away. The camp would be named in honor of the famous frontiersman Brigadier General Christopher "Kit" Carson.

Such a monumental undertaking in the region was unprecedented. Peak employment during construction reached 12,000 people, and the total payroll of the joint venture companies was $7,758,000. Seen from the air, Camp Carson has a design of a long arc that conforms to the local topography, an intentional plan that minimized grading and leveling.[7] Even so, about 1.5 million cubic yards of materials were moved and leveled for 600 buildings. The truck and mechanical repair yard built in the center of the project ran twenty-four hours each day. To adhere to the tight timetable, most structures were prefabricated on site at a lumberyard and then erected into the barracks and other buildings. The initial site used 84 million board feet of lumber, and 53 miles of main pipeline trenches were dug, with over 16 miles of connector line ditches and 43 miles of sewer lines. Added to this were 4.7 miles of storm drainage and nineteen miles of gas lines, after which streets were graded atop it all using 300,000 cubic yards of gravel.[8] The army then asked for additional mule stables and structures to house prisoners of war, raising investment to over $50 million. At the time, the project was called "the greatest boom period in history" for the city.[9] The construction team met their deadline under budget, with the first sections turned over to the Eighty-Ninth Infantry Division on June 2, 1942, six weeks before the camp was activated.

Of course, the impact on the local economy over and above the enormous construction effort was equally profound. In August 1942, the quartermaster signed contracts for 120,000 tons of coal annually, to be filled by El Paso County mines and others to the south, with deliveries of seven carloads daily.[10] The camp would hire 1,100 civilians, 800 of whom had already been employed by July 1942.[11] After payday, up to 5,000 soldiers were expected to fill downtown drinking and eating establishments on a Saturday night in September 1942.[12] These numbers would increase as more GIs filled the camp. Both the Broadmoor and the Antlers became de facto war facilities that wined and dined the top brass. For the generals, Colorado Springs was a pleasant respite, made comfortable because the military was respected in the community.[13] The personal ties forged between the Colorado Springs and service elites proved highly valuable in later local efforts to preserve and extend military capacity.

Maximum troop numbers reached 43,000 in 1943. All told, 104,165 men trained at Camp Carson during World War II. At its height during the war, Camp Carson Hospital was the largest in the country, servicing over 9,000 patients. By extension, Camp Carson also administered Camp Hale, the training site near Leadville for alpine ski troops working in cold weather conditions that operated from 1942 to 1965. Also, approximately 10,000 German prisoners of war were interned at Camp Carson, most providing local agricultural labor for eighty cents per hour pay.[14] The prisoner facility, chosen at Carson for its remote location, was populated mostly from German soldiers captured in the North Africa campaign.

Prior to the creation of the US Air Force in 1947, both the army and navy maintained their own aerial units. As part of the Camp Carson deal, the army also opened an Army Air Base. The city had built a civilian airport in 1925, and as early as 1941 the federal government had leased part of it and built facilities for training fighter pilots.[15] The army then leased most of the city airport in 1942 as Camp Carson was coming online, contracted with the city to build a $72,000 water pump at Prospect Lake in July to supplement the gravity-fed water lines, and built new barracks and renamed the site Peterson Field on December 13.[16] The field trained pilots during the war.

The city purchased the old Methodist Sanatorium complex on east Boulder Street and leased it to the army for an aerial photography reconnaissance unit in early 1942.[17] The Army Air Forces sought a more central location for the Second Air Force from its home in Spokane, Washington, so established Ent Air Force Base and moved the Second Air Force to the old sanatorium site in June 1943.[18] This expansion brought another large group of officers and personnel to Colorado Springs. Peterson Field continued to support all flying activities associated with Ent.

The fate of Camp Carson looked bleak after the war. As early as 1945 the camp hosted no Army Division, drawdown expanded, and the facility nearly closed as the number of troops dwindled to 600 in 1946.[19] However, at the end of the Korean War, the army consolidated facilities nationally and chose to upgrade, rather than close, Camp Carson. In 1954 the post designation was upgraded from camp to fort and again hosted a division. By 1956 it was the single-largest contributor to the Colorado Springs economy, employing 2,000 civilians, purchasing local supplies and utilities, and hiring contractors for construction improvements. The federal government also pays local school districts grants to compensate for students living on federal land who don't contribute property taxes to fund public schools.[20]

Colorado Springs and Fort Carson, "The Mountain Post," have evolved in a mutually dependent relationship ever since. The continual upgrades to facilities on the site were a crucial element that assisted the army to transition from conscripted soldiers to an all-volunteer force in the 1970s; the city also played a role in this national effort by providing a welcoming environment for recruits. Like any long-term commitment between two partners, there have been rough spots along the way. In the 1970s, concerns arose with the disproportionately high crime rate attributed to GIs from the post, water pollution into Fountain Creek, and high rates of child abuse in military families.[21] Throughout the existence of Fort Carson, the army and Colorado Springs city leaders and political representatives have maintained supportive and trusted relationships. Following military funding cycles, Fort Carson was repeatedly threatened with closure or reduction in size over the years; each attempt generated strong community and political support. The Vietnam War saw troops increase to over 24,000 and the original site expand to 137,000 acres, but by 1975 the potential loss of a brigade of approximately 3,800 troops—over 15 percent of those stationed at the time—caused the local state representative to call for a letter-writing campaign to Congress to avert a "crisis of frightening magnitude" with "staggering" financial repercussions.[22]

In the 1980s, much opposition intensified around the army's desire to expand and create a new maneuver and training grounds in southeastern Colorado. The army wanted over 200,000 acres to run tank and other heavy machinery drills. They narrowed down potential locations to three but finally chose what is now the Piñon Canyon Maneuver site in Las Animas County, about 130 miles southeast of the post. Ranchers and other local landowners in particular led the charge against the new site, reinforced by their state representatives. Disappointed by the perceived lack of state support and that politicians weren't asking the "true questions" about Fort Carson's economic influence, the army said it didn't want to use "scare tactics" but warned of the potential for closure if it didn't get the land.[23] After an environmental impact statement and lengthy legislative sessions, Congress authorized the money in 1981 to acquire the land and reached final approval in 1983.[24] Part of the agreement was that the army would not seek any further expansion in the future and would not use live artillery fire on the site. The army used its power of eminent domain in over half of the land purchases, which created bitter resentment, with thirty-three landowners taking it to court over disputed purchase prices.[25] After settling all cases and conducting extensive wildlife, environmental, and archaeological inventories, the army built a rail-loading yard and new facilities on site. Training operations started in 1985.[26]

During the debate, the main support for the Piñon Canyon expansion came from the Colorado Springs and Pueblo Chambers of Commerce, plus business and political representatives of Colorado Springs. Fort Carson chose a Broadmoor Hotel Board of Directors member for their "Good Neighbor" Award in 1981 for his Piñon Canyon support, citing his recognition that the "Army and civilian community are one in the same, and one big team."[27]

Following a total of five rounds of Base Reallocation and Closure (BRAC) reviews between 1988 and 2005, more than 130 major military installations were closed or designated to alternative land uses by 2015.[28] As a part of the shuffling of military personnel from closed installations to those remaining open, Fort Carson saw dramatic growth from 13,000 active duty soldiers in 2003 to approximately 26,000 soldiers by 2012.[29] By 2005, nearly 8,000 soldiers boosted troop levels to Vietnam-era highs, prompting $155 million spending for expansion construction in the biggest boom ever undertaken on the post.[30] This also led to off-base housing construction in the Security-Widefield area south of the city.[31] The fort alone was responsible for about 10 percent of the economic activity in the Pikes Peak Region.[32] The fort is also a popular post for soldiers, who appreciate being close to a city of Colorado Springs' size, where they can easily assimilate while off duty and blend into a community supportive of the military. Said one soldier, "Soldiers and civilians mix so well because almost everyone is from somewhere else. We are all transplants. So few of us are natives, so we all get along."[33]

The rapid growth in the first decade of the twenty-first century put new pressure on the army to again expand training maneuvers at Fort Carson. One response was to commence live-fire training at the Piñon Canyon Maneuver site in 2004, breaking the promise made when the facility was established.[34] Then in 2006, renewed conflict erupted over a proposal to expand the Piñon Canyon Maneuver site twofold, enlarging it into what would be the largest army training ground in the country and again reneging on initial promises not to expand. The army framed this expansion as a matter of urgent national security. Landowners created an opposition campaign after leaked maps showed the army's long-term plans to buy out and occupy the entire southeastern corner of Colorado, all the way to the Oklahoma and Kansas borders—an area the size of New Jersey! The army downplayed this "rogue" map but was remarkably arrogant about its rights and needs for expansion, and remarkably silent about how decisions were made and what its long-term plans would be.[35] Despite a rural ranching population

FIGURE 7.1. Army missile at the county courthouse (now Pioneers Museum) in 1960 encouraging enlistment but also symbolically illustrating the strong relationship between the city and the army. *Source*: Colorado Springs Pioneers Museum.

generally supportive of the military, the army's campaign was fraught with conflict and poorly presented or communicated. The opposition campaign, using a David-versus-Goliath narrative, sowed distrust with the army's intentions and succeeded in halting the expansion: as of late 2013, Congress put the project on hold.

Fort Carson today remains an integral part of Colorado Springs (figure 7.1). As of 2018, it employs about 4,500 civilian and contract workers, hosts over 23,000 military personnel (70% of whom live off post), and brings over $2 billion to the local economy through salaries, contracts, utility payments, grants, and other expenses.[36] The many services offered veterans provide a welcoming community and subsidies that serve to attract over 50,000 military retirees to the region. But as influential a role as the army plays in the city, it is the air force that came to define the city's relationship with the military.

THE CROWN JEWEL: THE UNITED STATES AIR FORCE ACADEMY

World War I raised awareness for the influence aeronautics would play in modern warfare. Although airplanes played a relatively small role in that conflict, by as early as 1918 military leaders in the United States were calling for an independent military branch dedicated to aerial warfare. The nascent Air Service was upgraded into the Air Corps in 1926 but remained as branches of the army and navy. After the massive aerial role in World War II, the National Security Act of 1947 established an independent and coequal US Air Force, which began operating on September 18, 1947.[37] Such an expansion of the nation's military required years of planning to determine the mission of this new service, budgets, recruitment levels, facilities, and a host of other major issues. Among them was the question of what to do about a new military academy, similar to those in West Point for the army and Annapolis for the navy. An initial report in early 1949 called for the creation of such an academy, and a site selection board was established in November 1949, to assess potential locations for this new institution. The competition began among hundreds of candidates to land this lucrative venture.

Selecting Colorado Springs

Local businessman Joseph Reich, owner of a downtown restaurant, read about the potential for a new air force academy one morning in 1949 and liked the idea of locating the facility in Colorado Springs. The postwar economy was slow, with Camp Carson in major drawdown mode that drained support for local business as troops left town. Unemployment was high, stores were closing, and houses were vacant. Reich and other businessmen took their ideas to the Chamber of Commerce, which enthusiastically supported an initiative to influence air force decision makers. The chamber built on their success from landing Camp Carson in 1942 and brought a level of expertise not seen in other places:

> Some of the members of the Citizen's Committee established by the Chamber of Commerce in 1954 had served together in 1942 when Camp Carson had been established. They cut their teeth on that project and learned the subtle technique of dealing with political and military leaders on a huge project involving millions of dollars. They also learned the importance of total community involvement.[38]

The Chamber of Commerce sprang into action, organizing a committee comprised of a core group of supporters to influence the air force. They produced initial fact sheets and got on the phone with influential people in Washington.

An initial site selection board for the academy studied 354 possible sites and included Colorado Springs as one of eight finalists.[39] While the Site Selection Board was conducting their review, the air force continued to grow rapidly. As part of its organizational planning, in 1950 the air force decided to consolidate widely distributed fighter bases and establish a centralized Air Defense Command. Charles Tutt Jr., a protégé of Spencer Penrose, ran the Broadmoor Hotel after Penrose died in 1939. His son, Thayer Tutt, was an air force lt. colonel at the Pentagon during World War II and knew many top leaders. He also served as chairman of the Chamber of Commerce's Military Affairs Committee while increasingly taking responsibilities for running the Broadmoor. Largely through Thayer Tutt's and other city leaders' personal relationships with top military personnel, Colorado Springs was selected to house the Air Defense Command.[40] Of great importance was the welcome reception the Tutts always provided to military personnel at the Broadmoor Hotel. Building on the reputation generated with army personnel during the war, the Broadmoor again became the entertainment and influence-peddling capital: "In the minds of many people, especially military people, Colorado Springs and the Broadmoor were synonymous."[41] But the generals were attracted to Colorado Springs not solely because of the Broadmoor clique, but also through the larger promotional campaign and incentives offered through the Chamber of Commerce: "The town's promotional effort was by this time slick, innovative, and unabashedly pro-military."[42] The city offered the idled and available Peterson Air Field on attractive terms and pledged to build housing. The Chamber bankrolled the congressional campaign of J. Edgar Chenoweth, a promilitary Republican to ensure support in Washington and continued their Military Housing Office through 1951 to appease concerns among air force officials. The location of the Air Defense Command in Colorado Springs, with access to Peterson Field, certainly helped the city in its quest to acquire a new air force academy.

Colorado Springs boosters and members of the Chamber of Commerce committee working to acquire the academy pressed their contacts in the Pentagon and White House: "Being good, influential Republicans, other key members of the committee had direct access to top officials of the Eisenhower administration. One or two could even pick up the telephone and talk to President Eisenhower himself."[43] Members of the committee made more than thirty trips to Washington, and the Chamber of Commerce spent over $40,000 on the venture. In 1953, Chamber members learned that legislation would authorize the secretary of the air force to acquire donated lands. They influenced Governor Dan Thornton to call a special session of the state legislature for the sole purpose of establishing a

Colorado land acquisitions commission. Both houses quickly passed the authorizing legislation and appropriated $1million to be used to purchase land required for the academy, should a final decision be made to build it. The plan was that the state would then deed the land to federal government and be reimbursed at actual cost, a strong showing of support for the academy at the highest levels of the Colorado state government.[44]

Momentum continued for the creation of an air force academy, and finally, President Eisenhower signed the bill designating the creation of this new institution on April 1, 1954 "for the instruction and preparation for military service of selected persons who shall be known as Air Force cadets."[45] Immediately afterward the secretary of the air force, Harold Talbott, appointed a site selection commission to determine where to locate the new facility. The five members—two generals, one university president, on private-sector businessman, and famous aviator Charles Lindbergh—were charged to recommend one finalist if unanimous, or if not, narrow the list down to three finalists, from which Secretary Talbott would make the final decision. The commission received 582 proposals in forty-five different states. California alone had fifty-seven, Texas fifty-one.[46]

The commission evaluated all applicants according to a similar list of criteria: not less than 15,000 acres (to allow room for future expansion); natural beauty; within fifty miles of an urban center for access to educational, cultural, and religious resources; accessible to rail, air and highway; a climate minimizing extreme conditions and natural hazards; suitability for flight training; and costs (including access to water and utilities).[47] One section specifically stated: "The Air Academy will become a national monument as are West Point and Annapolis. In selecting the permanent location, consideration will be given to the natural beauty of the site and of the surrounding country."[48] After eliminating the majority of applicants, the Commission made site visits to 34 locations in 21 states, plus surveyed another 33 sites from the air. The president of the Colorado Springs Chamber of Commerce, future Governor John Love, led the city's recruitment effort, continually sending envoys to Washington. The Military Affairs Committee was renamed the Air Force Academy Foundation, which raised lobbying money and created a promotional brochure in 1954 for the site (figure 7.2). Relying on the new Blue River water delivery system, the committee secured a City Council commitment for 2 million gallons of water per day and also offered to donate Peterson Air Field.[49] Members aggressively used their connections with the military's top brass: "Mr. Tutt was personally acquainted with General Eisenhower and Secretary Talbott."[50] General William H. Gill, retired commander of Camp Carson who then became president of Colorado College, offered to share resources of the college while the new academy was getting established, including use of athletic fields. The chamber solicited and received cooperation and support from the Denver Chamber of Commerce and others across the state. It was an all-out effort.[51]

FIGURE 7.2. Brochure created by the Colorado Springs Chamber of Commerce in 1954 to promote Colorado Springs as the best site for the future Air Force Academy. *Source*: U.S. Air Force Academy, McDermott Library archives.

When the commission visited Colorado Springs, members first expressed concerns about flight training at over 6,000 feet, plus approach and take-off limitations and treacherous air currents from the nearby mountains. Charles Lindbergh rented a plane and flew the crew over the proposed site, alleviating concerns about flight altitude and winds and in the process generating awe amongst the reviewers from the breathtaking scenery of the Rampart Range foothills, with Pikes Peak behind, when seen from the air. The committee also sought to address reports of respiratory troubles that arose at Camp Carson during war. The chamber called on state medical officials, military surgeons, and the dean of the University of Colorado Medical School to gather and present data and records that disproved this problem.[52]

Finally the commission met on May 27, 1954. They relied in part on a memo recovered from the original Site Selection Board that favored Colorado Springs, but mainly from their own observations. Three members favored Colorado Springs, one opposed that location, and one was undecided. Opposition to Colorado Springs centered on the relative remoteness and lack of nearby opportunities and services due to the small size of the city. In June the commission therefore recommended three sites to Secretary Talbott, without any ranking: Alton, Illinois; Lake Geneva, Wisconsin, and Colorado Springs. Secretary Talbott accepted the recommendations and now had the task of deciding among the three. He planned visits to each city.

In Alton, the Chamber of Commerce strongly supported the plan, but local property owners voiced opposition. Concerned about losing their properties to a "federal land grab," or at the least a decrease in property values due to proximity to the new facility, they mounted a fierce campaign against choosing this site. The alumni group of Principia College, a nearby small liberal arts school affiliated with the Christian Science Church, voiced the same concerns and urged opposition. Part of these concerns were fomented and encouraged by an undercover operative from Colorado Springs. When Alton was receiving favorable consideration, Chamber president John Love asked local car dealer R. Soland Doenges to go visit for a reconnaissance survey. Rather than simply gather information, he grew a scruffy beard, wore sunglasses, dressed in rough clothing, and attended several of the protest meetings where he shouted out provocative questions to stir up angry landowners. He also participated in gatherings of Principia College alumni and encouraged them to send protest letters and telegrams, then talked with Alton newspaper reporters to generate opposition in the press.[53] Although the local congressional representative and the local paper strongly supported the proposal, the perceived public opposition concerned the secretary.

Similarly, in Lake Geneva, situated on a small lake with many resort homes and nearby dairy farms, property owners who would be affected by the new institution led the opposition. When the commission first visited, its members were met by a mob of protestors flying banners flatly stating they did not want the air force. Although the Chamber of Commerce, local politicians, and the local paper supported the facility, the city attorney filed suit to halt the process, and even representatives in the state legislature opposed the proposal.[54] Again, Secretary Talbott was reluctant to establish this critical component of the entire air force in a community that wasn't welcoming. Compounding the situation was the dislike for

Wisconsin senator Joseph McCarthy held by both Secretary Talbott and President Eisenhower, who were likely reluctant to award such a prize to his state.[55] The president had also expressed several times his preference for a western location, outside of the Midwest.

These two experiences stood in stark contrast to the enthusiastic welcome the commission and the secretary found in Colorado Springs. Upon arrival, both were met with welcome signs in downtown store windows, warm greetings from community members, banners celebrating the arrival of the air force, and a genuine sense of civic pride in the potential to host the new academy. Such a welcome was unusual for the military.[56] Added to this positivity might have been clandestine influence from President Eisenhower, who, while staying out of the decision-making process, did host informal discussions with the secretary about the new location and later admitted that he was "very anxious" that it should locate in Colorado.[57]

On June 24, 1954, air force secretary Talbott announced that Colorado Springs would become the new permanent location of the United States Air Force Academy.[58] With an organized sales pitch of over six years' duration, the coalition that spread throughout the state could finally claim success. Said Governor Dan Thornton: this was "the greatest day in the history of Colorado."[59]

Boosterism by Elites

Charles Tutt Jr., summarized the decision to locate the Air Force Academy in Colorado Springs: "We had the best location."[60] But clearly more went into the decision than simply the physical attributes of the land. This was not a passive process; the local committee and their collaborators went to great efforts to influence and convince the Site Selection Commission and the secretary of the air force to choose Colorado Springs. Their success led to a formula for the local boosters: an all-out effort on every conceivable front to win military facilities. They would continue to succeed with this strategy in future efforts; so successfully, in fact, that regional planners Ann Markusen and colleagues stated that "Colorado Springs is a creation of its boosters."[61]

Viewed from the perspective of the twenty-first century, it seems quite remarkable that a small group of men could plan and undertake such daring projects with profound impacts upon the city for ever after. Images come to mind of these business elites sitting in the tony El Paso Club smoking cigars and charting the future of the city, then making it happen. And in fact, there is a clear lineage from the scrappy city founders and their Colorado Springs land investment scheme, who through promotional boosterism successfully created the image of an upscale resort that attracted investment, to the twentieth-century capitalist class with concentrated power, focused on the Broadmoor Hotel and its club members, who were able to make important decisions about military-based growth with little community input or opposition. Needless to say, even though the standard narrative is that these new elites were community-minded actors concerned with the future of the city, they all stood to benefit personally from the growth and business that came with the military institutions. Never mentioned were the personal profits to be made by a small number of people, or any of the negative public externalities that might come with rapid growth, large military facilities adjacent to town, or a local economy dependent upon defense industries. The interests of a small but powerful group drove a process that was viewed as good for the whole community, the way things "should" work, the "normal" progress of development. In this way, they in fact came to define the means by which society functions and the natural order of the world.[62] As to the character of the place it created, this group of elite boosters left a lasting business ethic that would come to characterize the city. Beyond simply attracting military installations and commands, the boosters' efforts fostered an ethic that would define the main business activity of the postwar city: land development and growth. This ethic facilitated rapid urban expansion in the second half of the twentieth century and into the twenty-first century.

Designing a National Monument

The decision to locate the new Air Force Academy in Colorado Springs was a monumental event. Next came the process of how to build an institution intended to be, literally, a national monument. This would be one of the largest single educational projects ever designed in this country and, at the time, one of the largest ever government-funded projects.[63] More important, it needed to be a symbol representing the air force, as well as the agenda of the country overall during the Cold War era. Air force secretary Talbott wanted an institution in which the people of America will have faith and pride. The air force bought $3.75 million of land, in addition to the state's contribution of $1 million, to build this new institution (figure 7.3).

After lengthy competition and review, the architectural firm Skidmore, Owings, and Merrill of Chicago was selected in July 1954, to plan and build the site. This well-respected firm had made important architectural statements as early as the 1933 World's Fair, an event that sought to emphasize the active role of industry and science in creating a new-world order. The firm was up for the task, well aware of the national importance and difficulty of the project: "Our challenge is to produce a timeless beautiful thing that works."[64]

The language of science, a new-world order, timelessness, human progress, and emphasis on functionality that works all reflect modernist thought. Modernism sought to break from the shackles of the past, to liberate humanity from the chains of superstition and the rigidities of tradition inherited from the old European world. The belief was in a bright new future for humanity based on human intellect, rational thought, and technological progress. In architecture, this translated

FIGURE 7.3. Prior to building permanent facilities, the initial guard booth at the south entrance to the Air Force Academy used an improvised Gardiner tuberculosis hut. *Source*: U.S. Air Force Academy, McDermott Library archives.

into forms that emphasized sleek, efficient functionality, removing ornamental frills and wasteful additions that serve no purpose, and relying on the use of new building materials such as glass and steel. Modern architects shunned the neoclassical and beaux arts traditions with their historical references and heavy ornamentation. Modernist designers took inspiration from the early twentieth-century Bauhaus school in Germany and Swiss-French architect Le Corbusier, both of whom emphasized architectural forms that were functional, pure, and rationally designed. The philosophy is best illustrated by the International Style, intended to serve all of humanity as scientific progress ushered in a new and liberating, utopian world.[65] These ideas melded nicely with the academy architects' desires to also emphasize flight, a modern and technological invention, in an effort to reflect the purpose of the air force in the academy design.

FIGURE 7.4. Aerial image of the Cadet Area, illustrating the rational design, with gridlike structure organizing the layout. *Source*: Stewarts Commercial Photographers, © Pikes Peak Library District, 013-10461.

The Air Force Academy occupies 18,500 acres and is a largely self-contained town, with numerous housing sites, schools, and recreation centers, and a golf course, football stadium, airfield, and other amenities. But the focus of the academy today and during the design phase is the Cadet Area, the central academic hub with cadet housing, the library, the academic building, an administration building, recreation facilities, parade grounds, and the chapel. This is the core that attracted the architects' attention. They chose to site this central hub of the campus on a mesa directly abutting the sharp rise of the Rampart Range. The hub is situated at over 7,100 feet and visible from afar above the surrounding terrain, with the planners using classical references to the Acropolis in Athens as an analogy (figure 7.4). When designing this core area, the firm underscored the role of reason in organizing and ordering the natural site to reflect the dual purposes as primarily an engineering school and a military academy. Architect Walter Netsch was influenced by Japanese principles of design that built on multiples or divisions of a basic building unit, in this case a seven-foot-by-seven-foot block to which all solids and voids would relate. Twice this unit was the width of each cadet room; four times this unit became the standardized beam and structural

FIGURE 7.5. Design built upon a foundational grid size, buildings emphasized glass and steel, and landscaping was sparse. *Source*: Photograph by Guy Burgess, © Pikes Peak Library District, 357-4665.

bay size. The entire site used a visible expression of the structural grid to reinforce a geometry superimposed over the more chaotic natural forms. Glass and steel were the primary construction materials, with aluminum exteriors that alluded to aircraft (figure 7.5).[66]

Skidmore, Owings, and Merrill not only reflected modernist thinking and design, but they were among the cultural avant-garde pushing this new philosophy on the world. They intended a design that would show the progress of humanity over the past century, reinforcing the role of technology in the service of humankind. Principal partner Nathaniel Owings said the academy buildings should be "as modern, as timeless and as style-less . . . as efficient and as flexible in their basic layout as the most modern projected aircraft."[67] Louis Skidmore said, "Certainly this architecture is free from the shackles of the past . . . buildings which are basically honest, which express the task they are performing and which actually perform the task."[68] Partner John Merrill said the slick forms of the academy architecture symbolized the new technological defense capabilities that superseded the outdated

FIGURE 7.6. Administration building (left) and dining hall (right). *Source*: Stewarts Commercial Photographers, © Pikes Peak Library District, 013-11546 and 013-11547.

methods and traditions of the army and the navy.[69] And chief architect Walter Netsch stated, "Just as West Point, with its medieval fortress-like appearance, symbolizes the traditions of land warfare, so does the sharplined and soaring Air Force Academy represent the newest and swiftest military science."[70]

The initial public presentation of the design took place at the Colorado Springs Fine Arts Center on May 13, 1955. The exhibit was highly choreographed, leading visitors through stations with artwork, models, dioramas, photographs, and inspirational quotes, starting and ending at a design of the campus master plan. The design was also released through architectural and popular journals. Propaganda photos portrayed a pristine city in which the individual was subordinated to the ordering grid.[71] The professional architectural community reacted favorably, calling it visionary. Political representatives, not so much.

Unaccustomed to the sharp rectangular shapes, aluminum and glass facades, and barren parade grounds of modernist design, many members of Congress balked at funding such a plan. Some advocated for using local stone facades to reflect the Colorado setting; others criticized the excessive amount of paved areas and lack of landscaping. Said a local Colorado representative, Byron Rogers, "It would appear to be an appropriate edifice for a modern factory," or a "glorified supermarket"[72] (figure 7.6). Others deemed it inhumane, an embodiment of government bureaucracy and the regulatory nature of military institutions (which actually describes pretty well the purpose of the facility). After partial funding and numerous delays, eventually Congress deferred to the expertise of the architects and construction began in 1955. Over $250 million went into the physical construction of the academy.

Gaining approval of the initial plan was difficult, but even more intense controversy arose with the next phase, which would build the centerpiece of the entire Cadet Area and the symbolic center of the entire academy: the chapel. While the chapel was always a lightning rod for criticism since the first unveiling of the Cadet

Area design, architects were able to deflect concern over the chapel design in the first phase because it was not in the initial appropriations from Congress. But soon came judgment day.

Before design and construction of the chapel even began, much discussion took place about who this building would serve. Was this to be for all religions? For Protestants only? Did the academy need multiple chapels for different religions? The decision came that there would be one chapel only, with spaces for different religions and denominations based on air force percentages: 25 percent Catholic, 72 percent Protestant, 3 percent Jewish.[73] This raised the sensitive concern whether the federal government was favoring one religion over another. While relying upon overall air force percentages of religious affiliations lent an air of credibility—giving the appearance of a rational decision-making process—the design nonetheless left an obvious hierarchy among the religions. The Protestant chapel sat atop the others in the spacious 1,200-person sanctuary, with a 100-seat choir loft. The Protestant chapel took in the full grandeur of the towering spires' interior. The Catholic sanctuary was underneath the main floor, without view of the lofty ceiling, seating a 500-person congregation with an 80-seat choir loft, and the Jewish sanctuary shared the lower floor, hosting 100 persons. There was a final All Faiths Room provided for smaller religious meetings, also on the lower floor (figure 7.7). While this arrangement has worked, conflicts have arisen throughout the years about who can use the main Protestant chapel for weddings or other ceremonies, particularly with non-Christian cadets or graduates requesting the space.[74]

Long, drawn-out battles took place in Congress over the chapel design and cost, with initial approval finally coming by 1958 and construction starting mid-1959. One area of potential controversy was why a religious facility would be the focus of a public institution at all? Was the federal government sanctioning a religious institution in seeming violation of the separation of church and state? Despite this apparent contradiction, that topic in fact was not a concern at the time. In the context of the Cold War against "Godless" communism, religion took on a key role in the struggle for western democracy, and a house of worship seemed appropriate for the new military academy.[75] A promotional booklet printed by the Air Force Academy said, "As modern airmen brush wings with infinity there is an increasing awareness of an ordered universe, a Divine Designer."[76] A subsequent air force publication stated:

> The cadet chapel is the centerpiece of our academy, as such it is a constant reminder of our academy's fourth pillar, spiritual development, and that we are a nation under God dedicated to the promotion of peace and goodwill among all nations of the world. The young men and women who come and study here do so in order to prepare themselves to protect freedom—freedom which is God's gift to all people.[77]

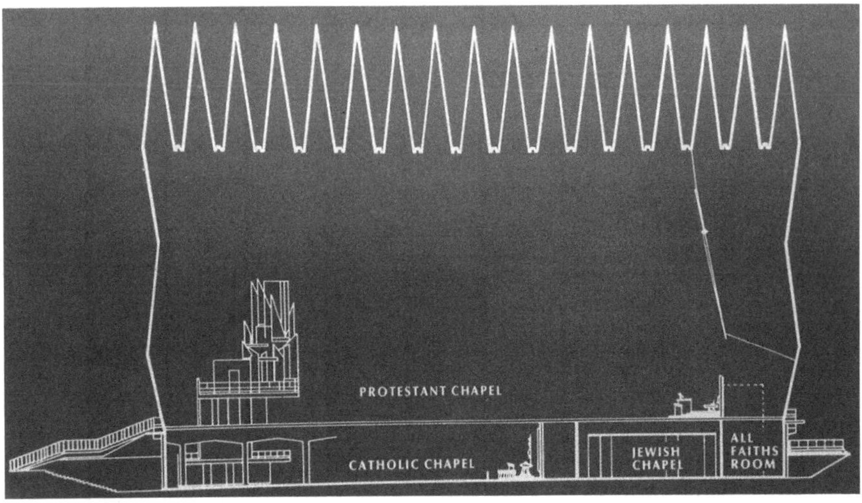

FIGURE 7.7. Air Force Academy Cadet Chapel design showing the partitioning of space between Protestant, Catholic, Jewish, and all faiths sanctuaries. *Source*: Colorado Springs Pioneers Museum.

While the appropriateness of a chapel as academy centerpiece was settled, the architects did struggle, however, with building a structure that references religious tradition and provides monumental symbology, two traits that conflicted with their modernist design philosophy. Architect Walter Netsch's solution was a structure with seventeen spires made up of three vertically interlocking tetrahedrons, each seventy-five feet long, rising to a height of 150 feet above the granite pediment. While the spires represent soaring aircraft wings, others see a reflection of the peaks of the Rocky Mountains rising immediately behind the site.[78] The chapel also sat prominently in the Cadet Area, contributing to its monumentality and again symbolically reflecting a modern-day Acropolis. The spires were clad in aluminum to evoke flight, yet between each spire was a one-foot wide row of stained-glass windows to respect traditional elements of a religious sanctuary (figure 7.8).

The chapel finally completed in the summer of 1963, criticism of the design was brutal. Colorado governor Edwin Johnson called it an "ugly duckling" and "monstrosity," saying "The paganistic distortion conceived by them as a place of religion is an insult to religion and Colorado."[79] Other criticisms called the building a row of tipis, a giant accordion, and a "polished aluminum monstrosity" completely incompatible with the natural grandeur of the Rocky Mountains.[80] Professional architects were again more endearing, but now nearly a decade after the academy project began, some again questioned the appropriateness of a religious chapel as the center of an academic and military institution. Despite these criticisms, the chapel is now considered an architectural masterpiece that is nationally

FIGURE 7.8. Air Force Academy Cadet Chapel, with seventeen spires soaring 150 feet tall. The three interlocking tetrahedrons can be seen on its northern end. The chapel has become the iconic symbol of the academy. *Source*: Colorado Springs Pioneers Museum.

recognized. It was listed as the fifty-first most popular building in the country by the American Institute of Architects in 2007. Time has shown that the building has successfully served the intended role of the iconic symbol of the academy.

Despite the critiques of modernist planning for creating stark buildings and places that are devoid of character, intimidating, dehumanizing, and generally unfriendly, strictly as a master-planned expression of modernist architecture, the academy is a jewel that one cannot help appreciating. It has great value as an example of place representing ideology, a pure reflection of an underlying philosophy.[81] The ability of Skidmore, Owings, and Merrill to work with a blank slate allowed them to create a masterpiece that appropriately reflects and symbolizes the mission of the United States Air Force and the regimented life of the cadets. The purpose of the academy stands in clear display, creating a certain beauty and synergy between design and function. In recognition of the special characteristics of this place, the Cadet Area of the academy was designated a National Historic Landmark on its fiftieth anniversary in 2004—an ironic designation given its intent to symbolize the future but fitting nonetheless.

The Academy and Colorado Springs

The United States Air Force Academy is intricately linked to the identity of Colorado Springs. After all, there is only one Air Force Academy in the entire country, and it is here. Planners Ann Markusen and colleagues label it "the postmark of Colorado Springs."[82] Right off the bat, city officials knew that a big payoff would accrue to the tourism sector from the free publicity and advertising that would come with the academy.[83] Another impact on the regional economy was to lend an air of academic credibility that supported the growing aerospace defense industries in the city. While Colorado College had long predated the Air Force Academy as the institution of higher education in town, its liberal arts curriculum and small size do not produce the computer programmers, aerospace and mechanical engineers, database developers, or other technical positions needed for the aerospace fields. Yet while the academy did bring academic credibility, and despite the accolades of technological excellence attributed to and emanating from the academy, in reality this institution also does not provide workers for the high-tech sector. Cadets follow a highly regimented program with little activity off campus, and then serve their commission in the air force away from Colorado Springs. The institution is not a mill for skilled employees seeking work locally. Nonetheless, local air force facilities and defense industry firms do interact with academy cadets and leaders in symbiotic ways that support the overall air force mission.

Throughout the subsequent years, the academy has had to adapt to larger societal movements in America. As the air force grew into a crucial pillar of the military, the Cadet Wing expanded from its initial capacity of 2,529 cadets to 4,417 in 1964.[84] This required the construction of new cadet housing buildings on campus, which generally fit into the overall design of the original Cadet Area but still caused architects at Skidmore, Owings, and Merrill to complain that the additions violated their vision. Military conscription ended in 1973, requiring the armed forces to broaden the scope of whom they recruit. Next came the battle for women's rights, including the struggle to ratify the Equal Rights Amendment among the states. These societal changes prompted President Ford to sign a law in 1975 admitting women into the military academies. The Air Force Academy began accepting women in 1976, with the first class of 157 women graduating in 1980 (figure 7.9).[85] Then in response to the concerns from the accrediting boards, to strengthen the academic credentials and to broaden the liberal arts education at the military academies, in 1992 Congress directed the academies to hire civilian faculty with doctoral degrees, to reach a goal of at least 25 percent by the year 2000. While this goal has been reached, accreditation concerns continued into the twenty-first century due to a heavy reliance on a rotating cadre of captains without doctoral degrees teaching classes at times outside of their academic fields.[86]

The academy went through a series of struggles in the twenty-first century, some similar to those occurring at other public institutions of higher education, others reflecting its unique mission. The strict honor code was challenged by cheating scandals, then came drug and sexual abuse cases in the early 2000s.[87] After exposure of sexual assault scandals in 2003, the iconic "Bring Me Men"

FIGURE 7.9. Julie Richardson arrives in 1976 with the first class of women admitted to the academy, in front of the iconic "Bring Me Men" sign that once greeted new doolies. *Source*: U.S. Air Force Academy, McDermott Library archives.

sign that greeted new doolies was taken down and replaced with "Integrity First. Service Before Self. Excellence in All We Do."[88] Later, dozens of cadets complained of an environment of religious intolerance. Overt evangelizing by born-again Christians was seen to be encouraged and promoted by leadership, causing a constitutional conflict at a supposedly secular institution. The football coach hung a banner, "I am a member of Team Jesus Christ."[89] Cadets said the slant toward Christianity and disrespect of other beliefs permeated the institution and created bias and persecution: "If you wanted to advance and get leadership positions, you better get in with the Jesus crowd."[90] A review team brought in from Yale University issued a report in July 2004 that found that stridently evangelical themes challenged the pluralistic environment of basic training and said the "overwhelmingly evangelical tone . . . encouraged religious divisions rather than fostering spiritual understanding."[91]

While in some respects the academy is no different from many public universities in these scandals, its symbolic national role, reputation as an elite institution, and dual military/academic mission create a unique context that exacerbates more typical problems found elsewhere while generating new ones of its own. A related tension is the need to secure a military installation on what is a public academy. Although well funded, the academy relies on foundations and revenues for some of its operations, in particular to support athletics. Prior to the September 11, 2001, terrorist attacks, the academy was the most visited man-made tourist destination in the state, attracting as many as 1.4 million visitors annually. Access to the campus was severely restricted afterward. By 2006, gates were reopened in the hopes of boosting the sagging tourist numbers, which lowered gift sales at the Visitors Center.[92]

As with any institution, times change and challenges come forth. So far, the academy has met those challenges. After more than fifty years, the academy is still held up as jewel of the country and asset of the city and state. At its fiftieth anniversary in 2004, a study found that the academy payroll, indirect jobs, and service spending total more than $561 million, plus spending by tourists and visitors to athletic events. It employs nearly 10,000 military and civilians, with another 3,500 jobs off base dependent upon spending from its workers. It remained the region's second biggest tourist draw, boosting the reputation and image of the city. It is responsible for about 5 percent of the jobs in El Paso County and about 10 percent of the local tourism industry.[93] It is a vital contributor to the regional economy but, more important, a vital component of the very identity of the city as a bastion of freedom.

AIR FORCE FACILITIES: PETERSON, CHEYENNE MOUNTAIN, AND SCHRIEVER

With increasing concerns about the Soviet Union during the Cold War, and with active conflict during the Korean War, the Air Force Air Defense Command was established in 1951, and the Ent Air Force Base was reopened as its headquarters. The facility oversaw, among other things, a network of permanent radar stations built along the coasts and in Canada. With the increasing threat of intercontinental

FIGURE 7.10. Aerial image of Ent Air Force Base in 1959. The base was converted to the Olympic Training Center in 1978. *Source*: Colorado Springs Pioneers Museum.

ballistic missiles, this relationship with Canada grew more intimate. The North American Aerospace Defense Command (NORAD) formed in September 1957, to control all continental air defense, and headquartered at Ent. Ent Air Force Base began with one permanent building: the old Methodist Sanatorium built in 1926 on Boulder Street. This became the NORAD headquarters (figure 7.10).

The Cold War and the increasingly technical military capabilities of the Soviet Union brought profound changes to the nation's airspace defense needs. Radars and fighter planes defending the coasts were no longer adequate: An all-out nuclear attack of intercontinental ballistic missiles targeting anyplace in the country would allow approximately eighteen minutes to respond. This new reality drove the need for new technologies, facilities, and organization, creating what came to be called the military-industrial complex: an interwoven system of production linking the Pentagon, the armed services, private contractors, and politicians.[94] President Eisenhower coined the phrase in his 1961 farewell speech, warning the nation of the threat to democracy he saw from the coalition of actors who would come to control the federal purse as the country became more and more militarized with ever more sophisticated technologies. As the federal government increasingly relied on the private sector for both military hardware, such as aircraft and missiles—and technical expertise from engineers, computer programmers, and telecommunications experts—the locations of the military facilities and the industries to support them shifted from the old industrial manufacturing core to the South and West, an extraordinarily rapid industrial expansion into what has been called the "Gunbelt."[95] Colorado Springs became the city that epitomized this transformation, with reliance on defense spending as its primary economic driver.

In a stunning example of Cold War logic, the Department of Defense devised an audacious plan to create the ultimate installation to monitor air defense and provide for a secure center that would continue running in the event of an attack. On May 18, 1961, construction began on NORAD's underground Combat Operations Center inside of 9,500-foot-tall Cheyenne Mountain on the southwestern edge of town, just past the Broadmoor Hotel complex. In one of the most outstanding Cold War engineering feats, tunnels were blasted into the solid granite eastern-facing walls, removing over 700,000 tons of rock. Caverns hollowed out for the new facility were reinforced with concrete domes and supporting arches. Behind two 3-foot-thick, 23-ton steel blast doors, the nerve center of the continent's defense against enemy attack would be eleven steel buildings, three stories tall, comprising more than 3,500 tons of steel plates, all sitting atop more than 900 steel springs that act like shock absorbers. It included a hospital, a 6-million-gallon water reservoir, and a ten-megawatt power plant with 500,000 gallons of diesel fuel to keep the generators running for thirty days. Later additions grew the facility to fifteen buildings using 7,000 tons of steel on 1,319 springs. In all, there were nearly three miles of tunnels and three main chambers.[96]

"America's Atomic Mountain" was fully operational by April 1966.[97] At the time, it was virtually indestructible. Using satellites, radars, and other sensors, information from all over the world is brought together at Cheyenne Mountain's Space Defense Operations Center to enable the resident four-star general to advise the president in case of an attack. Despite the design for maximum protection, the indestructability did not last long, as the Soviet Union increasingly built more powerful atomic bombs, with greater accuracy to target them. Soon it was recognized that a direct hit would destroy the entire mountain, facility and all. In later years, nuclear-armed cruise missiles evolved with the capacity to fly right up the tunnel entrance and explode inside the base. The encompassing mountain provided a symbolic feeling of safety, and certainly looked secure, but over time came to serve no real protective role.

The air force continued consolidating facilities, and Ent Air Force Base closed in 1976. The city and Department of Defense organized a land swap in 1978 whereby Ent was exchanged for land adjacent to Peterson.[98] Peterson Air Field was upgraded to Peterson Air Force Base, and the command center and personnel moved there. In 1978, the old Ent Air Force Base became the Olympic Training Center, with some military barracks repurposed for athletes, and the US Olympic Committee headquarters moving into the old NORAD building.

Central to the rise of the Gunbelt was the air force's strategy for outsourcing contracts to private firms rather than the traditional in-house design and development preferred by the army.[99] Colorado Springs had begun recruitment of high-tech manufacturing plants in the 1950s, when the city opened the Garden of the Gods Industrial Park on the northwestern edge of town and landed branch plants for two important firms: Kaman Sciences in 1957, and Hewlett Packard in 1962, followed quickly by firms such as Western Electrodynamics, Burroughs, and Maytag Electronics.[100] These firms pioneered the relocation of scientists and engineers to the city and laid the foundation for a high-tech industrial base that emerged in the 1970s, which in turn became the basis for contemporary defense contractors. In the case of Hewlett Packard, founding partner David Packard was born in Pueblo and wanted to locate a plant in Colorado Springs but was hesitant due to the lack of a nearby research university. Given his industrial clout and local familiarity, he met Governor McNichols about the need for a local major university, who then worked with local leaders to establish UCCS at the old Cragmor tuberculosis sanatorium in 1965. In addition to recruiting professionals in science and engineering nationally, Hewlett Packard relied on blue-collar assembly workers it found in abundance from, among others, spouses of Fort Carson soldiers, and over time tapped into the engineering school at UCCS for high-tech talent.

By the mid-1980s, community leaders expanded initiatives to diversify the economy and attract industries, including branch electronic plants. They claimed to have attracted 150 companies, adding 700 manufacturing jobs alone from 1970 to 1985 and earning the city the nickname "Silicon Mountain," a play on the Silicon Valley high-tech hub around San Jose, California. The city was a leader in semiconductor design and manufacturing, from which evolved a modest-sized agglomeration of technical branch plants.[101] But soon after, manufacturing jobs—particularly in the silicon chip industry—outsourced overseas, and firms left town. Leaders again turned their attention to the military, which was benefitting from the Reagan-era buildup.

As the militarization of space assumed an increasingly strategic role, Air force brass comfortable in Colorado Springs encouraged the Pentagon to transition the city's air defense communications facilities into space defense. An early success was the creation of the Air Force Space Command in 1982 headquartered at Peterson Air Force Base.[102] The Pentagon repeatedly restructured the military space programs over the next decades, creating a joint US Space Command in 1985 at the top of the chain. Its main mission was to weave space technology into the military's everyday work of fighting wars. The rapid expansion into space required a new facility built in 1983, for security reasons located about ten miles east of Peterson on the isolated plains. Falcon Air Force Station, renamed in 1998 to Schriever Air Force Base, became the headquarters for missions, among other tasks, to oversee the global positioning system (GPS) satellites and the military missions of the space shuttle program. The $2 billion Consolidated Space Operations Center at Schriever became operational in 1985 and employed more than 1,900 military and civilian personnel, with an affiliated Space Warfare Center dedicated in 1993.[103] Defense against missiles in space led Colorado Springs to strengthen its defense industry functions. Notably, space programs require perpetual research and investment in partnership with private-sector firms, ensuring the gravy train kept coming from federal coffers. A process of institutionalized innovation was set in motion, all flowing from the federal trough.

An agglomeration of space defense facilities matured in the mid-1980s to serve the larger national market from a base in Colorado Springs. The list of defense contractors with operations in town includes all the major national firms, for example, Braxton Technologies, Booz Allen Hamilton, Raytheon, Boeing, Northrop Grumman, Harris, and Lockheed Martin. Much of the local costs involve labor, requiring hundreds of programmers typing code each day. By 1985 Colorado Springs housed 35,000 military personnel, plus 7,300 civilian federal employees. Its military payroll of $507 million was almost one-half of the state's total, providing jobs for more than 60,000 people.

In the twenty-first century, space became even more central to the Department of Defense, with the secretary of defense vowing to make air force "the executive agent for space," and Colorado Springs vying to become the executive home.[104] At the start of 2002, a four-star general in Colorado Springs commanded the Air Force Space Command, the US Space Command, and NORAD. Peterson and Cheyenne Mountain brought in $618 million to the local economy, employing 5,692 military and 3,470 civilian workers, while Schriever brought $294 million and hired 2,026 military and 2,016 civilian workers. Colorado Springs had reached the apex, the space defense capital of the country, even though the original US Space Command was disbanded in 2002 and the Cheyenne Mountain Operations Center was placed on "warm standby" in 2006 as control was consolidated at Peterson.

Despite losing the coveted US Space Command and the downgrading of the Cheyenne Mountain Complex, Colorado Springs can still claim to be the nation's space capital. The Colorado Springs–based Air Force Space Command has about 40,000 personnel assigned to bases and satellite ground stations around the world and is responsible for the operation of the GPS, communications, and missile-warning satellites. Many of these functions are controlled at nearby Schriever Air Force Base. The North American Aerospace Defense Command and Northern Command remain headquartered at Peterson Air Force Base and continue to play the central role in air, space, and missile defense: "A great deal of our network is in Colorado Springs," said a vice president for Boeing's Missile Defense Systems.[105] Finally, in 2019, President Trump created a new US Space Command, eventually to be the Space Force, an entire new branch of the armed forces, and Colorado Springs was announced as its interim headquarters. The military expects large growth in the next decade.

THE DEFENSE ECONOMY

For the first seventy years of the city's history, the military played no role whatsoever in the economy or land use. For the second eighty years, the military has become the dominant economic driver, with facilities occupying large expanses in the metropolitan area, and active duty personnel, civilian defense contractors, and military retirees fundamentally shaping the social environment (figure 7.11). How did this dramatic transformation come about?

Regional planners Mia Gray and Ann Markusen point to the success of "recruit and parlay," a process whereby the city transformed assets recruited for one era into inputs for another.[106] The initial success of Fort Carson established a military-friendly environment and excess supply of blue-collar workers; the nascent Air Defense Command helped attract the Air Force Academy, which in turn attracted more air force facilities and a high-tech sector that brought skilled professionals and associated defense contract firms to the city. The initial stages—particularly attracting Fort Carson, Ent Air Force Base, and the Air Force Academy—were driven by a well-planned and organized local booster effort. Afterward, national defense imperatives and military leaders' preference for Colorado Springs drove the agglomeration of aerospace defense facilities in the city. Today the city has one of the highest concentrations of high-ranking military personnel in the nation.

Military-friendly cities also serve as favorable retirement communities. In Colorado Springs, retired military are a large percentage of the regional population and strongly contribute to the social ambiance. The Economic Development Corporation (EDC) estimates about 54,000 veterans live in the metro area, and Fort Carson claims 98,000 veterans live in Congressional District 5, the third-largest number in the country.[107] The city was recently ranked second nationally

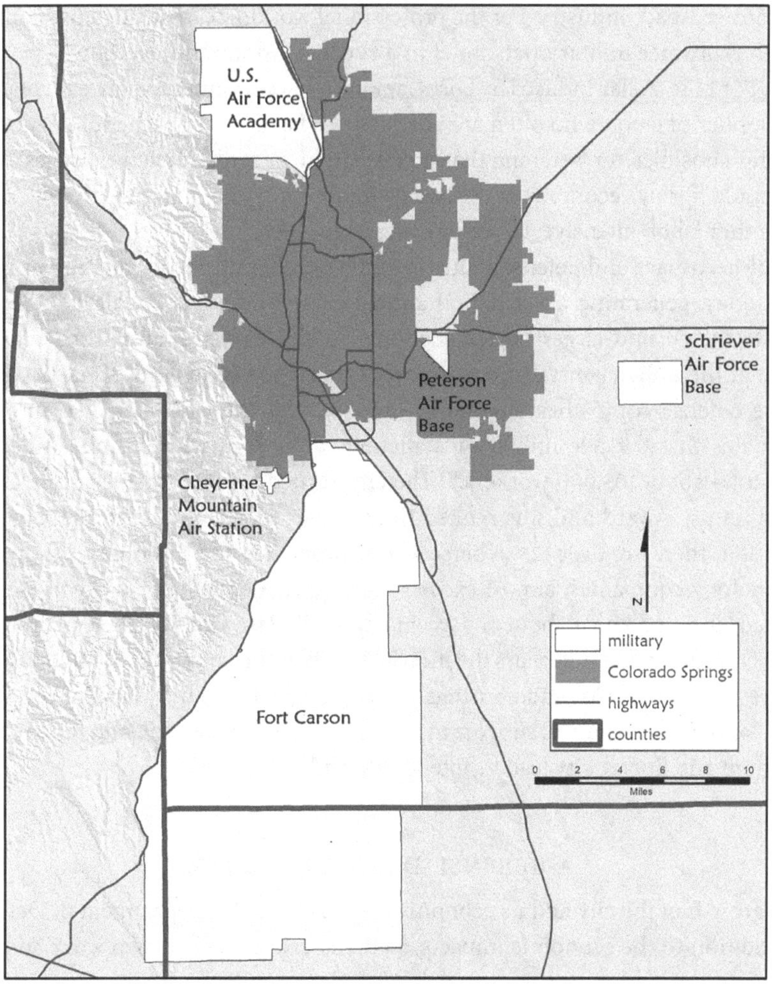

FIGURE 7.11. Map of the military facilities in Colorado Springs. *Source:* Cartography by author.

for military veterans.[108] The Pikes Peak Chapter of the Retired Officers Association is the largest in the country, with nearly 4,000 active members.[109] In addition to the military-friendly environment, an important attractor is federal programs and services that subsidize military personnel after they leave the service. Benefits that lower the cost of living include veterans' health care, post and base exchanges, recreational facilities and golf courses, and other services targeted toward veterans. Members of the military and their families can lay claim to some of America's most generous social welfare programs.[110]

Rather than leaving town when finished active duty service, and rather than retiring, thousands settle into civilian life here, creating a skilled workforce perfect for the aerospace industry. For the professional workforce, many defense contractors hire former military personnel in a revolving door and overflow phenomenon. For blue-collar industries, Fort Carson today continues to play a pivotal role as supplier of labor, who often are adaptable to flexible work schedules, and with federal subsidies for veterans that enable them to settle for lower wages.[111] The Colorado Springs economy in the twenty-first century has grown with call centers and other labor-intensive, lower-paying service jobs.[112]

The aerospace and defense industry is the number one economic driver in the city today, generating a $12 billion annual economic impact. Colorado Springs boasts the second-largest space economy in the United States. Total employment at the military installations in town totaled 52,662 in 2016. Some 240 aerospace defense companies operate in the city, and the Chamber of Commerce estimates that the five military installations combined with all related defense jobs total about 105,000 workers.[113] The city earned the Great American Defense Community Award and was ranked the number four city for defense jobs.[114] In addition, there are over 125 cybersecurity companies and 140 other information technology companies, almost exclusively defense dependent.[115] Defense-sector-related labor income is about 41 percent of total El Paso County labor income, and with contracts and multipliers the industry probably accounts for about half of the entire economy.[116] Colorado Springs has been called "the holy land of the Space Age," and, of importance, support for the military is interwoven into the image of freedom and liberty city leaders like to project.[117]

A DEFENSE-DEPENDENT CITY

The growth of the city and its economy owe much to the Department of Defense. In addition to the economic impacts, soldiers, cadets, and airmen work and volunteer in the community and are valued citizens, while the facilities provide cultural and recreational services to the greater population. But along with these positive influences, concerns arise at both the local and national level from excessive reliance on the military. The most pressing local concern is the overreliance economically on defense spending. City leaders have tried since the 1970s to diversify the economy, but it remains as dependent on federal defense spending as ever. The proverbial warning to not put all of your eggs in one basket may come home to roost when this spending is cut, bases close, or new defense imperatives change the focus from the local expertise to some new priority. Even in the high-tech private sector, jobs have not spilled over from the defense contractors to support strong diversity of other information technology or professional industries. Colorado Springs saw rapid declines in information technology and professional and business services from 2000 through 2015, with many young professionals leaving the city for Denver and other booming economies: "The job market in

Colorado Springs is not one for technical professionals unless you are military or former military" said a local worker in the information technology field.[118]

The great irony of course is that local leaders are vocal and strong supporters of the free market capitalist system and at the forefront promoting limited government, yet the city lives almost entirely on the federal dole. A high-level hypocrisy undermines the credibility of civic and business leaders who push the free market mantra. A 2013 study from the Brookings Institution and the *Washington Post* found Colorado Springs the most federally dependent big city in the country, with 19 percent of the labor force receiving federal paychecks.[119] A local study in 2011 found federal spending per El Paso County resident was nearly 70 percent more than the national average and contributed to about one-third of the economy.[120] So long as the gravy train continues, local leaders overlook this contradiction between philosophy and reality. And there is reason for optimism, at least from a macroeconomic viewpoint: This taxpayer spending is fertilized by the continual threat of war. Whether that means a war on communism, a war on drugs, a war on terrorism, a war on immigrants, or any other nebulous threat, investment on technological upgrades, increased fighting capacity, and more destructive weapons will seemingly never end, ensuring that the federal purse will remain open.

In Colorado Springs, two population characteristics of military dependency also affect the social environment. The first is the transient nature of active duty personnel. Soldiers and airmen are routinely reassigned to new positions around the world, and troops are deployed overseas. The reality is a short duration in any one place, leaving little connection and commitment to where you happen to be living at the time. Investment in housing is minimal, and fleeting place ties create little motivation for volunteer work in schools or elsewhere in the community. Given that over 25,000 solders are posted to Fort Carson, and 70 percent live off post, many local residents rarely develop strong connections to Colorado Springs. The second demographic is the large military retirement community, over 50,000 local citizens. Living on a fixed income, this community tends to be extremely tax averse and, without young children, unmotivated to support public schools. Commitment to local philanthropic organizations is weak, and resistance to publicly funded services is strong. Together these two bodies, over 10 percent of the local population, maintain connections to Fort Carson and the air force bases but much weaker ties to the civic life of the city overall.

Perhaps Colorado Springs leaders should not worry too much about being overly reliant upon Department of Defense spending—this trend is happening nationally. Since the attacks on September 11, 2001, budgets for most nonmilitary foreign-affairs-related government agencies and institutions have been essentially stagnant, and domestic spending on civilian social welfare programs has been slashed, but during the same time period the defense budget skyrocketed to historically high levels.[121]

The military has become the de facto last outpost of Big Government paternalism in the United States.[122] The military is becoming all that's left: the last federal institution standing.[123] This position means the military is asked to increasingly take on roles it never did before: nation building, diplomacy, cultural interpretation, disaster relief, environmental restoration, drug eradication, and policing the border, among others. Many of these efforts will be led from Colorado Springs. But someday we might be concerned that we ask the military to do too much, for as former Pentagon employee Rosa Brooks commented, "If your only functioning government institution is the military, everything looks like war."[124]

8

Liberty

> Colorado Springs stands for freedom, perhaps more than any other American city.
>
> —*COLORADO SPRINGS GAZETTE*, 2012[1]

Colorado Springs was founded and grew within the context of the larger Rocky Mountain region. As the West was settled and became more familiar to Americans to the east, its reputation grew to be the region that rewards individual enterprise, independence, and freedom. The iconic self-made men and women of the West became ingrained into the image of the place and the very identity of the people. The West embodies the concept of liberty fundamental to the core values of our nation. Yet liberty means different things to different people. As we have seen, liberty for health seekers meant freedom from disease. In another instance, liberty means freedom from repression. Colorado Springs, along with the rest of the region, attracted immigrants fleeing the stifling constraints of culture, religion, and work in eastern cities and industries. The West was the place to shape your life according to your own wishes, seek new opportunities, and start anew. As has been for immigrants time and again, the allure of liberty is a compelling draw. In Colorado Springs, liberty has come to mean freedom from rules and regulations that impede the ability to make money. This belief is supported through a free-market-oriented political culture with a strong adherence to private property rights, resistance to taxes, and limited government intervention in the economy. The antiregulatory ideology directly translates into a built environment of low-density, suburban housing commonly called urban sprawl.

DOI: 10.5876/9781646421688.c008

AFRICAN AMERICAN FOUNDATIONS IN COLORADO SPRINGS

Long neglected, the story of the African American experience in the West has gained sufficient attention to become an established topic of study. From the Buffalo Soldiers who were integral to US military operations during the Indian wars to independent farmers or ranchers and utopian community settlers, African Americans participated in the settlement of the West, and of Colorado Springs, from the earliest days.[2] In fact, George Motley, a civilian orderly in General Palmer's Civil War regiment, accompanied Palmer on his arrival to the as-yet-unfounded city in 1869 and remained until his death in 1916.[3]

The newfound freedom for African Americans in the post–Civil War era did not create immediate flight out of the South. Many ex-slaves had no means to travel or knowledge of where to go, so for most the only option was life as sharecroppers or tenant farmers on lands where they had long lived. Racial animosity and Jim Crow terrorism kept many Black people permanently indebted to white landowners and unable to flee. Labor shortages during World War I, when European immigration was curtailed and American soldiers went to fight in Belgium and France, stimulated mass migration of Black people out of the rural South into the northern and western industrial cities. However, sizeable numbers of Black families also fled the South and headed west in search of opportunities prior to the northern migrations of the twentieth century. Some of these people helped establish Colorado Springs.

Miner and cook David Polk Reed and family came from Kansas in 1872, the first Black family to move to the city, with many more to soon follow. The Black community suffered from de facto segregation and racial bias that determined where they could live and what jobs they could occupy, but the social climate was certainly preferable to the outright violence afflicting the Jim Crow South. The most prevalent jobs available were porters, janitors, teamsters, or common laborers, along with waiters and cooks and some skilled tradesmen. Hundreds worked the coal mines north of the city, or in the railyards for the numerous railroad companies. Some owned businesses, particularly barbershops, restaurants, and boardinghouses, or they worked as blacksmiths.[4] Women worked as household servants or washerwomen, or took in laundry. There were a few boardinghouses that were open to Black people near the downtown hotels, but the majority of African American residences were segregated to the industrial zones along the railway lines and in the floodplains. Therefore several concentrated African American neighborhoods developed, along Shooks Run, in the east along the Santa Fe line, particularly south of Pikes Peak Avenue, in the southwest along the D&RG line near the Conejos Street neighborhood, and in a small concentration on the near west side (figure 8.1). These segregated spaces, while among the least desirable in the city, were a step above the typical post–Civil War African American "shantytowns" that grew in cities across the country as "cabins in the creek bottoms."[5] The Colorado Springs neighborhoods offered a sense of

FIGURE 8.1. Number of African Americans, 1879–1905. Each circle is a unique address, the size of the circle the number of times that address was listed. Addresses for the same resident were only recorded in the first year listed. Many of the locations were boarding homes or other types of rooms for rent, so many people might list the same address while living in separate rooms. *Source*: City Business Directories, Colorado Springs Pioneers Museum; cartography by author.

community with tightly clustered houses, both self-built and others professionally constructed. The African American urban neighborhood was a relatively modern phenomenon and liberating for those brought up on southern plantations.

The overall Black population was small but continued to establish itself and push against barriers to integration. Payne Chapel, of the African Methodist

Episcopal Church, was the first Black congregation and remained influential in the community for many years. The church was established in 1876, in the Pueblo Avenue stone building that still stands today built in 1890 (albeit now serving as a brewery).[6] Saint John's Baptist Church began in 1878 and was a second early congregation of importance for the African American community. The community created Black Masonic lodges and integrated into schools, with the first Black graduate from the Colorado Springs High School (today Palmer High School) in 1885 and the first Black graduate from Colorado College in 1906. Several attempts at tuberculosis sanatoriums dedicated to African Americans operated as early as 1910. In 1887 one of the eight police patrolmen was Black, the first African American newspaper briefly ran in 1891 with others to follow, and the first Black constable was elected 1897. Some African Americans were highly skilled professionals, such as Charles Collins, who ran a riding school in 1889, and Dr. Richard Sudyam Grant, physician and surgeon who arrived in 1904. K. D. Stroud started his own hauling business and eventually a trucking company by the 1920s.[7] The city opened a chapter of the National Negro Business League in 1902 and a chapter of the NAACP in 1918.

Despite gains, the African American community still suffered discrimination. Students were integrated into public schools but were not allowed to participate in clubs or team athletics until 1925, and the school district did not hire a Black teacher until 1954. The high school principal at first excluded Black students from the new school cafeteria in 1916, but public protest quickly removed that restriction. Children were excluded from Boy Scouts, the YMCA and YWCA, and Black residents were not served in restaurants or hotels and were segregated to the balcony in theaters. Despite such indignities, one movement for racial tolerance shone a ray of hope for minorities in Colorado Springs during a particularly dark period in the state's history. The Ku Klux Klan wielded great influence and power in Denver and in state politics in the 1920s. In 1925 Governor Morley and the House of Representatives answered to the state Grand Dragon, Dr. John Galen Locke. Administrative appointments were made to Klan loyalists and appropriations to most state agencies cut, arousing the ire of two state senators from El Paso County who led a fight against Klan-backed legislation.[8] City leaders woke up after a near win by Klansmen in municipal elections on April 6, after which the Civic League quickly formed to fight Klan influence in El Paso County.[9] Thousands of local residents signed on with this movement that spread statewide, and Colorado Springs arose as the leader and home of an anti-Klan rebellion.[10] Klan leaders in state government vowed to undermine Colorado Springs elected representatives and eliminate any support for the city.[11] The *Gazette* ran articles and editorialized against this menace, calling it a civic duty to purge government of this threat to democracy.[12] Eventually Klan influence diminished in the state. Although the anti-Klan movement was largely led by business interests worried

TABLE 8.1. African American population

	Colorado Springs		*El Paso County*	
Year	*Number*	*Percentage*	*Number*	*Percentage*
1880	133	3.1	159	2.0
1890	439	3.9	571	2.7
1900	875	4.1	1,033	3.2
1910	1,107	3.8	1,330	3.1
1920	1,005	3.4	1,088	2.5
1930	965	2.9	1,096	2.2
1940	1,057	2.9	1,122	2.1
1950	1,176	2.6	1,230	1.7
1960	3,172	4.5	5,069	3.5
1970	7,045	5.2	12,226	5.2
1980	11,961	5.6	19,058	6.2
1990	19,610	7.0	28,257	7.1
2000	23,677	6.6	33,670	6.5
2010	26,253	5.7	38,492	6.2

Source: US Census Bureau.

about the ill effects on attracting commerce and industry, there were genuine concerns about racial tolerance, social tranquility, the general prosperity, and the very real threat to representative governance. The community stance against the Klan, while largely unknown today, stands as a bright moment in the city's history.

The African American community grew from its early foundation, but despite the overall accommodating environment, there was little to attract new Black migrants in the 1920s, as better jobs were readily available in factories in the northern industrial cities, nor during the Depression of the 1930s, when few jobs were available anywhere. Population numbers stagnated or declined (table 8.1).

World War II changed the demographic picture of the city, when the first troops arrived at Camp Carson in May 1942. The army remained segregated until an executive order signed by President Truman in 1948, so many services developed to serve Black troops. Out of the demand to serve the growing Black community arose one of Colorado Springs' most famous entrepreneurs, Fannie Mae Duncan. An immigrant to the city as a young girl from Oklahoma in 1933 with her widowed mother and siblings, Fannie Mae Bragg worked to support the family as she completed school at North Junior High and Colorado Springs High School, where she was the first in her family to graduate in 1938. She married Ed Duncan after graduation, then landed a job at the Post Exchange (PX) soda fountain for Black troops at Fort Carson. This work exposed her to the food and

FIGURE 8.2. Everybody Welcome at the Cotton Club, circa 1965. *Source*: Colorado Springs Pioneers Museum.

entertainment service industry and also strengthened her desire to run her own shop. She secured a loan from a wealthy Broadmoor resident Ed had worked for and opened Duncan's Café and Bar at 25 West Colorado Avenue in 1948. With continued success (despite the death of Ed), she bought the neighboring building and expanded the operation into the Cotton Club, named after the famous Harlem establishment (figure 8.2). Fannie Mae Duncan overcame an initial refusal by city manager Earl Mosley to grant her a business license on the grounds of being both a woman and African American, and later resistance from the police chief Irvin Bruce to the desegregated, mixed Black and white crowds who enjoyed the club. She convinced Chief Bruce that she was in the right and afterward posted the famous "Everybody Welcome" sign on the door to the club. Said Fannie Mae, "Good friends come in every color."[13] Fannie Mae Duncan expanded her business into a barbershop, gift store, beauty shop, and more, but it was the Cotton Club that was her legacy. Top-tiered acts such as Fats Domino, Louis Armstrong, Lionel Hampton, Duke Ellington, Bo Diddley, Little Richard, Count Basie, and B.B. King played shows at the club, and comedian Flip Wilson credited Fannie Mae for giving him his start while serving as a GI at Fort Carson.

The city slowly eliminated racial segregation after activists challenged the theater segregation and restaurant exclusion policies. Mayor Earl Mosley signed a 1947 city order that finally permitted Black children to swim in the Monument

Valley public pool every day, rather than once per week on a designated day and that eliminated discrimination in city-owned facilities. Yet for much of the success of the Cotton Club, Fannie Mae Duncan remained disillusioned that the Black performers at her club could not stay in city hotels. In fact, throughout the early twentieth century, African Americans could not stay in many towns overnight across the country, leading to the creation of the *Negro Motorists Green Book*. This guide for African American travelers listed safe lodging in a sort of underground directory published from 1936 to 1966. Colorado Springs had numerous listings, with one house consistently listed over many years at 418 East Cucharras Street, which unfortunately burned down in 2014.[14] To address the lodging problem for her guests, Fannie Mae Duncan purchased an 1891 Victorian mansion destined for demolition and moved it in three pieces to her home at 615 North Corona Street in the Shooks Run neighborhood. With forty-three rooms and 8,000 square feet, the house became a place for her to board guests playing at her club. The home became a point of pride in the Black community.[15]

While the vestiges of overt segregation were largely gone by the 1960s, housing remained a problem area as redlining and other discriminatory practices excluded Black people from much of the market. But progress continued as the first Black City Council member was elected in 1969, and in 1983 Leon Young became vice mayor. A blow for the historic African American landscape of the city came in the 1970s, however, when the national craze for urban renewal swept city planners. Urban renewal authority planners targeted the "blighted" sections of the city south of Colorado Avenue for renewal. As happened throughout much of urban America in the 1960s and 1970s, the modernist zeal for renewal meant wholesale destruction of the dense urban fabric that grew organically over decades to be replaced with large-scale, institutional structures occupying entire city blocks. And by no coincidence, the landscapes deemed "blighted" were usually minority neighborhoods with low-income housing and a plethora of shops and businesses to serve that community. Colorado Springs was no exception, and the blocks from Sierra Madre Street to Weber Street south of Colorado Avenue, the areas of historically African American concentrations, were bulldozed (figure 8.3). In the heart of this zone was the Cotton Club, razed in 1975. Today the city's legacy to urban renewal are numerous large office buildings, the Pikes Peak Center, the Sun Plaza, the County Courthouse and Jail, and County Office buildings—large institutional structures that, in the spirit of modernism, created a clear break from the past and embraced supposed rational progress. The scale and use of these buildings kill street activity as they present an imposing, sterile face to the pedestrian with limited access and monotonous walls lining the city block. Today's vibrant pedestrian zone hits an abrupt halt as one walks south on Tejon Street and reaches Colorado Avenue and the urban renewal projects, until shops again pick up three or four blocks south (i.e., if pedestrians are determined enough to walk

FIGURE 8.3. Aerial photo looking north, circa 1948, showing neighborhoods later torn down for urban renewal. The blocks highlighted have completely changed, as did others adjacent to the east, west, and south, plus many other individual lots throughout the downtown. Even the county courthouse, now the Pioneers Museum, was on the list for demolition. The Cotton Club was on Colorado Avenue just off this image to the west. *Source*: Colorado Springs Pioneers Museum.

past the judicial complex and parking garages). The Cotton Club and the many other shops in the small-scale buildings that foster human interaction were sacrificed in the name of modernity and a bright vision for a clean urban future. Along with the destruction of other important buildings such as the Burns Theater and the Gazette Building on Pikes Peak Avenue (not to mention the Antlers Hotel), the urban fabric now is unfortunately severely overrun with surface parking lots or large impersonal institutional structures where once stood shops, club, houses, and businesses—the stuff that encourages human mingling and makes a commercial zone function (figure 8.4).

Much of the early African American neighborhoods are gone, particularly the largest in what was then the southeast of the city. Urban renewal again took some of those as the Lowell neighborhood developed after South Junior High closed in 1983, but most simply fell to redevelopment as businesses and light industry paying higher rents replaced old housing stock.[16] The neighborhoods around the AT&SF depot were particularly hard hit as clearance slowly removed nearby houses. Housing that remains in the neighborhood along south Cascade Avenue towards Mill Street gives a clue to the character of the old blue-collar districts of

FIGURE 8.4. Changes in the urban landscape resulting from urban renewal projects. West side, 100 block South Nevada Ave (top); west side, 100 block South Tejon St. (middle), west side, 200 block Tejon St. (bottom). *Source*: Colorado Springs Pioneers Museum; photos by author.

the city. With a stroll through the old Shooks Run neighborhood, one can see African American churches and Masonic Lodge remaining despite demographic change to predominantly white residents. The Payne Chapel remains as a historic landmark at Pueblo and Weber Streets, though perhaps less appreciated as so by the brewery patrons.

PUBLIC TRANSPORTATION TROLLEYS

As Colorado Springs became more settled, and the railroads, mills, coal mines, and other industries required labor, working-class neighborhoods grew around the downtown and on the west side. Although small in area by twenty-first-century norms, the distances across the city quickly became too great to walk

FIGURE 8.5. Early trolley on Pikes Peak Avenue in front of the Antlers Hotel. *Source*: Colorado Springs Pioneers Museum.

when going to and from work. The tyranny of space was again proving a barrier to mobility in a growing city. Because cars were not yet available in the earliest days and horses were a luxury few could afford, some means of private or public transport became necessary.

The owners of the Colorado Midland Railroad, with their railyard workshop at what is today 21st Street, started the first horse-drawn trolley line to get laborers from Colorado Springs over to their workshops. The Colorado Springs & Manitou Street Railway began in November 1887, with a line that by 1888 ran from the Santa Fe Depot on Pikes Peak Avenue west to 28th Street in Colorado City, along Colorado Avenue. Another route ran a line along Tejon Street. The company incorporated as the El Paso Rapid Transit Company in 1889, after which lines were electrified and extended to Manitou Springs and other destinations, including Roswell and the Broadmoor (figure 8.5).[17] There was even a short-lived line to the base of Palmer Park to tap into the Boulevard Park speculative land development project, but by 1892 lack of travel shut that down and the eastern extension ended in Knob Hill. The company built a powerhouse for the lines at Moreno and Cascade, along with a car barn and shops at Moreno and Tejon Streets.[18]

The trolley company suffered through the recession after 1893. Upgrades were neglected; the lines continued to serve the city but required attention.[19] In 1901, Winfield Scott Stratton, ever attentive to the needs of the working class, bought the company and used his considerable fortunes from Cripple Creek to reinvigorate the city trolley system under the guise of the Colorado Springs Rapid Transit Railway Company, later the Colorado Springs and Interurban Railway Company.

He spent over $2 million to create one of the best transit systems in the country.[20] Lines were greatly extended, including a popular route to Stratton Park at the entrance to Cheyenne Canyon, where bands played in the pavilion on weekends. This line also provided access to the Boulevard Park baseball stadium in Ivywild, home of the Millionaires team, and "Bathhouse John" Coughlin's zoo and amusement park along Cheyenne Creek. Prospect Lake, Evergreen Cemetery, and eastern neighborhoods were connected; a new power plant was built on Sierra Madre Street; and twenty-nine luxury trolley cars were built in the shops on Tejon and Moreno between 1905 and 1911.[21]

Stratton was committed to the project and ensured his legacy continued after he died. The company kept fares low, extended new lines throughout the city, and took out $225,000 group life insurance on its employees—the first corporation in Colorado, and the first street railway in the United States, to do so. It also financed a home-buying plan for its employees; within ten years, 85 percent of its workers owned their own homes.[22] The line was profitable until 1911.

At the height of the trolley's success, the line served nearly all parts of the city. Mobility means liberty, the ability to work and live in a place one prefers. The city was well served by public transit with mixed-use, walkable neighborhoods and easy access to nearby schools, grocery stores, parks, and other services (figure 8.6). The bungalow houses popular in the first decades of the twentieth century were about 1,000-square-foot homes (the national average in 1950 was 983 square feet), often sold as kits from Sears Roebuck and other stores for home assembly. Colorado Springs was a city of quaint little neighborhoods, with diverse land uses in dense settings, the type of neighborhoods that New Urbanists planners of the twenty-first century try to replicate in urban environments today (figure 8.7).[23]

Despite the commitment to the trolley company, it could not compete with changing technologies.[24] The first Model T was released by the Ford Motor Company in October 1908, and the affordability of this mass-produced icon caused rapid expansion of commercial and private automobile ownership. Buses began competing with trolleys in 1926; they proved more flexible to plan and open routes for and cheaper to operate. Stratton Park also closed in the late 1920s, and after systematically shutting down unprofitable lines, all trolley operations ceased by April 1932. The Colorado Springs Bus Company began operations the next month. Most tracks were torn up as the automobile became the dominant form of transport in America.

URBAN SPRAWL

In twentieth-century America, nothing represented freedom more than the personal automobile. The suburban dream, popularized by the iconic laid-back, outdoor living of Southern California in the first half of the twentieth century,

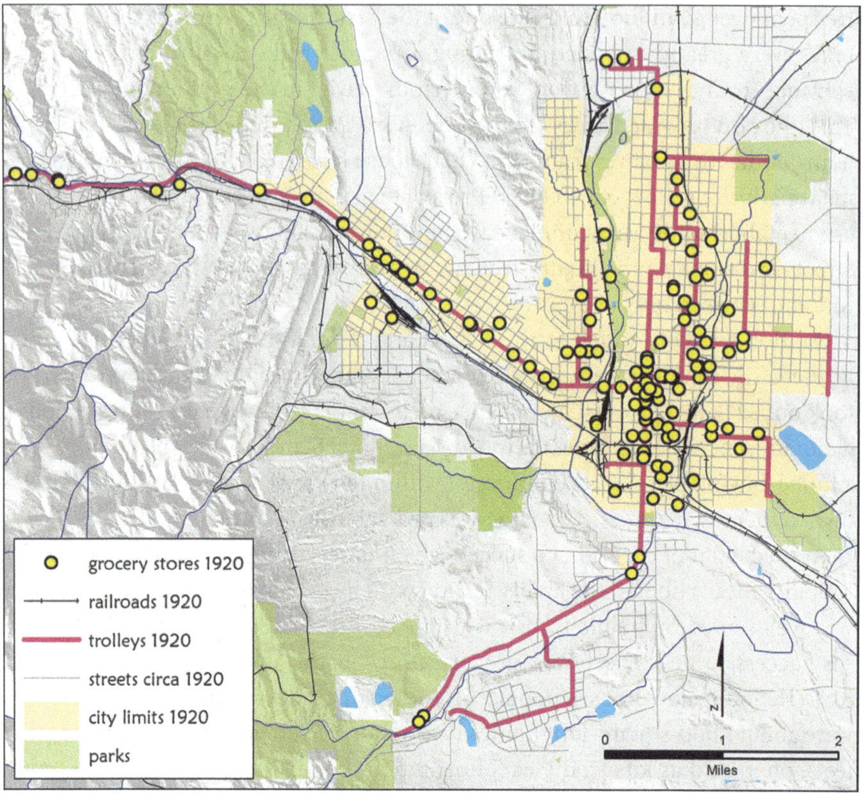

FIGURE 8.6. In 1920 there were 135 neighborhood grocery stores and nearby public transit that fully served the city, including access to parks. *Source*: City Directory, 1920, Colorado Springs Pioneers Museum; cartography by author.

swept the nation, and the car made it all possible.[25] Federal loan guarantees from the Federal Housing Administration (FHA) and the Department of Veterans Affairs (VA) provided the means to home ownership, and the suburban standalone house in a residential tract became the urban pattern, including that in Colorado Springs.

The demise of the streetcar system did not immediately lead to wholesale adoption of automobiles and rapid suburbanization in Colorado Springs. The Great Depression kept wages and employment low and temporarily stifled growth. Post–World War II, however, saw the great boom in the city that went along with the population boom in the country. An infusion of defense spending injected wealth into the town and attracted defense contractors. Add the campus for the University of Colorado in 1965, the Olympic Training Center in 1977, and a healthy manufacturing base in the 1980s, and the city attracted new businesses and many migrants. Colorado Springs went on an annexation spree

FIGURE 8.7. Brochure promoting home ownership, mid-1940s. Said the text, "In this serene land of far horizons, where life is gracious and unhurried, human and material values naturally assume their proper perspective." The suburban ideal was powerful in Colorado Springs. *Source*: Colorado College Tutt Library, Special Collections.

to incorporate peripheral areas into the city limits (figure 8.8). The net result: the population changed from just over 45,000 in 1950 to more than 416,000 in 2010, and the density decreased from about 4,800 persons per square mile to just over 2,000 as houses got larger and more spread out (table 8.2). Added to these numbers are the even lower-density ex-urban McMansions built in northern El Paso County outside of the city limits that now spread to the Douglas county line.

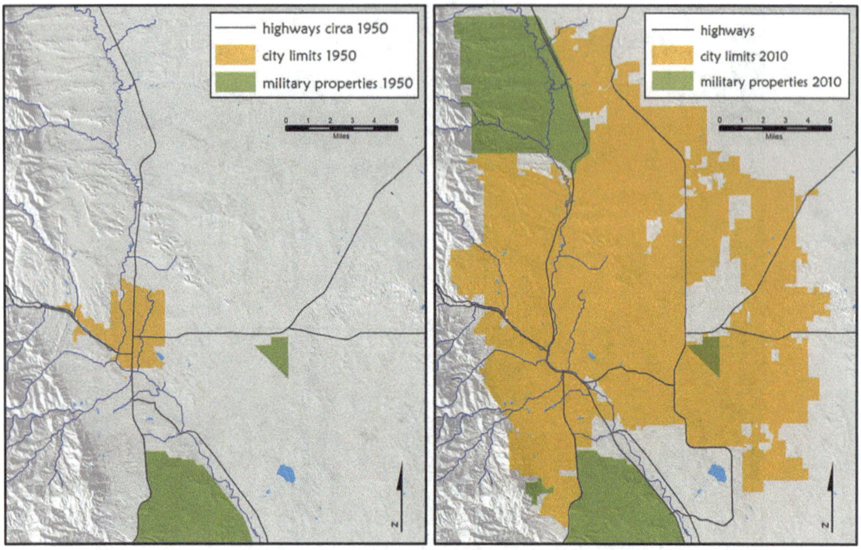

FIGURE 8.8. City annexation, 1950 (left) to 2010 (right). *Source:* Cartography by author.

TABLE 8.2. Colorado Springs historical population and area

Year	*City Population*	*County/Metro Population*	*City Incorporated Area (sq. mi)*	*City Density (persons per sq. mi)*
1900	21,085	31,602	7.0	3,012
1910	29,078	43,321	7.2	4,039
1920	30,105	44,027	8.2	3,671
1930	33,237	49,570	8.2	4,053
1940	36,789	54,025	8.2	4,486
1950	45,472	74,523	9.5	4,787
1960	70,194	143,742	16.4	4,280
1970	135,501	235,972	63.5	2,134
1980	215,150	309,424	109.3	1,968
1990	281,140	397,014	183.2	1,535
2000	344,076	491,750	186.0	1,850
2010	416,427	645,613	194.8	2,138

Source: U.S. Census Bureau, City of Colorado Springs.

Automobile transportation infrastructure tried to keep up. The main highway north to Denver originally ran along Cascade Avenue, past Roswell on the north end of the city and across Monument Creek, through the Pikeview coal camp and roughly following the railroad tracks and over Monument Hill (figure 8.9). After the disastrous 1935 flood that took out nearly every bridge in the city, the highway

FIGURE 8.9. Old bridge crossing Monument Creek on the Denver Highway that connected to Cascade Avenue, circa 1915. Image on the right shows bridge ruins near Mark Dabling Blvd. *Source*: Colorado Springs Pioneers Museum (left), photo by author (right).

route moved from Cascade to Nevada Avenue, avoiding Monument Creek until the gap between Popes Bluffs and Austin Bluffs near Pikeview. But these early highways were insufficient for the growing mobility and speeds of automobiles. A national interstate highway system was first explored in Congress in 1944, culminating in the Federal Aid Highway Act signed by President Eisenhower in 1956 that envisioned and propelled the interstate system to connect urban centers. Interstate 25 was planned as the principal route along the Colorado Front Range.

Interstate 25 roughly followed the train tracks from Monument Hill south into the northern suburbs, but how to route the twelve-mile path through the heart of the city was up for debate. Interstates take up enormous amounts of land, and there was no linear void of unused space traversing the city. Three routes were considered: one along Union Boulevard on the (at that time) east edge of town, one along Shooks Run following the AT&SF tracks, and a third on the west side of Monument Creek, called the Walnut Street route.[26] Of course, following the existing highway along Nevada Avenue and through the wealthy and well-positioned Old North End neighborhood was not considered at all, given the political clout of the neighborhood residents. The chosen route followed the path of least resistance, which meant Walnut Street along the west side of the creek, through lower-income areas (figure 8.10). The state acquired 503 acres on 321 separate parcels from 236 property owners to clear land for the interstate.[27] Overlaying aerial images and historic maps on the current land use identifies approximately 500 structures that once existed on 300 city blocks ultimately torn out (figure 8.11). Continued widening and expanding the Interstate and its exits over the years solidify the barrier this transportation corridor forms between the downtown and the near west side (figure 8.12). One casualty after the interstate was completed in 1960 was the old Conejos Street neighborhood, the city's original Jewish quarter and later a close-knit Hispanic barrio (figure 8.13). Today no houses remain in this working-class neighborhood that was isolated and hemmed in by railroads, the

FIGURE 8.10. Interstate 25 being constructed, aerial view looking south circa 1959. The image shows the Nevada Avenue interchange, where the interstate splits from the old highway route and goes west of Monument Creek. The settlement to the right of the interstate in the foreground is the Pikeview coal-mining town, the open land to the left would become part of the UCCS campus. *Source*: Colorado Tourist Brochure Collection, Colorado College Special Collections.

city power plant, other industrial expansion from the east, and the new interstate from the west.

Cheap land on the eastern fringes of town drove housing expansion as the suburban ideal was sold to American consumers. No longer were neighborhoods built one house at a time by independent builders, resulting in a somewhat organic landscape that characterizes older neighborhoods, but rather developers tapped into economies of scale through mass production to build extensive tracts of residential neighborhoods. The suburban settings typically contained a limited number of house models replicated over and over in single-use residential zones. Along with these new tracts came the high-speed arterial routes to move commuters around and corporate big-box stores and restaurant franchises in strip malls that characterize suburban America.

Colorado Springs quickly took on a suburban character. As in much of the country, this suburban craze was partially driven by white flight as wealthier Anglos fled the more crowded and diverse downtown in search of bigger houses, better schools, and segregated spaces. One result was a hollowing out of the urban core,

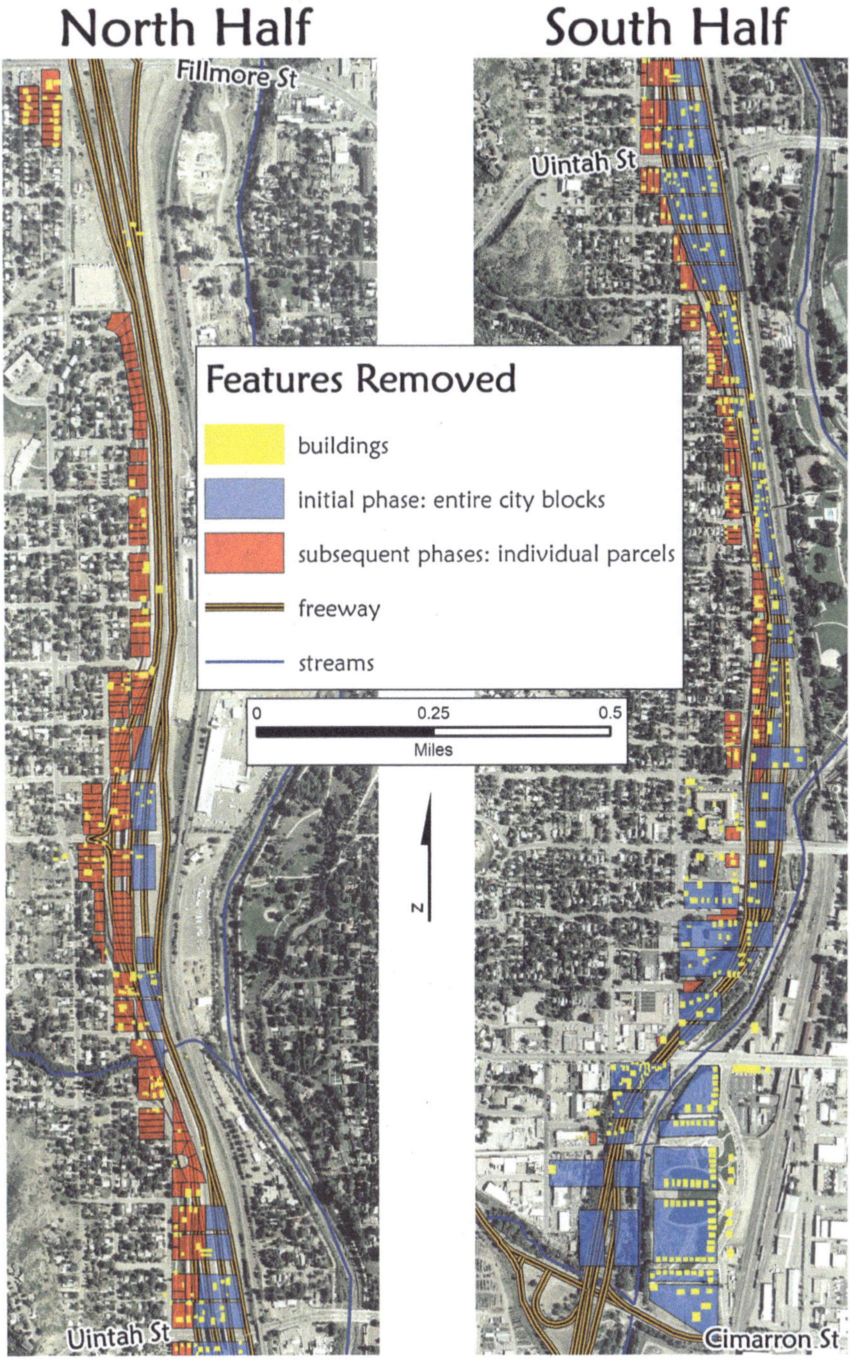

FIGURE 8.11. Removal of buildings, city blocks, and property parcels for Interstate 25, first completed in 1960. *Source*: Data compiled by author from historic imagery and maps, cartography by author.

FIGURE 8.12. The raised lanes and wall from expansion and widening of Interstate 25 creates a rigid barrier between the downtown and the near west side. *Source*: Photo by author.

FIGURE 8.13. Conejos street neighborhood, showing individual houses, 1909 (left), and photo of kids playing on "the dragon" in Conejos Park, 1958, shortly before the interstate came through. *Source*: USGS (left), Photograph by Myron Wood, © Pikes Peak Library District, 002-10405 (right).

affecting older neighborhoods (figure 8.14). As downtown population decreased and suburban population increased, Colorado School District 11 was forced to simultaneously close downtown schools while building, along with all of the other public school districts, new suburban ones (figure 8.15). This rapid expansion of the city with lower and lower densities creates new urban challenges: increased

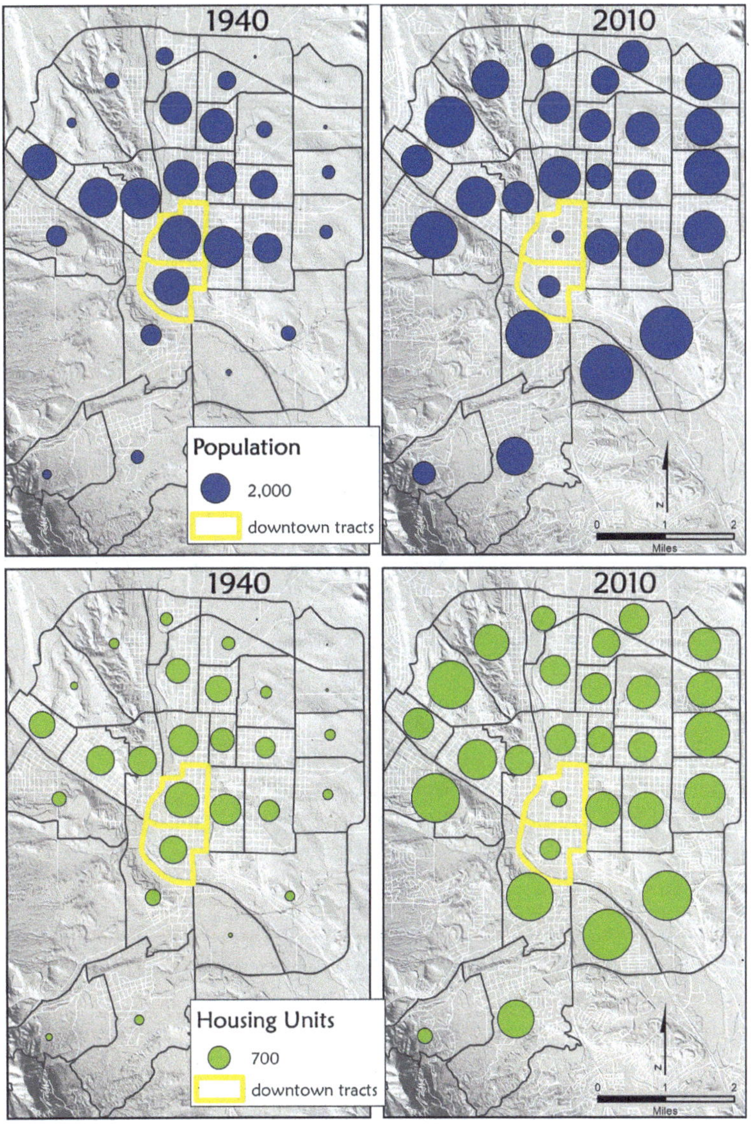

FIGURE 8.14. Population change (top) and housing unit change (bottom), 1940–2010, in twenty-eight census tracts that cover the oldest parts of the city. The two downtown census tracts show decline. *Source*: U.S. Census Bureau, historic data compiled by author; cartography by author.

asphalt pavement generates flashy and polluted runoff that erodes the banks of Fountain Creek, productive ranchland and environmentally sensitive spaces are paved over, greater distances traveled via automobile contribute to poor air quality, police and emergency responders are forced to cover wider areas, public transit is not cost effective in low-density settings, new parks and schools are expensive

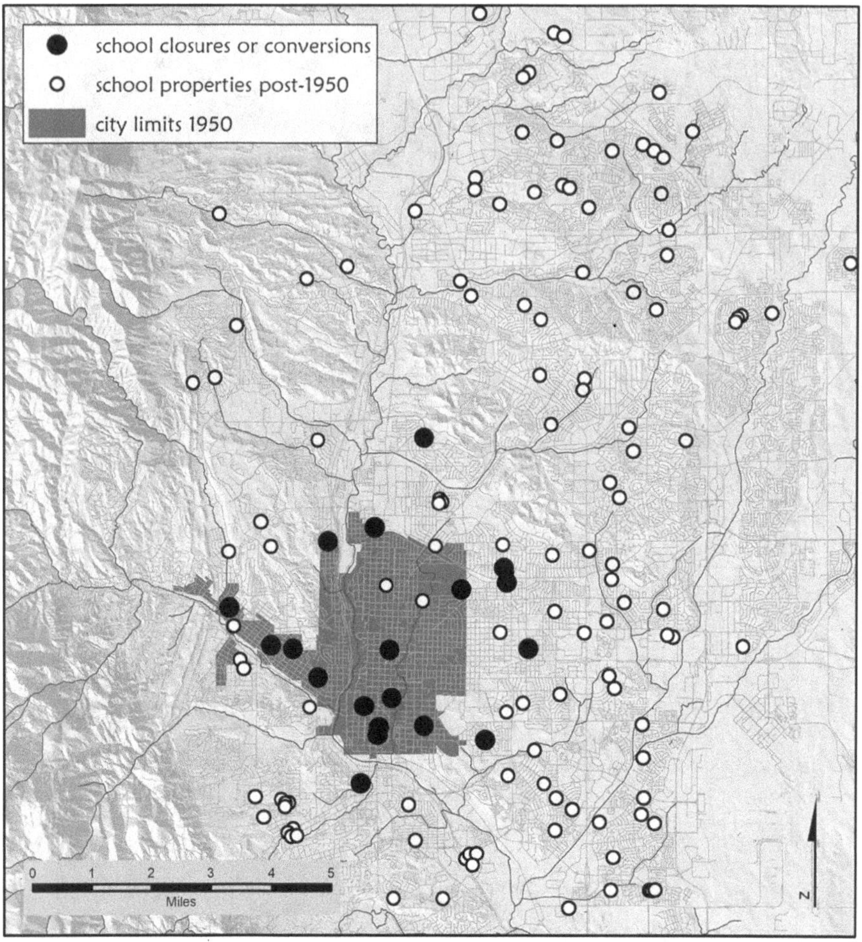

FIGURE 8.15. Schools close in the older neighborhoods while new ones open in the suburbs. *Source:* Cartography by author.

to build, and commuters are increasingly stuck in traffic jams for more hours each day. Public health officials increasingly point blame at these built environments for reducing the opportunity for children to walk outdoors, in part contributing to the rapid increase in childhood obesity seen nationally.[28] The pattern of suburban development segregates different land uses across such great distances today in Colorado Springs that automobile ownership is virtually required (figure 8.16). In 1995, the Pikes Peak Area Council of Governments estimated that residents drove an average of 11.4 million miles each day—thirty-five miles for every person and well above national norms.[29] Since 1995, annual urban vehicle miles traveled have increased by 50 percent.[30] While the popularity of the private automobile was built upon the image of personal freedom it provides, consider that teens,

FIGURE 8.16. The low-density, suburban tract home development that expands the urban fringe makes car ownership mandatory for Colorado Springs commuters. *Source*: Photo by author.

elderly, impoverished, or disabled peoples who cannot drive or cannot afford a car are severely restricted in their mobility, requiring others to drive them about or spending great time waiting on an insufficient public transit system. Dependence upon automobiles is not liberating for many.

The concerns with rapid urban sprawl were forefront in the political sphere from the late 1980s through the 1990s. Even in very Republican El Paso County, a 1988 campaign brochure to reelect a sitting Republican County Commissioner lamented that

> property taxpayers have suffered from the need to finance the building of new schools, parks, and libraries; to maintain a continually growing system of roads and streets, and to develop and maintain expensive drainage systems made necessary by rapid growth. Well-planned growth, rather than spontaneous urban sprawl, is imperative. Urban sprawl and huge developments on the prairie create severe demands for services—new school buildings, new parks, new or improved roads, new drainage systems. Unless growth is well-planned, the financial drain on you, the property taxpayer, becomes more and more burdensome.[31]

Another commissioner campaign ad in 1990 said that "the number one issue facing us today is growth and development" and called for strong master planning.[32] "We've become a community of cul-de-sacs" said city councilman Bill Guman in a *Gazette Telegraph* feature labeled "Sprawlorado Springs," stating that the city could be the poster child for car dependence.[33] Concern was raised that the costs of urban sprawl were not paid by those creating it. Given the low property taxes in Colorado Springs and the gross inefficiencies associated with low-density residential areas, the city struggles to adequately provide services. Mayor Suthers recognized in 2018 that residential property taxes don't pay for the services and infrastructure required.[34] Municipalities such as Colorado Springs end up subsidizing growth

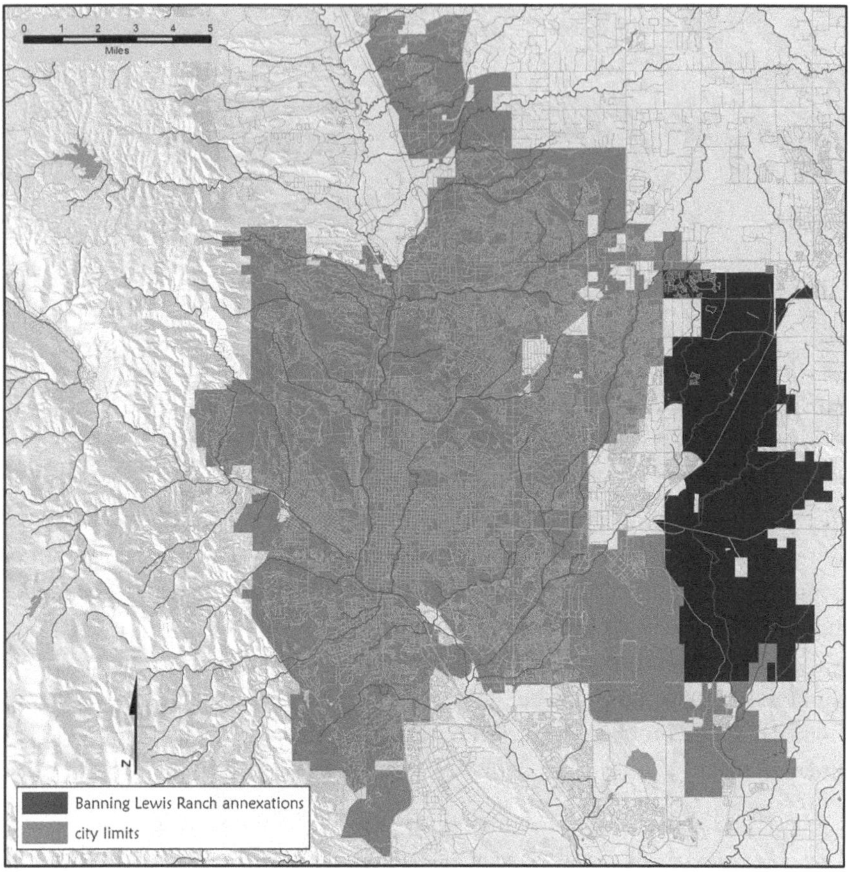

FIGURE 8.17. The Banning Lewis Ranch, annexed by the city in 1988. *Source*: Cartography by author.

by undercharging for new infrastructure, roads, schools and parks, and services. This is a classic case of concentrated benefits with dispersed costs; the few who build these projects gain much at the expense of the many who pay small enough amounts through their property and sales tax to not really notice. The externalities of growth are not fairly paid for by those who create it, with one former city councilor bemoaning policies that "allowed the development community to build poor and inadequate road and stormwater infrastructure and then ask citizens for new taxes . . . to go back and fix it."[35] Concerned citizens advocate for higher impact fees charged up front to developers and home buyers to pay for the cost of growth.

The story is perhaps best illustrated by the Banning Lewis Ranch, an enormous tract of land annexed into the city in 1988 on the east side (figure 8.17). Developers first envisioned 175,000 people at full buildout in this annexation alone. Because of the concerns with urban sprawl, the city annexation agreement imposed impact fees on the Banning Lewis property that sought to shift the costs of the suburban development to the builders and buyers, rather than to taxpayers in general. Requirements were more strict than in other areas of the city to pay for roads, drainage, and parks and trails, plus provide land for fire and police stations and a site for public transit.[36] Shortly after the annexation the Savings and Loan crisis hit Colorado Springs hard. The city became known as the foreclosure capital of the country, and the planned developments did not happen. Banning Lewis property has passed through numerous owners, two that went bankrupt. Then with the Great Recession of 2008, concern for urban sprawl diminished as growth came to a halt. The Banning Lewis property was bought by one of the region's largest homebuilders and developers in 2014. By 2018 the city was again growing, and developers pointed out that houses were being built in unincorporated El Paso County farther east, leapfrogging over the Banning Lewis tract. The narrative then constructed was that costs from excessive regulations were driving urban sprawl beyond city limits, an unintended consequence of urban-planning policies that were supposed to rein in sprawl. So a revised annexation agreement on the Banning Lewis properties was approved by City Council in April 2018, to remove the higher impact fees and align development with other city-planning policies. The new vision is for a lower density than originally proposed, now targeting 62,000 residents, and the claim is that this approach will generate $49 million over and above the cost of developing and servicing the area over the next thirty years because "methods for how development pays for itself have evolved since the 1980s."[37] Opponents argue that the city is again, in fact, back in the business of subsidizing urban sprawl in low-density, suburban settings.

While reduced regulations on Banning Lewis development will lower house prices, buyers might give thought to the viability of those investments. After the 2008 Great Recession, studies found that houses on the suburban fringe lost value at twice their metro average, while housing in denser, walkable neighborhoods held their value much better. Foreclosures were much more prevalent in suburban settings, with the two cities most dependent on urban sprawl as their means of growth, Las Vegas and Phoenix, suffering the worst foreclosure crisis in the nation.[38] Given that the massive $1 billion-plus Southern Delivery System was built exclusively to provide water for this growing part of the city, developing Banning Lewis is seen as necessary to justify those expenses paid by current city residents.

Regardless of the fiscal accounting as to whether suburban expansion pays for itself or not, the perverse reality in Colorado Springs, and most of suburban America, is that we now build cities to accommodate cars more so than people (figure 8.18). The sheer amount of space dedicated to roads, parking structures, and the three-car garage in the suburban home is immense.[39] Crossing wide arterial suburban streets in the city such as Powers Blvd. is unsafe, barriers such as

FIGURE 8.18. Welcome to the University of Colorado—No humans allowed. Because cars are privileged over people at intersections and numerous other spaces in the urban environment, we see such absurdities like that shown above. *Source*: Photo by author.

walls and fences often prevent walking or riding, auto accidents are rampant, and traffic gets perpetually worse. Colorado was ranked second in the country for road rage fatalities in 2018.[40] In the United States, the irony is that we have some of the worst traffic in the lowest-density cities. Even an urban infill project, the University Village shopping center, promoted as a mixed-use, pedestrian-friendly, and sustainable "funky" village across from the UCCS campus and at the gateway to the downtown, ended up as a big-box strip mall focusing on an enormous lot of 3,300 parking spaces, over 1,000 more than city code required.[41] The costs to maintain low-density development are enormous, from the inefficiencies for heating and cooling stand-alone houses (subsidized by the US Navy to keep global flows of oil readily available),[42] to the water consumption needed for suburban lawns and the public health effects from nonwalkable spaces.

Perhaps equally troubling is the effect on the urban core, and the role that a strong downtown should play in forging an urban identity and uniting a diversity of people in functional public spaces. Suburbs are privatized worlds, whereas cities thrive on a strong public realm—the famed piazzas in Italy, the Zócalo of Mexico City, the street cafés of Paris, the sidewalks of New York. Since post–World War II, America has largely forgotten how to build urban settings with strong public spaces that encourage human gathering and interaction. Much of suburban growth was

FIGURE 8.19. In what was the hot new retail district of the 1980s now sit abandoned big-box stores in a sea of pavement. Many suburban strip malls have a life expectancy of only about twenty-five years, leaving blighted and wasteful spaces interspersed throughout Colorado Springs and much of urban America. *Source*: Photo by author.

not even designed for longevity: the shiny, new suburban commercial spaces built in the 1970s and 1980s have devolved into abandoned big-box stores in seas of unused parking lots, as seen all along south Academy Boulevard, where commercial vacancy rates reached 50 percent in some areas (figure 8.19).[43] Cities around the country that grew rapidly during the auto era—such as San Jose, Phoenix, or even Las Vegas—lack a definable downtown and sense of place. For a metropolitan area with over 700,000 people, the Colorado Springs downtown Central Business District is far undersized, a direct function of the era of suburbanization and private automobile transit when the city greatly expanded. City boosters recognize the need for a strong downtown identity and are actively working to build a sense of place around the urban core. A city's quality-of-life attributes—increasingly focused on walkable, urban centers—attract young professionals and industries that rely on them.[44] While trends and preferences for housing and urban living are shifting and the city's downtown is undergoing vital growth and investment, most housing continues to be built at the urban fringes, particularly on the high-end northern edges, where new homes average more than 3,800 square feet.[45] Projections are for this development to continue.[46] Even with a robust investment in the Central Business District, the overall suburban pattern, once laid down, has come to define the city, especially as suburban growth outpaces infill.

THE GROWTH MACHINE

As Colorado Springs exploded with suburban growth from the 1960s through today, the standard narrative is that land development is merely the workings of supply and demand in a benign competitive setting.[47] Suburban tract housing and urban sprawl simply reflect consumer demand in a market economy. But as seen with the energy exerted by boosters to attract military installations to the city, the development process is not passive. Sociologists John Logan and Harvey Molotch argue that places are in fact the creations of activists, or entrepreneurs, who push hard to alter market functions in ways that influence urban development.[48] The actors in this process comprise the "growth machine." People who use their time and money to participate in local development decisions are the ones who, in vast disproportion to their representation in the population, have the most to gain or lose in land use decisions. Therefore local business coalitions form to exert control over the land development process in ways that benefit their personal interests while shaping the perception of these projects as a public good. Through their mutual interests in perpetuating growth, they work to dampen opposition within the city or region through their ability as experts in the field to control the public conversation.[49] Entrepreneurs are able to portray growth as inevitable and good. The social value of urban growth becomes naturalized—growth brings jobs, expands the tax base, pays for urban services, and is a fundamental requirement for prosperity.

In the Colorado Springs context, the small group of local business elites responsible for first attracting large military facilities morphed into a growth industry dominated by land developers who hold great sway in shaping the future of the city. Land development decisions supposedly take place in a rational process whereby data and options are objectively analyzed for optimal solutions, but in fact, the very concept of "rationality" is constructed by those with power over the process.[50] The growth machine constructs a widely accepted simplification of the world, where the leaders come to define what can and cannot be done.[51] Preconceived ideas of a small-but-powerful group become the reality. The need for growth becomes taken for granted, with developers working in this context free to venture into speculative projects with near impunity. Land developers in Colorado Springs have used their influence to ensure limited restrictions and regulations on any land development project. Hidden from the conversation are the personal profits for a small number of people in the growth machine coalition and negative public externalities produced by urban growth.

Actors such as universities, newspapers, utilities, or local sports teams that normally do not engage in real estate development as their primary mission may join growth machine coalitions to promote their own interests, particularly because they are strongly affected by local place characteristics.[52] For example, the recent "City for Champions" grant received for tourism promotion from Colorado Office of Economic Development saw all three of the local higher education institutions play a role. The Air Force Academy, a federal institution in the department with the largest share of the federal discretionary budget, gets state money to build a new visitors' center near the north entrance gate, even though one currently exists in the Cadet Area. The University of Colorado Colorado Springs gets money to build a new sports medicine center, where the "tourism" component here is the supposed attraction from around the country for patients who will seek out the world-class facilities. Finally, Colorado College gets money to build a new ice hockey arena adjacent to campus, also supposedly attracting tourists even though the facility will be smaller than the World Arena, where their team currently plays.

Coalitions of stakeholders routinely align around specific projects that will benefit them, as seen with the aforementioned University Village urban renewal project on Nevada Avenue across from the UCCS campus. In an effort to rid the lands adjacent to campus from perceived blight, the university became an active partner in promoting a taxpayer-subsidized infrastructure needed to build the shopping center.[53] The urban renewal authority, a quasi-governmental agency operating outside of the oversight of the city planning offices, often plays the coordinating role in bringing stakeholders together to navigate the development process and construct the narrative used to justify a project's benefit—in the case of University Village, that of a sustainable, mixed-use, urban infill project (as opposed to what resulted, a car-oriented, big-box shopping center). In another project, the agency rationalized the need for taxpayer-supported "urban renewal" on the undeveloped periphery of the city, claiming blight existed (a precondition required to authorize this agency) in part because urban infrastructure such as sidewalks and curbs were not present. The city pushed for this project—another suburban shopping center—as a way to partially finance a stretch of our major highway bypass in the northeast part of the city. The result is again taxpayers subsidizing private development of urban sprawl, this time in the name of urban renewal.

The context in which people receive images and other materials of place promotion is important. The dominant antiregulatory, small government political culture of Colorado Springs facilitates cohesion around the growth machine ideology, which in turn reinforces and reproduces the greater conservative political culture. As a result, the deregulated development process with little opposition leads to a predictable and generic urban landscape that has come to define much of the Colorado Springs built environment.

POLITICAL CULTURE

While suburbanization and urban sprawl occurred in all US cities over the past half century or more, the prevalence of unconstrained growth has been particularly acute in Colorado Springs.[54] Why might this be? Home builders will tell you that they are just responding to market demand; they are building the product American consumers want. Suburbia is an expression of liberty! While the growth machine concept challenges the notion that suburban sprawl is simply a reflection of the free market at work, and other urbanists generate data showing that suburban tract homes are not what most consumers want, the free market argument holds great sway in Colorado Springs and reflects the predominant, limited government, antiregulatory political philosophy.[55] Certainly one dimension that drives low-density suburbanization is based on the political culture of this city.[56] Colorado Springs is well known in the state and nationally as a very conservative city, ranked fourth nationally in 2014.[57] Republicans outnumber Democrats two to one in El Paso County. The US Congressional District has been Republican since its creation in 1970, with the *Denver Post* referring to the representative in 1986 as an "ultraconservative," a trend that continues and is a point of pride for the current Congressman.[58] The population is distrustful of government, is very tax averse, and tends to defer to the private sector to resolve disputes and guide society and the economy. This tendency gives great influence to the private sector, and from the very founding of the city, the principal business endeavor has been real estate development. Developers today have great influence in the city, bankrolling City Council election campaigns, dominating the Planning Commission, and repeatedly pressuring city government to restructure (once even eliminate) city-planning offices to reduce government oversight and create an environment more friendly to builders.[59] A citizen concerned about declining water levels in wells in the rapidly growing north El Paso County expressed dismay in 2002 that there seemed to be no regulatory oversight to growth: "The developers shouldn't have absolute power, and I'm afraid they do."[60]

The conservative political culture in Colorado Springs has deep roots but also many modern additions. General Palmer set the initial tone, from the very founding the city as a speculative real estate venture. The support for free enterprise and increasing business influence grew with the railroads, particularly the Colorado Midland. With little trust in the weak federal government, local leaders gravitated to the business community for leadership. Even more than the railroads, however, the probusiness ethic soared with the boom of gold mining at Cripple Creek, when local capitalists took the lead in ownership and development of the largest gold district in the country. The labor wars of 1893 and 1903 exacerbated the rigid divisions between capital and labor and motivated local Republican Party supporters to form a cohesive and uniform block of politicians to influence state-level politics that continues to this day. Local Republicans ensured Cañon City businessman James Peabody was elected governor in 1903, then Colorado Springs banker and oil executive Oliver Shoup was elected in 1918 and served until 1923. Upon his return to Colorado Springs, Shoup allied with local business to push a free market agenda and promote private enterprise. For example, he took out full-page ads in the *Gazette* and promoted a citizen's committee to oppose the city purchasing the electric company and converting it to a public utility in 1924. The *Gazette* called the argument put forth by the "socialistic" City Council for a public utility "as specious as any document that ever went out from a Socialist organization seeking to abolish private enterprise for the theoretical advantages of public ownership."[61] Shoup's campaign failed, but the influence of the business community in Colorado Springs, allied with the Republican Party and the *Gazette* editorial board, remained strong and continued to grow.

There is also the general context of the Rocky Mountain West, where a strong libertarian streak has long prevailed. The iconic independent frontiersman, cowboy, homesteader, or miner creates to this day an image of rugged independence, a self-made survival skill that requires no outside assistance. Western interests seeking local control battled the federal government over use and development of the public domain in a series of "sagebrush rebellions" over the years. In the 1880s the conflicts began over federal irrigation projects, in the 1890s over the Forest Service's administration of timber reserves, in the early twentieth century over grazing rights and the creation of the Bureau of Land Management (BLM), and by the 1960s over designating land as wilderness areas.[62] The conflicts continued into the twenty-first century, with vigilantes occupying a national wildlife refuge and armed confrontations with BLM rangers over grazing fees. The mythic vison of this independent streak gave rise to conservative attitudes, which emphasize local control, and a sense of western coherence. To westerners, place means individuality, a way of distinguishing the self with a strong antigovernment, antiauthoritarian streak.[63] Colorado Springs upholds this western, conservative ethic.

An underlying philosophical foundation of conservative thought emphasizes the imperfectability of man, ultimately drawing upon the Original Sin of the Adam and Eve biblical tale. Humans by nature are inherently flawed, reflected in poor behavior and choices they often make. For conservatives, the tragic course of human history testifies to man's basic moral weaknesses and shortcomings.[64] Conservatives therefore tend to oppose radical plans to reorganize society, particularly from government, that promise to construct some type of utopian living. Because of their view of human nature, they believe such plans must eventually fail. Conservatives, then, are generally skeptical about what government can do to help solve humankind's problems.[65] They doubt the ability of governmental policies and programs to radically improve the human condition. Conservatives recognize the need for government, particularly to control the impulses of deviant behavior, but ultimately order and stability depend on the individual to practice virtue and responsibility. The roadblocks to perfectability are found within each human, not in the external environment.

The evolution of this foundational thought led to classical liberalism, a movement toward greater liberty from monarchical or theocratic control. Classical liberalism is built on the foundation of English political economy, which maintained that maximum efficiency, full production, and the common good are best served by the rational pursuit of self-interest in a competitive environment of free markets.[66] Any intervention by the state only serves to distort the functioning of free competition and inhibit personal freedoms. This conservative viewpoint differs greatly from twentieth-century liberalism, which has come to mean the expansion of state power in the pursuit of perceived social welfare, not necessarily liberation of the individual from outside control.[67] By the twentieth century, conservative philosophy diverged along two lines. The "traditional" wing emphasized social order, adherence to cultural traditions, and respect for authority and was much more willing to cede power to the government to enforce societal norms. The "libertarian" wing was more concerned with maximizing individual liberty, with adherents fearful of the state and its ability to restrict personal freedoms. The libertarians hold a much higher respect for the inherent good of humans and believe people can self-regulate their behavior to act responsibly without the need for the state enforcing codes of behavior, which they see as coercion and ultimately a form of violence.[68] These two competing factions generally aligned under the umbrella of the Republican Party, but at times they stand opposed on topics such as civil liberties, military intervention, and the role of the state at enforcing behavior.

The live-and-let-live mentality of the West evolved into a mainstream, moderate Republicanism, with elements of both traditional conservativism and a libertarian orientation. Western Republicans were in general a moderating influence on the party, often supporting New Deal programs, with a strong isolationist wing that even opposed entering into World War II.[69] Perhaps the pragmatic, moderate Republican mentality is best epitomized by John Love, Colorado's thirty-sixth governor and from Colorado Springs. A political unknown, he won the 1962 election against an incumbent Democrat during a time of economic prosperity largely through his personal connection to a broad diversity of Colorado citizens made while campaigning. Renowned as a no-nonsense, honest straight-talker who spoke informally and without scripted messages, he went on to become Colorado's only three-term governor. In his inaugural speech, he pledged a limited government and praised the "great virtues of self-reliance, initiative, and ambition," calling for all government possible to be kept at the local level.[70] While his platform pushed free enterprise and personal liberty and warned against the dangers of an expanding federal government, he also was a champion for public education, environmental protection, and placing constraints upon haphazard urban growth.[71] Love was the lone western official to not back Barry Goldwater for the Republican presidential nomination in 1964. In many ways, he was a protégé of Dwight "Ike" Eisenhower, president from 1953 to 1961. Ike, whose wife was from Colorado and who maintained close ties to the state, epitomized the 1950s era of bipartisanship and centrist, pragmatic politics. Mainstream Republicans of the time, following conservative principles, were willing to compromise and even adjust goals to be able to best function in an imperfect realm of existence. Yet such Republicans were, to the more right-wing elements of the party, sellouts and frauds—liberals in disguise. Many conservatives had long-simmering fury about Roosevelt's New Deal, and these concerns about "collectivism" and the expansion of the state boiled over with the Cold War, when anticommunism became the defining theme of a growing conservative movement. This grew to mean not simply a rejection of a Soviet-style organization of society but also of federal regulations, the welfare state, and liberal political culture. "Anticommunism" often meant opposition to the United Nations, trade unions, or any sort of planning.[72] The labels "communist" or "socialist" became symbolic epithets directed against the entire complex of bureaucratic, metropolitan, multiethnic, and Democratic forces feared and despised by the Right.[73] They saw bipartisanship as one of the fundamental flaws of postwar politics.[74] Robert Welch, the founder of the John Birch Society, came to the conclusion that because President Eisenhower had served under Roosevelt and was backed by eastern Republicans, he was, in fact, a communist.[75] Joe McCarthy undertook his maniacal purge of communists from the State Department and other institutions until his overzealousness led to censure in 1954.

Such beliefs did not just appear from nowhere in the 1950s. Nationally, media activists dissatisfied with the liberal consensus they saw in mainstream Republicans pushed a more conservative agenda through the Mannion Forum radio show, William F. Buckley's *National Review* that launched in 1955, and other radio and print outlets. These and other media activists popularized the term "liberal media bias," believing that conservative voices were being silenced.[76] Despite the journalistic paradigm of objectivity, and federal regulations such as the Fairness Doctrine, which mandated alternative views be represented in print and televised media, right-wing media activists felt persecuted. To them, they *were* the alternative voice; they saw no need to present liberal views through their outlets. Theirs was the response to what they saw as slanted reporting that dominated American media. These early conservative outlets were overtly partisan and stressed the legitimacy of presenting positions based on ideological integrity. The result was a different way of knowing the world, weighing evidence, and evaluating fact or truth. That evaluation relied not on the source's impartiality but on the assumed biases of the writers, editors, and publishers involved in the media enterprise. And with what they saw as coordinated attacks on the Right, they helped construct the Right's oppositional identity with a populist appeal: "Conservatives fashioned a narrative not of a political faction attempting to change policy but of an epic, high-stakes struggle between the coordinated forces of oppression and the embattled, noble right."[77]

Colorado Springs had national influence in this media movement from the Right. One influential person to push radical libertarian, even anarchist, ideas was Raymond Cyrus Hoiles. In the 1920s, R. C. Hoiles owned a newspaper in Ohio in which he exposed crooked bidding between the local government and contractors.[78] After his house was bombed, he moved to Santa Ana, California, in 1935 and bought the Santa Ana *Register* (later the Orange County *Register*). He named his company Freedom Newspapers, later Freedom Communications, and bought a dozen papers throughout the country, including the Colorado Springs *Gazette Telegraph* in January 1946. Hoiles wrote a daily column in the *Gazette* throughout the 1940s and 1950s, where he frequently quoted passages from books and speeches of libertarian thinkers, responded to readers' questions, and advocated his position. He engaged in the public forum to attempt persuasion, and the editorial page was filled with daily columns from other Freedom Communications writers with complementary viewpoints. Despite the overall civil and informed tone of his columns, the content was radical for the time and place. He believed public schools were the "grassroots of our troubles . . . the primary tyranny" because they were based on force rather than voluntary persuasion, robbery rather than love, thereby breeding hate and reinforcing collectivist ideas.[79] A public school teacher is little more, he contended, than "an inmate of a house of prostitution."[80] He said that "being a member of a board of education is a dirty, mean, immoral job."[81] The only moral that public colleges could possibly pass along is that "might makes right," showing an inherent disrespect for the dignity of man, out of harmony with God's laws.[82] To Hoiles, all taxation was robbery that condemned citizens, through government coercion, into slaves, and he called for all government functions to be privatized, including the military.[83] Collective bargaining of unions violated nonmembers' rights to work and the individual capacities of each worker; unions challenged free enterprise with labor czars who sought to fatten their own pocketbooks and impose power over the slaves they held captive.[84] True to his beliefs, he shut down the paper from January 27–29, 1947, over a collective-bargaining dispute, locked out the unionized typographic workers from the *Gazette Telegraph* (who formed an alternative paper, the *Free Press*), and hired all new, nonunion workers.[85] *Time* magazine later accused Hoiles of barely paying subsistence wages to his new typographic workers.[86]

Hoiles argued that the essence of Christianity is the importance of the individual and railed against the Federal Council of Churches of Christ in America who, in a Declaration of Economic Justice, called for "organized cooperation" among different denominations rather than competition between them: "The late Duce might have cited that as the charter for his corporative state. Stalin unquestionably would declare that his barbarous tyranny is built to these specifications. Hitler would have accepted them without the addition of a comma."[87] He argued that the crash of the Great Depression was due to one thing, and one thing only: "Government interference with human initiative."[88] When the city proposed new recreation facilities to combat juvenile delinquency, Hoiles saw this as the state coveting power to compel other people to comply against their will.[89] And of the Republican candidates Dewey and Warren nominated to run against Harry Truman for president in 1948, he condemned them for being "in favor of most every socialistic move such as minimum wages, collective bargaining, socialized medicine and Federal assistance in education," continuing the New Deal scheme of collective robbery.[90] Such statements caused a stir among readers and the quiet, mainstream, probusiness Republicans of Colorado Springs, but for decades these opinions filled the editorial pages of the city's largest newspaper and certainly had influence on the overall political climate.[91]

In 1954, Hoiles hired Robert LeFevre to be the editorial writer for the *Gazette Telegraph*. LeFevre was born in Idaho in 1911, tried out acting in Hollywood for a while, hustled as a traveling salesman and con man during the Depression (he was also bailed out through jobs with the Works Progress Administration, despite his hatred for the federal government), then fell in with a mystical cult called The Mighty "I AM," whose leader considered himself the reincarnation of George Washington and had some cosmic connection with Mount Shasta in California.[92] This group pushed a crypto-Nazi ideology, called for the death of Franklin Roosevelt, and eventually was indicted for mail fraud in 1940, after which LeFevre turned state witness and joined the army.[93] After the war LeFevre, who also had experience running radio stations and busting unions, worked as a news director for a Fort Lauderdale TV station, where he gained notoriety in 1954 by condemning, in the spirit of the McCarthy purges, the *Girl Scout Handbook* for praising the UN Universal Declaration of Human Rights.[94] After arriving in Colorado Springs, LeFevre continued the radical libertarian editorials in the *Gazette Telegraph*. When the County Zoning Commission took an active role planning for the new Air Force Academy in 1954, LeFevre accused it of attempting to "play God and tell less fortunate mortals how they can use their property."[95] He regularly wrote the standard fare such as "the power to tax is the power to enslave," leading to a general perversion of society and that this country will never be safe until a stake is driven through the heart of the international vampire, the United Nations.[96] When Congress was considering censure for Senator Joe McCarthy, the *Gazette Telegraph* published a petition for all to sign in support of the senator, warning that an unjust decision against McCarthy "could be helpful only to the communists and their Soviet masters."[97]

LeFevre had a position of great influence in the community but was unsatisfied with simply writing propaganda pieces—he sought to influence a new movement in society. In 1956 LeFevre started the Freedom School just north of Colorado Springs, in the Douglas County foothills. LeFevre had three female groupies from his I AM days that remained with him throughout the years, along with his wife, and together they built a campus of rustic cabins in the pines to create an institution dedicated to the study of human freedom. The curriculum was to be a sort of capitalist boot camp to explore the true meaning of liberty.[98] He ran one- and two-week sessions, mostly for wealthy businessmen, that espoused the evils of big government. Class materials taught that truly free individuals will govern themselves when they practice volunteerism and responsibility and that private property is the basis of human freedom. One of LeFevre's disciples was Charles Koch, who insisted that all his brothers attend the school and who became a trustee and donor in 1964.

LeFevre sought to upgrade the Freedom School into an accredited institution offering graduate degrees "teaching the fundamentals of private property, free market activity."[99] Despite no formal academic credentials, he proposed to convert the school into the Rampart College in 1963. Not surprisingly, the state denied accreditation. When the school was first proposed, LeFevre met with eighty local business leaders at the Antlers Hotel to solicit $5 million in funding.[100] The local business community became bitterly divided over the proposed school.[101] The Chamber of Commerce Executive Committee viewed the college as a new enterprise with a payroll that would contribute to the local economy and issued a statement welcoming the school on March 14, 1963. Some members of the chamber strongly dissented this opinion, publicly stating that the chamber should not extend a welcome to "a man whose written and spoken words indicate he wants to tear down and destroy practically everything which makes this community today."[102] The *Free Press*, the competitor to the *Gazette Telegraph* and long rival, took up the charge against the proposed Rampart College, publishing editorials from February through May 1963, calling the Freedom School nothing but a propaganda mill for a vicious and selfish philosophy, "attempting to undermine the very foundations upon which this nation is constructed."[103] The local chapter of the American Association of University Women published a front-page statement opposing the new school, calling them an extremist group, and local radio station KVOR published and voiced strong opposition.[104] Letters in opposition from citizens were published in the *Free Press* in March and April 1963.[105] When *Time* magazine ran an exposé on Hoiles and LeFevre in April 1963, the recently retired mayor of Colorado Springs, William Henderson, regretted that the city received nationwide publicity "advertising to the world that we are a home of crackpots" (figure 8.20).[106] Worse for Henderson was the perception that the city aids and abets these men's questionable objectives. He saw the *Gazette Telegraph* as the greatest deterrent to new industry locating in the city.

The Freedom School campus suffered from disastrous floods in 1965 and, despite promoting the principles of the free market, was never profitable as a private enterprise. The wealthy donors who kept the school open finally lost faith, and it closed by 1968. Over a thousand people attended the Freedom School and it had a lasting effect, particularly on the Koch family, who today have great influence across many dimensions of society and government to promote an agenda that seeks an unrestrained capitalism free from government oversight, a vision that is, at its core, fundamentally at odds with democracy as a form of government.[107] Although many considered LeFevre a charlatan, his strength was the power of personality

WEDNESDAY MORNING FREE PRESS

FREE PRESS BUILDING TELEPHONE 633-3881

COLORADO SPRINGS, COLORADO WEDNESDAY, APRIL 17, 1963 NO. 73

The Country Parson

"Machines may have some advantages over man; although they can't love their neighbors—neither can they hate them."

Ex-Mayor Criticizes Effect Of Rampart College Here

Three Of Five 'Freedom School' Scholarship Winners Connected With The U.S. Armed Services

Says We Are Made To Look Like 'Home Of Crackpots'

FIGURE 8.20. Ex-Mayor Henderson blasts Rampart College in the *Free Press* headline, April 17, 1963. *Source*: Pikes Peak Library District, Special Collections.

that some called "spellbinding."[108] LeFevre ultimately lost credibility with a nascent but more mainstream libertarian movement due to his extreme pacifism and belief that any retaliatory force was never justified. He tried to run the Rampart College as a mail-order propaganda supplier from Southern California and started new outreach activities to the surfers and hippies of the region that included a convert, Dana Rohrabacher, later congressional representative from Orange County until 2018, who played guitar and preached the gospel of the free market. LeFevre eked along as a libertarian proponent until his death in 1986.

The influence of the Freedom School and the *Gazette* on Colorado Springs conservative thought was gradual, as seen by the opposition the proposal to convert it into Rampart College generated even in the early 1960s, but these outlets did create a fertile environment for the "New Right" conservatism that blossomed in the 1990s. A sampling of Republican campaign brochures from the 1960s through the 1990s shows trends in campaign literature affected by both time and geography. Early messages, especially for statewide offices, are far more moderate than what would come later. A 1966 reelection brochure for Governor John Love states his conviction that "our willingness and ability to support public education" is of paramount importance to the state—a far cry from R. C. Hoiles's calls to abolish public education.[109] A Republican US senator in 1974 called for support of solar energy and a tax on low-gas-mileage cars, and the state attorney general called for strengthening consumer protection and the environment—hardly contemporary GOP positions. Yet at the geographic scale more local to Colorado Springs, even early campaign literature from the 1970s touts conservative messages: the call for local governance and focus on the individual (1974 county commissioner), denouncing federal regulations and promoting the need to have faith in God and the free enterprise system (1976 US congress representative), reducing the taxpayer burden and welfare costs (1976 county commissioner), and reducing federal and state bureaucracies and regulations (1978 state representative). By the late 1980s and 1990s the messages moved rightward: maximum privatization of functions, enable free enterprise to meet transportation needs, investigate all welfare programs, no new taxes or expansion of state agencies (1986 state senator), oppose an Equal Rights Amendment and forbid state employees to strike (1986 state representative), privatize government services (1988 state representative), make English the official language (1990 state representative), and never increase taxes (1990 state representative). By the 1990s even statewide offices reflected this rightward shift, with 1990 gubernatorial candidate John Andrews pushing his "Freedom Agenda," which called for reducing taxes, extending school vouchers, curbing teacher unions, and upgrading services through competitive contracting with the private sector.[110]

The Freedom Communications media conglomerate that owned the *Colorado Springs Gazette* was just one example of strong connections that exist between Colorado Springs and Orange County, California. Defense contractors from Southern California are also major investors in Colorado Springs, which has long been a destination for migrants leaving the Golden State. The evangelical megachurch was invented in Orange County and has become a staple element of suburban Colorado Springs. The resultant automobile-oriented suburban landscape built in Colorado Springs mimics that found in Orange County, with both housing an educated, affluent, and largely white demographic. Media pundit Ed Quillen went so far as to coin Colorado Springs "the eastern-most extension of Orange County, California."[111] These connections and the similarities in the historical development between these two places play a major role in the Colorado Springs conservative political culture.

An early stronghold of right-wing activism, particularly libertarian-oriented support for the 1964 Barry Goldwater campaign, took root in Orange County in Southern California. Harvard historian Lisa McGirr argues that part of the explanation for this place-specific movement was due to both the rapid growth from migration and the built environment itself. Orange County grew tremendously from a very small population on vast ranches and fruit orchards into a giant suburb of Los Angeles. The embrace of laissez-faire capitalism placed strong emphasis on private development of private spaces, with little regard for public or community spaces or any identifiable urban core. The built environment reinforced privacy, individual property rights, home ownership, and isolation at the expense of public space and town centers. The environment we build—the cultural landscape—reflects our values, but we also internalize those values into the very identity of each and every one of us as we traverse through those landscapes.[112] Without public institutions and social spaces, such isolation weakened community engagement and normalized the ethic of individualism. Orange County suburban dwellers reported feeling disconnected, with the fragmented spaces creating disorientation and feelings of emptiness.[113] This void, or lack of place connection, found in social gathering spaces, combined with the very newness of the people there, meant that values and mores were up for grabs at the very time that the social, economic, and cultural changes of the 1960s were challenging traditions and belief systems.[114] Whereas national liberal leaders foresaw expansion of federal functions as a means to improve the lives of citizens, expand personal freedoms, tear down racial hierarchies and rework gender relations, others in the 1960s saw turmoil, disruption, and a threat to the social order that they knew from their midwestern upbringing.[115] The formation of the local political culture also took place during the Cold War, with many Orange County residents working for defense contractors that promoted a collective opposition to communism and all related types of statist institutions.

The new modern suburban consumer setting of Orange County seemed to threaten older family and church values many had grown up with, thereby reinforcing their importance. The uncertainty of societal change in a new setting may have made them cling even more strongly to traditional moorings.[116] Fueled by conservative media outlets, these recent settlers in this new California landscape came to oppose what they perceived to be a decline in religiosity, morality, individual responsibility, and family authority. Although benefitting greatly from modernity and federal intervention, particularly defense spending, they rejected secularism, relativism, and egalitarianism. America, they believed, had an organic, benevolent order that would function well if not for tampering by liberal elites. Liberalism threatened to undermine economic well-being and freedom when the state spent resources to distribute wealth downward in society in the name of equity—a social decline, they argued, that went hand in hand with the growth of centralized federal power:

> Thus, America's problems were not the result of any inherent limitations of a capitalist economy or inequalities in American life, but rather were due to liberal tampering with an otherwise harmonious, self-sustaining system. Capitalism, this argument went, would run smoothly if not for an overgrown state. Family, morality, and religion would be intact if liberal elites had not encouraged permissiveness and secularism.[117]

Political activism—fueled in part by media agitators warning of the ever-present communist threat to liberty, and by extension, the federal state's infringement on personal freedoms—became a binding force that created a place identity and gave meaning to the community.

This analysis of the rise of the New Right in Southern California reveals remarkable similarities to the situation in Colorado Springs from the 1960s through today, where rapid growth in nondescript, generic suburban housing tracts creates little sense of place. Many of these tracts are segregated into "gated communities," isolating the residents from outsiders and creating highly controlled spaces with homogeneous socioeconomic profiles. While Orange County evolved from nearly nothing, migrants to Colorado Springs came into a community (albeit small in the 1950s) with an already-established Republican base, and the *Gazette* regularly editorialized on libertarian values, personal liberty, and free market principles. (The editorial page motto was "Colorado's most consistent newspaper.") The economy depends on defense spending, with a heavy military presence that strengthened an anticommunist, and antistatist ethic. The rapid expanse of the suburban fringe generated a newness of people in an lonely void, with lack of place connections that likely favored receptivity to the larger political culture. Republican political candidates in this new 1970s landscape sought legitimacy by emphasizing their midwestern values, "a native of Indiana's Farm Country," or coming from Nebraska, Oklahoma, and Iowa.[118] This nascent conservative identity attracted like-minded immigrants, especially given that by the 1990s, Colorado Springs became the preferred destination for Southern California "refugees" fleeing what to them had become an oppressive, Democratically controlled California state bureaucracy and an increasingly nonwhite county.[119] Influential Southern California immigrant Number One: Douglas Bruce.

Douglas Bruce came to Colorado Springs in 1986 after several tax disputes in California with the Internal Revenue Service. Once in Colorado Springs he bought and managed several rental properties in the region. In 1988, he began work on a "Taxpayers Bill of Rights," or TABOR proposal, to limit the revenues governments can collect and the amount they can spend. He successfully led a campaign that passed such restrictions for Colorado Springs in 1991, then, on the third try, led the TABOR campaign that won state approval in 1992. This state constitutional amendment has had a profound effect upon city, county, and state governance in Colorado. The law links increases in revenue spending to population and inflation changes, prohibiting any amount over the growth in those two variables. Furthermore, during times of economic downturn, when budgetary spending typically decreases, the base value is reduced accordingly, referred to as the "ratcheting down" effect. Governments therefore often see an overall decline in their spending capabilities even as growth later occurs. While any political jurisdiction can vote to "de-Bruce" and permit their government to keep excess funds over and above the upper limit, the net outcome has been a huge restriction on the growth of government—exactly the intended purpose. To avoid collecting more revenue than permitted by TABOR, Colorado Springs has been forced to reduce its property tax levy nine times since 1990.[120] Loved by some and hated by others, TABOR is an economic reality all Colorado elected officials must deal with—and a legacy Colorado Springs passed onto the rest of the state.

Because TABOR has kept property taxes low, and a relatively unregulated development process fosters rapid growth, one benefit for Colorado Springs is that the cost of living is very affordable compared to urban centers such as Denver and Boulder. Many people are attracted to the city because they can buy a home here; others find appeal in the lack of regulation over their personal lives. The tradeoff, of course, is poor public services and a landscape that reflects the freewheeling growth machine. Weak oversight of building sites led to over two dozen houses sliding down the slopes in the western foothills from landslides and expansive soils.[121] Until a recently approved tax for road improvements, street potholes drew daily complaints; meanwhile the Environmental Protection Agency, the Colorado Department of Public Health and Environment, and city of Pueblo have an ongoing lawsuit against the city for water runoff infractions that violate clean water standards.[122] The bus system still doesn't serve much of the city and requires thoughtful planning and long waits for commutes even in places it does serve. Homeless services are far too few, as seen by the camps of people living along all city streams and railroad beds. Colorado Springs is also heavily dependent upon sales taxes to make up for low property taxes, a regressive revenue source that disproportionately hits the lower income. This reliance on sales taxes creates great fiscal problems during recessions, as seen after 2008—the city was forced to stop trash collection or watering for parks and street medians, many trees died in the urban forest, up to one-third of the street lights were turned off, and city employees were laid off, including police and firefighters. By 2013, the city faced a $1.3 billion infrastructure backlog. Local columnist John Hazlehurst speculated that TABOR had made the city "ungovernable," and in 2016 a local business recruiter cited the external image of the city as "dysfunctional," with a negative political culture and tired infrastructure.[123] Business leaders bemoaned the loss of young, educated people who fled the city for better opportunities in Denver—the city lost 3,500 workers from 2013 to 2014, with the largest declines in professional and technology sectors.[124]

Bruce himself remains a controversial character. He regularly filed lawsuits against Colorado Springs for illegally increasing spending without voter approval, sometimes successfully and other times not. He went on to become a county commissioner in 2004, where he argued with the other commissioners, and later a state representative, where he was censured for kicking a reporter. He has been called a slumlord and repeatedly cited by the city for unkempt properties, then cited for contempt of court while challenging the constitutionality of city code enforcement, all of which he considers a vendetta to punish him for his antitax activism.[125] In 2011 he was convicted of money laundering and tax fraud felonies, spending 180 days in jail. To the rest of the state, he epitomizes the harsh, right-wing extremist image many equate with El Paso County and Colorado Springs.

Doug Bruce may be an extreme case, but he is not alone in pushing a local conservative legislative agenda. Colorado Springs and El Paso County were often at the forefront of new initiatives later tried at the national scale. School vouchers and school choice programs were implemented here long before entering into the national debate; the city has privatized or outsourced many functions, including its fleet services, emergency responders, trash collection, and the city hospital. El Paso County issues the most concealed gun permits of any county in the state, and it has the lowest average property tax rate for all of the Colorado Front Range urban counties, below the statewide average and less than half of the national average.[126] The city's 2015 budget noted that Colorado Springs spends less per capita ($718) than any comparable city, and the largest school district reports a $1,300 decline in teacher pay for the 2014–2015 year, with salaries $9,000 below the national average.[127] Local political science professor Josh Dunn wrote, "Colorado Springs was the Tea Party before there was a Tea Party."[128] A 2012 *Gazette* Editorial sums it up: "The local culture is overwhelmingly pro-military, pro-gun, pro-religion, pro-family, pro-business, and pro-life . . . Yes, it is Nirvana."[129]

While the *Gazette* editorial board may view Colorado Springs as paradise on earth, the increasingly strident tone of the right wing has made life uncomfortable for those they oppose. The "liberal elites" included among academia, the media, federal bureaucrats, or eastern, urban sophisticates have become the target of the Right, which has taken on a neopopulist flavor, claiming to be the voice of the forgotten common folk.[130] Following Federal Communication Commission deregulations in the 1980s, a second wave of right-wing media activists have arisen on both radio and later television that greatly contribute to this New Right movement. Unlike in the early era when conservative media was the outcast fringe, these new players are now the gatekeepers of the conservative movement, with a penchant for political purity, turning social issues such as abortion and gun control into litmus tests for candidates. They specialize in the politics of opposition. Anybody advocating for public services or spaces, planning, or government programs of nearly any kind are labeled "socialists," and even though the "liberal media bias" is still a standard sacrificial target, there is now no legitimate claim to the outsider status of conservative media: A 2007 study found 91 percent of news/talk radio shows were conservative, and Fox News was literally inside of the Trump White House.[131] Nonetheless, in 2018 the complaint of persecution continued, with a new focus on technology companies such as Google for supposedly biased search algorithms, again relegating the conservative voice as victim despite any evidence for the claim. Fealty to ideological purity is of paramount importance, with nonbelievers seen as the "enemy of the people." This media coverage has led to events such as UCCS faculty bombarded with vitriol, even death threats, for teaching about climate change, revolutionary history deemed unpatriotic, or the ethics of a "post-truth" rhetoric—all attempts to silence dialogue. Inflammatory, antimilitary messages were posted on campus, only to find these were a hoax created by two veterans in the community in an attempt to provoke agitation against the university and its perceived politically correct culture. In 2019, the University of Colorado (CU) interviewed former Minnesota congressman Mark Kennedy for president of the four-campus system. Survey responses from 2,812 faculty, students, staff, and administrators found 82.1 percent expressed concern that he would have difficulty meeting expectations, and the faculty council pointed out misstatements and incorrect information in his record. To this CU regent Chance Hill, from El Paso County, called the opposition a smear campaign from a "far leftist mob—who, in my opinion, represents a mentality as dangerous to this nation's future as any foreign threat we face."[132]

Hostilities intended to punish nonbelievers were also directed to targets off campus. A mentally deranged "solider for the children" killed three people in town while attacking the local Planned Parenthood office. Local state senator John Morse was recalled for the first time in state history in a special election because of his vote in the state legislature to impose limits on the capacity of gun magazines after another tragic mass-shooting in the state. El Paso County representative Gordon Klingenschmitt proclaimed an attack on a pregnant woman the curse of God for the practice of abortion, and that only people going to heaven are entitled to equal treatment under the law. Heavily armed, self-designated citizen "patriots" stood guard outside of a military recruitment center to protect the soldiers inside since policy requires they be unarmed while working. The local Justice and Peace Commission offices were vandalized, materials stolen, and members threatened for their opposition to war in Iraq.[133] The list goes on.

In 1999, John Love reflected in his memoirs on the rise of the Right with the Goldwater campaign, and its lasting effects: "I had less a quarrel with Goldwater's ideology than I did with the general conservative hysteria . . . This political attitude has permeated the GOP for years and has concerned me about the future of the party."[134] This recent partisanship is a long way from the tolerance and compromise that underpinned mid-twentieth-century conservatism, with some seeing a damaging image of intolerance as the reputation of Colorado Springs: "Our branding was a big problem . . . we were getting such negative press across the country."[135] Added to this is the paradox that while preaching a libertarian ethic, we would expect leaders to embrace market-driven disruption, yet Colorado Springs has been remarkably resistant to certain types of change and innovation: The coal-burning power plant remains open in the heart of the downtown, with sulfur dioxide and other emissions listed as "unclassifiable" due to lack of monitoring; all the while wind and solar power bids outperform coal for new facilities elsewhere in Colorado.[136] An innovative and now very successful startup company building solar community gardens left town and moved to Denver due to local political resistance, as did a jamboree celebrating and promoting tiny houses as a potential solution for low-income and homeless shelter.[137] Retail marijuana stores are prohibited in the city; meanwhile two highly profitable stores in neighboring

Manitou Springs have contributed mightily to that town's revenues. Leaders have also been more than willing to commit a cardinal sin against libertarian principles—using government to intervene in market forces—when it comes to subsidizing business. The $53 million to keep the US Olympic and Paralympic Committee is one example, utilizing public funding for urban renewal infrastructure that benefits private developers (including the new shopping center at the urban periphery) is another, and the resistance to increased impact fees that subsidize sprawl yet a third. An entrenched conservatism outweighs the libertarian faction of the local Republican Party. Part of this tendency toward more social conservatism rather than free market libertarianism may be due to another vital dimension of the Colorado Springs social environment: the influence of the evangelical Christian community.

9

God

> Throughout the centuries God has chosen different cities for different tasks. Colorado Springs has been chosen to refresh and globalize Christianity.
>
> —PASTOR TED HAGGARD, 1995[1]

The heavy influence of the military in Colorado Springs, its business-oriented political culture, its western libertarian ethic with allegiance to antitax and limited government politics generated a strong conservative basis for the city. A final element that boosted its conservative image was the rise of the Christian Right and an agglomeration of evangelical religious institutions in the city, particularly in the 1990s and first decade of the 2000s. Local leaders of the Christian Right with national influence pushed the city toward a much more socially conservative place than it had previously been and stamped an image of the city as the "Evangelical Vatican" among outsiders that persists to this day.[2]

AMERICAN EVANGELICAL ROOTS

America is more religious than any other western postindustrial country. The tense relationship between religion and the government was a central concern to the founding fathers who wrote the Constitution, so much so that the First Amendment specifically deals with this matter. Written in a time when the dangers to liberty that accrue when a government sanctions one religion over another were all too evident, and in a place where many had fled specifically to avoid religious persecution by political powers, the First Amendment makes clear that "Congress shall make no law respecting an establishment of religion or prohibiting the free exercise thereof." The effect of this bold statement was to give all

DOI: 10.5876/9781646421688.c009

religions a free rein, where no one need belong to or involuntarily support any faith or congregation against their will. The United States created a free market for religions, where citizens as consumers can shop around for the congregation that suits their personal needs and interests. This competitive environment explains the flourishing of different sects as lay preachers, entrepreneurs, prophets, visionaries, and even cult leaders competed for followers.

That the First Amendment was seen as a protection by minority Christian groups is evident in the staunch support of the Danbury Baptists in Connecticut for the election of Thomas Jefferson, a deist who did not believe in the fundamental scriptures of the New Testament and was attacked as a heretic by political enemies during his presidential campaign of 1800. These Baptists, long persecuted under the laws of a state-sponsored Congregationalist Church, sought and secured guarantees from Jefferson upon his inauguration that he would support religious liberty guaranteed in the First Amendment. Jefferson's 1802 letter to the Danbury Baptist Association affirmed his commitment to the First Amendment by offering his famous interpretation that it created a "wall of separation between church and state."[3] Both Jefferson and the Baptists in Connecticut recognized that separating religion from the state strengthens both and, vice versa, that sanctioning any religion as an official arm of the state corrupts both. Evangelicals, and Baptists in particular, have been the primary beneficiaries of religious pluralism in America.[4]

Although the First Amendment guarantees freedom to worship for *any* religion, of course the dominant religious belief of most early Americans was some form of Protestant Christianity. The competitive atmosphere generated by the First Amendment led Protestant Christianity to fragment into numerous organized and experimental churches as America was settled. Particularly in the Appalachian frontier, utopian movements and new religions came and (mostly) went. One notable exception to the fleeting nature of new religions was the Church of Jesus Christ of Latter Day Saints, founded by Joseph Smith in upstate New York in 1830 when he published *The Book of Mormon*. Long persecuted, the saints survived by fleeing in exile to what is now Utah, creating a truly American religion that flourishes today. Others were not so successful, with groups such as the Shakers, Harmonites, and Amana Colonies trying to create new utopias in this new land but ultimately failing.

Christianity flourished in the nineteenth century through revivals held along the frontiers of the new country. Traveling lay preachers held these gatherings to spread the gospel and convert followers. Preachers were dynamic entertainers, relying on voluntary conversions. Speaking to and for the common folk lent a populist cast to their message and introduced an anti-intellectual strain into evangelicalism.[5] Established congregations with formal hierarchies of authority were shunned; revivalists criticized the wealth and pretensions of their professional clergy and called them oppressors of the poor. The lay preachers simplified theological complexities to a clear message that all are sinners, lost without God and condemned to hell, but those who repented and claimed salvation would gain everlasting life. The emphasis at revival meetings was the experience of a new birth, of being born again. Spiritual democracy in this populist religion meant all were capable of controlling their own lives.[6] In America, postrevolutionary notions of equality led to an expansion of sects that promised salvation to all, rather than to some preordained selection of adherents.

The common name that came to be used by these Christian revivalists was evangelical. The word comes from the Greek *evangel*, or "good news"; it refers to the New Testament or simply the Gospel. An evangelical is committed to evangelism, or bringing others into the faith, and stresses the importance of this conversion, or being born again. Because evangelicals believe in the personal relationship between each person and their savior, they maintain a quest for piety in all manners of life and at least initially maintained a strong suspicion of wealth, worldliness, and any sort of formal, ecclesiastical pretension.[7] By the late nineteenth century, evangelical groups were generally pessimistic about the future of civilization and possessed an intense supernaturalism, or the belief in those aspects of the New Testament such as the Holy Trinity, the virgin birth, and the bodily resurrection of Jesus.[8]

One major divide in the Christian denominations came about over differing interpretations of when the Second Coming of Jesus would occur. Postmillennialism is the belief that Jesus will return only after believers construct the millennial kingdom, the thousand-year reign of heaven on earth, after which a tribulation period will take place leading to the great battle with Satan at Armageddon. Antebellum preachers came to believe in premillennialism, an interpretation that sees the world as increasingly sinful and doomed, to which Jesus returns and the Rapture occurs in which the faithful ascend to heaven prior to the tribulations and the ultimate battle at Armageddon.[9] This belief means that Jesus could return at any moment. Premillennialism offers hope for believers in what they see as an otherwise dismal worldly situation. These different interpretations for the end of times are important because of the influence they have on Christian engagement with the political sphere. The fundamental conflict boils down to this dilemma: should adherents withdraw from a mainstream they see as hopelessly corrupt, or should adherents selectively engage with society to create conditions appropriate for Christ's kingdom?[10] Premillennialist thinking denies human responsibility for the reform and betterment of society here on earth and acts as a brake on reform efforts, since it regards such efforts as fruitless attempts to thwart God's plan for human history.[11] Controversy over whether Rapture would come before or after the Tribulations depended on a high degree of certainty about biblical dates and the identity of biblical figures and places, so there could be no compromise, and disputes arose between the differing factions.

As more liberal interpretations of the scriptures became popular alongside modernizing trends in society, a reaction arose among a powerful faction of the Christian community: the fundamentalists. In the 1910s and 1920s, the rise of fundamentalism sought a return to New Testament simplicity, believing in the authenticity of miracles, the coming Rapture, the virgin birth, and other of the supernatural elements of doctrine. This was a fundamental protest against liberal theology, an almost militant strain of antimodernism that required separation from those insufficiently pure:[12] "Fundamentalist churches offered shelter from 'worldliness,' the saving remnant and rightful heirs to American civilization. Whether martyrs or potential conquerors, militancy became important to their sense of identity."[13] A central tenet of fundamentalism is the devout belief that the Bible was "inerrant," or absolutely and literally true. As the word of God, the scriptures could not be questioned. Civilization was in an inevitable decline; prophecy clearly stated that Christ would return to restore his kingdom in Jerusalem after the battle of Armageddon. History was seen to be firmly in God's hands, with the outcome inevitable. For fundamentalists, Satan was always appearing in new guises so that the world was under perpetual threat.

By the middle of the twentieth century, Billy Graham became the voice of the evangelical community, uniting the disparate Protestant groups under his evangelical umbrella. Originally adhering to the premillennialist separation mentality, Graham's mission was to convert, evangelize, and wait for the Second Coming. A firm believer of this impending event, in 1951 he said, "We may have another year, maybe two years, to work for Jesus Christ, and [then] . . . its [*sic*] all going to be over." Later in 1953, he prophesized that "we are living in the latter days," but by then his attitudes about engagement with the political world were changing.[14] Graham allied with President Eisenhower to forge a connection between religion and patriotism, all reinforced by the imperatives of the Cold War. Godless communism translated into a force of Satan, providing the perfect opportunity for Christian theology to mix with worldly politics. Throughout the 1950s, Graham's revivals frequently highlighted the threat of communism and nuclear war, framing the global struggle as a battle to the death between Christ and the Antichrist. In Eisenhower's election, he saw that "God is giving us a respite, a new chance."[15] The stage was set for the rise of the Christian Right.

COLORADO SPRINGS FOUNDATIONS

Colorado Springs became headquarters to early players in the business of spreading Christianity, largely through decisions made by individual firms rather than any organized and concerted effort to create a religious-based economy. The first of these was Young Life, a Christian ministry that targets middle school adolescents through college students to introduce them to Jesus Christ. They are an ecumenical group, working with many different churches and Christian organizations around the world.

Young Life was founded in 1941 by Jim Rayburn in Gainesville, Texas, seventy-five miles north of Dallas, as a Bible study club for high school kids. Ministry members believe in "contact work," going to where kids are and meeting with them on their own terms in order to gain their trust and earn the right to spread the word of Christ. Camping has been a core program from the beginning, and Young Life acquired several Colorado ranches, including two properties in the Arkansas River Valley, near Buena Vista and about two hours west of Colorado Springs. The organization moved to Colorado Springs in 1947 to be closer to the Colorado land they own, making it easier to manage and access their properties for camping retreats and summer programs.[16] Young Life now owns and runs thirty-two camps worldwide, and through numerous outreach programs interacts with over 2 million kids annually in over 100 countries, relying on more than 39,000 volunteers working with staff.[17] In 1986 Young Life moved closer to downtown into the former Shepard's Citations Building on Cascade Avenue. It remains one of the largest Christian organizations in the city, employing about 200 people, and has active chapters with many programs throughout the United States.

In 1933, Dawson Trotman founded an interdenominational Christian service in Southern California he named the Navigators. Its focus is proselytizing; members concentrate on recruiting and training laymen to further spread the word of Christ. Outgrowing their buildings near Los Angeles, in 1952 Trotman asked the leader of Young Life in Colorado Springs, Jim Rayburn, to be on the lookout for property for the Navigators.[18] Trotman was simultaneously helping Billy Graham find a new conference headquarters and came to Colorado Springs in 1953, when he was told that the old estate of General Palmer, Glen Eyrie, might be available. Billy Graham's organization agreed to buy the property, with a plan for the Navigators to use it until Graham was ready to develop it. It was envisioned as a spiritual retreat. Graham later had second thoughts and told Trotman that God wanted the Navigators to have the spot.[19] This purchase posed a monumental challenge for Trotman as the price was far more than he had considered possible. His group had to raise $108,000 in six weeks and assume annual payments of $26,000. Through concerted effort, hard work, and a little luck, the final donation came through on the last day to secure a loan, and the Navigators purchased the estate for their new home in 1953. The narrative published by the Navigators attributes this to nothing short of a divine miracle: "It would have been impossible but for God and His reassuring promises."[20]

The Navigators incorporated in the state of Colorado as a nonprofit in 1956.[21] They see themselves as an outreach organization of Christians traveling through life here on earth, whose purpose is to make disciples and have them become disciple makers. Rather than large group proselytizing, they prefer one-on-one intense work "to win young men to Christianity and train them as dedicated, disciplined Christians,"[22] recruiting on college campuses, the military, and in the professional world. "To Know Christ . . . and to make him known" has been their founding message.[23] The theological underpinning of the Navigators clearly aligns with fundamentalist teaching: "Today we as Christians live on an enemy-occupied planet. Satan is prince of this world. We are in spiritual warfare against Satan and his hosts."[24] In addition to missionary work, they conduct year-round training sessions, weeklong summer conferences and seminars for adults and young people, distribute correspondence course and Bible study materials, and hold summer camps for junior high boys and girls. They own and run Eagle Lake Camp, one hour west of Colorado Springs. Several dozen staff members live on the campus, the rest live in town, where many of the group's funders also live. The Navigators work in over 100 countries and employ nearly 4,000 people worldwide, including more than 750 in Colorado Springs.[25]

Glen Eyrie was General Palmer's home, a spectacular estate with a sixty-seven-room, 1905 Tudor castle at its heart, located in a magnificent setting adjacent to Garden of the Gods at the entrance to Queen's Canyon (figure 9.1). After Palmer died in 1909, the estate went through three owners but remained mostly unoccupied or used as a summer home intermittently. When it was sold in 1953 to the Navigators at a reduced price, the Navigators' intent was to develop it as a center where people could nurture and renew their relationships with God and with one another, offering warm hospitality to a variety of Christian groups. They consider it "home" for more than 3,000 missionary staff serving in the United States and abroad on military bases, on college campuses, and in communities.[26]

Another early Christian business in the city was Compassion International, an organization that focuses on feeding and supporting orphans and impoverished children around the world. Everett Swanson began Compassion International after he became troubled by the poverty and orphans he saw in Korea during the Korean War. Founded in Chicago in 1952, the organization moved to Colorado Springs in 1980. Their original headquarters is now home of the Beth-El Nursing College at UCCS; Compassion built their new Global Ministry Center headquarters in northern El Paso County in 2001.

Compassion International recruits donors to sponsor a needy child then works to provide food, schooling, medical attention, mentoring, training, and Christian instruction. All of Compassion International's work is channeled through local churches in the areas of need. Other work includes public education films, presentations, and publications.[27] With over $200 million in annual revenue the organization hires nearly 500 local employees. By 2018 it had reached over 2 million children in twenty-five countries.[28]

FIGURE 9.1. Glen Eyrie castle, built in 1905, and estate grounds in the Rampart Range foothills. This was General Palmer's home, now the headquarters for the Navigators. *Source*: Colorado Springs Pioneers Museum.

Several smaller organizations also located in Colorado Springs by the 1980s, such as International Students, Inc., which focused on converting international exchange students at American universities to Christianity. The organization occupied the old tuberculosis sanatorium at Star Ranch in 1972 and employs about twenty-five. Others locating in the city were the World Evangelical Fellowship and the High Flight Foundation.[29] A group based in Manitou Springs, Summit Ministries, began in 1962 and ran two-week summer encampments for teenagers. John Birch Society member and local Christian activist David Noebel became director in 1974, and though he once proclaimed that rock music was used by communists to render youth useless, he grew the ministry to the extent that by 1991 the organization had 1,500 enrollments.[30]

Despite these early players in the Christian industries in Colorado Springs, religion was not an outsized factor in shaping the city's political culture or personality, nor did these groups generate a reputation for the city as a Christian-focused economy and culture. Through the 1980s, churches were fairly mainstream and represented a cross section of established traditions: "Unlike California, notorious for its many cults, most of the religious interest in Colorado Springs runs along well-established traditions. Most religious people are involved in churches of long standing or those which have developed out of old traditions," said a local newspaper reporter in 1980.[31] That would change in the 1990s.

RISE OF THE CHRISTIAN RIGHT

As in many other dimensions of American society, the 1960s caused great disruption in the evangelical community, leading to a sense of crisis. Concerned with the dangers of liberalism, conservative factions in the Southern Baptist Convention purged the organization of moderates and took an increasingly uncompromising stance on the need for the country to return to biblical law.[32] The most influential leader at the national level became the fundamentalist Jerry Falwell, preacher and founder of the Thomas Road Baptist Church in Lynchburg, Virginia, and later founder of Liberty University, a powerhouse in conservative politics today. As Falwell became increasingly concerned with the moral degeneracy of the nation, he moved away from his original position of separating the church from politics. To Falwell, it was no longer acceptable for Christians to separate and wait for Rapture; Christians needed to act to save the nation from secular humanism. His preaching took on a strident militaristic tone: "The Christian life is to be a competitive, combative life," and "The local church is an organized army equipped for battle, ready to charge the enemy."[33] The evangelical community shunned politics no more, and the Christian Right as a political force emerged.

While the overall social atmosphere of the 1960s and the Cold War influenced the shift toward political involvement by the evangelical community, scholars have identified one precipitating event that shook the community out of its complacency and spurred a virulent reaction: In 1970 the Internal Revenue Service (IRS) announced they would deny tax-exempt status to racially segregated private schools.[34] Since forced desegregation of public schools in the 1950s and the later passage of the Civil Rights Act of 1964, many southern communities had created private "segregation schools" to educate white students outside of the public school system. While southerners had long complained of federal intrusion on states' rights and a lack of respect for southern traditions, they tolerated federal mandates because they could adapt through such strategies and continue a segregated educational environment. The IRS initiative was a direct threat to their ability to circumvent federal law; it shattered any hopes that Christians could isolate themselves inside their own institutions and teach what they pleased. Bob Jones University in South Carolina became the first target of the IRS, and its tax-exempt status was revoked in 1976 (this was later rescinded, and the IRS stopped the policy). Concurrent with these political events were less rigid interpretations among evangelicals about exactly when Rapture would occur, thereby opening a space for the Christian Right to become more involved in society and agitate to shape the political realm.[35]

Prodded by friends and supporters, Jerry Falwell formed the Moral Majority in 1979, designed to mobilize Christians into a political force to fight a "holy war."[36] The size, determination, and rapid ascent of the Christian Right in the 1980s took the nation by surprise. Evangelicals who had previously felt alienated from the larger American society were now empowered. Billy Graham allied with the new movement, and despite his unfulfilled predictions in 1951 that the end of the world was imminent, in 1979 he again proclaimed, "I believe God has shown me that unless we have a change in America, we have a thousand days as a free nation . . . three years."[37]

The evangelical sermon was always undertaken as a performance, so preachers in the 1970s were eager to exploit changing media technologies and airwave deregulation to reach a wider audience via television. Chief among those new televangelists was Pat Robertson. Son of a US senator, Robertson created the Christian Broadcasting Network based in Virginia Beach and used it to market his premier show, the *700 Club*. This show reached millions, became the longest-lived religious program on the air, and led to personal earnings in the hundreds of millions of dollars. On the show Robertson would proclaim miracle healings among his audience and make grandiose claims, including the miracle that his power of prayer had diverted Hurricane Gloria away from its path toward Virginia (instead hitting Long Island). He preached that natural disasters in America reflected God's anger over legalized abortion, bans on school prayer, and homosexuality. He published books rife with conspiracy theories, including an accusation that George H.W. Bush was unwittingly assisting "an occult-inspired world socialist dictatorship . . . under the domination of Lucifer and his allies."[38] Satan-worshiping occultists "secretly ruled America," he wrote.[39] Intellectual Christian theologian Francis Schaeffer called him a "certified lunatic."[40] Despite his seemingly far-out proclamations, such was the influence of Robertson through his media empire that Republican presidential candidates sought his support.

The great influence Pat Robertson had on Colorado Springs was to push Christian beliefs into the realm of politics even further than Jerry Falwell had. In 1986 Robertson ran in the presidential primaries to become the Republican Party's candidate, using the slogan "Restore the Greatness of America through Moral Strength."[41] Ultimately his campaign failed for a variety of reasons. The first was bad timing of poor publicity among the televangelists community. Fellow Pentecostal preacher Oral Roberts's claim that God would "call him home" and make him jump off a tower if followers didn't immediately contribute $8 million to save his university in Tulsa was ridiculed; Jim and Tammy Faye Bakker's Charlotte-based PTL Club was exposed as an elaborate Ponzi scheme rife with exorbitant spending, drug abuse, sexual affairs, and hush money payments (Jim Bakker was convicted of twenty-four counts of fraud and conspiracy, including theft of $158 million); then popular fundamentalist and preacher of righteous behavior Jimmy Swaggart was caught taking a prostitute into a New Orleans motel. All of this convinced much of the public that these Christian media figures were charlatans. More important for Robertson's campaign were his own actions. Robertson drew criticism for his support of the most brutal military leaders from the Central American civil wars, including born-again General Efraín Ríos Montt in Guatemala, brainchild and director of the scorched-earth program that the United Nations later labeled genocide of Maya Indians, and El Salvador's Roberto D'Aubuisson, banned by Congress from entering into the United States for directing right-wing death squads, and whom Robertson referred to as a "very nice guy."[42] The press challenged the more audacious claims made throughout his career, such as the faith healing of cancer or other ailments. For instance, reporters wanted to know if he could divert Soviet missiles through prayer once he was president the same way he did for Hurricane Gloria. Robertson was not used to being questioned in such a manner; the press was a much different audience than his devoted followers, who never challenged his many proclamations. In defense, Robertson took on the role of victim and accused reporters of religious bigotry.

The Christian Right reached its apogee of power in the 1990s and early 2000s, both in Colorado Springs and nationally. After Pat Robertson's failed 1986 campaign, he went on to form the most influential Christian political group, the Christian Coalition, led by Ralph Reed. The Christian Coalition worked with lay evangelicals to mobilize and train Christians for effective political action. Its strategy was to be active in local politics in order to build a movement from the ground up.[43] Again based in Virginia, the coalition started its first chapter in solidly Republican Orange County, California. Reed described his voter mobilization program as a covert military operation that sought to "take back America" to the way it was before God was banned from the classroom.[44] Ralph Reed's Christian Coalition was very involved in 1994 Republican Party congressional wins, saying, "Our movement is now in many ways thoroughly integrated and enmeshed into the machinery of the Republican Party."[45] The Christian right reached its height of strength and influence with the election of George W. Bush in 2000, who invited evangelicals into positions of governance.[46]

An important shift occurred among leading evangelicals in the 1990s when many began preaching prosperity theology that legitimized wealth and worldly success. Faith in God, combined with positive thinking and optimism, will deliver monetary wealth, good health, and victory over life's difficulties, so the thinking went. Advocates preached a fusion of self-healing through positive thinking and American can-do pragmatism that thrives under capitalism. Whereas a pillar of the evangelical movement in the nineteenth century was a backwoods populism that maintained a strong suspicion of wealth and pretentious titles, a perpetual quest for piety, and simplicity in life, televangelists became the chief apologists for financial success at the end of the twentieth century. To this thinking, wealth and status were seen a reflection of God's blessings, a reward for true believers. This theological shift lent support for the televangelists' strategy of promising worldly goods in the name of Jesus to financial supporters of their shows, and it also served to justify the televangelists' own fortunes and sometimes-extravagant lifestyles.[47] This form of trickle-down religion also meshed perfectly with trickle-down economics in vogue with the Reagan presidency, inviting thoroughly modern and well-to-do believers in places such as Colorado Springs and Orange County, California, into the evangelical fold.

With their rise to power during their era of maximum influence, the Christian Right took up as their main target sexual politics and feminism. Rapidly changing views of women in society were utterly disconcerting to conservative Christians. Christian authors, ministers, and commentators preached that women could achieve fulfillment, true femininity, and liberation only by submission to their husbands. Of all feminist demands, abortion was seen as the most threatening.[48] In addition to being seen as murder, abortion violated the ideal of feminine domesticity and remains a rallying call for Christian political activists. Intense opposition led to acts of domestic terrorism from groups such as Operation Rescue, members of which (including a former guest on Colorado Springs–based James Dobson's Christian radio program) assassinated abortion doctors.

While the Christian Right was obsessed with sexuality in general and abortion specifically, topping the list of concerns was homosexuality. While long preaching against the sins of succumbing to sexual temptations and adultery, the Christian Right saw homosexuality as a sin of a higher order, a perversion of nature, an abomination to God, an act deserving of imprisonment or perhaps death. As the AIDS epidemic was accelerating in the early 1990s, its disproportionate impact on the gay community was seen as wrath of God on homosexuals, retribution for the "war on nature" their illicit acts generated.[49] Jerry Falwell and others of the religious Right called for quarantine of AIDS victims.

The feminist movement and changing gender norms were seen by the Christian Right as a conspiracy by secular humanists to erase Christianity from society. They viewed all of these related topics as a concerted effort to reprogram sexuality and gender roles through pop culture and again saw themselves as persecuted.[50] The ascendency of the Christian Right was a national phenomenon, but several of the most influential and key actors in the movement were based in Colorado Springs, generating a perception among many that the city was driving the Christian political agenda from what was dubbed "the Vatican of American Evangelicalism."[51]

COLORADO AMENDMENT 2

For two decades beginning in the 1990s Colorado Springs gained national attention from political actions taken by local members of the Christian evangelical community. The first that thrust the city to the forefront of the Christian Right–inspired culture wars was the writing and promotion of Amendment 2 to the state constitution; it prohibited "minority status, quota preferences, protected status or claim of discrimination" for homosexuals.[52] Colorado for Family Values, an advocacy group led by local car dealer Will Perkins, wrote the legislation and pushed the agenda. Perkins and others in the organization claimed this was not homophobic and did not promote an antigay agenda: they were merely insisting that gays shouldn't get "special rights" that might lead to quotas being established for hiring or when assessing discriminatory practices. After all, they claimed, the gay community already enjoyed the same civil rights protections as all Americans, why should they be afforded more?[53]

Part of what drove Colorado for Family Values to create this amendment was that the cities of Denver, Boulder, and Aspen had already created legislation forbidding discrimination against homosexuals in jobs or housing. Amendment 2 would repeal those existing laws, even though such a move violated a treasured conservative principle of local rule and power distributed away from centralized state or federal bodies. More important, in Colorado Springs, the City Council–appointed Human Relations Commission recommended the council vote on an ordinance to ban discrimination of minorities in 1991, which Perkins saw as an attempt to legislate protected status for homosexual behavior.[54] Colorado for Family Values felt it needed to make a stand to prevent the further spread of antidiscriminatory laws based on sexual orientation and to defend their belief in Christian values.

Put on the statewide ballot in 1992, the amendment was approved by 53 percent of Colorado voters on November 3. Taken aback, opponents of the amendment were shocked out of their complacency, and reaction was swift. A coalition of opponents quickly filed suit in the Denver District Court to throw out Amendment 2 on the grounds that it violated federal equal protection laws, plus state rights of home-rule and legislative power.[55] The court issued an injunction that halted its implementation while the case worked its way through the legal system, saying it violated the fundamental right of gays and lesbians to participate equally in the political process.[56]

Opponents organized boycotts of the city, Perkins' car dealership, and the entire state. "Hate is not a family value" was one local rallying cry.[57] Groups such as the US conference of mayors cancelled conventions, cities issued travel bans to Colorado for their public employees, movie stars lent their names in protest, and businesses and nonprofits changed plans to relocate to the state.[58] Colorado gained the moniker "the Hate State," while Colorado Springs was called the city of hate and bigotry.[59] Boycott leaders saw success, claiming that by the end of 1993 Amendment 2 had cost the state $119.7 million, making it the most expensive civil rights violation in US history. Denver alone lost thirty-one conventions worth $38 million, and Colorado Springs tourism officials tallied their losses at eighteen groups—including the US Conference of Mayors—worth a total of $2.2 million.[60] The Broadmoor eliminated sixty jobs because of convention cancellations.[61]

In addition to the direct economic impact, the city's image took a hit and private businesses found increasing difficulty recruiting new talent. Global competition demands a work environment in which employees feel valued, safe, and heard, and the same goes for the community in which the firm is located, said one high-tech manager in Colorado Springs. Citing recruiting efforts that had already suffered, another local director said, "Whether we like it or not, the perception of Colorado Springs by the rest of the nation and the rest of the world is very negative at this point in time."[62] One local financial investment company working in California was asked to remove mention of being from Colorado Springs from its promotional literature; another business consultant feared the city had become the "laughingstock" of the nation: "In the 20 years I've lived here, I've never seen anything so destructive going on in this community," said a local businesswoman.[63]

The Colorado Springs gay community responded by coming out of the closet in unprecedented numbers: "I see Amendment 2 as one of the most positive things that has ever happened to our [gay] community," said one member. The gay activist group Ground Zero formed to focus opposition and challenge stereotypes and misperceptions about gays and lesbians: "Colorado for Family Values has created its worst nightmare: a vocal and organized gay and lesbian community in its own backyard," said a spokesman for Ground Zero (figure 9.2).[64] Local activists Amy Divine and Douglas Triggs started the Citizens Project, an organization formed in 1993 to monitor conservative religious groups in the city, using the phrase (and bumper stickers) "Celebrate Diversity." Their mission to maintain "traditional American values of separation of church and state, freedom of religion and speech, pluralism, individuality, and tolerance and compassion for others" sought to promote tolerance in a city wracked by ill will and distrust, a city, the founders said, that doesn't always embrace diverse points of view.[65] The local weekly alternative newspaper, the *Colorado Springs Independent*, launched in 1993 to counter the reporting from the *Gazette*, particularly its editorial page.[66] Public Broadcasting Service journalist Bill Moyers ran a show on Colorado Springs and Amendment 2, painting a picture far from the "live-and-let-live image of the New West the chamber of commerce would like to present to the national TV audience."[67] *Springs Magazine* wrote that not since the voters of Colorado elected to forgo being an Olympic site in 1972 has the state received so much international exposure.[68] Many Coloradans came to resent Colorado Springs for bringing hardship and shame upon the state.[69]

In October 1994, the Colorado Supreme Court struck down Amendment 2 in a 6–1 decision. The justices ruled it unconstitutional, violating the US Constitution's equal protection clause, because the amendment "singles out one form of discrimination and removes its redress from consideration by the normal political process."[70] The decision was challenged by Colorado attorney General Gale Norton and taken to the US Supreme Court, where in May 1996, it was struck down as a violation of the Fourteenth Amendment: "A state cannot so deem a

FIGURE 9.2. Ground Zero, the gay and lesbian support group from Colorado Springs that formed after passage of Amendment 2, marching at the front of a gay rights demonstration in Washington, DC, in 1993. *Source: Denver Post* (1993), September 19.

class of persons a stranger to its laws," said Justice Anthony Kennedy for the 6–3 majority opinion. He said that singling out the state's homosexuals "in a solitary class" was inexplicable on any basis other than "animus" and that prejudice is not a valid justification for a policy that creates special burdens for one group not placed on others.[71]

Attorney General Norton called the court's decision insulting to Colorado voters. The vice president of Colorado Springs–based Focus on the Family accused the justices of "judicial activism," while president of the Family Research Council Gary Bauer blamed "an out-of-control unelected judiciary."[72] Nonetheless, the Supreme Court decision was the final blow, and the amendment never became law. It did, however, leave long-lasting effects on the city's image and reputation.

JESUS SPRINGS[73]

While Colorado for Family Values and Amendment 2 grew out of the local Christian community, that base was simultaneously growing and intensifying in the early 1990s through deliberate strategies undertaken by city leaders. After an economic downturn in the 1980s, when declines in the personal computer market affected local silicon chip manufacturers and military funding for space initiatives also fell, the city looked for new strategies to stimulate the economy. The Chamber of Commerce had created the Economic Development Corporation (EDC) in 1970 to recruit private businesses to Colorado Springs, and this group, based on advice from the economic development consulting firm PHH Fantus they hired, decided to target the nonprofit sector for environmentally clean businesses that would diversify the existing economic base.[74] The assistant director of the EDC and member since 1984 was Alice Worrell, who grew up in the evangelical church and "speaks their language."[75] To Worrell, a specific slice of the nonprofit industries in America seemed a good fit: Christian parachurch organizations. These are not churches, but support firms that comprise the business of religion, be it anything from missionary groups, orphanage supporters, Bible and Christian text publishers, producers of Christian educational materials and workshops, film and other media producers, youth outreach organizations, ministry training, radio talk show producers, and many more. As early as 1988, Worrell took the lead through aggressive recruiting to help evangelical groups relocate, relying on her upbringing by Christian college teachers: "There were lots of names I knew from living on evangelical college campuses all my life."[76]

One target geographic area was Southern California, a hub of conservative voters and Christian organizations.[77] In 1989, California tightened tax exemptions on religious organizations, at the same time that Colorado loosened theirs by extending the definition of religious worship (which already enjoyed tax exemptions) to an activity "in furtherance of religious purposes" as determined by the organization.[78] This change meant the Christian parachurch organizations would enjoy the same tax-exempt status that churches already relied upon.

Worrell and the EDC relied on the state's tax exemptions and the city's conservative culture to attract new Christian organizations. She highlighted the presence of the early religious groups such as the Navigators and Young Life, in the city since 1947, to show a favorable base that would welcome new Christian organizations. Since most religious organizations operate on a tight budget, the EDC also used low labor and housing costs as inducements, citing the affordability and family-oriented climate of the city.[79] The campaign worked—many religious groups envisioned a comfortable fit into the conservative political climate. Many felt kinship with the already established and ever-growing number of Christian parachurch organizations.[80]

By 1991 there were already enough Christian parachurch organizations in the city for them to enjoy agglomeration economies, or savings that businesses in similar economic sectors enjoy from locating nearby to each other. These savings come from access to supply firms for the industry, sharing of information, specialized labor who know the business, savings from travel when many firms are in one place, and specialized services that arise through the concentration of the industry. For instance, International Media Systems is a local production company that was doing about one-third of its business in 1991 with local evangelical organizations, one of many local vendors, including accountants, printers, lawyers, hotels, freelance writers, graphic designers, and travel agents who specialize in serving Colorado Springs evangelical organizations: "Ministry Organizations like to work with professionals who share their world view and their beliefs."[81] When a Los Angeles transplant, Every Home for Christ, announced a $3.5 million headquarters in northern Colorado Springs, it said it would add a $3 million office complex to offer space for smaller ministries so they could enjoy lower operating costs through shared resources.[82] A Christian book publisher who relocated from Southern California said, "A lot of authors I work with come through this town and being here saves me an incredible amount of travel and expense."[83] In 1992 the evangelical group Youth With a Mission relocated from Amsterdam to Colorado Springs. The director of research said, "We believe that being part of a community of so many other agencies and ministries with shared international focus can only be beneficial . . . This new location will improve communication and networking that can in turn mean more effectiveness in our ministries."[84] The Navigators, Promise Keepers, and Campus Crusade for Christ worked in a synergistic way that benefitted each other through shared staff and information.[85] By 1991 there were thirty-three Christian evangelical organizations in the city, paying more than $45 million in wages to about 2,200 workers.[86] Over seventy religious ministries had relocated to Colorado Springs by 1995 and over ninety by 2014.[87]

The religious environment in Colorado Springs quickly changed, particularly as local evangelical groups became overtly political. By 1994 the local chapter of the Christian Coalition was the largest in the state, and members were thrilled at the November congressional victories for Republicans and their "Contract With America" agenda: "We helped elect the candidates God wants in office," said a local member.[88] The rapid influx and concentration of evangelical organizations created a new social dynamic that empowered evangelicals to express their political muscle at the local level. Influence was initially felt in the public arena when local evangelicals took the lead in helping establish charter schools in the 1990s.[89] Longtime residents, including mainstream Republicans, grew concerned that fundamentalist groups instructed members on how to exert their values in areas from public schools to federal legislation. The unified block of Christian activists carried undue influence.[90] Citizens Project reported in 1991 that self-esteem books were removed from shelves of an elementary school after evangelical parents complained that they contained New Age philosophies. A group called "Cowboys for Christ" objected to their kids studying Greek mythology, then sued to force the school to teach Bible-based morality. The city's largest school district received calls from "concerned Christians" who complained about gay and pagan panelists at a high school diversity conference, prompting officials to cut them from the program.[91] Parents pressed for textbook changes at local schools, then schools cut back Halloween festivities over protest about the pagan origin. Parents wanted evolution removed from the curriculum, filing lawsuits to demand creationism be taught; citizens concerned with the increased religious influence in schools complained that police officers openly wore crosses on their uniforms.[92] The superintendent of an affluent school district in northern El Paso County reported that the growing influence of the religious Right cast a shadow over local classrooms. Teachers were increasingly afraid to deal with tough issues, which the superintendent worried would lead to self-censorship out of fear of conflict with Christian activists.[93]

In addition to the activism focused on schools, local rabbi Howard Hirsch complained of the "disenfranchisement of other points of view," while a Congregational Church reverend, James White, called the religious Right "tolerance-impaired."[94] Downtown pastors claimed they had never seen the churches so divided. As a result, the Pikes Peak Inter-Religious Clergy Alliance formed to be a counterweight to the evangelical groups.[95] President Phyllis Wannemacher of the Colorado Springs Education Association resented that the new evangelicals were coming into the community and saying, "Stop what you're doing, we want you to be like us."[96] "If you don't agree with them, you're evil," said a local Republican leader.[97] Marcy Morrison, a local Republican heavyweight and then-mayor of Manitou Springs, felt the entire strategy to recruit the evangelical nonprofits was flawed, a misunderstanding from a consulting firms' message: "They told us, 'Folks, you must diversify, look for different kinds of jobs for your people. Don't put your eggs in one basket again like you did with the military and then microchip companies.' But I think we've done exactly that again with religious organizations."[98]

The strength of the evangelical community grew in the 1990s, even as resistance also assembled. By 1997, the EDC had issued a study reporting that the city has a reputation of being controlled by "religious zealots," causing "significant detriment to recruiting talented young people [who] fear the imposition on the general public of extreme beliefs through schools and through government."[99] The EDC stopped their policy of recruiting religious nonprofits in 2002 over concern about bad publicity.[100] But by then, the policy had already created a robust evangelical presence in the city, and one organization in particular carried the most weight and exerted the most influence at the national level: Focus on the Family.

Focus on the Family

Focus on the Family is a Christian ministry that offers advice and counseling for marriages, relationships, child-rearing, and more, all based on biblical principles. The ministry publishes books and other literature, provides telephone and email counseling, produces digital media, and most, important, conducts a daily radio telecast. It has been called a "Christian radio ministry."[101] All of their work is intended to "protect . . . against destructive social influences" and "promote biblical truths worldwide."[102] The organization formed in 1977 by James Dobson in Southern California. Dobson graduated from what is now the Point Loma

Nazarene University, then went on to earn his doctorate from the University of Southern California (USC) in child development. He served on the faculty in the School of Medicine at USC for fourteen years, focusing on marriage counseling and pediatrics. The son of a traveling evangelical preacher, Dobson felt the call to proselytize and published his highly influential book *Dare to Discipline* in 1977. He went on to publish twenty-six books plus others that he coauthored.

Dobson left his faculty position to dedicate his time fully to Focus on the Family, which became more political in its messages and advocacy throughout the 1980s and beyond. Dobson served as advisor to both President Reagan and George H.W. Bush in the 1980s.[103] Like much of the Christian Right, Dobson focused his angst on feminism because of the threat he saw it posed to the traditional family structure. In his 1975 book entitled *What Wives Wish their Husbands Knew about Women* Dobson makes the bold assumption that he knows what women want and is the authority to speak for them. His advocacy for respecting women and women's work is a call to accept traditional gender roles as "God-designed."[104]

In 1982 Dobson and Focus lent their support for the Family Research Council, a conservative think tank in Washington, DC, that lobbied legislators. He devoted renewed attention to this organization in 1989 when he hired Gary Bauer, former advisor to Ronald Reagan and used it to monitor legislation and federal policies on family affairs. Through a network of state family councils with a half million on their mailing list, these two leaders revitalized the Family Research Council into the most powerful Christian Right lobby group. It rose to become one of the three largest evangelical political organizations.[105]

Focus had grown out of its facilities in Pomona by 1991. Already a major player of the Christian Right, Focus was recruited by the Colorado Springs EDC to relocate to Colorado Springs as the key part of the EDC's overall nonprofit recruitment strategy. To entice the ministry's $70 million annual operation to Colorado Springs, the El Pomar Foundation broke with its policy against funding religious groups and awarded Focus a $4 million grant to subsidize their move.[106] Focus's initial office opened in June 1991, in temporary facilities while it built a permanent campus at the north end of the city. At the time it had about 725 employees in California and expected to save approximately $5 million per year because of the local agglomeration economies.[107] Landing Focus on the Family solidified Colorado Springs' reputation as the national, and worldwide, Christian center.

In September 1993, Focus completed and moved to its new forty-seven-acre campus in the Briargate neighborhood. In a show of the strong ties between the Air Force Academy and the local evangelical community, the academy parachute team delivered keys to Dobson to officially open the new building.[108] Conveniently ignoring the $4 million subsidy given to the organization, a video accompanying ministry's 1993 annual report stated: "The beautiful forty-seven acre campus and home of Focus on the Family is not the result of any great scheme of man

FIGURE 9.3. Focus on the Family generates so many tourist visits that it merits its own exit sign on Interstate 25. *Source*: Photo by author.

but is truly from the hand of God."[109] The site grew to eighty-eight acres with a 25,000-square-foot Welcome Center and employed over 1,300 people.[110] Boasting its own zip code and exit sign from the interstate, Focus on the Family has become one of the most popular tourism sites in the region, with about 250,000 visitors annually (figure 9.3).[111] The Welcome center includes a giant tubular slide to a lower floor for kids to play with a replica World War II plane to climb through. The upper floor has the expansive bookstore, theater, and information about the organization, including displays for the TrueU.org program, an alternative to university teaching on philosophy, sociology, history, and other subjects designed to present the biblical worldview and "a place to discover the truth."

From his new campus, Dobson built a powerful media empire, "The most effective social and political vehicle of the national Christian Right."[112] His daily radio program had an audience of over 5 million listeners and his books sold over 16 million copies, with filmed lectures reaching a wider audience than that by any other evangelical outlet.[113] Magazines and newsletters achieved a circulation of 3 million.[114] Dobson promoted the traditional family, opposed feminism for breaking traditional gender roles, and spoke out strongly against both abortion and homosexuality. Focus on the Family, while new to Colorado Springs in 1991, lent vital support to Colorado for Family Values and the Amendment 2 campaign. By the end of the 1990s Dobson's network of organizations rivaled the Christian Coalition for political influence. This clout and his own force of personality and general appeal made him the most influential leader the movement ever had.

Not content to let the Family Research Council do all his political work, Dobson split the public policy division apart from Focus on the Family so the former, called Focus on the Family Action, could directly engage with politics while the remaining Focus on the Family division could maintain its tax-exempt status. By 1998 his policy network had thirty-four state affiliates and more than 2 million members.[115]

Such was the clout of James Dobson by the late 1990s that virtually every Republican presidential hopeful traveled to Colorado Springs to seek his blessing. These visits began in earnest leading up to the 1996 presidential election. From April to July of 1995, four of the nine Republican presidential candidates had visited Dobson in Colorado Springs, with more afterward. Said a spokesman for candidate Pete Wilson, "He runs the most influential religious broadcast in the country, aimed straight at conservative voters."[116] Dobson took on the Republican Party for not being aggressive enough in their support of biblical values, listing policy failures such as the inability to restrict abortions and failing to block funding for the National Endowment for the Arts (NEA): "I'm talking about the moral foundation to the universe. Things we know are right."[117] He threatened Republican leaders he would abandon the Republican Party and try to take as many of his 5 million radio listeners as he could with him if they continued to "betray" evangelical voters who helped put them in office.[118] Known for never compromising, Dobson continued to be the major player in the cultural wars through the early 2000s, including regular meetings and counsel with George W. Bush after his 2000 election.

With the Bush presidency, fear that drove right-wing activism diminished. Family Research Council membership declined sharply, as did funding for Focus, in part due to discredited programs such as the "Love Won Out" conversion therapy conferences designed to convert gay men and women to a heterosexual lifestyle and the resignation of longtime *Focus* radio show cohost Mike Trout after an extramarital affair.[119]

Dobson may have reached the height of his national influence in about 2005, as did the influence of the Christian Right in Colorado Springs, "Home of the greatest concentration of fundamentalist Christian activist groups in American history."[120] Over one-third of religious adherents in the county were aligned with evangelical churches. Religious visitors filled over one-third of hotel bookings in 2000.[121] About ninety Christian nonprofits were located in town with a combined revenue of nearly $1 billion. Compassion International was the largest, with a revenue of nearly $217 million, followed by Young Life, Focus on the Family, the Navigators, and Cook Communications.[122] These top three each ranked in the state's top twenty nonprofits in 2005, larger than US Olympic Committee and the University of Colorado Foundation. These organizations hired about 3,800 people, with perhaps another 1,300 jobs generated from these industries as a multiplier effect, but their influence on the local and national social environment was even larger.[123] The industry concentration enabled very specialized niche firms to operate profitably, for example, Mission Training International, which brings future missionaries to the city to conduct hostage exercises to prepare for hostile engagements overseas.[124] The *Gazette* was a constant supporter of most local initiatives driven by the Christian Right, especially in its editorial and opinion page that went far to solidify the city's reputation for entrenched conservatism. A Christian charity watchdog director said these groups were not merely important players, but they are the country's leviathans: "I would put Colorado Springs as the nation's most influential Christian city."[125] While Focus on the Family was one of the main actors, a local megachurch also played an outsized role.

New Life Church

Ted Haggard grew up on an Indiana farm and graduated from Oral Roberts University in 1978. He was an associate pastor at a large church in Baton Rouge, Louisiana, when he visited a missionary friend in Colorado Springs in 1984. During that visit, his friend prophesized that Haggard would build his own church in town. Ted climbed the slopes of Pikes Peak, prayed, waited for a revelation, then felt called by God to move to the city.[126] He and his wife started humbly in 1985, preaching in basements with lawn chairs for pews, then slowly moving from one rental office complex to another as his congregation grew. At one time the church rented space in a strip mall with a bar, liquor store, and massage parlor as neighbors.[127] Colorado Springs, like much of urban America, is plagued with abandoned big-box stores in strip malls that were once the hot shopping districts but now typify corridors of urban blight, no longer competing with ever-larger stores in newer areas with higher incomes. As a result, startup churches are a common rental for these spaces, and New Life was one of many (figure 9.4).[128]

When he first arrived, Haggard found many New Age spiritualists in town that he considered devil worshipers, 1960s-era leftovers of a satanic community. Through aggressive evangelism that included actively confronting sinners and Satanists, his flock grew and Haggard believes they chased most occultists out of town, which he attributed to a miracle. Eventually he purchased a thirty-five-acre lot north of the city to build the New Life Church. More than a church, it grew into a giant complex as followers multiplied. Haggard called it a place for those who love the Lord but can't stand church.[129] New Life became one of the nation's most important megachurches.

FIGURE 9.4. "Jesus Heals Cancer" at the Victory World Outreach, an evangelical church occupying a big-box shell on South Academy Boulevard, 2000. *Source*: photo by author.

The megachurch phenomenon grew to maturity in Orange County, California. As the laid-back, outdoor living of southern California took off across America in the early twentieth century and led to the car-oriented, suburban landscapes of today, new landforms to cater to the automobile were invented.[130] The first drive-in church began in 1955 in Garden Grove, with a combined walk-in and drive-in built in 1961. These institutions scaled up into multimillion-dollar operations, building upon the California lifestyle by using rock music, relaxed and informal attire, light shows, giant video screens, and other entertainment devices. The congregations are huge, but the evangelical focus is on personal redemption through a relationship with Jesus. This cultural innovation combined a therapeutic style of worship using contemporary music and fashion with highly designed and focused worship services that catered to the individualistic suburban lifestyles. By the 1990s, Orange County was home to the country's highest concentration of megachurches and a host of influential evangelical preachers who contributed to a resurgence of born-again Christianity.[131] One of the largest and most influential is the Saddleback Valley Community Church, headed by pastor Rick Warren. Started in a high school auditorium in Laguna Hills, California, the church built its first campus in nearby Lake Forest. This institution reflects its suburban setting by creating a dispersed, multinodal, multiscaled network with an emphasis on weekly small group meetings in members' homes. The geography of suburbia is fundamentally integral to the religious action. Saddleback's dispersed services give the everyday places of work, play, and shopping a spiritual significance, making the fragmentation of suburbia meaningful. Multiple different services target specific demographics. Warren writes in his influential book *The Purpose Driven Life* that "it's not about you," that life is not simply for personal gratification, yet the church is purposefully organized to meet the individualized needs of suburban lifestyles.[132] In many ways, it is completely about you, creating performances that center on the individual. Unique to the world, the megachurch goal is to provide religious consumers with as many choices as possible.[133]

In suburban Colorado Springs, replete with seas of tract housing, big-box stores, and wide arterial roads whizzing commuters about, the New Life complex grew into the largest church in the city. Boasting some 14,000 members in the mid-2000s, the multibuilding complex has a 7,500-seat worship auditorium at its center but uses tactics similar to Saddleback and other influential megachurches, with services custom-tailored to different ages and demographic groups and a focus on small group meetings in homes. All this was Pastor Ted's domain, evidence of God's blessings. Haggard preached a prosperity theology, free market form of Christianity, linking his church to the miracle of capitalism and free market competition: "Pro-free markets, pro-private property . . . That's what evangelical stands for."[134] He preached that the Christian home is in a constant state of war against the forces of Satan, said that liberal Christianity is a failed ideology, and coined the motto "Cooperation without compromise" in his aggressive lobbying against gay marriage.[135] He was an early and vocal supporter for Amendment 2, telling Bill Moyers in his PBS report that homosexuality is "immoral," citing the Bible as his source.[136] Haggard grew popular with national media, regularly appearing on cable TV shows and in print, and gained such clout that he had weekly calls with George W. Bush after the 2000 election.

In 1998 Haggard had a vision to build a World Prayer Center, which was completed that year. The $5.5 million, 55,000-square-foot building on the New Life campus is a center that focuses targeted prayer to help those in need and assists Christianity to reach remote corners of the world. The center hosted full-time, on-site intercessors who have been called by God to pray for a living, but requests were also sent to the world prayer movement, comprising about 50 million people in 120 countries who answer prayer requests. The Prayer Center provides space for other Christian ministries and affiliated conferences. With a direct view to the US Air Force Academy (and painted in the same silver and blue colors), the vernacular for the center is the "spiritual NORAD," with adherents likening the spread of Christianity as going to war. They see concentrated prayer working to subdue demonic spirits so that God's kingdom can triumph on earth.[137]

Haggard organized the Association of Life-Giving Churches, offshoots affiliated with New Life and its evangelical theology, which grew to about 300 churches nationwide. With his wide-reaching influence, Haggard was elected in 2003 as president of the National Association of Evangelicals, which represents 45,000 churches and over 30 million believers as the nation's most powerful religious lobbying group. By 2005, he was easily James Dobson's equal in terms of national influence: "No pastor in America holds more sway over the political direction of evangelicalism than does Pastor Ted, and no church more than New Life."[138]

Despite its size and prestige, New Life Church was not the only megachurch in town. For instance, the Woodmen Valley Chapel hosts a congregation of over 5,000 with casual services offering music, lights, and giant video screens for full entertainment.[139] Church pastor Tomberlin stated that God raised Colorado Springs to be a strategic center and wants Colorado Springs to be influential for the entire country. He encouraged members to express their Christianity in the public realm and to help the church distribute Christian Coalition voter materials. Pastor Tomberlin said that members should be insulated from the world, but not isolated, yet the locations of these megachurches, in the affluent suburbs north of the city—away from the chaotic, messy, diverse, and sinful city center—by design isolate the flock from urban diversity. These suburban enclaves house people of similar race and class in privatized worlds, sheltering evangelicals from conflict with different people with different lifestyles encountered in public spaces. Some believers see more urban places as demon possessed, potentially affecting people who simply traverse through them. When author Jeff Sharlet was writing an article on the New Life Church for *Harper's*, he was warned against going downtown when seeking places to eat and instead directed toward the chain eateries on the big suburban arterial roads. The downtown, he was told, is "confusing," a place to which many church members rarely ventured.[140] The suburban locations for these megachurches are a strategic retreat, where believers plant churches as outposts circling the enemy.

The Fall

In November 2006, a self-proclaimed male prostitute in Denver revealed that Ted Haggard had been soliciting his services every month or so over the past three years, with visits that included purchasing and using crystal methamphetamine.

Mike Jones, his accuser, said Haggard's hypocrisy motived him to go public after he grew tired of hearing his antigay messages.[141] The news broke like a thunderclap throughout the nation but hit particularly hard among the New Life community and other evangelicals in Colorado Springs. Many could not believe the news—the *Gazette* ran the headline "Shock. Disbelief. Denial." James Dobson accused the media of unconscionable behavior, reporting unfounded rumors in a shameful attempt to influence voter initiatives supporting gay rights in an upcoming election.[142] Haggard originally denied the accusations, but as his story continued to evolve, he eventually admitted to all.

At the peak of his power and called the most prominent evangelical in the nation, Haggard had to put himself on administrative leave from the New Life Church and resign as president of the National Association of Evangelicals.[143] A panel that took over temporary leadership for New Life Church investigated the matter and sent Haggard into exile for rehabilitation in Phoenix. New Life members retreated inward as they questioned the very foundations of their belief. The Pikes Peak evangelical empire that Haggard and others had built quickly crumbled. Membership at New Life Church declined by over 40 percent to around 8,000.[144]

Business and civic leaders again fretted about the city's image as national and international media descended upon the city. "It just reinforces the conservative image (of the city)," a local businessman said about the intense media coverage.[145] The coverage made it one of the biggest stories to ever come out of Colorado Springs.[146] This scandal broke shortly after the city had already been generating headlines through sex and religion scandals at the Air Force Academy, then one elected official insulted single moms on national TV and another stated that only white Americans are "normal." Added to this, the ongoing controversy over Amendment 2 was still relatively fresh in national attention: "For a community our size, we do garner a great deal of media" said the president of the Convention and Visitors Bureau. A local defense contractor president said, "it makes it hard to recruit young, single people."[147]

While the episode brought personal disgrace to Ted Haggard and shame to the New Life congregation, the event marked the beginning of a change in the relationship between evangelical groups and the community. What followed was a marked introspection among local evangelicals and lessening of overt political activity.[148] By 2007, local Republicans were increasingly unhappy with extremism; the president of EDC admitted the reputation of the Springs as intolerant remained widespread.[149] Moderate Republicans in Colorado Springs, uncomfortable with the close entanglement between religious organizations and the party, hoped their voice could now be heard.

James Dobson stepped down as Focus on the Family Director in February 2009. Contributions and listeners had been flat since 2000, and the organization trimmed its budget and eliminated ninety-six positions in 2003.[150] Losing money, employees shrank from a high of around 1,400 to 700 by 2010 as sales declined and the base demographic was aging. Dobson's replacement, Jim Daly, tried to reach a younger audience in a move toward more hands-on social services to transcend politics. Despite the move away from overt political activities, Dobson continued his daily radio broadcasts and maintained the partisan attacks. In 2010 the Focus on the Family board asked Dobson to resign from the flagship radio show.[151]

A RENEWED CHRISTIANITY

The decline of the two big evangelical leaders in Colorado Springs was fairly abrupt, but even before the cataclysmic revelations of Ted Haggard's hidden life, change was taking place in the evangelical political sphere nationally. Prior to George W. Bush's reelection in 2004, prominent evangelicals published books accusing the Christian Right of confusing politics for religion in its quest for power, leading to a culture of intolerance. One leader reflected that attempts to restore morality though the political process had failed.[152] *Christianity Today* editorialized in 2006 their concerns that the word "evangelical" is increasingly shorthand for right-wing US politics.[153] Both Jerry Falwell and James Dobson found that when becoming aggressively political, membership and contributions declined. The Christian Right was further harmed when Jerry Falwell, two days after the terrorist attacks of September 11, 2001, said on *700 Club* that abortionists, pagans, feminists, gays, the ACLU, and all who support a secular America helped the attack to happen by mocking God. Pat Robertson responded, "Well, I entirely concur."[154] Tired of such harsh condemnations, membership in evangelical movements declined. By 2009, popular Southern California megachurch leader Rick Warren declared the Christian Right dead.

In a criticism of the megachurch phenomenon, Christian minister and author Skye Jethani has argued that the core values of consumerism are incongruent with Christian life. He writes that the satisfaction of our personal desires should not be our goal in life, and the church does not exist to supply spiritual goods and services to religious consumers: God is not a commodity that exists to make you feel better. He worries that the institutionalized, businesslike management of megachurches has taken precedent over the transcendent calling of Christian ministry, and while more people are reporting they are drawn to Christ, they reject the antigay, antiwomen, and overtly political affiliation with the Republican Party that is too exclusionary.[155] "The world I was dreaming about was not the world my church was dreaming about," said one young evangelical to the *New York Times*.[156]

Young Christians in particular are looking for a more authentic religious experience. Concerns over homelessness, poverty, imprisonment, refugees, racism, and a seemingly perpetual state of warfare are more important than partisan politics and the consumer lifestyle. Environmental issues, particularly global warming—a topic the conservative Right still denies is real—loom larger in their psyche.[157] Premillennialists in the Christian Right had long ignored environmental conservation because their apocalyptic thinking deemed stewardship unnecessary—when Rapture occurred, the earthly condition would be irrelevant. Younger evangelicals now take environmental matters seriously, if for nothing else than to alleviate suffering among the poor who will be disproportionately affected by climate change. Their new calling is their Christian duty to work for the common good, to build community as an expression of their faith.

Local radio journalist Noel Black interviewed young evangelicals in Colorado Springs for a 2015 show episode entitled "After the Evangelical Vatican."[158] He found many disillusioned with the political stances of New Life Church and the cult of personality that existed around Ted Haggard. Seeking new ways of expressing Christianity, two ex-members opened the Wild Goose, a coffee and drink meetinghouse downtown to create community engagement. They sought to create a parallel culture to the hardline evangelicals. Others sought out a more liberal congregation, flocking to the First Congregational Church, one of the well-established downtown churches from the initial days of the city. It became a refuge for former New Lifers looking for something more open, especially among those who felt forced out for voicing doubts. Skeptical of viewing the church through a consumer lens, they are suspicious of the "slick" performances and aren't looking to be entertained in their worship.

Switchback Coffee owner Brandon DelGrosso says that as a follower of Jesus, he doesn't have a problem with the term "evangelical," just the politicized version of that term: "Anytime religion has become politicized, it has always been horrible." To him when the church becomes intertwined with the state, people follow because it is advantageous, not because they believe. As an example of this renewed expression of faith, Switchback Coffee Roaster and Café in the downtown lists their values as believing that all people belong and that we are better together, and they seek to build connections to unite their neighborhood.[159] This statement of values, along with the "Safe Space" sign for all gender identities on the wall of the shop, tell you right away that this expression of Christianity differs greatly from the message that drove the 1990s-era Christian Right and its focus on political influence. While starting his coffee roaster, and later café, was strictly a business decision to fill a local demand for good coffee, there is no doubt that DelGrosso's faith has shaped the business. "Jesus hung out with the lowly oddballs, the outcast, those that were hated. He was called a drunkard, a sinner. But he never had a condemning word come out of his mouth. As a follower of Jesus, I want to live like that. So through this coffee shop, I want to share my table with all people so that everyone feels accepted, that everyone belongs."[160] Tyler Hill, also a follower of Jesus and coowner of Loyal Coffee in downtown Colorado Springs, says that youth today don't want the government to represent their spirituality; they are more concerned with what Jesus taught: love your enemy, care for the poor, help refugees. He sees a strong generational divide in the Christian community: "The wounds we suffered from the Old Guard are deep. We were tricked, they didn't really care about me." While his copartners do not all share his faith, they do share a common vision. Through the Loyal Coffee Shop slogan "community by way of coffee," Hill says, "We want to offer up a dose of kindness and humanity. We want to manifest beauty. We want you to know that we care about you, that you are seen, heard, loved."[161] The vision and actions of Christian entrepreneurs such as Hill and DelGrosso are working to transcend boundaries in the community, to heal the wounds, rather than creating more divisions.

POST-EVANGELICAL COLORADO SPRINGS

In 2002, *Christianity Today* proclaimed Dallas the capital of American evangelicalism, taking the title away from Colorado Springs.[162] The publication stated that Christianity is an influential subculture in Colorado Springs, whereas in Dallas it *is* the culture. Evangelicals in Colorado Springs do remain an influential subculture and a solid part of the community, but now there is increasing diversity and different perspectives within the community. Despite the negative press the city received, the EDC effort did generate jobs and an economic niche that continues to attract Christian companies and the services that support the industry.[163] The wealthy northern suburbs, where most megachurches are located, are, by and large, stable and prosperous additions to the city.

Some argue the Christian influence in the city was exaggerated to begin with. Surveys showed that in 2005 at the height of Haggard's influence, El Paso County residents were less inclined to go to church than those in the state overall.[164] For total religious adherents in 2010, El Paso County was far behind liberal Boulder and Denver counties![165] Political scientist Josh Dunn has concluded that the evangelical influence on urban politics is overstated and that politics have largely failed social conservatives in Colorado Springs, with their influence slowly declining since the passage of Amendment 2.[166]

Despite less aggressive politics, a quieter media voice, and perhaps declining influence, the Colorado Springs evangelical community has not disappeared and maintains a strong presence. The national antiabortion group Personhood USA said Colorado Springs is "always our biggest base of support."[167] Evangelical influence can be seen through the political support for Gordon Klingenschmitt, a former navy chaplain court-martialed and discharged in 2006. He runs a TV show and ministry, the *Pray in Jesus Name Project*, that has been labeled a hate group by the Southern Poverty Law Center. He proclaims that gays are not going to heaven and wrote a book about the multiple demons ruling President Obama.[168] Klingenschmitt said of Jared Polis, now Colorado governor but at the time the state's first openly gay US congressman, that his goal is for Coloradans to "endorse his sodomy and . . . join ISIS in beheading Christians."[169] Despite these and many other extreme claims, he was elected to the Colorado House of Representatives for an El Paso County district from2015 to 2017. Local Democratic Party leaders complain that Klingenschmitt just furthers the reputation of Colorado Springs as the "capital of crazy."[170] Mr. Klingenschmitt ran for City Council in 2019. While successful in fundraising, out of a twelve-candidate field to elect three he came in fourth place.

Like any one person or any one group, the evangelical community comes with both its good and bad sides. Longtime columnist and city observer John Hazlehurst wrote: "Living in a city so heavily influenced by the Christian right means living with a ruling class of intermittently loony Republicans, as well as their seriously wacko hangers-on. But it also means living in a law-abiding city of comparatively careful drivers, clean streets, well-kept homes, good schools, and safe, pleasant neighborhoods."[171]

Because Colorado Springs was viewed as the "Evangelical Capital" of the country and had garnered so much media attention, The Civilians theater troupe from New York City came to explore the topic and create a play entitled "This Beautiful City" based on the Colorado Springs experience.[172] This remarkable performance brought in the voice of players from all sides of the drama, with actors quoting New Life members, Ted Haggard's confession, atheists who had bricks thrown through their window, activists denying there should be a separation of church and state, opponents to evangelizing at the Air Force Academy, powerful stories from an ex-drug addict whose life was saved when born again, tales of demons at work in the community, and more. The play captures the emotions, turmoil, arguments, and passion that unfolded in Colorado Springs. Toward the end, a transgender woman talks of losing her job after telling her workmates she could no longer live as a man and was tired of running from herself. Despite losing everything, she talks of her love for the city that she helped design and build in her professional career, and, tellingly, she stated, "If there is one thing I have learned, from all this hell I've been through, it is that now, I see the people." When asked by her friends why she doesn't just move somewhere she would be more welcomed, her response beautifully captures the image that Colorado Springs, as an embodiment of the Rocky Mountain West ethic, at one time projected and one day might once again represent:

> You know what, this is America, and I like it here. I like seeing Pikes Peak out my front door. And I will be doggonned, if some guy is going to tell me where I can or can't live. The moment we have to run and hide, and live in the shadows, that is the moment we have lost our liberty, and it is not going to happen, not on my watch. You didn't get permission from me to be who you are, so damn sure I'm not gonna get permission from you to be who I am.

Amen.

10

Place

> It is given to a hundred cities to be manufacturing centers, but what do they make that is comparable to your scenery and your air?
>
> —CHARLES MULFORD ROBINSON, 1905[1]

Colorado Springs has been a key player in the creation of the American West. The city has also helped shape the ongoing discourse of nation building, the stories this country tells about itself. It has had an outsized influence, beyond what most would expect for a city of its size located far from the power centers of the nation. There is something about the place that sets it apart. What is it that makes Colorado Springs unique, that creates its identity, its sense of place? Answering that has been the challenge of this book, yet distilling out its sense of place remains elusive.

SENSE OF PLACE

The meaning of the phrase "sense of place" can be interpreted from two different perspectives. The first interpretation attributes a sense of place to the locality itself. This perspective is concerned with the characteristics of a place, in this case a city, so it refers to an image projected by the architecture of its buildings, the spatial arrangement of the built environment, its natural setting, and the social milieu or political culture of its governance and inhabitants. The second perspective understands sense of place as a characteristic of a person, a part of each individual's identity as she, he, or they develop place attachments and feelings about home or other places of special importance. This perspective emphasizes the ways that people experience, use, and understand place.[2] The emphasis of this book has been on the former—the special characteristics that make Colorado Springs unique. Having

DOI: 10.5876/9781646421688.c010

said that, it is impossible to disentangle these two perspectives, because the built environment affects our personal identity. As we traverse through our everyday landscape, we are bombarded with imagery and symbolism that reflect a certain set of values and ideals, which we in turn internalize to form our perception of the world and how it ought to be organized. Our built environment therefore shapes our sense of place, and we then continue to create places that reflect that sense of place, that value system. In essence, culture—a human construct—is embodied in our landscapes, which then help to further formulate culture, our understanding and value system that shapes our lifestyle. Geographer Edward Soja coined this the "socio-spatial dialectic," the interplay between our world, how it looks, how we organize it, and our personal identity about who we are and where we belong.[3]

The perspective that a locality has certain characteristics that create its sense of place derives from ancient notions of the "spirit of place," expressed in the Latin phrase *genius loci*.[4] This term refers to a belief in a local guardian divinity, a supernatural presence, where any place derived much of its unique quality from the presence and protection of this spirit. Visitors and inhabitants were thought to become aware of this benign presence as their feelings about a place developed. Their sense of place is a quality that emerges from the characteristics of that place, something that cannot be enumerated but yields a special status to the place being experienced.[5] In our modern world we typically dismiss the notion of a spiritual guardian, yet we still recognize that some places have an attraction which gives us a certain indefinable sense of well-being. A visit to such a place can be a significant event; we are refreshed and elated each time we are there. The food, smells, sounds, climate, landforms, architecture, and local customs intertwine to generate a special feeling. We develop attachment to these places and they become a very part of our personal identity.

Seminal landscape scholar J. B. Jackson reiterated this connection between the spirit of place and an individual's sense of place by emphasizing a sense of time. He believes that through ritual, or repeated routine, we build a sense of place. A shared experience through a custom of repeated ritual is a celebration of reverence. A feeling of fellowship with those who share the experience is built into the phrase *genius loci*: "It is our sense of time, our sense of ritual, which in the long run creates our sense of place, and of community."[6] As our urban environments are constantly undergoing change, a cyclical sense of time, the regular recurrence of events and celebrations gives us reassurance and a sense of unity and continuity. History and geography interact to form our sense of place.

Doreen Massey also attributes a sense of place to the routines and activities that occur in that place. She says that places are not a "thing" at all but rather a constellation of processes. They are not intrinsically coherent, merely a locus for the generation of new configurations where we confront the challenges of negotiating a diverse world.[7] This perspective may be a universal truth, a condition of all urban settings, yet there is no doubt that places differ—geography does still matter. In our globalized world of advanced capitalism, cities are those places that host the locus of activities, and each city negotiates these activities differently. At any given place history builds upon itself, so events that occur in a place, and the landscapes that accrue during those events, alter the character of future events at that same place, building a palimpsest of features and traditions that shape the contemporary social environment and appearance—its sense of place.

So what gives Colorado Springs a sense of place? Each chapter of this book has examined important dimensions of the city's history, geography, and their contribution to its identity. From the many events that shaped this story, capital accumulation has been a defining theme of the city from its very beginning. Despite the enormous profits generated from real estate sales, health services, coal extraction, and coke production, founding the CF&I steelworks in Pueblo, the D&RG and Midland Railroads, control of Cripple Creek gold extraction and processing, and federal defense spending, wealth generation was long sustained by exploiting its environmental capital—generating profits from the beauty of its natural environment, and building a cultural landscape to support that resource. In short, it has long profited from Pikes Peak and built an urban infrastructure to sustain that relationship. These different dimensions can be distilled into three factors that shape Colorado Springs: (1) the built landscape, which in Colorado Springs translates into the importance of the historic downtown, (2) the values of the people, here a local culture has evolved that values freedom and liberty expressed through policies of limited governance, and (3) the natural environment, which in Colorado Springs means the lasting relationship between the city and Pikes Peak.

A VIBRANT DOWNTOWN

Colorado Springs went through several rough decades from the 1990s through the early 2010s. The city lost silicon chip design and manufacturing firms that had diversified its economy, it was labeled as an intolerant and unwelcoming headquarters of the Christian Right, its landscape became characterized by monotonous urban sprawl with generic chains and short-lived big-box stores—even becoming the prototypical setting for Eric Schlosser's book *Fast Food Nation*—and the recession of 2008 hit the city so hard that basic municipal services people expect were halted.[8] Young professionals fled the city, and newcomers never arrived. *Denver Post* columnist Ed Quillen summed up the city as "an economy based on defense spending, a haven for aspiring fundamentalist ayatollahs and a geography dominated by the automobile."[9]

And yet, what a difference a decade or two makes. Colorado Springs rebounded from the 2008 recession to such an extent that it now ranks as one of the country's most desirable and attractive places to live and work. Some accolades include first

FIGURE 10.1. Boutique shops, restaurants, and clubs in the revitalized historic downtown core. *Source*: Photo by author.

place in Most Desirable Places to Live and in Fastest Growing City for Millennials, and other high rankings for job growth, business friendly policies, and balanced lifestyle.[10] The image of intolerance is fading, the economy is diversifying, young professionals are again moving here, and the downtown is booming (figure 10.1).

With the economic rebound from the 2008 recession, growth in downtown Colorado Springs has been impressive. Three new hotels, four new apartment complexes, and numerous restaurants are either built or planned. The Olympic Museum opened in 2020 and a downtown professional soccer stadium in 2021, and visionary renderings by architects project a thriving condo, hotel, and entertainment district in the city's southwestern industrial zone. Nearly $864 million was invested in downtown projects from 2013 to 2018.[11] When the coal power plant closes in 2023, an enormous tract of land will open along Fountain Creek.

Investment in the downtown is an important and very promising sign. For decades now the downtown has been undersized for a metropolitan area of about 700,000 as suburban growth drew commerce away from its historic core. As more young professionals reject long commutes and the large, stand-alone suburban house, they seek urban living: "Concentration, not dispersion, is the elixir of urbanity."[12] The city now attracts housing and jobs to its core to create a dynamic urban environment. The success of the downtown is fundamental to the identity of the overall metropolitan area. The downtown is the place that projects the image of the city to the rest of the world. Its public spaces are for all residents, commons to use and enjoy that bring community together. As urban designer

Jeff Speck advises, cities with limited resources need to pick their winners and focus on the places where investment can make a real difference and the city can maximize its return on investment.[13] That place is downtown, which shapes the city's reputation and creates the sense of place attributed to the entire metropolitan area. It is the heartbeat of the region.

A thriving downtown not only produces economic dividends, but a well-designed urban environment also generates a happiness dividend.[14] Physicians and public health workers well know that exercise such as simply walking leads to better physical health, but increased exercise also generates a positive mental outlook that combats depression and loneliness and that boosts self-esteem. People are happier when they socially engage with others, even unintentionally bumping into people you may know. "Cities were created to bring things together," wrote Speck, and urban environments that promote walking and human interactions generate a feeling of belonging and connection to place.[15] People are most happy when they don't feel excluded, when they feel that the city is theirs and they belong. The downtown commercial core, including its public spaces, engage citizens with the city and enable them to feel a part of something larger than themselves. In addition, people are happy when they see and surround themselves with beauty. While the natural setting of Colorado Springs is unparalleled for its beauty, the ugly boxes designed for obsolescence in strip malls with giant paved lots create a bleak suburban landscape amidst this natural splendor. In downtown, the historic architecture, the arts on the street program, its public spaces and museums, numerous street festivals, the summer flower planters, and the winter holiday decorations all use beauty to enliven the ambiance and enable public interaction. The downtown offers an antidote to isolation and detachment. The built environment is an expression of our humanity; it should be a source of joy for visitors and residents alike. Colorado Springs needs to continually strengthen its historic core to avoid becoming placeless, another generic landscape, another sprawling Atlanta, Phoenix, or Los Angeles (figure 10.2).

Despite the success of the downtown in recent years, many citizens oppose aspects of this development. Citizens complain most of bike lanes constricting car mobility, a topic that generated more letters to the editor at the *Gazette* than any in the history of the city.[16] One popular meme among opponents is that "we don't want to be like Boulder," the liberal neighbor to the north.[17] But we might reconsider the value of streets as public spaces, since they are funded by taxpayers. When women of the Civic League invited planning consultant Charles Mulford Robinson to visit and give urban-planning recommendations in 1905, he suggested that the city not consider the street merely a means of transportation, but rather "you should make it an out-of-doors room, inviting people to loiter there, to sit in the sunshine and enjoy the views."[18] Downtown streets can be designed for more uses than simply high-speed car traffic.

FIGURE 10.2. Locally owned shops and restaurants in historic buildings with street art create an exciting and beautiful urban environment to stroll and enjoy. *Source*: photo by author.

Functional alternatives to the single occupancy vehicle are not simply quaint idealistic dreams given the uncertainties brought by climate change but will become increasingly necessary. Urbanists such as Peter Calthorpe point out that smarter and sustainable forms of urbanism will bring the most effective solutions to climate change.[19] Urbanity generates efficiencies, and if Colorado Springs can utilize smart design and alternative technologies in a vibrant urban downtown to reduce its ecological footprint, it could be a national leader well poised for an increasingly hot and arid environment.

LIBERTY AND LIMITED GOVERNANCE

Colorado Springs emerged from the Rocky Mountain libertarian ethic of self-reliance. This beacon of liberty attracted African American migrants, health seekers, and formed movements of national importance such as women's suffrage. The early twentieth-century headquarters of Colorado's radical feminism was Colorado Springs, where the Woman's Party formed in 1916.[20] Leadership of activists Caroline Spencer, Natalie Gray, and Berthe Arnold were at the forefront of suffrage protests in Washington, DC; each were arrested over the course of the two-year demonstrations, thrown into Washington, DC, jails with abysmal conditions, and subjected to harsh treatment. But through their leadership, the

Nineteenth Amendment was passed on August 6, 1920.[21] The appeal of liberty that burns bright in Colorado Springs had lasting influence on the entire nation.

This quest for liberty evolved into an antiregulatory, low-tax, probusiness political culture. This culture does not necessarily mean a purely libertarian ethic respecting personal and market freedoms—socially conservative leaders have been very willing to restrict and regulate unwanted behaviors and to intervene in the market economy to subsidize or support favored businesses. This version of freedom really relates to freedom from regulations that might restrict profit making. Palmer's land development projects, railroads, and industrialization were interwoven to use place for profit. The industrial past generated a business culture that promotes free enterprise and sees opportunity and answers in the private sector. The belief in an antiregulatory politics directly translates into the urban sprawl that characterizes the built environment. Colorado Springs leaders were quick to react to some threats against a business-friendly environment, such as during the labor wars in Cripple Creek, or when the Ku Klux Klan attempted to take control of local politics. They have also pushed new agendas to promote limited governance and probusiness polices, such as sponsoring passage of TABOR tax relief and with early and sustained support for the Tea Party and national politics of the Right. To this day, when many people think of Colorado Springs, it is this image of conservative politics that comes to mind.

Colorado Springs leaders were slower to respond to other threats to the business culture such as the anarchy advocated by Robert LeFevre or the image of intolerance that came with evangelical political influence, though some did speak out. One conceptualization of freedom that unifies the business community is support for the military. The armed forces are seen as defenders of freedom. This belief has shaped Colorado Springs into one of the most military-friendly cities in the country, and the Air Force Academy projects an image of freedom through military might to the nation. As national defense spending and militarization of the country continually increase, Colorado Springs is a focal point and key player in those initiatives.

Mayor John Suthers has become a tireless booster of the city since elected in 2015. Reelected in 2019, this avowed "limited government guy," has stabilized the political environment, with investors feeling more confident and potential migrants more comfortable moving to the city.[22] The limited governance culture brings both challenges and benefits; for example, fiscal constraints from low tax revenues will continue to hinder public works. As Mayor Suthers said in 2018, "Our property taxes are so low . . . that it doesn't produce enough revenue to take care of the infrastructure." Continually building vast tracts of residential homes costs the city more to provide services and infrastructure than it makes on property taxes in return: "We don't want a bunch of residential properties that aren't accompanied by revenue-producing properties. The reality of the world right now, property taxes don't do it and I don't see that changing," said the mayor.[23]

This deficit means the city relies heavily on sales taxes to fill its coffers, a strategy that brings its own problems. During recessions, as seen in 2008, revenues plunge to such an extent that basic services and jobs are cut.

Sales taxes are regressive, disproportionately affecting the poor more than the wealthy, and one challenge that at least partially results from limited governance is growing inequality. While this disparity reflects national trends, inequality is exacerbated through the city's expectation that market forces, rather than public services, will satisfy basic social conditions. A point-in-time survey of homeless people counted about 1,300 in 2016, not including those living with friends. Most of these homeless people were unsheltered; about 170 were military veterans.[24] Encampments sprout up and grow along the creeks and abandoned railways through town. Law enforcement makes them move along, then they reappear a few days later. Shelters and services do not meet demand, and these people's quality of life is poor. Downtown businesses suffer when customers avoid the area due to panhandlers and congregations of homeless people on street corners. The city had a shortage of 8,000 affordable housing units in 2017 with a long wait-list.[25] In addition to the homeless concentrations downtown, poverty concentrates in southeastern Colorado Springs, a region replete with abandoned shops and run-down housing units. Southeast Colorado Springs has about a fifth of the city's population, yet accounts for 30 percent of the violent crimes.[26] Residents in southeast Colorado Springs report some of the highest rates of poor physical health and mental distress in the state.[27] This part of the city is characterized by large arterials such as the Martin Luther King Bypass and the Milton Proby Parkway, which create pedestrian barriers, isolating neighborhoods and disconnected spaces. Some attribute these poor designs to weak regulations.[28] Urban planners and city leaders have worked to make the suburban setting more urban, creating hubs of interconnected activity. As an example of what could be done, the city of Lakewood worked successfully with private developers to transform a blighted suburban mall into a suburban downtown, but such a joint venture using public funds violates the free market philosophy prevalent in Colorado Springs. While Mayor Suthers stressed the city is best served by letting free market forces determine this area's economic future, the reality is that private-sector retailers and developers prefer wealthier neighborhoods, where risk is lower and returns on investment higher.[29] Lack of private investment for housing and transportation needs of low-income residents is a market failure, one that will likely lead to continued neglect and growing inequality in the city's southeast.

When the city, local school districts, or other public enterprises bring tax initiatives to the voters of Colorado Springs, they are routinely denied. Simply put, residents are very skeptical of publicly funded services. As political scientist professor Josh Dunn has said, "A tax increase is never just a tax increase in Colorado Springs. Instead it is an invitation to reconsider the very foundations and purposes of government."[30] Of the state's 272 municipalities, 230 have voted to end revenue caps imposed by the 1992 TABOR law, allowing local governments to keep revenues that otherwise would be refunded to residents and to spend them on providing services.[31] Colorado Springs is one of the few municipalities that has not overruled TABOR. Part of the reluctance to fund public services may arise from a peculiar characteristic that developed in Colorado Springs. In a 1996 master's thesis, Lyn Peterson attributed the lack of generosity in supporting taxpayer-funded public programs to the tradition in Colorado Springs of relying on a wealthy benefactor to solve the city's problems.[32] General Palmer gave land for churches and parks, plus subsidized the Antlers Hotel and the Cragmor Sanatorium that is now UCCS, among other generosities. Spencer and Julie Penrose built the Pikes Peak Highway, the Broadmoor, a municipal swimming pool, and the zoo and established the Fine Arts Center. Winfield Scott Stratton built the Mining Exchange Building, a public transportation system, and Stratton Park and subsidized the post office and county courthouse that is now the Colorado Springs Pioneers Museum, plus other philanthropic donations. In short, perhaps citizens in Colorado Springs have come to expect someone to sweep in and save the day. And in fact, there now is another superrich actor, Philip Anschutz. A billionaire who started in the oil business, he expanded into the railroad industry. In an all-too-fitting twist, he purchased Rio Grande Industries in 1984, the holding company of General Palmer's Denver & Rio Grande Railroad, which he leveraged to purchase the Southern Pacific Railroad and merged both with the Union Pacific Railroad in 1996. Afterward he grew his business empire in telecommunications, then entertainment and sports. Notoriously private and offering few public statements about his vision for the city, he nonetheless now owns the Broadmoor Resort, the *Gazette* newspaper, the Pikes Peak Cog Railway, and the Seven Falls tourist attraction. He has greatly expanded the offerings of the Broadmoor to include a rustic lodge atop Cheyenne Mountain, a ranch in Pike National Forest, a fly-fishing retreat on the Tarryall River, and horse stables for riding opportunities. The Broadmoor recently swapped land with the city in a highly controversial move opposed by many, in which the city gave away a 189-acre open-space parcel that citizens voted to purchase in 1885. Anschutz has quietly built a small local empire, controlling the most influential businesses in the city.[33] Whether Anschutz becomes the next wealthy benefactor remains uncertain, but that model has certainly been the city's tradition.[34]

Despite pressing challenges the city must face, clearly Colorado Springs has been successful and continues to grow. What appear as constraints to some are advantages for others. The prime benefit to Colorado Springs of low property taxes and unregulated development is affordability. The city has a better affordability index than the state overall, with median house value about half that of Boulder, the state's liberal icon. The suburban neighborhoods of the city are by and large safe and rewarding places to live. They remain the dominant housing option for most of the city's inhabitants. Many suburban residents enjoy the freedom that comes with driving, the privacy of their stand-alone home; they appreciate the modern schools and affordable houses, the convenient shopping centers and neighborhood parks, and the communities of young families. For them the suburban dream remains real, along with the belief that residents should celebrate the opportunities the city offers.

Many residents also take great pleasure living in an environment relatively free from intrusive regulations. There are no mandates in Colorado Springs to recycle, undergo vehicle emission tests, carry reusable bags to the grocery store, or pay your employees more than the state minimum wage. Land developers need not conform to strict design standards for buildings, nor set aside a certain number of housing units as "affordable," thereby raising the price of the remaining units. Such interventions in the free market are seen as unwelcome distortions that would impede the most efficient allocation of resources. Gun ownership and concealed carry permits are prevalent, shopping centers provide convenient car access, and utility rates are low. People are considered free-thinking agents who are best able to make decisions about how to live their lives. They will either benefit or suffer based on their own choices made as informed adults, without others telling them how they should live or what they can or cannot do. All are expected to carry their own weight and not rely on government services to bail them out.

The predominant philosophy of Colorado Springs' residents is that everyone should be held accountable for their actions. The freedom to make rational and informed choices is privileged over government-imposed mandates and restrictions on behavior. If people believe that carbon emissions or pollution are problems, they should then voluntarily change behavior to reduce those impacts. There is no need for laws that mandate behavior. But while this philosophy sounds great in theory, the impacts of behavior are often obscured and externalized, letting those who enjoy such "freedoms" off the hook. For example, those who choose to drive gas-guzzling trucks are not held accountable for their carbon emissions, those who choose not to recycle are not held accountable for plastic pollution in the oceans, and those who soak bluegrass lawns with water are not held accountable for habitat loss to native trout in western slope streams. The lack of full environmental accountability to offset negative externalities represents another market failure. While Colorado Springs residents are not the only abusers of these failures by any means, the emphasis placed on market forces to solve environmental problems in our local political culture yields a high per-capita impact. Environmental degradations from climate change have yet to become so glaring that choices must be restricted through government regulations, but that day may soon come.

As Colorado Springs moves forward, Mayor Suthers is leading the charge to generate a business-friendly environment, develop the downtown, and overcome the image of intolerance the city once had so that all feel welcome. He is a reincarnation of the pragmatic, mainstream Republican. In addition, young entrepreneurs in the city are reinterpreting Christianity in new and meaningful ways that bridge divides and unite the community. At a time when the Republican Party is moving ever rightward nationally, Colorado Springs in many ways is doing the opposite. Maybe, as has happened in the past, the local manifestation of conservativism will shape and influence national politics as Colorado Springs implements policies and positions that are later adopted nationwide.

PIKES PEAK

While the political culture is a defining theme for Colorado Springs, ever present is Pikes Peak, which continues to shape the very identity of the city. The mountain is the reason for the city's location. Few other cities have a natural landscape that rises more than 8,000 feet in vertical relief in just ten horizontal miles. A 1980s-era tourism map produced by the Downtown Partnership labeled the city "A Metropolis at the foot of a Majesty." The mountain is the source for much of its water, and this water shapes the urban forest canopy and sustains the ability to house nearly 700,000 people. Its snowcap is not only an inspiration to look at but a reminder of the fragility of the environment. The sunny, dry, and cool climate attracts migrants today just as it always has. The mountain shapes the weather: each summer day starts with brilliant blue skies, slowly clouds build up from the rising air currents, then thunderstorms break free from the bonds of the slope and roll past the city on their way to Kansas. The recreation economy continues to drive events, generate jobs, and shape an urban identity. On Pikes Peak slopes people ride bikes, ski, and hike, and in its streams and reservoirs they fish. They walk, drive, or take the cog railroad to its summit, and gold is still extracted from its Western Slopes. Spiritualists relish in nature to refresh themselves; recreationists relax in the pines. Marketers promote its beauty and therapeutic effects, while military recruits and Olympic athletes train in the high altitude. Colorado Springs capitalizes on sports industries while adopting the Olympic City brand. "America's Mountain" remains a very symbol of liberty, meshing perfectly with the city's identity. It is the western frame of view that all residents look at each day, a point of reference and familiarity that signifies home. Pikes Peak is inseparable from Colorado Springs. The city continues to profit from the peak.

As a contemporary expression of the importance of Pikes Peak to local identity, a search of whitepages.com found 2,076 businesses referencing "peak," "mountain," or similar themes, nearly 10 percent of all named businesses in the metro area. Business owners themselves identify with this reference, expecting that "peak" symbolism will attract customers who also identify with the label as an expression of local vernacular identity.[35] The mountain silhouette or representational imagery is used in countless business and public agency logos. The city

FIGURE 10.3. Chamber of Commerce promotional materials, circa 1925. *Source*: Colorado Springs Pioneers Museum.

logo itself is a clever adaption of the five Olympic rings into five slope faces of a mountain (see figure 6.21). These mountain representations show that Pikes Peak is a symbolic landscape, one that reflects the importance of the human-nature connections driving the city's sense of place.[36]

Pikes Peak has been the most consistent icon used to promote Colorado Springs since its foundation. The city marketed Pikes Peak to create its sense of place long before other western amenity-based towns began branding images of their natural landscapes. Colorado Springs is a city of the Rocky Mountain West, and the ever present Pikes Peak is what cultural geographer Kevin Blake calls a "peak of identity" that defines the Colorado Springs region (figure 10.3).[37] As the Summit

House atop Pikes Peak is rebuilt and scheduled for completion in 2021, the visitor experience will be enhanced and further tie the city and mountain together.

Colorado Springs has been called the City of Sunshine, City of Homes, Silicon Mountain, City of Champions, City of Millionaires, Newport in the Rockies, America's Switzerland, the Fountain Colony, Olympic City USA. In hindsight, it seems somewhat of a shame that city founders adopted the label "springs," since there is no such water feature. More curious is why these founders didn't use something about the mountain, some reference to alpine, rampart, sierra, snowy, or similar metaphor. Perhaps the city should rename itself to reflect its location at the foot (*pie* in Spanish, pronounced "pee-ā") of the Ute's Sun Mountain (*Tava*), the *pie de Tava*: "Piedetava!" Why not construct a new identity, free from the shackles of the past, looking to a bright new future? That is the way of the West, always moving optimistically forward, building a new society such as symbolized by the utopian vision for the Air Force Academy. Or better yet, let it just embrace its past, its landscape, its culture, its mountain, blemishes and all, and continue to build a welcoming place of opportunity where Great Plains meet Rocky Mountains, where land touches sky, where the city profits from the peak.

Notes

PREFACE

1. John Stilgoe, *Outside Lies Magic: Regaining History and Awareness in Everyday Places* (New York: Walker and Company, 1998), 2.

CHAPTER 1: GRASS

1. Helen Hunt Jackson, *Bits of Travel at Home* (Boston: Roberts Brothers, 1898), 224; Isabella L. Bird, *A Lady's Life in the Rocky Mountains* (Norman: University of Oklahoma Press, 1960 [1873]), 152.

2. For example, see descriptions in Walter Prescott Webb, *The Great Plains* (Boston: Ginn and Company, 1959 [1931]).

3. For discussions of the new language and representations needed to describe the West to East Coast audiences, see Anne Farrar Hyde, *An American Vision: Far Western Landscape and National Culture, 1820–1920* (New York: New York University Press, 1990).

4. Webb, *Great Plains*, has an entire section devoted to how the tradition of the Great American Desert came to be.

5. Quoted in Webb, *Great Plains*, 156–157.

6. Webb, *Great Plains*, 158.

7. See J. Victor Moreno-Mayar, Lasse Vinner, Peter de Barros Damgaard, Constanza de la Fuente, Jeffrey Chan, and Jeffrey P. Spence, "Early Human Dispersals within the Americas," *Science* 362 (2018): 1128–1139.

8. Roche Lindsey, instructor, UCCS anthropology, personal communication, July 2014. This site was being excavated during the summer of 2014.

9. For good histories of the plains and its inhabitants, see Elliott West, *The Contested Plains: Indians, Goldseekers, and the Rush to Colorado* (Lawrence: University Press of Kansas, 1998);

and Anne Farrar Hyde, *Empires, Nations, and Families: A History of the North American West, 1800–1860* (Lincoln: University of Nebraska Press, 2011).

10. Hyde, *Empires, Nations, and Families*, gives a good account of the multicultural world of William Bent and his family.

11. "Springs of Manitou Held Sacred Centuries Ago," *Colorado Springs Gazette*, January 23, 1918, 60.

12. See, e.g., William J. Palmer, "The Founding of Colorado Springs," *Colorado Springs Gazette*, August 10, 1896, 13, in this twenty-fifth anniversary edition. See also Dave Hughes, "Controversy in Colorado—Colorado's Indian Wars Revisited," in *Remembering West Word*, ed. Suzanne Schorsch (Colorado Springs: Old Colorado Historical Society, 2012), 170–172; and H. S. Rogers, "A Brief Historical Sketch of the Founding and Building of the County Seat of El Paso County, Colorado," in *Annual Report and Financial Statement, 1901–1902* (City of Colorado Springs, 1902), 220.

13. See Patricia Nelson Limerick, *The Legacy of Conquest: The Unbroken Past of the American West* (New York: W.W. Norton and Company, 1987); or Donald Worster, *Rivers of Empire: Water, Aridity, and the Growth of the American West* (New York: Pantheon, 1985). See also Hyde, *An American Vision*.

14. LeRoy R. Hafen, ed., *Ruxton of the Rockies* (Norman: University of Oklahoma Press, 1950).

15. Manly R. Ormes, *The Book of Colorado Springs* (Colorado Springs: Denton Printing Company, 1933).

16. *Colorado Springs Gazette*, January 1, 1888, 11.

17. *Colorado Springs Gazette*, January 1, 1888, 11.

18. William Wyckoff, "Mapping the 'New' El Dorado: Pikes Peak Promotional Cartography, 1859–1861," *Imago Mundi* 40 (1988): 32–45.

19. *Colorado Springs Gazette*, January 1, 1888, 11; Rogers, "A Brief Historical Sketch," 211 and 213; Palmer, "The Founding of Colorado Springs," and Dave Hughes, "An Original Fosdick Plat Found," in *Remembering West Word*, ed. Suzanne Schorsch (Colorado Springs: Old Colorado Historical Society, 2012), 2–7.

20. Marshall Sprague, *Newport in the Rockies: The Life and Good Times of Colorado Springs* (Athens, OH: Swallow Press, 4th ed., 1987 [1961]).

21. Hunt Jackson, *Bits of Travel at Home*, 225.

22. William Jackson Palmer, "The Westward March of Emigration in the United States, Considering in Its Bearing upon the Near Future of Colorado and New Mexico," in *Legends, Labors and Loves of William Jackson Palmer*, ed. T. Blevins, D. Daily, C. Nicholl, C. P. Otto, and K. S. Sturdevant (Colorado Springs: Pikes Peak Library District, 2009 [1874]), 143.

23. Ormes, *Book of Colorado Springs*; Sprague, *Newport in the Rockies*; Rogers, "A Brief Historical Sketch."

24. Curt Arthur Poulton, "A Historical Geographic Approach to the Study of the Institutionalization of the Doctrine of Prior Appropriation: The Emergence of Appropriative Water Rights in Colorado Springs, Colorado" (PhD diss., University of Minnesota, 1989), 90.

25. "A Year Ago," *Colorado Springs Gazette*, January 4, 1873, 3.

26. Tim Scanlon, "Some Perspectives on 100 Years of Comprehensive Planning in Colorado Springs," preface in the 2020 reprint of Charles Mulford Robinson, *A City Beautiful Dream: The 1912 Vision for Colorado Springs* (Colorado Springs: Pikes Peak Library District, 2020 [1912]), 9–26.

27. Palmer, "The Founding of Colorado Springs."

28. "Colorado Springs," *Colorado Springs Gazette*, January 4, 1873, 4.

29. R. Laurie Simmons and Thomas H. Simmons, *Historical and Architectural Survey of Downtown Colorado Springs, 2003–04* (Denver: Front Range Research Associates, 2004), 18.

30. Palmer, "The Founding of Colorado Springs," 10.

31. Palmer, "The Founding of Colorado Springs," 10–11.

32. Simmons and Simmons, *Historical and Architectural Survey*.

33. Poulton, "A Historical Geographic Approach," 103.
34. "Colorado Springs in 1871," *Colorado Springs Gazette*, April 19, 1873, 1.
35. *Colorado Springs Gazette*, April 19, 1873, 2.
36. "Colorado Springs," *Colorado Springs Gazette*, January 4, 1873, 4.
37. "Colorado Springs," 4.
38. Rogers, "A Brief Historical Sketch," 212.
39. "El Paso County," *Colorado Springs Gazette*, January 4, 1873, 4.
40. *Colorado Springs Gazette*, April 26, 1873, 2.
41. *Colorado Springs Gazette*, April 15, 1873. See also Rogers, "A Brief Historical Sketch," 221.
42. Hunt Jackson, *Bits of Travel at Home*, 224.
43. See the discussion of Colorado Springs in William Wyckoff, *Creating Colorado: The Making of a Western American Landscape, 1860–1940* (New Haven, CT: Yale University Press, 1999).

CHAPTER 2: WATER

1. Donald Worster, *Rivers of Empire: Water, Aridity, and the Growth of the American West* (New York: Pantheon, 1985), 7.
2. Susan B. Carter. "Labor Force," in *Historical Statistics of the United States: Millennial Edition*, ed. Susan B. Carter, Scott S. Gartner, Michael Haines, Alan Olmstead, Richard Sutch, and Gavin Wright (New York: Cambridge University Press, 2005).
3. John W. Powell, *Report on Lands of the Arid Region of the United States* (Cambridge, MA: Harvard, 1983 [1879]).
4. Karl Wittfogel, *Oriental Despotism: A Comparative Study of Total Power* (New York: Vintage, 1981).
5. For a rich analysis of water rights in New Mexico, see Eric P. Perramond, *Unsettled Waters: Rights, Law, and Identity in the American West* (Berkeley: University of California Press, 2019).
6. Donald Meinig, *The Shaping of America: A Geographical Perspective on 500 Years of History*, vol. 3, *Transcontinental America, 1850–1915* (New Haven, CT: Yale University Press, 1988).
7. Marc Reisner, *Cadillac Desert: The American West and Its Disappearing Water* (New York: Penguin, 1993).
8. Patricia Nelson Limerick, *The Legacy of Conquest: The Unbroken Past of the American West* (New York: W.W. Norton and Company, 1987).
9. See, e.g., the 1960 map "Early Irrigation Ditches and Their Water Rights," showing historic irrigation ditches in El Paso County, courtesy of the Colorado Springs Pioneers Museum. Also see the *Weekly Gazette*, July 19, 1890, 7, for a list of ditches and priorities.
10. Worster, *Rivers of Empire*: see page 90 for this discussion on the Doctrine of Prior Appropriation.
11. Curt Arthur Poulton, "A Historical Geographic Approach to the Study of the Institutionalization of the Doctrine of Prior Appropriation: The Emergence of Appropriative Water Rights in Colorado Springs, Colorado" (PhD diss., University of Minnesota, 1989), 1.
12. Michael Holleran, *Historic Context for Irrigation and Water Supply Ditches and Canals in Colorado* (Denver: University of Colorado, 2005). See also Dick Stenzel, "An Irrigated Legacy: The Union Colony," in *Citizen's Guide to Colorado's Water Heritage* (Denver: Colorado Foundation for Water Education, 2004), 19–23.
13. Colorado Foundation for Water Education, *Citizen's Guide to Colorado Water Law* (Denver, 2009).
14. Poulton, "A Historical Geographic Approach."
15. Worster, *Rivers of Empire*, 92.
16. Worster, *Rivers of Empire*, 141.

17. See Gray Brechin, *Imperial San Francisco: Urban Power, Earthly Ruin* (Berkeley: University of California Press, 1999), for a discussion of water and land speculation in the San Francisco context.

18. Manly R. Ormes, *The Book of Colorado Springs* (Colorado Springs: Denton Printing Company, 1933). Ormes said the town center was originally planned to be where Colorado College now lies, but two seventy-foot wells produced no water (73). Also, drinking water came from wells and at the springs in the Monument Valley and at the Riggs Ranch just south of town (72).

19. Poulton, "A Historical Geographic Approach." The El Paso Canal was conveyed from the Colorado Springs Company to city ownership on August 21, 1877.

20. "Our Mountain Water System," *Colorado Springs Gazette*, December 31, 1899, 5. See also Colorado Springs Water Department, *Report of the Colorado Springs Water Department, April 1905–December 1906* (Colorado Springs, 1907); see section entitled "A Brief History of the Colorado Springs Water System."

21. Ormes, *Book of Colorado Springs*. Note that historic maps show the Boulder Street Reservoir several blocks west of current park boundaries, so the original reservoir and the current park are not exactly overlapping.

22. Poulton, "A Historical Geographic Approach," 169. Poulton documents the legal battles of the El Paso Canal well, including conflicts with 1861 water rights in the Harmes Ditch (taking water from Fountain Creek) that predated the El Paso Canal (253).

23. "City Water System," *Colorado Springs Gazette Telegraph*, April 18, 1962; Colorado Springs Water Department, *Report*. Ormes, *Book of Colorado Springs*, states, "Whether the town should institute its own water system, or whether the function of water supply should be intrusted [*sic*] for development and ownership to private enterprise was bitterly contested" (39); he also cites Walter C. Frost reporting to the city auditor, September 1902: "The founders of this city were confronted at the outset with the water problem, and one of the first questions arising was whether the town should institute and own a water system, or whether the function of water supply should be entrusted to private enterprise. This question was hotly, even bitterly contested, and credit is largely due to the efforts of Mr. Matt France, that the policy of public ownership was then adopted," (75).

24. Poulton, "A Historical Geographic Approach." Note that the city was incorporated in September 1872, thereby enabling it to issue municipal bonds.

25. See discussion in Brechin, *Imperial San Francisco*.

26. Carl Smith, *City Water, City Life: Water and the Infrastructure of Ideas in Urbanizing Philadelphia, Boston, and Chicago* (Chicago: University of Chicago Press, 2013).

27. Michael Rawson, *Eden on the Charles: The Making of Boston* (Cambridge, MA: Harvard Press, 2010).

28. Patricia Nelson Limerick, with Jason L. Hanson, *A Ditch in Time: The City, the West, and Water* (Golden, CO: Fulcrum, 2012), 56.

29. Limerick, *A Ditch in Time*, 56.

30. Brechin, *Imperial San Francisco*, 99.

31. Colorado Springs Utilities, "Water Historic Timeline," 2010, provided courtesy of Gary Bostrom, chief water services officer.

32. "Water Works Report," *Colorado Springs Gazette*, May 1, 1888, 3. This was a report from city engineer H. I. Reid to John Himebaugh, chairman of the Committee on Water Works.

33. Poulton, "A Historical Geographic Approach," 172. See also Ormes, *Book of Colorado Springs*, 77, but he reports the year as 1890, not 1889. Also note the "Water Historic Timeline" says this intake was moved upstream in 1907, but the purpose is unclear, since the city lost rights to water in Bear Creek in 1895.

34. *Colorado Springs Gazette*, December 31, 1899, 17, report from water commissioner J. C. St. John. Other sources for this story include Poulton, "A Historical Geographic Approach,"

317–329; Ormes, *Book of Colorado Springs*; Gazette, "Our Mountain Water System"; and Jan Hoegh, "Utilities History Fraught with Countless Problems," *Colorado Springs Gazette Telegraph*, 1970, unknown date, accessed in the Colorado Springs Pioneers Museum.

35. Poulton, "A Historical Geographic Approach," 165. Beaver Creek flows south into the Arkansas River. Ruxton Creek flows into Fountain Creek, which then also flows south into the Arkansas. So while the South Slope project was a diversion between minor watersheds, both creeks eventually reach the Arkansas—it was not a transmountain diversion across the Continental Divide, which would come later.

36. *Gazette*, report from water commissioner.

37. Ormes, *Book of Colorado Springs*, 77. Note: although the city was now conscientious about securing water rights, it did not always do so before work was begun, as was the case on Beaver Creek. After the Bear Creek and Broadmoor lawsuits, one would think securing such rights would come first.

38. "Mountain Water System," *Sunday Gazette and Telegraph*, January 1, 1905, 30.

39. Gazette, "Our Mountain Water System" and report from water commissioner. Also see Edwin A. Sawyer, *The Present Water Supply of Colorado Springs* (Colorado Springs, 1901). This document was a report filed on August 2 to go into the "Century Chest" time capsule, opened in 2001. Mr. Sawyer was a local engineer.

40. Marshall Sprague, *Newport in the Rockies: The Life and Good Times of Colorado Springs*, 4th ed. (Athens, OH: Swallow Press, 1987).

41. Sawyer, *Present Water Supply*, 11.

42. See Colorado Springs Utilities, "Water Historic Timeline," and Poulton, "A Historical Geographic Approach."

43. "2014 Water Tour" document published by the Colorado Springs Utilities.

44. Letter from H. I. Reid, engineering consultant, to William Lloyd, secretary of the Myron Stratton Home, 1917. Stratton Collection, box 79, Colorado Springs Pioneers Museum Archives.

45. "South Suburban Imposes Further Water Restrictions," *Colorado Springs Gazette*, June 25, 1954, 1; "Myron Stratton Water Department and Brookside Water Company Merge," *Free Press*, April 11, 1953, 1; "Council Votes to Buy South Suburban Water," *Colorado Springs Gazette*, September 28, 1965, A1.

46. "Broadmoor Development to Cost $1,000,000; Pipe Beaver Creek Water 16 Miles to Three Big Tracts," *Colorado Springs Gazette*, August 30, 1925, 1.

47. Note: the company was formerly the West Monument Land and Water Co., later the Austin Bluffs Land & Water Co., and then just Northfield Water.

48. "Austin Bluff," *Colorado Springs Gazette*, January 1, 1889, 7. This trolley company incorporated in 1890, a consolidation of two earlier lines.

49. *Gazette*, "Austin Bluff," 7.

50. Frederick T. Henry, *You Never Miss the Water until the Well Runs Dry, or, the Colorado Springs Municipal Water System Emphasizing the Saga of the Blue River Project* (internal memo, Colorado Springs Utilities, 1955); "Contract Signed for Underground Water Supply," *Colorado Springs Gazette*, June 23, 1954, 1; "Suit Filed to Stop Sale of Clear Springs Ranch Water to Colorado Springs," *Colorado Springs Gazette*, August 3, 1963, 1; Lianne Shupp and Gary Shupp, "Altering Nature's Way: Colorado's Costly Water Problem," *Colorado Springs: A Magazine for the Pikes Peak Region and Southern Colorado*, August 1978, 4–7, 41–42; W. J. McGlasson, "City Can Purchase Water, Legal Battle," *Colorado Springs Gazette Telegraph*, May 19, 1976, B1; Poulton, "A Historical Geographic Approach," 125; Colorado Springs Utilities, "Water Historic Timeline."

51. Sawyer, *Present Water Supply*, 11.

52. Limerick and Hanson, *A Ditch in Time*, 116.

53. Prior to completing all pipelines and the Montgomery Reservoir for the Blue Rivers system, water was sent down the South Platte River to store in Eleven Mile Reservoir. It then was

released downstream to Lake George, where pumps there and again at Florissant sent the water to the North Slope Reservoirs (Hoegh, "Utilities History Fraught with Countless Problems"). Although use of pumps for Blue River water was only a brief interlude, these pumps were again called on during a 1963 drought, when water from Lake George supplemented meager flows from the Blue. See "Water Users Spending Selves into Bankruptcy," *Colorado Springs Gazette Telegraph*, July 7, 1963.

54. Henry, *You Never Miss the Water.*

55. Henry, *You Never Miss the Water.*

56. This diversion, including the Roberts Tunnel, was begun in 1946 and completed in 1962.

57. This information on Denver's role in the Blue River Project comes from Limerick and Hanson, *A Ditch in Time*, 143–162.

58. Henry, *You Never Miss the Water.*

59. Henry, *You Never Miss the Water*; Poulton, "A Historical Geographic Approach"; Colorado Springs Utilities, "2014 Water Tour."

60. Limerick and Hanson, *A Ditch in Time*, 57; and as an example of how wildly wrong the experts can be at forecasting water demand, one report in 1976 found that even with an expanded Twin Lakes system, two new Fry-Ark projects, tapping into the Eagle River, and a Phase II and III of the Homestake Project (none of which were ever built), demand would still exceed supply for El Paso County by 2003, see Russell K. Livingston, John M. Klein, and Donald L. Bingham, *Water Resources of El Paso County, Colorado* (Colorado Water Conservation Board: Colorado Water Resources Circular No. 32, 1976).

61. Limerick and Hanson, *A Ditch in Time*. Note: Denver eliminated the so-called Blue Line that excluded outlying areas in 1960.

62. Ed Sealover, "Over the Mountains and through the Woods, Water Flows to You," *Colorado Springs Gazette*, January 2, 2004, 1; Shupp and Shupp, "Altering Nature's Way"; Janie Vonderlage, "Springs Utilities," *Colorado Springs Gazette Telegraph, 1980*, n.d., accessed in the Colorado Springs Pioneers Museum.

63. Vonderlage, "Springs Utilities"; "Water Holds Key," *Free Press*; Glenn Urban, "City Major Supplier of Region's Water Resources," *Colorado Springs Gazette Telegraph*, February 24, 1980, CC 5; Poulton, "A Historical Geographic Approach," 178.

64. Barry Noreen, "Water Project Faces New Hurdle," *Colorado Springs Gazette Telegraph*, December 29, 1992, B1; Barry Noreen, "City's Wilderness Stance Angers Brown," *Colorado Springs Gazette Telegraph*, December 29, 1992, B1.

65. Michelle Fulcher, "Springs Crowd Supports Homestake Water Project," *Colorado Springs Gazette Telegraph*, June 10, 1982, 22.

66. Jim Buynak, "Homestake II Clears Another Hurdle," *Colorado Springs Gazette Telegraph*, April 6, 1992, B1. See also Noreen, "Water Project Faces New Hurdle"; Fulcher, "Springs Crowd Supports Homestake Water Project."

67. Colorado Springs Utilities, *SDS: Water for Generations* (White Paper, Colorado Springs, 2014); Noreen, "Water Project Faces New Hurdle."

68. Colorado Springs Utilities, "Water Historic Timeline."

69. Michael C. Hinderlider, various memos and reports on the geology and Twin Lakes reservoir expansion, folders 33–35, Hinderlider Collection, Colorado History Hart Research Library, Denver, 1948. Also see letter from Wallace Doe to Hinderlider, February 12, 1959, on the legal status of the reservoir expansion, new canals, and records on diversion quantities through the Independence Pass Tunnel. Finally see report in folder 287 on the canals and reservoirs in the lower Arkansas Valley.

70. W. J. McGlasson, "City Water Could Support 539,000," *Colorado Springs Gazette Telegraph*, n.d., February 1977; Urban, "City Major Supplier of Region's Water Resources"; Colorado Springs Utilities, "Water Historic Timeline."

71. Poulton, "A Historical Geographic Approach," 181.

72. Matt Jenkins, "Water Warrior," *High Country News* 44, no. 5 (2012): 14–20.

73. Colorado Agricultural Water Alliance, *Meeting Colorado's Future Water Supply Needs* (Denver, 2008).

74. Reisner, *Cadillac Desert*. Reisner lays out a damning condemnation of the blind ambition that led the Bureau of Reclamation, and the Corp of Engineers, to build ecologically damaging and economically irrational projects.

75. Jedediah S. Rogers, *Fryingpan-Arkansas Project* (Washington, DC: Bureau of Reclamation, 2006).

76. Michael C. Hinderlider, "Report of the State Engineer," folder 289, Hinderlider Collection, Colorado History Hart Research Library, Denver, 1926. This report predates investigation by the Bureau of Reclamation but lays the groundwork for potential diversions from the Taylor River into the Arkansas Valley that would be the basis for the Gunnison-Arkansas project.

77. Rogers, *Fryingpan-Arkansas Project.*

78. "Letter from O.R. Smith to R.L. Parshall," January 18, 1953, and "Letter from R.L. Parshall to A. Batson," February 3, 1953, both found in folder 42, Hinderlider Collection, Colorado History Hart Research Library, Denver.

79. "Water Conflict: Battlefield," *Colorado Springs Gazette*, February 23, 2003, p. A9. Also see www.secwcd.org.

80. Henry, *You Never Miss the Water.*

81. "PanArk Diverted Water 25% Short of Projected Demands," *Herald Democrat*, June 16, 1967.

82. "PanArk Diverted Water 25% Short of Projected Demands."

83. . "PanArk Diverted Water 25% Short of Projected Demands," 7.

84. Reisner, *Cadillac Desert*, 301, 309.

85. See https://dola.colorado.gov/demog_webapps/dashboard.jsf for state projections. For inflated numbers used by Colorado Springs Utilities, see sdswater.org, or see Colorado Springs Utilities, *SDS: Water for Generations.*

86. David Vickers, "New Water Pipeline Project Eyed by CSU," *Cheyenne Edition*, March 24, 2000, 1; Ed Sealover, "Newspaper, Salazar Team to Fight Reservoir Expansion," *Colorado Springs Gazette*, March 31, 2005, 1.

87. Colorado Springs Utilities, "Water Historic Timeline"; Colorado Springs Utilities, *SDS: Water for Generations.*

88. Dan Wilcock and Rick Tosches, "Pipe Dreams," *Colorado Springs Independent*, March 10, 2005, 16.; Bruce Finley, "Fifty-Mile Pipeline Gets Final Piece: A $841M Diversion," *Denver Post*, March 19, 2015, 4A.

89. Colorado Springs Utilities, "2014 Water Tour." Other sources claim the city will increase capacity by 50; see Wilcock and Tosches, "Pipe Dreams."

90. Pam Zubeck, "Choppy Waters," *Colorado Springs Independent*, May 2, 2012, 15; "SDS—On Time and Under Budget," *CSU Connection*, June 2014; Finley, "Fifty Mile Pipeline"; Pam Zubeck, "On the Line," *Colorado Springs Independent*, January 27, 2016, 14.

91. Poulton, "A Historical Geographic Approach," 340.

92. These numbers were generated when Colorado Springs began its Stormwater Enterprise in order to calculate the percentage of each city parcel in impervious surfaces. They include the surface area of city streets. Data courtesy Jeff Besse, city of Colorado Springs.

93. Ed Sealover, "City Wants Clean Streams," *Colorado Springs Gazette*, April 9, 2002, Metro 1.

94. The Taxpayer's Bill of Rights was in initiative begun in Colorado Springs by Doug Bruce, and approved statewide in 1992. The law stipulates that at all levels of government, tax revenues can only increase from year to year based on inflation and population increase. Any revenues collected above that amount must be returned to taxpayers. Any new increases above that amount

must be approved in a voter referendum. The city tried to call the Stormwater Enterprise a "fee," not a "tax," but that is a distinction without difference, hence the court ruling.

95. John Hazlehurst, "Keep an Eye on Pueblo," *Colorado Springs Independent*, February 6, 2013, 8.

96. Summit Economics, *White Paper Exploring Potential Solutions to Regional Stormwater Challenges* (Colorado Springs, 2012), 6.

97. American Society of Civil Engineers (ASCE), 2012, 2012 Infrastructure Report Card for the Colorado Springs Area, http://www.asce-scbranch.org.

98. John Hazlehurst, "Fearing Clogs in the Pipeline," *Colorado Springs Independent*, November 26, 2014, 8.

99. "Ado Over Stormwater," *Colorado Springs Independent*, May 2012.

100. Pam Zubeck, "Clear Path for SDS," *Colorado Springs Independent*, April 13, 13.

101. Wilcock and Tosches, "Pipe Dreams"; http://sdswater.org.

102. Pam Zubeck, "The Jenkins Family Empire," *Colorado Springs Independent*, November 19, 2014, 22.

103. Summit Economics, *Economic Impacts of the Southern Delivery System on the Regional Economy of Colorado Springs, Pueblo, and Surrounding Areas* (Colorado Springs: Center for Regional Advancement, 2011), 14.

104. Summit Economics, *Economic Impacts*, 14.

105. Black and Veatch, LLC, *Water Resource Plan for Colorado Springs Utilities* (Colorado Springs Utilities, 1996).

106. Raquel Rutledge, "City Ponders New Rules to Save Water," *Colorado Springs Gazette*, February 19, 1998, 1.

107. Barry Noreen, "Water Projects Getting Smaller," *Colorado Springs Gazette*, September 9, 2002, A1; Black and Veatch, *Water Resource Plan*.

108. Based on rough accounting calculations from various sources: Black and Veatch, *Water Resource Plan*; Colorado Springs Utilities, "2014 Water Tour"; Wilcock and Tosches, "Pipe Dreams."

109. Bill McKeown, "Water Supply Low—And Dropping Quickly," *Colorado Springs Gazette*, January 23, 2004, 1.; "Conservative Beliefs Only as Deep as a Dry Well," *Colorado Springs Gazette*, October 7, 2002, A1.

110. Limerick and Hanson, *A Ditch in Time*: "The engineering achievements of the nineteenth and twentieth centuries transformed American life so completely that they erased from view the limitations that natural conditions once exerted over settlement" (49); Poulton, "A Historical Geographic Approach": "Public officials and professional water managers do their job so well that the average citizens can live out their daily lives in the west without being aware that a miracle of resource management is taking place" (4).

CHAPTER 3: AIR

1. "Colorado City," *Sunday Gazette Telegraph*, January 1, 1905, 25–26.

2. Louis R. Ehrich, "Search for Health," *Colorado Springs Gazette*, January 1, 1888, 6. Mr. Ehrich first published this essay as "Health Resorts for Lung Troubles" in the *New York Tribune* on May 22, 1887; he wrote the essay on May 8, 1887, in Colorado Springs. It was reproduced in the *Gazette* as cited here.

3. Sheila M. Rothman, *Living in the Shadow of Death: Tuberculosis and the Social Experience of Illness in American History* (New York: Basic Books, 1994).

4. Thomas Dormandy, *The White Death: A History of Tuberculosis* (New York: New York University Press, 2000).

5. Katherine Ott, *Fevered Lives: Tuberculosis in American Culture since 1870* (Cambridge, MA: Harvard University Press, 1996), 36.

6. Billy M. Jones, *Health Seekers in the Southwest, 1817–1900* (Norman: University of Oklahoma Press, 1967), 24. See all of ch. 1 in this excellent history for the discussion of the pervasive fevers and disease of settlers in the Mississippi Valley, and their constant search for healthy places.

7. Rothman, *Living in the Shadow of Death.*

8. Jones, *Health Seekers in the Southwest.*

9. Ott, *Fevered Lives*, 40.

10. Frederick I. Knight, paper read to the Boston Society of Medical Observation, March 5, 1888. Reproduced in George Rex Buckman, *Colorado Springs, Colorado: Its Manifold Attractions as a Health Resort, A Pleasure Resort, A Scenic Center, and a Residence City (Together with a Collection of Medical Facts Concerning Colorado Springs)* (Colorado Springs: Gazette Printing Company, 1892), 42.

11. On aseptic atmosphere, see "Colorado Springs, Colo.: The City of Sunshine," *Colorado Springs Gazette*, January 1, 1902, 88. Promotional ad written by the secretary of the Chamber of Commerce.

12. Clinton Wagner, "Colorado Springs and Davos Platz Compared as Winter Health Resorts," paper read to the New York Academy of Medicine, October 20, 1887. Reproduced in Buckman, *Colorado Springs, Colorado*, 47.

13. Rothman, *Living in the Shadow of Death*; Jones, *Health Seekers in the Southwest.*

14. Rothman, *Living in the Shadow of Death.*

15. Ott, *Fevered Lives.*

16. As Rothman, *Living in the Shadow of Death*, explains on 157, many people use the terms "sanitarium" and "sanatorium" interchangeably, but they had different meanings in the nineteenth century. A sanitarium was a health resort; a sanatorium was a medical institution established for the treatment of tuberculosis.

17. Ott, *Fevered Lives*; Dormandy, *The White Death.*

18. Rothman, *Living in the Shadow of Death.*

19. Rothman, *Living in the Shadow of Death*, 194.

20. Ott, *Fevered Lives.*

21. Dormandy, *The White Death*; Ott, *Fevered Lives.*

22. "Colorado Springs in 1872," *Colorado Springs Gazette Telegraph*, November 18, 1990, I8 and I9. This citation was a hand-drawn map reproducing the city landscape in 1872, with annotated text explaining historical facts about the sketches on the map. Art and research by John Wagner.

23. Matt Mayberry, "On a Cough and a Prayer: The Modern Woodmen Sanatorium and the Tuberculosis Industry in the Pikes Peak Region," in *Doctors, Disease, and Dying in the Pikes Peak Region*, ed. Tim Blevins, Dennis Daily, Sydne Dean, Chris Nicholl, Michael L. Olsen, Katherine Scott Sturdevant, and Amy Ziegler (Colorado Springs: Pikes Peak Library District, 2012), 248.

24. "A Description of Colorado, El Paso County, and Colorado Springs," *Colorado Springs Gazette*, January 4, 1873, 4.

25. S. Edwin Solly, *Manitou, Co. U.S.A.: Its Mineral Waters and Climate* (St. Louis: John McKittrick, 1875); S. Edwin Solly, *The Health Resorts of Colorado Springs and Manitou* (Colorado Springs: Gazette Publishing, 1883).

26. "A Brief History of a Great Natural Health Resort," *Weekly Gazette*, January 4, 1890, 5.

27. Jones, *Health Seekers in the Southwest*, attributes this moniker to Mr. Frank Fossett on page 160.

28. Iza Duffus Harry, *Between Two Oceans; or, Sketches of American Travel* (London: Hurst and Blackett, 1884), 231, quoted in Ott, *Fevered Lives*, 41.

29. B.F.D. Adams, "Contagiousness of Phthisis," in Buckman, *Colorado Springs, Colorado*, 52.

30. Douglas R. McKay, "The History of Nordrach Ranch: Colorado's First Sanatorium of the Open Air," *Colorado Magazine* 56, nos. 3 and 4 (1979): 179–195.

31. Quoted in Buckman, *Colorado Springs, Colorado*, 19.

32. Douglas R. McKay, *Asylum of the Gilded Pill: The Story of Cragmor Sanatorium* (Denver: State Historical Society of Colorado, 1983), 4. McKay cites the *Colorado Springs Gazette*, January 1, 1905, for this quote. Dr. Shepard ran frequent ads for his tent cottage homes, e.g., see *Colorado Springs Gazette*, January 1, 1910.

33. Henry W. Hoagland, *My Life* (Pomona, CA: Progress Bulletin, 1940), 80, cited in Chris Nicholl, "Matters of Life and Death: Dr. Charles Fox Gardiner and Colorado's Early Tuberculosis Physicians," in Blevins et al., *Doctors, Disease, and Dying in the Pikes Peak Region*, 139–178.

34. McKay, "The History of Nordrach Ranch," 180; City of Colorado Springs, *Revised Ordinances of the City of Colorado Springs*, section 3, article 2, 1896, 72.

35. Andrew Gulliford, "Come Only If Rich: The Health Seeker Movement in Colorado Springs" (manuscript, Colorado College, 1974), 6–9, Colorado College Tutt Library, Special Collections.

36. E. J. White, "Colorado Springs and Its Climatic Attractions," *Colorado Springs Gazette*, January 1, 1902, 12.

37. E. J. White, "Colorado Springs and Its Climatic Attractions," 12.

38. R. K. Hutchings, "Some Facts Concerning . . . Colorado Springs," in *The Colorado Springs Region as a Health Resort: High Altitudes for Invalids*, ed. Charles Fox Gardiner and Gilbert McClurg (Colorado Springs: Chamber of Commerce, 1898), 26.

39. Gardiner and Gilbert, *The Colorado Springs Region as a Health Resort*, 49, where this essay was reproduced.

40. McKay, "The History of Nordrach Ranch," 181.

41. "Bellevue Sanitarium Ready to Receive Patients," *Weekly Gazette*, February 22, 1890, 3.

42. Joanne F. Ruth, *We Are Beth-El Nurses: A Heritage of Caring at the Foot of Pikes Peak* (Colorado Springs: Cheri Gillard, 2016).

43. Bob Hoff and Lynn Gilfillan-Morton, *The History of Health Care in the Pikes Peak Region* (Bloomington, IN: Authorhouse, 2005). On the National Preacher's Home, see John Stokes Holly, *The Invisible People of the Pikes Peak Region: An Afro-American Chronicle* (Colorado Springs: Friends of the Pikes Peak Library District and Friends of the Colorado Springs Pioneers Museum, 1990).

44. "Many Large Institutions for the Care of the Sick," *Gazette Telegraph*, January 1, 1905, 109 (supplement).

45. "Printers Home," *Weekly Gazette*, March 29, 1890, 3.

46. Hoff and Gilfillan-Morton, *History of Health Care in the Pikes Peak Region*.

47. Lynn A. Gilfillan-Morton, "Women of Health and Caring in the Southern Rockies," in Blevins et al., *Doctors, Disease and Dying in the Pikes Peak Region*, 75–109.

48. Charles Fox Gardiner, "The Sanatory Tent and Its Use in the Treatment of Pulmonary Tuberculosis," *Transactions of the American Climatological Association* 18 (1902): 209–221, repr. in Blevins et al., *Doctors, Disease and Dying in the Pikes Peak Region*, ed. 179.

49. Gardiner, "The Sanatory Tent," in Blevins et al., *Doctors, Disease and Dying in the Pikes Peak Region*, 180.

50. Gardiner, "The Sanatory Tent," 180.

51. Gardiner, "The Sanatory Tent," 181.

52. Gardiner, "The Sanatory Tent," 183.

53. McKay, "The History of Nordrach Ranch," 184.

54. White, "Colorado Springs and Its Climatic Attractions," 12.

55. McKay, "The History of Nordrach Ranch," 186.

56. McKay, "The History of Nordrach Ranch," 185.

57. McKay, *Asylum of the Gilded Pill.*

58. McKay, *Asylum of the Gilded Pill.*

59. McKay, *Asylum of the Gilded Pill.* 82.

60. Mayberry, "On a Cough and a Prayer."

61. Mayberry, "On a Cough and a Prayer." 251.

62. *Guide to the Pikes Peak Region* (Colorado Springs: Starrett and Snyder, May 1913), 35.

63. Hoff and Gilfillan-Morton, *History of Health Care in the Pikes Peak Region*; "Young Life Group Transfers National Headquarters Here," *Colorado Springs Gazette Telegraph*, December 14, 1947, 1; "Young Life Buys 645 Acre Club Property in Canada," *Colorado Springs Gazette Telegraph*, January 5, 1954, 1.

64. Ruth, *We Are Beth-El Nurses.*

65. Hoagland, *My Life*, in Nicholl, "Matters of Life and Death," 167.

66. McKay, *Asylum of the Gilded Pill.*

67. McKay, "The History of Nordrach Ranch."

68. Gilfillan-Morton, "Women of Health and Caring."

69. Ruth, *We Are Beth-El Nurses.* The location of Beth-El was within the city limits, in an eastern zone annexed in 1890. The location was chosen prior to the 1910 ordinance, and Beth-El was a general-purpose hospital, not exclusively a TB sanatorium. These likely explain the seeming contradiction of opening the site within the city limits at the same time that Sunny Rest was forced to move farther east. The later opening of the Methodist TB sanatorium in 1926 was surely due to the proximity of Beth-El (both Methodist owned), but also likely due to a decrease in hostility against tuberculars by that date.

70. Joanne F. Ruth, "Nurse . . . Nurse . . . Do We Have a Nurse?" in *Bigwigs and Benefactors of the Pikes Peak Region*, ed. H. Jordan, T. Blevins, D. Daily, S. Dean, C. Nicholl, and M. Olsen (Colorado Springs: Pikes Peak Library District, 2017), 263–299.

71. "Winning Health in the Pikes Peak Region," marketing promotional brochure (Colorado Springs, Colorado Springs Chamber of Commerce, 1923).

72. Dormandy, *The White Death.*

73. Mayberry, "On a Cough and a Prayer."

74. McKay, "The History of Nordrach Ranch," 179.

75. Buckman, *Colorado Springs, Colorado*, 5.

CHAPTER 4: METAL

1. Quoted in Robert G. Athearn, *Rebel of the Rockies: A History of the Denver and Rio Grande Western Railroad* (New Haven, CT: Yale University Press, 1962), 5.

2. Robert E. Riegel, *The Story of Western Railroads: From 1852 through the Reign of the Giants* (Lincoln, NE: University of Nebraska Press, 1964 [1926]).

3. Robert E. Gallamore and John R. Meyer, *American Railroads: Decline and Renaissance in the Twentieth Century* (Cambridge, MA: Harvard University Press, 2014).

4. Riegel, *The Story of Western Railroads.*

5. Dee Brown, *Hear That Lonesome Whistle Blow: Railroads in the West* (New York: Holt, Rinehart, and Winston, 1977). See also Riegel, *The Story of Western Railroads.*

6. Richard C. Overton, *Gulf to Rockies: The Heritage of the Fort Worth and Denver—Colorado and Southern Railways, 1861–1898* (Austin: University of Texas Press, 1953).

7. Riegel, *The Story of Western Railroads.*

8. Overton, *Gulf to Rockies.*

9. George L. Anderson, *General William J. Palmer: A Decade of Colorado Railroad Building, 1870–1880* (Colorado Springs: Colorado College Publications, General Series No. 209, Study Series No. 22, 1936).

10. Brown, *Hear That Lonesome Whistle Blow.*

11. Brown, *Hear That Lonesome Whistle Blow.*

12. Anderson, *General William J. Palmer.*

13. Anderson, *General William J. Palmer.*

14. Athearn, *Rebel of the Rockies.*

15. William A. Bell, "The Denver & Rio Grande Railroad: An Address Given to the Employees, January 28, 1920," in *Legends, Labors and Loves of William Jackson Palmer*, ed. T. Blevins, D. Daily, C. Nicholl, C. P. Otto, and K. S. Sturdevant (Colorado Springs: Pikes Peak Library District, 2009 [1920]), 101.

16. William Jackson Palmer, "The Westward March of Emigration in the United States, Considered in Its Bearing upon the Near Future of Colorado and New Mexico," in T. Blevins et al., *Legends, Labors and Loves of William Jackson Palmer*, 139.

17. Anderson, *General William J. Palmer*, 121.

18. Palmer, "The Westward March of Emigration," 179.

19. Brown, *Hear That Lonesome Whistle Blow.*

20. Numerous authors discuss the development of South Pueblo, including Athearn, *Rebel of the Rockies*; Brown, *Hear That Lonesome Whistle Blow*; and H. Lee Scamehorn, *Pioneer Steelmaker in the West: The Colorado Fuel and Iron Company 1872–1903* (Boulder, CO: Pruett Publishing Co, 1976). Note that while the D&RG terminal was on the south side of the Arkansas River in 1872, today it is not. After the 1921 flood, the river channel was rerouted to its current path, whereas prior to 1921 the river ran where the Riverwalk is today, separating the town from the railyards.

21. The connection to Cañon City was not completed until 1874.

22. Athearn, *Rebel of the Rockies*; Anderson, *General William J. Palmer.*

23. Keith L. Bryant, Jr., *History of the Atchison, Topeka, and Santa Fe Railway* (New York: Macmillan, 1974). Note that the coalfields in southern Colorado were also attractive to the AT&SF, hence their lines running toward both Pueblo and Trinidad. They could use coal to generate revenue while they continued to extend lines farther west.

24. The "Rio Grande War" is documented by many historians, including Bryant, *History of the Atchison, Topeka, and Santa Fe Railway*; Athearn, *Rebel of the Rockies*, and Riegel, *The Story of Western Railroads.*

25. A short connecting line was built by the Texas, Santa Fe & Northern to connect Española to Santa Fe, which the D&RG bought in 1895, finally completing its connection to the New Mexico capital.

26. Morris Cafky, *Colorado Midland* (Denver: Rocky Mountain Railroad Club, 1965).

27. Athearn, *Rebel of the Rockies.*

28. "Rio Grande Plans," *Weekly Gazette*, February 22, 1890, 1; Riegel, *The Story of Western Railroads.*

29. Gallamore and Meyer, *American Railroads.*

30. Overton, *Gulf to Rockies.*

31. Scamehorn, *Pioneer Steelmaker in the West.*

32. Scamehorn, *Pioneer Steelmaker in the West.*

33. Scamehorn, *Pioneer Steelmaker in the West.*

34. Many more coking sites came online in subsequent years, particularly west of Trinidad.

35. Scamehorn, *Pioneer Steelmaker in the West.*

36. Scamehorn, *Pioneer Steelmaker in the West*; Overton, *Gulf to Rockies.*

37. Jonathan Rees, *Representation and Rebellion: The Rockefeller Plan and the Colorado Fuel and Iron Company, 1914–1942* (Boulder: University Press of Colorado, 2010); Thomas G. Andrews, *Killing for Coal: America's Deadliest Labor War* (Cambridge, MA: Harvard University Press, 2008).

38. Robert Ormes, *Tracking Ghost Railroads in Colorado* (Colorado Springs: Century One Press, 1975).

39. Overton, *Gulf to Rockies.* The evolution of this railroad was the Denver, Texas & Gulf Railroad Co. on May 28, 1885, then the Denver, Texas & Ft. Worth on April 12, 1887. The connecting line coming from Texas was the Ft. Worth & Denver City, with a connection near the Canadian River. On April 1, 1890, the Union Pacific, Denver & Gulf consolidated both lines into the larger UP system. This became the Colorado & Southern Railway in 1896 and was then sold to the Chicago, Burlington & Quincy system in 1908.

40. Cafky, *Colorado Midland.*

41. Cafky, *Colorado Midland.*

42. The Midland tracks reached Buena Vista in route to Leadville on July 13, 1887. Because the company did not want to waste fuel by descending all of the way into Buena Vista, only to climb again up to Leadville, the track passes east of town, on Midland Hill, a 450-foot higher elevation, where a stage shuttled people between the tracks and town. Locals today hike and ride along the old track, and tunnels puncture the cliffs on the east side of the Arkansas River just north of town.

43. Cafky, *Colorado Midland.*

44. Athearn, *Rebel of the Rockies.*

45. Cafky, *Colorado Midland.*

46. Cafky, *Colorado Midland.*

47. Thomas J. Noel and Cathleen M. Norman, *A Pikes Peak Partnership: The Penroses and the Tutts* (Boulder: University Press of Colorado, 2000).

48. "Midland Road Is Nearly Gone," *Colorado Springs Free Press*, May 13, 1949, 7.

49. Overton, *Gulf to Rockies.*

50. See Bryant, *History of the Atchison, Topeka, and Santa Fe Railway*, ch. 4, for an excellent discussion of Fred Harvey and his partnership with the AT&SF to create the Harvey House restaurants.

51. "Work to Begin Soon on Santa Fe Depot," *EL Paso County Democrat*, April 28, 1916, 1.

52. "A Piece of City's Past to Step into the Future," *Colorado Springs Gazette*, March 8, 2015, B1.

53. "Tracks Going, Trains May Still Be Running," *Gazette Telegraph*, December 11, 1973, D1.

54. "Track Removal Granted 120-Day Extension," *Gazette Telegraph*, October 2, 1974, D4.

55. "Railroads Coming," *Colorado Springs Gazette*, April 8, 1888, 1.

56. Brown, *Hear That Lonesome Whistle Blow.*

57. "Resident Recalls Roswell Suburb," *Colorado Springs Gazette*, October 14, 1974, B1.

58. "Rock Island Plan Derails Springs-Limon Route," *Colorado Springs Gazette*, June 6, 1982, D1.

59. Noel and Norman, *A Pikes Peak Partnership.*

60. "Famous Short Line Will Be Sold Tomorrow," *Colorado Springs Gazette*, October 15, 1922, 1.

61. "The Colorado Springs and Cripple Creek District Railway," *Facts Magazine* 27, no. 25 (1901), 3.

62. Promotional brochure for the Colorado Springs and Cripple Creek Railroad, "Through the Heart of the Rockies into the Land of Gold," 1915, Starsmore Center for Local History, Colorado Springs Pioneers Museum.

63. Robert G. Taylor, *Cripple Creek Mining District* (Palmer Lake, CO: Filter Press, 1973).

64. Tivis E. Wilkins, *Short Line to Cripple Creek* (Golden, CO: Colorado Railroad Museum, 1983).

65. Morris Cafky and John A. Haney, *Pikes Peak Trolleys: A History of the Colorado Springs Streetcar System* (Colorado Springs: Century One Press, 1983).

CHAPTER 5: ROCK

1. Marshall Sprague, *Money Mountain: The Story of Cripple Creek Gold* (Boston: Little, Brown and Co., 1953), 293.

2. Robert Guilford Taylor, *Cripple Creek Mining District* (Bloomington: Indiana University, printed in Palmer Lake: Filter Press, 1973).

3. Taylor, *Cripple Creek Mining District.*

4. Sprague, *Money Mountain.*

5. Frank Waters, *Midas of the Rockies* (Denver: University of Denver Press, 1949). See also Sprague, *Money Mountain.*

6. At least four reputable sources report a population of 50,000 or more for the mining district by 1900, but none of those entries cite their source for that number. The 1900 US Census lists 29,000 for all of Teller County, the vast majority of whom were living in the mining district. Given the transient nature of the labor, this number is likely an undercount. However, that does not justify the inflated claim of 50,000 people.

7. Roger Hadix, *Baseball in Colorado Springs* (Charleston, SC: Arcadia, 2013).

8. Sprague, *Money Mountain.*

9. *Colorado Telegraph*, June 16, 1901; cited in Waters, *Midas of the Rockies*, 253.

10. Waters, *Midas of the Rockies.*

11. Thomas J. Noel and Cathleen M. Norman, *A Pikes Peak Partnership: The Penroses and the Tutts* (Boulder: University Press of Colorado, 2000). See also Marshall Sprague, *Newport in the Rockies: The Life and Good Times of Colorado Springs*, 4th ed. (Athens, OH: Swallow Press, 1987).

12. *City Directory of Colorado Springs, Colorado City, and Manitou* (Colorado Springs: Giles Directory Company, 1900).

13. Manly R. Ormes, *The Book of Colorado Springs* (Colorado Springs: Denton Printing Company, 1933). See also Sprague, *Money Mountain.*

14. Waters, *Midas of the Rockies*; Sprague, *Newport in the Rockies.*

15. *Colorado Springs Gazette*, October 6, 1900, 5.

16. Taylor, *Cripple Creek Mining District.*

17. Taylor, *Cripple Creek Mining District.*

18. Taylor, *Cripple Creek Mining District.*

19. Noel and Norman, *A Pikes Peak Partnership.*

20. Tivis E Wilkins, *Short Line to Cripple Creek* (Golden: Colorado Railroad Museum, 1983).

21. "New Smelter Deal Is Consummated," *Colorado Springs Gazette*, March 21, 1900, 1.

22. Noel and Norman, *A Pikes Peak Partnership.*

23. Irving Howbert, "What Some Colorado Springs Men Say about Colorado Springs," *Colorado Springs Gazette*, January 1, 1902, 11.

24. Wilkins, *Short Line to Cripple Creek.*

25. "Almost Finished," *Colorado Springs Gazette*, September 15, 1906, 5.

26. Taylor, *Cripple Creek Mining District.*

27. Wilkins, *Short Line to Cripple Creek.*

28. Taylor, *Cripple Creek Mining District.*

29. Waters, *Midas of the Rockies.*

30. "Annual Edition," *Colorado Springs Gazette*, February 18, 1912.

31. Taylor, *Cripple Creek Mining District.*

32. William Jackson Palmer, "Letter to the Citizens of Colorado Springs of the Twenty First Century," in *Legends, Labors and Loves of William Jackson Palmer*, ed. T. Blevins, D. Daily, C. Nicholl, C. P. Otto, and K. S. Sturdevant (Colorado Springs: Pikes Peak Library District, 2009 [1874]), 197.

33. George G. Suggs, *Colorado's War on Militant Unionism: James H. Peabody and the Western Federation of Miners* (Detroit: Wayne State University Press, 1972); William G. Thomas, "Howbert, Waite, and the Ladies: The Colorado Gubernatorial Election of 1894," in *Bigwigs and Benefactor of the Pikes Peak Region*, ed. H. Jordan, T. Blevins, D. Daily, S. Dean, C. Nicholl, and M. Olsen (Colorado Springs: Pikes Peak Library District, 2017), 205–239.

34. Sprague, *Money Mountain*; Sprague, *Newport in the Rockies*; Suggs, *Colorado's War on Militant Unionism*.

35. "To Arms!" *Colorado Springs Gazette*, May 30, 1894, 1. See also Sprague, *Newport in the Rockies*.

36. Thomas, "Howbert, Waite, and the Ladies."

37. Sprague, *Money Mountain*; Suggs, *Colorado's War on Militant Unionism*; Thomas, "Howbert, Waite, and the Ladies."

38. Robert W. Larson, *Populism in the Mountain West* (Albuquerque: University of New Mexico Press, 1986).

39. The source for most of the information in this paragraph is Suggs, *Colorado's War on Militant Unionism*.

40. Taylor, *Cripple Creek Mining District*; Sprague, *Money Mountain*.

41. Scot Martelle, *Blood Passion: The Ludlow Massacre and the Class War in the American West* (New Brunswick, NJ: Rutgers University Press, 2007), 45. Martelle quotes from a letter Director L. M. Bowers wrote to company headquarters in New York on April 12, 1909.

42. Terrence Haverluk, "Chile Peppers and Identity Construction in Pueblo, Colorado," *Journal of the Study of Food and Society* 6, no. 1 (2003): 45–59; H. Lee Scamehorn, *Pioneer Steelmaker in the West: The Colorado Fuel and Iron Company 1872–1903* (Boulder, CO: Pruett Publishing Co, 1976).

43. Thirteenth Census of the United States, *Volume II: Population 1910* (Department of Commerce: Bureau of the Census, 1910).

44. *City Directory of Colorado Springs, Colorado City, and Manitou* (Colorado Springs: Giles Directory Company, 1900).

45. Colorado Springs Chamber of Commerce, *Daily Doings in the Pikes Peak Region* 9 (July 1919): 43.

46. Three sources were identified and used to compile these numbers, all from the Tri-Community Parish Records at the Sacred Heart offices in Old Colorado City: Book I: *Old St. Mary's*, which lists place of birth on selected marriage records; *Burials, Oct. 1891–Dec. 1916*, which lists location of natality through 1904; and *Liber Matrimonium, July 2, 1917–1957*, which lists the place of baptism for selected entries. For the latter, data collection stops after 1931, when foreign born nearly cease. The burial records also provide rich qualitative information about age and cause of death, including numerous entries listing railroad or smelter accidents.

47. "Coal," *Colorado Springs Gazette*, January 1, 1888.

48. Ormes, *Book of Colorado Springs*.

49. R. La Motte, "Tracing the Steady Progress of Colorado Springs through the Development of Its Public Utilities," *Colorado Springs Gazette and Telegraph*, January 1, 1905, 26.

50. Ormes, *Book of Colorado Springs*.

51. "CSLH&P Co Second Largest Employer and Taxpayer in City," 1921 unknown newspaper source accessed in the Starsmore Center for Local History, Colorado Springs Pioneers Museum, vertical file "Cities and Towns—Colorado Springs—Municipal Utilities." Also see Samantha Meigs, *One Hundred Years of Electric Service in Colorado Springs, 1886–1986* (Colorado Springs: Department of Utilities, Electric Transmission and Distribution Division, 1987).

52. "Council Turned Socialistic," *Colorado Springs Gazette*, April 2, 1924, 4

53. *City of Colorado Springs, Mining Report: Colorado Springs Coal Field, A Guide for Future Land Use* (Colorado Springs: Planning Department, Geology Section, 1967).

54. H. K. Ellingson, "75-Mile Rail Line Hauls Coal from Depths of Pikeview Mine" *Colorado Springs Gazette Telegraph*, November 23, 1947, 8C.

55. Matt Mayberry, "To Power a City: Coal Mining in Colorado Springs" (Colorado Springs: Pikes Peak Library District, in review).

56. Ellingson, "75-Mile Rail Line."

57. Douglas McKay, *Asylum of the Gilded Pill: The Story of Cragmor Sanatorium* (Denver: State Historical Society of Colorado, 1983); "Gets 30 Days for Selling to Youths: Papeton Bootlegger Was Caught by Posse Led by Dr. Shaefer," *Colorado Springs Gazette*, April 2, 1924, 1.

58. H. S. Rogers, "A Brief Historical Sketch of the Founding and Building of the County Seat of El Paso County, Colo," in *Annual Report and Financial Statement, 1901–1902* (City of Colorado Springs, 1902), 244; H. C. Harmon, "Rapid Development of the Coal Industry in Colorado," *Colorado Springs Gazette and Telegraph*, January 1, 1905, supplement, 32; Colorado Springs Chamber of Commerce, *Daily Doings in the Pikes Peak Region*, 43; *Fifteenth Census of the United States*, vol. 3. *Population 1930* (Department of Commerce: Bureau of the Census, 1930).

59. Dames & Moore, *Colorado Springs Subsidence Investigation*, vol. 1, *Executive Summary* (Denver: Colorado Division of Mined Land Reclamation, 1985).

60. Dames & Moore, *Subsidence Investigation*, 17.

61. Dames & Moore, *Subsidence Investigation*, 15.

62. Jim Bates, "Cave in Forces Evacuation," *Colorado Springs Sun*, March 29, 1979, 1.

63. *City of Colorado Springs, Mining Report*.

64. "Pikeview Coal Mine will Cease Operations July 1," *Colorado Springs Gazette Telegraph*, June 4, 1957, 1:6.

65. Bill Vogrin, "What Lies Beneath: Springs' Coal-Mining History Leaves a Maze of Tunnels—and Potential Problems," *Colorado Springs Gazette*, September 27, 2012.

66. "Mrs. Lipsey Recalls Hassell Iron Works History," *Colorado Spring Gazette Telegraph*, June 19, 1957, 19:1.

67. Ormes, *Book of Colorado Springs*.

68. All of Teller County had only 2,495 people in 1960. Numbers are from the *1960 Census of Population and Housing* (Department of Commerce: Bureau of the Census, 1960).

69. Robert Rhatigan, "Preservation or Disneyfication? The Colorado Limited Gaming Act of 1990 and Its Effects on the Historic Landscape and Character of Black Hawk, Central City, and Cripple Creek, Colorado" (MA thesis, University of Colorado Colorado Springs, 2008).

CHAPTER 6: FUN

1. This quote was originally printed in the *Greeley Tribune* but reprinted in William J. Palmer, "Founding of Colorado Springs," *Colorado Springs Gazette*, August 10, 1896, 14.

2. Anne Farrar Hyde, *An American Vision: Far Western Landscape and National Culture, 1820–1920* (New York: New York University Press, 1990).

3. Hyde, *An American Vision*, 14.

4. Hal Rothman, *Devil's Bargains: Tourism in the Twentieth-Century American West* (Lawrence: University Press of Kansas, 1998).

5. Rothman, *Devil's Bargains*. See also Marguerite S. Shaffer, "Seeing America First: The Search for Identity in the Tourist Landscape," in *Seeing and Being Seen: Tourism in the American West*, ed. D. Wrobel and P. Long (Lawrence: University Press of Kansas, 2001), 165–193.

6. William Jackson Palmer, "The Westward March of Emigration in the United States, Considered in Its Bearing upon the Near Future of Colorado and New Mexico," in *Legends, Labors and Loves of William Jackson Palmer*, ed. T. Blevins, D. Daily, C. Nicholl, C. P. Otto, and K. Scott Sturdevant (Colorado Springs: Pikes Peak Library District, 2009 [1874]), 137–182.

7. Hyde, *An American Vision*.

8. Marshall Sprague, *Newport in the Rockies: The Life and Good Times of Colorado Springs* (Athens, OH: Swallow Press, 1987).

9. Hyde, *An American Vision*.

10. *Fountain Colony: Villa La Font*, author unknown, 1926, 1–2, Starsmore Center for Local History, Colorado Springs Pioneers Museum.

11. "Manitou Springs," *Colorado Springs Gazette*, January 1, 1888, 10.

12. "Manitou Springs," 11.

13. Juanita L. Breckenridge and John P. Breckenridge, eds., *El Paso County Heritage* (Dallas: Curtis Media Corp, 1985), 75. See also Hyde, *An American Vision*, 160.

14. "Pikes Peak Region," promotional brochure from the Colorado & Southern Railroad, 1924, Starsmore Center for Local History, Colorado Springs Pioneers Museum. See also "Build $50,000 Bath House at Manitou This Spring," *Colorado Springs Gazette*, January 1, 1905, 7.

15. "Pikes Peak Region," 1924. On the issue of energy costs to heat the Manitou mineral baths, the most recent rendition is the 2015 opening of the nearby Sun Water Spa, which relies on solar power to heat the water.

16. William Philpott, *Vacationland: Tourism and Environment in the Colorado High Country* (Seattle: University of Washington Press, 2013).

17. Patricia Nelson Limerick, "Seeing and Being Seen: Tourism in the American West," in *Seeing and Being Seen: Tourism in the American West*, ed. D. Wrobel and P. Long (Lawrence: University Press of Kansas, 2001), 39–58.

18. "Manitou Springs," *Colorado Springs Gazette*, January 1, 1888, 10.

19. Quotes and information about these tourist attractions come from business promotional brochures over various years accessed from both the Starsmore Center for Local History, Colorado Springs Pioneers Museum, and the Colorado College Tutt Library, Special Collections.

20. Leah Davis-Witherow, "Marketing the Mountain: Pikes Peak in the Popular Imagination," in *To Spare No Pains: Zebulon Montgomery Pike and His 1806–1807 Southwest Expedition*, ed. T. Blevins, M. Mayberry, C. Nicholl, C. P. Otto, and N. Thaler (Colorado Springs: Pikes Peak Library District, 2007), 217–238.

21. *Colorado Springs Gazette*, July 4, 1891, 4.

22. This quote is attributed to Teddy Roosevelt when he took the Short Line trip in 1901. The quote has been reproduced repeatedly; here I cite a promotional brochure from the Colorado Springs and Cripple Creek Railroad "Through the Heart of the Rockies into the Land of Gold," 1915, Starsmore Center for Local History, Colorado Springs Pioneers Museum.

23. Eric Swab, "The Legend and History of Fred Barr," in *Bigwigs and Benefactors of the Pikes Peak Region*, ed. H. Jordan, T. Blevins, D. Daily, S. Dean, C. Nicholl, and M. Olsen (Colorado Springs: Pikes Peak Library District, 2017), 99–126.

24. Troy R. Lovata, "Tourism as Built for the Tourists: The Anasazi Cliff Dwellings of Manitou Springs, Colorado," *International Journal of Historical Archaeology* 15 (2011): 194–205. See also Rothman, *Devil's Bargains*.

25. From business promotional brochures, Colorado College Tutt Library, Special Collections.

26. Rothman, *Devil's Bargains*. For another excellent analysis of constructed authenticity, see Chris Wilson, *The Myth of Santa Fe: Creating a Modern Regional Tradition* (Albuquerque: University of New Mexico Press, 1997).

27. Lovata, "Tourism as Built for the Tourists."

28. Hyde, *American Vision*. Also see Marguerite S. Shaffer, "Seeing America First: The Search for Identity in the Tourist Landscape," in *Seeing and Being Seen: Tourism in the American West*, ed. D. Wrobel and P. Long (Lawrence: University Press of Kansas, 2001), 165–193.

29. Erinn Barnes, "Unwitting Benefactors: American Indians and Tourism in the Pikes Peak Region, 1890–1930," in H. Jordan et al., *Bigwigs and Benefactors of the Pikes Peak Region*, 173–203.

30. Promotional brochure for the Shan Kive, 1912, Colorado College Tutt Library, Special Collections.

31. Hyde, *American Vision*.

32. Bill McKenzie, "Antlers Hotel—Three Generations of Taste-Catering Inn-Keeping," *Free Press*, February 2, 1969, 58–59, "City and County in Motion" Sunday supplement.

33. Leland Feitz, *The Antlers: A Quick History of Colorado Springs' Historic Hotel* (Denver: Golden Bell Press, 1972); Judith R. Finley, "Hustling the Tourists: Early Automobile Sightseeing in the Pikes Peak Region," in *Enterprise and Innovation in the Pikes Peak Region*, ed. T. Blevins, D. Daily, S. Dean, C. Nicholl, and M. L. Olsen (Colorado Springs: Pikes Peak Library District, 2011), 212–227.

34. Promotional business brochure, Colorado College Tutt Library, Special Collections.

35. Promotional business brochure, Colorado College Tutt Library, Special Collections.

36. "Colorado Hotels, Lodges, and Guest Ranches," promotional brochure published by the Rock Island Railroad, Colorado College Tutt Library, Special Collections.

37. First quote Hyde, *An American Vision*, 172; second quote "At the Foot of Pikes Peak," unknown author ca. 1893, promotional photo booklet with accompanying text intended to entice 1893 Chicago World's Fair travelers to Colorado Springs, Starsmore Center for Local History, Colorado Springs Pioneers Museum.

38. Thomas J. Noel and Cathleen M. Norman, *A Pikes Peak Partnership: The Penroses and the Tutts* (Boulder: University Press of Colorado, 2000).

39. Noel and Norman, *A Pikes Peak Partnership*.

40. Joyce B. Lohse, "The Penrose Legacy: Ventures, Vogue, and Vagary," in Jordan et al., *Bigwigs and Benefactors of the Pikes Peak Region*, 127–171.

41. The original lodge fell into disuse, suffered from vandalism, and was demolished in 1973. The Broadmoor built a new lodge in the early twenty-first century that offers luxury lodging amidst the pines.

42. Penrose gave the zoo to city in 1938; it is now an independently run nonprofit with no city support.

43. Rothman, *Devil's Bargains*: auto numbers cited on 146.

44. Finley, "Hustling the Tourists," 215.

45. Richard H. Jackson and Mark W. Jackson, "The Lincoln Highway: The First Transcontinental Highway and the American West," *Journal of the West* 42, no. 2 (2003): 56–64.

46. "Publicity Starts Work on Pikes Peak Highway," *Colorado Springs Gazette*, September 3, 1914, 5; "Pikes Peak Ocean-to-Ocean Highway Pronounced Finest Road in Existence," *Colorado Springs Gazette*, August 10, 1914, 5; Citizens of the Pikes Peak Region for the Creation of the Ocean to Ocean Highway Association, 1939, resolution to form, business minutes accessed from the Starsmore Center for Local History, Colorado Springs Pioneers Museum.

47. "Use Envelopes to Advertise Merits of City of Sunshine," *Colorado Springs Gazette*, January 5, 1906, 5.

48. Davis-Witherow, "Marketing the Mountain."

49. "Chamber of Commerce to Give Away 20,000 More Cards Today," *Colorado Springs Gazette*, July 8, 1911, 1.

50. "Publicity Campaign to Start Work at Once," *Colorado Springs Gazette*, February 11, 1915, 5.

51. "Colorado-to-Gulf Road One of the Most Important," *Colorado Springs Gazette*, January 16, 1914, 2; "Thousands Turn out to Welcome Springs–to–Gulf Highway Boosters on Return from 2,500-Mile Trip," *Colorado Springs Gazette*, May 28, 1914, 1; Katie Rudolph, "Bumps in the Road: The Spirit of Enterprise and the Sociability Tour of 1914," in *Enterprise and Innovation in the Pikes Peak Region*, ed. T. Blevins, D. Daily, S. Dean, C. Nicholl, and M. L. Olsen (Colorado Springs; Pikes Peak Library District, 2011), 114–147.

52. Archive notes, "Marketing the Mountain" exhibit at the Colorado Springs Pioneers Museum, Leah Davis-Witherow, curator of history.

53. Rudolph, "Bumps in the Road."

54. Rothman, *Devil's Bargains*; Limerick, "Seeing and Being Seen."

55. Finley, "Hustling the Tourists."

56. John A. Jakle, Keith A. Sculle, and Jefferson S. Rogers, *The Motel in America* (Baltimore: Johns Hopkins University Press, 1996); John A. Jakle and Keith A. Sculle, *The Gas Station in America* (Baltimore: Johns Hopkins University Press, 1994).

57. Larry Ford, *Cities and Buildings: Skyscrapers, Skid Rows, and Suburbs* (Baltimore: Johns Hopkins University Press, 1994).

58. Ford, *Cities and Buildings.*

59. William Wyckoff, "Denver's Aging Commercial Strip," *Geographical Review* 82, no. 3 (1992): 282–294.

60. W. G. Elmslie, "The Case against a Municipal Camp Ground at Prospect Lake," *Colorado Springs Gazette*, April 1, 1924, 8.

61. Nancy Lewis and Deborah O'Dell, *The Parks of Colorado Springs: Building Community, Preserving Legacy* (Dallas: Brown Books, 2011).

62. Jakle et al., *The Motel in America.*

63. Jakle et al., *The Motel in America.*

64. Rothman, *Devil's Bargains.*

65. Philpott, *Vacationland.*

66. "Ski Jumping Contest Scheduled for Today," *Sunday Gazette and Telegraph*, April 6, 1924, 15; "Ski Club Plans to Hold June Tourney," *Colorado Springs Gazette*, April 11, 1924, 1.

67. Philpott, *Vacationland.*

68. Annie Gilbert Coleman, *Ski Style: Sport and Culture in the Rockies* (Lawrence: University Press of Kansas, 2004).

69. Philpott, *Vacationland*, talks about tourist "consumption" of ski towns, but for the best source for consumerism and identity construction, see Naomi Klein, *No Logo* (New York: Picador, 1999).

70. Coleman, *Ski Style*; Philpott, *Vacationland.*

71. Lewis and O'Dell, *Parks of Colorado Springs.*

72. "Monument Park—Bower of Beauty in the Heart of the City," *Colorado Springs Gazette and Telegraph*, January 1, 1905, 7.

73. Charles Mulford Robison, *A City Beautiful Dream: The 1912 Vision for Colorado Springs* (Colorado Springs: Pikes Peak Library District, 2012 [1912]), 93.

74. *Colorado Springs Gazette*, February 24, 1918, 1. See also Lewis and O'Dell, *Parks of Colorado Springs.*

75. After the devastating 1935 Memorial Day flood, the Works Progress Association and Civilian Conservation Corps workers helped reconstruct the park. Flood control widened the channel, effectively removing sixty-five acres from use.

76. Lewis and O'Dell, *Parks of Colorado Springs.*

77. Outdoor Industry Association, *Technical Report* (Boulder, CO, 2018), accessed June 11, 2018, http://outdoorindustry.org/what-we-do/annual-reports/.

78. Outdoor Industry Association, *Technical Report*; also see *Colorado Springs Gazette*, March 16, 2018, A3.

79. Mia Gray and Ann R. Markusen, "Colorado Springs: A Military-Anchored City in Transition," in *Second Tier Cities: Rapid Growth Beyond the Metropolis*, ed. A. Markusen, Y. S. Lee, and S. DiGiovanna (Minneapolis: University of Minnesota Press, 1999), 311–332.

80. Colorado Springs Chamber of Commerce and EDC, Sports Industry Profile, 2018, accessed June 11, 2018, https://coloradospringschamberedc.com/.

81. Colorado Springs Convention and Visitors Bureau, accessed June 11, 2018, http://www.visitcos.com. See also "Pikes Peak Region Sets Tourism Records," *Colorado Springs Business Journal*, September 1, 2017, https://www.csbj.com/news/daily/pikes-peak-region-sets-tourism-records/article_c94f8d85-f5ed-5c8c-9e19-93ffeaf3563a.html.

82. For example, see Patrick T. Long, "For Residents and Visitors Alike: Seeking Tourism's Benefits, Minimizing Tourism's Costs," in *Seeing and Being Seen: Tourism in the American West*, ed. D. Wrobel and P. Long (Lawrence: University Press of Kansas, 2001), 70–90; Limerick, "Seeing and Being Seen"; Philpott, *Vacationland.*

83. Rothman, *Devil's Bargains*, 11.

84. Philpott, *Vacationland*, 8.

85. Davis-Witherow, "Marketing the Mountain," 218.

86. Both quotes from William J. Palmer, "Founding of Colorado Springs," *Colorado Springs Gazette*, August 10, 1896, 14.

CHAPTER 7: WAR

1. This is one of the many descriptions of the space economy local boosters attributed to the city. The quote appears in Ann Markusen, Peter Hall, Scott Campbell, and Sabina Deitrick, *The Rise of the Gunbelt: The Military Remapping of Industrial America* (New York: Oxford University Press, 1991), 175.

2. Mia Gray and Ann R. Markusen, "Colorado Springs: A Military-Anchored City in Transition," in *Second Tier Cities: Rapid Growth beyond the Metropolis*, ed. A. Markusen, Y. S. Lee and S. DiGiovanna (Minneapolis: University of Minnesota Press, 1999), 313.

3. US Army, *Fort Carson: A Tradition of Victory* (Fort Carson, CO: Public Affairs and Information Office, 1972).

4. US Army, *Fort Carson*, 10.

5. Markusen et al., *Rise of the Gunbelt.*

6. Army, *Fort Carson.*

7. Army, *Fort Carson.*

8. Ed Honnen, *Camp Carson: A Cow Ranch to a Military City* (Colorado Springs: Self Published, 1977); Ed Honnen owned a local construction company that subcontracted to build the camp.

9. "$50 Million Army Camp Projects Here Bring Boom Days Never Dreamed Of," *Camp Carson Mountaineer*, July 26, 1942.

10. "Coal Contract Let at Camp," *Camp Carson Mountaineer*, August 13, 1942.

11. "1,100 Get Jobs at Camp Carson," *Camp Carson Mountaineer*, July 30, 1942.

12. "Many Soldiers Paid Today, Will Throng City Saturday," *Camp Carson Mountaineer*, July 31, 1942.

13. Markusen et al., *Rise of the Gunbelt.*

14. US Army, *Fort Carson Directory and Guide* (Colorado Springs: Phillip T. Flaxman Publisher, 1960); Carol Bruce-Fritz and Kathryn Davis Gardner, *On the Home Front: Colorado Springs in World War II* (Colorado Springs: Colorado Springs Pioneers Museum, 1994).

15. US Air Force, Peterson Air Force Base Fact Sheet, February 1, 1980.

16. "$72,000 Paid city by Government," *Camp Carson Mountaineer*, July 28, 1942.

17. Bruce-Fritz and Davis Gardner, *On the Home Front.*

18. US Air Force, *Ent Air Force Base Directory and Guide* (Colorado Springs: Phillip T. Flaxman Publisher, 1958).

19. "An Ever-Changing Role," *Mountaineer*, April 25, 1989.

20. "Carson Biggest Factor in Colorado Springs Economy," *Mountaineer*, November 16, 1956.

21. Joyce Trent, "Report Shows High GI Crime Rate," *Colorado Springs Sun*, September 25, 1954, 1; George Gladney, "Ft. Carson Crime Rate Drops," *Colorado Springs Sun*, November 23, 1975, 1; "Carson Cited for Major Water Pollution Problems," *Colorado Springs Sun*, October 22, 1977, 1; Anthony Polk, "Fort Carson Shows High Child Abuse Rate," *Rocky Mountain News*, January 21, 1979, 6.

22. William Buzenberg, "Kramer Urges Campaign Opposing Possible Troop Transfer," *Colorado Springs Sun*, January 5, 1975, 5.

23. Nina Bondarook, "Panel Action on Carson Criticized," *Colorado Springs Sun*, February 15, 1980, 1-A.

24. Denise Gamino, "Study of Carson Options for Training Troops Due," *Colorado Springs Sun*, July 10, 1981.

25. David Havlick and Eric Perramond, "Militarized Spaces and Open Range: Piñon Canyon and (Counter)Cartographies of Rural Resistance," *Environment and Planning D: Society and Space* 33 (2015): 169–184.

26. Sue McMillin, "Army Ready to Move into New Training Area," *Colorado Springs Gazette Telegraph*, July 15, 1985, p. B1.

27. Jim Sanders, "Carson Names Wilmot 'Good Neighbor,'" *Colorado Springs Sun*, January 21, 1981, 3-D.

28. *Base Structure Report Fiscal Year 2003 Baseline* (Washington, DC: US Department of Defense, 2002); Defense Base Closure and Realignment Commission Report, vol. I (Washington, DC: US Department of Defense, 2005).

29. US Army, *Fort Carson Facts* (Colorado Springs: Fort Carson, 2012).

30. Tom Roeder, "Sites to Behold," *Colorado Springs Gazette*, October 10, 2005, Metro-1; Tom Roeder, "Fort Carson Scrambles to Handle Influx," *Colorado Springs Gazette*, May 14, 2005, 1.

31. Jane Reuter, "Carson's Growth Driving Housing Development," *Colorado Springs Gazette*, November 16, 2005, Metro-4.

32. David Bamberger, "Fort Carson's Impact Echoes throughout Area, State," *Colorado Springs Gazette*, October 10, 2004.

33. John Diedrich, "Soldiers Comfortable in Springs," *Colorado Springs Gazette*, March 15, 1999, News-1.

34. Havlick and Perramond, "Militarized Spaces."

35. Havlick and Perramond, "Militarized Spaces."

36. US Army, *Fort Carson Factsheet* (Colorado Springs: Fort Carson, 2018).

37. George V. Fagan, *The Air Force Academy: An Illustrated History* (Boulder, CO: Johnson Books, 1988).

38. Fagan, *The Air Force Academy*, 40.

39. Robert Allen Nauman, *On the Wings of Modernism: The United States Air Force Academy* (Urbana: University of Illinois Press, 2004).

40. Markusen et al., *Rise of the Gunbelt*.

41. Fagan, *The Air Force Academy*, 40.

42. Markusen et al., *Rise of the Gunbelt*, 180.

43. Fagan, *The Air Force Academy*, 46.

44. Fagan, *The Air Force Academy*, 46

45. Mack Miller, *Wild Blue U: The Story of the U.S. Air Force Academy* (New York: Collier Books, 1972), 6.

46. Fagan, *The Air Force Academy*.

47. Fagan, *The Air Force Academy*; Nauman, *On the Wings of Modernism*.

48. Nauman, *On the Wings of Modernism*, 12.

49. A congressman from California challenged the availability of sufficient water for the Colorado Springs site and asked for an investigation into the site selection process. See "Californian May Ask Probe of Academy Site Selection," *Colorado Springs Gazette Telegraph*, November 16, 1954, 1.

50. Markusen et al., *Rise of the Gunbelt*, 181.

51. "Springs Awarded Academy for Its 'Warm Welcome,'" *Free Press*, October 30, 1958, 24.

52. Fagan, *The Air Force Academy*.

53. Fagan, *The Air Force Academy*.

54. Fagan, *The Air Force Academy*.

55. Nauman, *On the Wings of Modernism*.

56. Markusen et al., *Rise of the Gunbelt*.

57. Fagan, *The Air Force Academy*, 48.

58. Air Force Academy Construction Agency, *Armed Forces Guide to the Colorado Springs and Pikes Peak Region* (Colorado Springs: Phillip T. Flaxman Publisher, 1958).

59. Miller, *Wild Blue U*, 7.

60. Fagan, *The Air Force Academy*, 47.

61. Markusen et al., *Rise of the Gunbelt*, 175.

62. B. Flyvbjerg, *Rationality and Power: Democracy in Practice* (Chicago: University of Chicago Press, 1998).

63. Nauman, *On the Wings of Modernism*.

64. Nauman, *On the Wings of Modernism*, 60. The quote is from partner Nathaniel Owings.

65. William Curtis, *Modern Architecture Since 1900*, 3rd ed. (London: Phaidon, 1996).

66. Information in this paragraph all from Nauman, *On the Wings of Modernism*.

67. Nauman, *On the Wings of Modernism*, 62.

68. Nauman, *On the Wings of Modernism*, 62.

69. Nauman, *On the Wings of Modernism*, 73.

70. Nauman, *On the Wings of Modernism*, 62.

71. Nauman, *On the Wings of Modernism*, 62.

72. Nauman, *On the Wings of Modernism*, 75.

73. Fagan, *The Air Force Academy*.

74. "Ex-Cadet Prompts Chapel Policy Change," *Colorado Springs Gazette*, February 16, 1999.

75. Nauman, *On the Wings of Modernism*, 108.

76. US Air Force, *The United States Air Force Academy Cadet Chapel*, color promotional booklet published by the Air Force Academy, 1978.

77. US Air Force, *The United States Air Force Academy Cadet Chapel*.

78. "Spires that Soar," *Time*, July 27, 1962.

79. Nauman, *On the Wings of Modernism*, 66.

80. Nauman, *On the Wings of Modernism*, 116.

81. John Diedrich, "Architect Builds on a Dream," *Colorado Springs Gazette*, March 17, 2000, Metro-3.

82. Markusen et al., *Rise of the Gunbelt*, 183.

83. Phil Robertson, "Springs Seen Boom Town but It's in Slow Motion," *Colorado Springs Gazette Telegraph*, November 16, 1954, 9.

84. Fagan, *The Air Force Academy*.

85. US Air Force, *Women in Motion: Celebrating 20 Years at the Air Force Academy* (Colorado Springs: USAFA Directorate of Public Affairs, 1996).

86. Personal correspondence with Dr. Terry Haverluk, professor of Geospatial Sciences at the Academy from 1996 to 2018, Colorado Springs, July 15, 2018.

87. John Diedrich, "Air Force Wants Closer Ties to AFA," *Colorado Springs Gazette*, October 4, 2002, Metro-1; Pam Zubeck, "Pentagon Blames AFA Brass," *Colorado Springs Gazette*, December 8, 2004, 1.

88. "Motto Behavior," *Colorado Springs Gazette*, September 25, 2004.

89. Pam Zubeck, "AFA Finds Faith Bias Roots Deep," *Colorado Springs Gazette*, November 20, 2004, 1.

90. Pam Zubeck, "Claims of AFA Religious Slant Nothing New," *Colorado Springs Gazette*, November 19, 2004.

91. Pam Zubeck, "Year-Old Report Warned of 'Evangelical Tone' at AFA," *Colorado Springs Gazette*, April 20, 2005, 1.

92. Tom Roeder, "For First Time since 9/11, AFA Will Open Gate," *Colorado Springs Gazette*, September 25, 2006, 1.

93. *50: Celebrating the U.S. Air Force Academy's Golden Anniversary* (Colorado Springs: Freedom Communications, 2004).

94. Markusen et al., *Rise of the Gunbelt*.

95. Markusen et al., *Rise of the Gunbelt*.

96. Ray Herst, "Steel City Being Built under Cheyenne Mountain," *Colorado Springs Gazette Telegraph*, December 5, 1963, 43.

97. US Air Force, *The Cheyenne Mountain Story*, promotional booklet, n.d.; "America's Atomic Mountain" slogan attributed to David Havlick, "Cheyenne Mountain, Colorado," in *People's Atlas of the Nuclear United States*, ed. Shiloh Krupar and Sarah Kanouse, a digital public humanities project (in progress). See https://web.northeastern.edu/nulab/peoples-atlas/.

98. "Land Near Peterson AFB Exchanged for Land at Ent AFB," *Colorado Springs Gazette*, January 26, 1978, A-1.

99. Markusen et al., *Rise of the Gunbelt*.

100. Colorado Springs Chamber of Commerce, *Report* (Colorado Springs, 1963); this is a lengthy booklet the chamber produced to attract industry to the city.

101. David Angel, *Restructuring for Innovation: The Remaking of the U.S. Semiconductor Industry* (New York: Guilford Press, 1994); Markusen et al., *Rise of the Gunbelt*.

102. "Air Force Space Command Celebrates 20th," *Satellite Flyer*, August 29, 2002.

103. "Space Center Counts Down," *Colorado Springs Gazette*, February 24, 1980, EE-1; Bob Shaw, "Panel to Explore Space Center Impact," *Colorado Springs Gazette*, July 25, 1982, Metro-1.

104. Mary Boyle, "New Clout for Springs," *Colorado Springs Gazette*, March 9, 2001, 1.

105. "Satellites Crucial to Warfare," *Colorado Springs Gazette*, May 12, 2003, Local-1; quote from Tom Roeder, "Flight Defines Springs," *Colorado Springs Gazette*, December 15, 2003, Life-1.

106. Gray and Markusen, "Colorado Springs," 312.

107. Colorado Springs Chamber of Commerce and Economic Development Corporation, *Key Industries*: https://coloradospringschamberedc.com/key-industries/aerospace-defense/, US Army, Fort Carson fact sheet, 2018.

108. See https://livability.com/topics/community/10-best-cities-for-veterans, accessed November 15, 2018.

109. Tom Roeder, "Flight Defines Springs," *Colorado Springs Gazette*, December 15, 2003, Life-1.

110. Rosa Brooks, *How Everything Became War and the Military Became Everything* (New York: Simon and Schuster, 2016).

111. Gray and Markusen, "Colorado Springs."

112. Wayne Heilman, "Springing from the Springs," *Denver Post*, December 29, 2014, 2A (originally published in the *Colorado Springs Gazette*).

113. Colorado Springs Chamber of Commerce and Economic Development Corporation, *Aerospace and Defense Industry Profile*: accessed November 15, 2018, https://coloradospringschamberedc.com/key-industries/aerospace-defense/.

114. May 23, 2016, accessed November 15, 2018, https://news.clearancejobs.com/2016/05/23/best-cities-defense-intelligence-jobs/.

115. Colorado Springs Chamber of Commerce and Economic Development Corporation, *Key Industries*: accessed November 15, 2018, https://coloradospringschamberedc.com/key-industries/information-technology/.

116. Summit Economics, LLC, *The Economic Impact of Department of Defense, Veterans and Military Retirees, and the Department of Veterans Affairs Activities in Colorado* (Denver, 2018).

117. Roeder, "Flight Defines Springs."

118. Quote from Heilman, "Springing from the Springs," 2A; "Jobless Rate in Springs Falls—Not in a Good Way," *Denver Post*, January 3, 2015, 13A (originally published in the *Colorado Springs Gazette*).

119. Tom Roeder, "Study: Springs Most Vulnerable City," *Colorado Springs Gazette*, October 3, 2013, A6.

120. Barry Noreen, "Limited Government Just a Lot of Talk Here," *Colorado Springs Gazette*, July 24, 2011, Local-1.

121. Brooks, *How Everything Became War*.

122. Brooks, *How Everything Became War*.

123. Brooks, *How Everything Became War*.

124. Brooks, *How Everything Became War*, 21.

CHAPTER 8: LIBERTY

1. "Freedom Fighters Flock to our City," *Colorado Springs Gazette*, April 25, 2012, A16.

2. Founded in 1910, Dearfield, Colorado, was one attempt at a utopian agricultural community for African Americans in Weld County.

3. John Stokes Holley, *The Invisible People of the Pikes Peak Region: An Afro-American Chronicle* (Colorado Springs: Friends of the Pikes Peak Library District and Friends of the Colorado Springs Pioneers Museum, 1990).

4. Holley, *The Invisible People of the Pikes Peak Region*.

5. Lisa Goff, *Shantytown, USA: Forgotten Landscapes of the Working Poor* (Cambridge, MA: Harvard University Press, 2016), 179.

6. "African Methodist Church," *Weekly Gazette*, July 12, 1890, 5.

7. John Stokes Holley, "The Strouds: A Most Remarkable Family," in *Bigwigs and Benefactors of the Pikes Peak Region*, ed. H. Jordan, T. Blevins, D. Daily, S. Dean, C. Nicholl, and M. Olsen (Colorado Springs: Pikes Peak Library District, 2017), 240–261.

8. "That the Place Might Go to a Kluxer," *Colorado Springs Gazette*, April 18, 1925, 4; "The Legislature and the Job Facing Voters," *Colorado Springs Gazette*, April 20, 1925, 4.

9. "Hundreds Sign up in Battle against Klan," *Colorado Springs Gazette*, April 17, 1925, 1; "League Goes into Action against Klan," *Colorado Springs Gazette*, April 18, 1925, 1. Note that an earlier civic league existed from 1909 to 1914 that advocated for women's suffrage and acted as a shadow government to scrutinize elected officials.

10. "Antiklan Sentimentality spreading," *Sunday Gazette and Telegraph*, April 26, 1925, 1.

11. "State Klan Sends SOS Call for Aid," *Colorado Springs Gazette*, April 23, 1925, 1.

12. "Neutrality Impossible When City Is Menaced," *Colorado Springs Gazette*, April 22, 1925, 4.

13. Kathleen F. Esmiol, "Chasing the American Dream: Fanny Mae Duncan and the Cotton Club," in *Enterprise and Innovation in the Pikes Peak Region*, ed. T. Blevins, D. Daily, S. Dean, C. Nicholl, and M. Olsen (Colorado Springs: Pikes Peak Library District, 2011), 316.

14. *Negro Motorists Green Book* (Victor H. Green and Co., 1940); https://digitalcollections.nypl.org/items/dcb66a80-83d3-0132-5b00-58d385a7b928 or https://delphi.tcl.sc.edu/library/digital/collections/greenbook.html. Also see Rhonda Colvin, "Some Americans Afraid to Explore," *Denver Post*, January 27, 2018, 14A (originally published in the *Washington Post*); Derek Alderman and Joshua Inwood, "Toward a Pedagogy of Jim Crow: A Critical Reading of the Green Book," in *Teaching Ethnic Geography in the 21st Century*, ed. L. Estaville, E. Montalvo, and F. Akiwumi (Washington, DC: National Council for Geographic Education, 2014), 68–78.

15. Esmiol, "Chasing the American Dream," 327.

16. "Parents Continue to Fight for South Junior High School," *Colorado Springs Minority Press*, March 11, 1983, 1.

17. Morris Cafky and John Haney, *Pikes Peak Trolleys* (Colorado Springs: Century One Press, 1983).

18. Manly R. Ormes, *The Book of Colorado Springs* (Colorado Springs: Denton Printing Company, 1933).

19. "The Electric Railway," *Colorado Springs Gazette*, December 31, 1899, 21.

20. Marshall Sprague, *Money Mountain: The Story of Cripple Creek Gold* (Boston: Little, Brown and Co., 1953).

21. Frank Waters, *Midas of the Rockies* (Denver: University of Denver Press, 1949); Cafky and Haney, *Pikes Peak Trolleys*.

22. Waters, *Midas of the Rockies*, 239.

23. E.g., see design principles advocate by the Congress of New Urbanism at www.cnu.org, or Smart Growth America at www.smartgrowthamerica.org.

24. The demise of streetcars in urban America was not just from free market competition with bus lines but was helped along by General Motors (GM), Standard Oil, Firestone, and other companies actively buying about twenty-five streetcar companies across the country and shutting them down, all in order to usher in buses using their products. These companies were found guilty in 1949 of conspiracy to monopolize interstate commerce under the Sherman Antitrust Act, but a sympathetic judge fined the GM treasurer a grand total of $1.

25. Donald Meinig, "Symbolic Landscapes," in *The Interpretation of Ordinary Landscapes*, ed. D. W. Meinig (New York: Oxford University Press, 1979), 164–192; Kenneth T. Jackson, *Crabgrass Frontier* (New York: Oxford University Press, 1985); D. J. Waldie, *Holy Land: A Suburban Memoir* (New York: W. W. Norton and Co., 1996).

26. *Commemorating the Opening of the Monument Valley Freeway, Colorado Springs* (Denver: Colorado Department of Highways, 1960), Pikes Peak Library District, Special Collections.

27. *Commemorating the Opening of the Monument Valley Freeway*.

28. Howard Frumkin, Lawrence Frank, and Richard Jackson, *Urban Sprawl and Public Health: Designing, Planning, and Building for Healthy Communities* (Washington, DC: Island Press, 2004); Richard J. Jackson, *Designing Healthy Communities* (San Francisco: Jossey-Bass, 2012); Janette Sadik-Khan, *Streetfight* (New York: Penguin, 2016).

29. John Branch, "Urban Design: Home Sweet Garage," *Colorado Springs Gazette Telegraph*, January 12, 1997, A5.

30. Bureau of Transportation Statistics, accessed August 20, 2108 at www.bts.gov, data compiled from US Department of Transportation, Federal Highway Administration, 1995–2016 Highway Statistics Washington, DC: Annual Issues.

31. "Re-elect Meier County Commissioner," political campaign brochure, 1988, Starsmore Center for Local History, Colorado Springs Pioneers Museum, Republican Party of Colorado Collection.

32. "Gary Shupp Republican for County Commissioner," political campaign brochure, 1990, Starsmore Center for Local History, Colorado Springs Pioneers Museum, Republican Party of Colorado Collection.

33. Branch, "Urban Design"; John Branch, "Urban Critics Question the Aesthetic of 'Sprawlorado Springs,'" *Colorado Springs Gazette Telegraph*, January12, 1997, 1.

34. Pam Zubeck, "Forging Ahead," *Colorado Springs Independent*, August 1–7, 2018, 15.

35. Pam Zubeck, "The Puppeteers," *Colorado Springs Independent*, November 16–22, 2016, 18–23; quote is from Joel Miller, page 22.

36. "BLR Annexation Agreement Comparison Table," city document, accessed August 3, 2018, https://coloradosprings.gov.

37. "Banning Lewis Ranch Annexation Amendment," proposal passed April 24, 2018, https://coloradosprings.gov/blr.

38. Christopher Leinberger, "Federal Restructuring of Fannie and Freddie Ignores Underlying Cause of Crisis," Urban Land, accessed February 10, 2011, https://urbanland.uli.org/economy-markets-trends/federal-restructuring-of-fannie-and-freddie-ignores-underlying-cause-of-crisis/.

39. Jane Holtz Kay, *Asphalt Nation* (Berkeley: University of California Press, 1997); James Howard Kunstler, *The Geography of Nowhere* (New York: Simon and Schuster, 1993).

40. Anna Staver, "Road Rage Fatalities: Colorado Ranks No. 2 in the Nation," *Denver Post*, August 2, 2018, 5A.

41. John Harner and Frank Kinder, "Placelessness in a Deregulated City: University Village in Colorado Springs," *Urban Geography* 32, no. 5 (2011): 730–755.

42. Catherine Lutz and Anne Lutz Fernandez, *Carjacked: The Culture of the Automobile and Its Effect on Our Lives* (New York: Palgrave Macmillan, 2011); these authors estimate 10 percent 25 percent of the entire annual military budget is dedicated to oil resource control.

43. "Academy Boulevard Corridor Conditions Assessment," City of Colorado Springs, City Planning and Community Development Department, September 12, 2007.

44. Jeff Speck, *Walkable City* (New York: North Point Press, 2012).

45. Cameron Moix, "City Anticipates Future Growth in North Colorado Springs," *Colorado Springs Business Journal*, February 24, 2017, http://www.csbj.com/2017/02/24/city-anticipates-future-growth-in-north-colorado-springs/.

46. "Small Area Forecast Report," Pikes Peak Area Council of Governments, July 2018, accessed August 5, 2018, www.ppacg.org.

47. Harvey Molotch, "The City as a Growth Machine," *American Journal of Sociology* 82, no. 2 (1976): 309–330.

48. John Logan and Harvey Molotch, *Urban Fortunes: The Political Economy of Place* (Berkeley: University of California Press, 1987).

49. Eugene McCann, "The Cultural Politics of Local Economic Development: Meaning-Making, Place-Making, and the Urban Policy Process," *Geoforum* 33, no. 3 (2002): 385–398.

50. Bent Flyvbjerg, *Rationality and Power: Democracy in Practice* (Chicago: University of Chicago Press, 1998).

51. Eugene McCann, "'Best Places': Interurban Competition, Quality of Life and Popular Media Discourse," *Urban Studies* 41 (2004): 1909–1929; Don Mitchell, *Cultural Geography: A Critical Introduction* (Oxford, UK: Blackwell, 2000).

52. Kevin Cox and Andrew Mair, "Locality and Community in the Politics of Local Economic Development," *Annals of the Association of American Geographers* 78, no. 2 (1988): 307–325.

53. Harner and Kinder, "Placelessness in a Deregulated City."

54. Author and documentarian Eric Schlosser chose Colorado Springs as the prototypical, suburban-oriented city replete with corporate commercial food franchises and chains for his 2001 book *Fast Food Nation*. He said the city served as metaphor for the evolution of the nation's fast-food industry. See Eric Schlosser, *Fast Food Nation: The Dark Side of the All-American Meal* (Boston: Houghton Mifflin, 2001).

55. Architecture professor and urban design consultant Anton Nelessen pioneered an innovative planning tool called "visual preference surveys" that regularly show few people prefer residential and commercial spaces most commonly built in suburban America today. See nelessen.com.

56. For a discussion of how political culture influences urban planning, see Amanda Johnson Ashley and Leslie Alm, "Western Regional Identity and Urban Development Policy: The View from Professional Planners," *Social Science Journal* 53, no. 2 (2016): 143–155.

57. Chris Tausanovitch and Christopher Warshaw, "Representation in Municipal Government," *American Political Science Review* 108, no. 3 (2014): 605–641; Joshua Dunn, "The Paradoxes of Politics in Colorado Springs," *Forum* 12, no. 2 (2014): 329–342.

58. This quote from the *Denver Post*, February 10, 1985, was reproduced on a political campaign brochure for Martha Ezzard for the US Senate race, Starsmore Center for Local History, Colorado Springs Pioneers Museum, Republican Party of Colorado Collection.

59. J. Adrian Stanley, "Foxes and Henhouses," *Colorado Springs Independent*, September 5–11, 2012, accessed September 17, 2012, www.csindy.com; "City Election Cash," *Colorado Springs Independent*, February 22–28, 2017, 17.

60. Barry Noreen, "Conservative Beliefs Only as Deep as a Dry Well," *Colorado Springs Gazette*, October 7, 2002, A1.

61. "Council Turns Socialistic," *Colorado Springs Gazette*, April 2, 1924, 4.

62. William Graf, *Wilderness Preservation and the Sagebrush Rebellions* (Savage, MD: Rowman and Littlefield, 1990).

63. Hal Rothman, *Devil's Bargains: Tourism in the Twentieth-Century American West* (Lawrence: University Press of Kansas, 1998).

64. William R. Harbour, *The Foundations of Conservative Thought: An Anglo-American Tradition in Perspective* (South Bend, IN: University of Notre Dame, 1982).

65. Harbour, *The Foundations of Conservative Thought.*

66. Michael W. Miles, *The Odyssey of the American Right* (New York: Oxford University Press, 1980).

67. Brian Doherty, *Radicals for Capitalism: A Freewheeling History of the Modern American Libertarian Movement* (New York: Public Affairs, 2007).

68. "You Can Control Yourself," *Colorado Springs Gazette Telegraph*, February 26, 1963, 6, editorial written by Robert LeFevre but unsigned.

69. Miles, *Odyssey of the American Right.*

70. Gordon G. Guass, "Limited Government' Pledged by Gov. Love at His Inaugural," *Colorado Springs Gazette Telegraph*, January 8, 1963, 1.

71. Donald L. Walker Jr., "John A. Love: The Story of Colorado's Thirty-Sixth Governor," *Historical Studies Journal* 17 (2000): 1–59.

72. Lisa McGirr, *Suburban Warriors: The Origins of the New American Right* (Princeton, NJ: Princeton University Press, 2001), 35.

73. Miles, *Odyssey of the American Right*, 224.

74. Nicole Hemmer, *Messengers of the Right: Conservative Media and the Transformation of American Politics* (Philadelphia: University of Pennsylvania Press, 2016).

75. Miles, *Odyssey of the American Right.*

76. Hemmer, *Messengers of the Right*, xiii.

77. Hemmer, *Messengers of the Right*, 124.

78. Doherty, *Radicals for Capitalism.*

79. R. C. Hoiles, "Education Built on Quicksand," *Colorado Springs Gazette Telegraph*, October 4, 1946, 4; R. C. Hoiles, "The Grassroots of Our Troubles," *Sunday Gazette Telegraph*, October 20, 1946, 4b.

80. "Time Blasts Hoiles," *Free Press*, April 16, 1963, 1.

81. "The Same Old Line," *Free Press*, April 5, 1963, 4.

82. R. C. Hoiles, "The Errors in Our Educational System," *Colorado Springs Gazette Telegraph*, November 4, 1946, 4; R. C. Hoiles, "Common Ground" column, *Colorado Springs Gazette Telegraph*, December 9, 1946, 4.

83. R. C. Hoiles, "Have We Strength of Character?" *Colorado Springs Gazette Telegraph*, October 1, 1946, 4; *Free Press*, "Time Blasts Hoiles," 1. See also William J. Schultz, "Freedom for Whom? Robert LeFevre, the Freedom School, and the Birth of Modern Libertarianism," paper presented at the Bigwigs and Benefactors of the Pikes Peak Region: The Freedom School and Mafia on the Front Range conference, Colorado Springs, Pikes Peak Library District, published February 19, 2015, https://www.youtube.com/watch?v=3SbRFCMfs4Y; and Noel Black and Jake Brownell, *Wish*

We Were Here Episode 16: Liberty's Pitchman—Robert LeFevre and The Freedom School, KRCC Radio Journalism production, June 17, 2016, Colorado Springs, https://www.cpr.org/podcast-episode/wish-we-were-here-episode-16-libertys-pitchman-robert-lefevre-the-freedom-school/.

84. R. C. Hoiles, "Personal Liberty Again Ignored," *Colorado Springs Gazette Telegraph*, October 3, 1946, 4; *Sunday Gazette Telegraph*, October 6, 1946, 5a; R. C. Hoiles, "Brother's Keeper," *Colorado Springs Gazette Telegraph*, November 7, 1946, 4.

85. "Striking Printers to Publish Paper," *Sunday Gazette Telegraph*, February 2, 1947, 1; "A New Paper Is Born," *Free Press*, February 3, 1947, 2.

86. *Free Press*, "Time Blasts Hoiles," 3.

87. R. C. Hoiles, "Religion Should Not Be Haven of Demagogs," *Colorado Springs Gazette Telegraph*, October 29, 1946, 4.

88. R. C. Hoiles, "Republicans Compromise Again," *Colorado Springs Gazette Telegraph*, July 2, 1948, 4.

89. R. C. Hoiles, "On Teaching the Ten Commandments," *Colorado Springs Gazette Telegraph*, November 1, 1946, 4.

90. Hoiles, "Republicans Compromise Again."

91. Ira E. Hoagland, "If This Be Freedom," *Free Press*, March 6, 1963, 4.

92. Doherty, *Radicals for Capitalism*, 312.

93. Black and Brownell, *Wish We Were Here Episode 16*.

94. Doherty, *Radicals for Capitalism*, 312. An investigation of the Girl Scouts may sound absurd but not so for the troop leaders called in for hearings in front of the House Un-American Activities Committee. One leader lost her job, and the Girl Scouts made changes to their guide book.

95. "Planner's Paradise," *Colorado Springs Gazette Telegraph*, November 12, 1954, 4.

96. "The Power to Enslave," *Colorado Springs Gazette Telegraph*, February 21, 1963, 20; "Who Owns This Country?" *Colorado Springs Gazette Telegraph*, November 30, 1954, 8.

97. "A Petition to the U.S. Senate," *Sunday Gazette Telegraph*, November 21, 1954, C2.

98. Black and Brownell, *Wish We Were Here Episode 16*.

99. "'Freedom' School by Any Other Name," *Free Press*, March 24, 1963, 4.

100. "Businessmen Hear Freedom School Expansion Proposal," *Colorado Springs Gazette Telegraph*, February 20, 1963, 1.

101. *Free Press*, "Time Blasts Hoiles," 1.

102. "C of C Director Blasts Group for Bid to Rampart College," *Free Press*, March 19, 1963, 1.

103. Free Press, "The Same Old Line," 4; "Would You Support Pornography?" *Free Press*, March 25, 1963, 4. Note that the *Free Press* became the *Colorado Springs Sun* in 1970, then was bought by the *Gazette* in 1986 and shut down.

104. "AAUW Raps Proposed 'Rampart College,'" *Free Press*, March 21, 1963, 1; Sheldon Singer, "A Major Mishap," *Free Press*, March 24, 1963, 1.

105. C. M. Holloway, "Chilling Similarity," *Free Press*, March 24, 1963, 5; Ernestine Parsons, "To the Editor," *Free Press*, April 3, 1963, 4.

106. "Ex-Mayor Criticizes Effect of Rampart College Here," *Free Press*, April 17, 1963, 1.

107. For an in-depth, well-documented, detailed analysis of this agenda, see Nancy MacLean, *Democracy in Chains: The Deep History of the Radical Right's Stealth Plan for America* (New York: Viking, 2017).

108. Doherty, *Radicals for Capitalism*, 319.

109. "Re-elect Governor John A. Love," political campaign brochure, 1966. Starsmore Center for Local History, Colorado Springs Pioneers Museum, Republican Party of Colorado Collection.

110. All examples in this paragraph are campaign brochures accessed at the Starsmore Center for Local History, Colorado Springs Pioneers Museum, Republican Party of Colorado Collection.

111. Ed Quillen, "Perhaps It's Time to Pretend That General Palmer Never Existed," *Denver Post*, May 11, 1999, 7B.

112. John Harner, "Place Identity and Copper Mining in Sonora, Mexico," *Annals of the Association of American Geographers* 91, no. 4 (2001): 647–667; Edward Soja, *Postmodern Geographies: The Reassertion of Space in Critical Social Theory* (London: Verso, 1989).

113. Justin G. Wilford, *Sacred Subdivisions: The Postsuburban Transformation of American Evangelicalism* (New York: New York University Press, 2012), 12.

114. McGirr, *Suburban Warriors*, 29.

115. McGirr, *Suburban Warriors*, 29.

116. McGirr, *Suburban Warriors*, 29.

117. McGirr, *Suburban Warriors*, 151.

118. All examples in this paragraph are campaign brochures accessed at the Starsmore Center for Local History, Colorado Springs Pioneers Museum, Republican Party of Colorado Collection.

119. A sample of state-to-state migration data as recorded by the Internal Revenue Service for 2000–2001, 2004–2005, and 2009–2010 consistently show California as the number one sending state for migrants to Colorado.

120. John Hazlehurst, "A New Kind of Power Struggle," *Colorado Springs Independent*, August 26–September 1, 2015, 9.

121. Ryan Maye Handy, "Homes Ride Slow Slide," *Denver Post*, April 24, 2016, B1; Billie Stanton Anleu and Maria St. Louis-Sanchez, "A Flawed System," *Colorado Springs Gazette*, April 29, 2016, 1.

122. Billie Stanton Anleu, "Pueblo Seeks to Join Lawsuit," *Denver Post*, February 9, 2017, 5a (originally published in the *Colorado Springs Gazette*); Pam Zubeck, "Burden of Proof," *Colorado Springs Independent*, August 23–29, 2017, 12.

123. John Hazlehurst, "Return of the Taxophobe," *Colorado Springs Independent*, August 14–20, 2013, 8; Pam Zubeck, "The Puppeteers," *Colorado Springs Independent*, November 16–22, 2016, 18–23.

124. Wayne Heilman, "Springing from the Springs," *Denver Post*, December 29, 2014, 2a; "Jobless Rate in Springs Falls—Not in a Good Way," *Denver Post*, January 3, 2015, 13a. Both of these articles were originally published in the *Colorado Springs Gazette*.

125. Hazlehurst, "Return of the Taxophobe"; Ray Flack, "Tempers Flare in Courtroom as Bruce Battles Charges," *Colorado Springs Gazette Telegraph*, August 20, 1993, B-4.

126. Colorado Property Tax Calculator, accessed August 20, 2018, smartasset.com/taxes.

127. John Hazlehurst, "A New Kind of Power Struggle," *Colorado Springs Independent*, August 26–September 1, 2015, 9; "Annual Report to the Public," 2017, Colorado Springs School District 11, accessed September 2, 2018, www.d11.org.

128. Joshua Dunn, "Who Governs in God's City?" *Society* 49, no. 1 (2012): 25.

129. "Freedom Fighters Flock to Our City," *Colorado Springs Gazette*, April 25, 2012, A16.

130. Harbour, *The Foundations of Conservative Thought*.

131. Hemmer, *Messengers of the Right*.

132. Meg Wingerter, "Faculty and Regent Toss Barbs over Mark Kennedy," *Denver Post*, April 30, 2019, 1A. In the CU system, regents are elected officials who have the highest authority to set policy and guide the university.

133. Raquel Rutledge, "Vandals Unable to Quiet Peace Vigil," *Colorado Springs Gazette*, October 21, 2002, Metro-1.

134. Walker Jr., "John A. Love," 37.

135. Zubeck, "The Puppeteers," 20.

136. Conrad Swanson, "Former Colorado Springs City Manager Calls for Shutting Coal-Fired Martin Drake Power Plant," *Colorado Springs Gazette*, June 22, 2018, 1; Judith Kohler, "Study: More Renewable Energy Can Save $600M," *Denver Post*, August 24, 2018, 14A; Aldo Svaldi, "Coal's Status as Dominant Source of Power Fading," *Denver Post*, August 22, 2018, 9A.

137. Matthew Schniper, "Tiny House Jamboree Outgrows the Springs," *Colorado Springs Independent*, May 17–23, 2017, 15; newsletters from SunShare to investors.

CHAPTER 9: GOD

1. Marc Cooper, "God and Man in Colorado Springs," *Nation*, January 2, 1995, 10.

2. Jeff Sharlet, "Soldiers of Christ: Inside America's Most Powerful Megachurch," *Harper's Magazine*, May 2005, 42.

3. "Letters between Thomas Jefferson and the Danbury Baptists (1802)," Bill of Rights Institute, https://billofrightsinstitute.org/founding-documents/primary-source-documents/danbury baptists/.

4. Randall Balmer, *Evangelicalism in America* (Waco, TX: Baylor University Press, 2016).

5. Balmer, *Evangelicalism in America*.

6. Frances Fitzgerald, *The Evangelicals: The Struggle to Shape America* (New York: Simon and Schuster, 2017).

7. Balmer, *Evangelicalism in America*.

8. Fitzgerald, *The Evangelicals*.

9. John Fea, *Believe Me: The Evangelical Road to Donald Trump* (Grand Rapids, MI: William B. Eerdmans Publishing, 2018).

10. Ann Burlein, *Lift High the Cross: Where White Supremacy and the Christian Right Converge* (Durham, NC: Duke University Press, 2002).

11. William Martin, *With God on Our Side: The Rise of the Religious Right in America* (New York: Broadway Books, 1996).

12. Martin, *With God on Our Side*.

13. Fitzgerald, *The Evangelicals*, 160.

14. Fitzgerald, *The Evangelicals*, 180.

15. Martin, *With God on Our Side*, 33.

16. Paul Asay, "God's Business," *Colorado Springs Gazette*, October 23, 2005, 1.

17. Young Life, accessed February 3, 2019, https://www.younglife.org/About/Pages/default.aspx.

18. The Navigators, "The Glen Eyrie Story," promotional brochure, 1973, Colorado College Tutt Library, Special Collections, ephemera, tourist brochures.

19. Donnie Smith, "Navigating from Los Angeles to Colorado Springs," *Colorado Springs Sun*, March 25, 1971, 7.

20. The Navigators, "The Glen Eyrie Story," promotional booklet, 1960, 7, Starsmore Center for Local History, Colorado Springs Pioneers Museum, Religious institutions: Navigators collection.

21. The Navigators, "The Navigators," promotional booklet, 1962, Starsmore Center for Local History, Colorado Springs Pioneers Museum, Religious institutions: Navigators collection.

22. The Navigators, "Valley of the Eagle's Nest," promotional booklet, 1962, Colorado College Tutt Library, Special Collections, ephemera, tourist brochures.

23. The Navigators, "Navigators."

24. The Navigators, "Navigators."

25. "Navigator's Co-founder, Trotman, Dies at 90," *Colorado Springs Gazette*, October 29, 2004, Metro-4.

26. Larry Nelson, "Glen Eyrie, Home of the Navigators," *Free Press*, March 8, 1970; Navigators, "Glen Eyrie Conference Center," promotional brochure, n.d., Starsmore Center for Local History, Colorado Springs Pioneers Museum, Religious institutions: Navigators collection.

27. Steve Rabey, "Springs Attracts Global Groups," *Colorado Springs Gazette Telegraph*, November 24, 1991, D-1.

28. Compassion International: accessed February 3, 2019, https://www.compassion.com/about /about-us.htm.

29. John Fetler, "Religious Groups Call Colorado Springs Home," *Colorado Springs Gazette Telegraph*, February 22, 1981, 8-E.

30. Martin, *With God on Our Side*.

31. John Fetler, "Colorado Springs: Cross Section of American Religion," *Colorado Springs Gazette Telegraph*, February 24, 1980, 10-G.

32. Fitzgerald, *The Evangelicals*.

33. Fitzgerald, *The Evangelicals*, 283.

34. Balmer, *Evangelicalism in America*.

35. Martin, *With God on Our Side*.

36. Fitzgerald, *The Evangelicals*, 291.

37. Martin, *With God on Our Side*, 206.

38. Fitzgerald, *The Evangelicals*, 416.

39. Martin Durham, *The Christian Right, the Far Right and the Boundaries of American Conservatism* (Manchester, UK: Manchester University Press, 2000), 117.

40. Fitzgerald, *The Evangelicals*, 368.

41. Fitzgerald, *The Evangelicals*, 383.

42. Fitzgerald, *The Evangelicals*, 385.

43. Martin, *With God on Our Side*.

44. Durham, *The Christian Right*, 170.

45. Fitzgerald, *The Evangelicals*, 422.

46. Fea, *Believe Me*.

47. Balmer, *Evangelicalism in America*.

48. Durham, *The Christian Right*.

49. Martin, *With God on Our Side*, 242.

50. Burlein, *Lift High the Cross*.

51. Steve Rabey, "Evangelical Groups Reach Out to the World from Springs Home," *Colorado Springs Gazette Telegraph*, November 24, 1991, A-1.

52. Dirk Johnson, "I Don't Hate Homosexuals," *New York Times*, February 14, 1993, 10.

53. Michael Booth, "Experts Assess the Issues in Amendment 2 Court Fight," *Denver Post*, February 12, 1992, 1.

54. Chet Harden, "Hate and Love: The Twisted Road from Amendment 2 to 'I do,'" *Colorado Springs Independent*, May 1–7, 2013, 18.

55. Michael Booth, "Coalition Files Suit against Amendment 2," *Denver Post*, November 13, 1992, 1.

56. Howard Pankratz, "Court Blocks Amendment 2," *Denver Post*, July 20, 1993, 1.

57. Bruce Finley, "Amendment 2 Sparks Boycott of Dealership," *Denver Post*, November 7, 1992, B-1.

58. Jeffrey Leib, "Unionists Cancel Convention over Amendment 2," *Denver Post*, November 19, 1992, 1.

59. D'Arcy Fallon, "Protestors Decry City of Hate," *Colorado Springs Gazette Telegraph*, January 17, 1993, News-1.

60. Angela Dire, "Boycott as Controversial as Amendment," *Colorado Springs Gazette Telegraph*, December 19, 1993, B-1.

61. Jeffrey Leib, "Springs Hotel Cuts 60 Jobs," *Denver Post*, March 6, 1993, C-1.

62. Joanna Schmidt, "Diversity in the Workplace," *Colorado Springs Gazette Telegraph*, February 21, 1993, E-1.

63. Jane Grandolfo, "Businesses in Springs Fight Fallout," *Colorado Springs Gazette Telegraph*, February 14, 1993, A-1.

64. Luis Aguilar, "Group Fights Myths about Gays," *Colorado Springs Gazette Telegraph*, January 31, 1993, News-1.

65. D'Arcy Fallon, "Citizens Project Founders Tap Public Interest," *Colorado Springs Gazette Telegraph*, February 14, 1993, News-1.

66. Kirk Woundy, "Start the Presses," *Colorado Springs Independent*, December 10–16, 2014, 21.

67. Joanne Ostrow, "Focus on Colorado Springs," *Denver Post*, November 18, 1993, E-1.

68. Cate Terwilliger, "Galvanized Gays," *Colorado Springs Independent*, May 22–28, 1996, 10.

69. Fallon, "Protestors Decry City of Hate."

70. Angela Dire, "This Colorado Cannot Do," *Colorado Springs Gazette Telegraph*, May 21, 1996, A-1.

71. Linda Greenhouse, "Gay Rights' Laws Can't be Banned, High Court Rules," *New York Times*, May 21, 1996, 1.

72. Greenhouse, "Gay Rights' Laws Can't be Banned."

73. While at a conference for the National Trust for Historic Preservation in Omaha in May 2002, colleague Judith Rice-Jones was speaking with a National Park historian from Denver who made the comment about Colorado Springs, "my liberal gay friends call it Jesus Springs."

74. Dirk Johnson, "Rise in Christian Right Divides a City," *New York Times*, February 14, 1993, 10; Burlein, *Lift High the Cross*; Cooper, "God and Man in Colorado Springs."

75. Alan Gottlieb and Virginia Culver, "A House Divided? Influx of Religious Groups Rattles Springs," *Denver Post*, November 15, 1992, C-1.

76. Burlein, *Lift High the Cross*, 175; Rabey, "Evangelical Groups Reach Out"; Eric Gorski, "Ministry's Impact Matter of Opinion," *Colorado Springs Gazette*, July 20, 2002, A-1.

77. Joanna Schmidt, "Ministry Plans Headquarters," *Colorado Springs Gazette Telegraph*, March 30, 1993, D-1.

78. Burlein, *Lift High the Cross*, 175.

79. Gottlieb and Culver, "A House Divided?," C-7.

80. Johnson, "Rise in Christian Right Divides a City."

81. Rabey, "Springs Attracts Global Groups."

82. Schmidt, "Ministry Plans Headquarters."

83. Schmidt, "Ministry Plans Headquarters."

84. Wayne Heilman, "Youth Ministry Moves Office to Springs," *Colorado Springs Gazette Telegraph*, July 22, 1992.

85. Eric Gorski, "Springs Hosting Major Gathering of Evangelical Christian Leaders," *Colorado Springs Gazette*, February 14, 1999, News-1.

86. Rabey, "Evangelical Groups Reach Out."

87. Joshua Dunn, "The Paradoxes of Politics in Colorado Springs," *Forum* 12, no. 2 (2014): 329–342.

88. Cooper, "God and Man in Colorado Springs," 9.

89. Dunn, "Paradoxes."

90. Johnson, "Rise in Christian Right Divides a City."

91. Fallon, "Citizens Project."

92. Thomas Heath, "In Colorado Springs, Religious Groups Have the Right of Way," *Washington Post*, December 25, 1994, A3; Cooper, "God and Man in Colorado Springs."

93. Virginia Culver, "Religious Right: An Education Damper," *Denver Post*, November 19, 1992, 5B.

94. Gottlieb and Culver, "A House Divided?," C-7.

95. Paul Asay, "Alliance Provides More Liberal Voice," *Colorado Springs Gazette*, September 25, 2004, 1.

96. Gottlieb and Culver, "A House Divided?," C-7.

97. Johnson, "Rise in Christian Right Divides a City," 10.

98. Gottlieb and Culver, "A House Divided?," C-1.

99. Citizen's Project, *Freedom Watch*, May 1997, 3.

100. Gorski, "Ministry's Impact."

101. Joanna Schmidt, "Focus on the Family Ready to Begin Springs Move," *Colorado Springs Gazette Telegraph*, April 19, 1991, C-7.

102. Focus on the Family, accessed March 18, 2019, https://www.focusonthefamily.com/about/foundational-values#mission.
103. Durham, *The Christian Right.*
104. Burlein, *Lift High the Cross*, 123.
105. Martin, *With God on Our Side*, 342.
106. Gorski, "Ministry's Impact."
107. Rabey, "Evangelical Groups Reach Out."
108. Pam Zubeck, "Air Force Academy Finds Faith Bias Roots Deep," *Colorado Springs Gazette*, November 20, 2004, 1.
109. Burlein, *Lift High the Cross*, 179.
110. Jane Grandolfo, "Focus Outgrows New Campus," *Colorado Springs Gazette Telegraph*, July 24, 1993; Andy Friedberg, "Breaking New Ground at Focus," *Colorado Springs Gazette*, October 9, 1998, A-1.
111. "Focus on the Family," *Colorado Springs Gazette*, September 27, 2002, Go!-3.
112. Cooper, "God and Man in Colorado Springs," 11.
113. Martin, *With God on Our Side.*
114. Fitzgerald, *The Evangelicals.*
115. Fitzgerald, *The Evangelicals.*
116. Jeff Thomas, "GOP Hopefuls Know Dobson's Clout," *Colorado Springs Gazette Telegraph*, July 9, 1995, A-1.
117. Michele Ames, "Dobson's Threat Leaves Much Up in the Air," *Colorado Springs Gazette*, February 14, 1998, A-1.
118. "Dobson Threatens to Defect from the GOP with Evangelical Voters," *Colorado Springs Gazette*, February 12, 1998, A-10, original author and publication in the *New York Times.*
119. "Focus on the Family: Through the Years," *Colorado Springs Gazette*, July 20, 2002, A-4.
120. Sharlet, "Soldiers of Christ," 41.
121. Paul Asay, "Book Cites Area Diversity on Religion," *Colorado Springs Gazette*, June 3, 2004; Erin Emery, "Evangelicals Filling Springs Hotel Rooms," *Denver Post*, May 24, 2000, 1A.
122. "Top 100 Colorado Nonprofits," *Rocky Mountain News*, June 9, 2007, 5.
123. Asay, "God's Business."
124. John Dicker, "Guerrillas for God," *Colorado Springs Independent*, April 3–9, 2003, 14.
125. Asay, "God's Business," 1.
126. David Kelly, "In Colorado, a Wellspring of Conservative Christianity," *Los Angeles Times*, July 6, 2004, E-1.
127. Sharlet, "Soldiers of Christ"
128. Raymond McCaffrey, "Storefront Salvation," *Colorado Springs Gazette*, April 10, 1999, Life-1.
129. Cooper, "God and Man in Colorado Springs."
130. Donald Meinig, "Symbolic Landscapes," in *The Interpretation of Ordinary Landscapes*, ed. D.W. Meinig (New York: Oxford University Press, 1979); John A. Jakle and Keith A. Sculle, *The Gas Station in America* (Baltimore: Johns Hopkins University Press, 1994).
131. Lisa McGirr, *Suburban Warriors: The Origins of the New American Right* (Princeton, NJ: Princeton University Press, 2001).
132. Justin G Wilford, *Sacred Subdivisions: The Postsuburban Transformation of American Evangelicalism* (New York: NYU Press, 2012), 71.
133. Skye Jethani, *Immeasurable: Reflections on the Soul of Ministry in the Age of Church, Inc.* (Chicago: Moody Publisher, 2017).
134. Sharlet, "Soldiers of Christ," 47.
135. Kelly, "In Colorado, a Wellspring of Conservative Christianity," E-6.
136. Ostrow, "Focus on Colorado Springs."

137. "Prayer Center Opens Doors for Grand Tour," *Colorado Springs Gazette*, September 18, 1998, News-1; Eric Gorski, "Lord, Hear Our Prayer," *Colorado Springs Gazette*, January 23, 1999, Life-1; Sharlet, "Soldiers of Christ," Dicker, "Guerrillas for God."

138. Sharlet, "Soldiers of Christ," 43.

139. Eric Gorski, "Megachurches Bring Worshipers Back into the Fold," *Colorado Springs Gazette*, April 4, 1999, News-1.

140. Sharlet, "Soldiers of Christ," 49.

141. Deedee Correll, "Accuser Wanted News Out before Election," *Colorado Springs Gazette*, November 3, 2006, A-7.

142. Paul Asay and Deedee Correll, "Shock. Disbelief. Denial," *Colorado Springs Gazette*, November 3, 2006, 1.

143. R. Scott Rappold, "Pastor's Influence Reaches around Globe," *Colorado Springs Gazette*, November 3, 2006, A-7.

144. Hartford Institute for Religion Research, hirr.hartsem.edu/megachurch/database.html; 2011 data were reported in Wilford, Sacred Subdivisions, appendix A, 169.

145. Rich Laden, "Business, Civic Leaders Fret about City's Image," *Colorado Springs Gazette*, November 4, 2006, A-1.

146. Andrew Wineke, "All Eyes on the Springs Thanks to Global News," *Colorado Springs Gazette*, November 4, 2006, A-11.

147. Laden, "Business, Civic Leaders Fret," A-12.

148. Joshua Dunn, "Who Governs in God's City?" *Society* 49, no. 1 (2012): 24–32.

149. Diane Carman, "Rehab for Springs' Anti-gay Image Is a Slow Dance," *Denver Post*, April 26, 2007, 5B.

150. Cate Terwilliger, "Finances Get Blurry for Focus on Family," *Denver Post*, February 23, 2003, B-1.

151. Fitzgerald, *The Evangelicals*.

152. "Religious Right Is Losing Faith in Political Work," *Colorado Springs Gazette*, March 9, 1999, repr. from article that first appeared in the *New York Times*.

153. Fitzgerald, *The Evangelicals*.

154. Fitzgerald, *The Evangelicals*, 466.

155. Jethani, *Immeasurable*.

156. Elizabeth Dias, "'God Is Going to Have to Forgive Me': Young Evangelicals Speak Out," *New York Times*, November 1, 2018, https://www.nytimes.com/2018/11/01/us/young-evangelicals-politics-midterms.html.

157. Dias, "'God Is Going to Have to Forgive Me.'"

158. Noel Black and Jake Brownell, *Wish We Were Here*, episode 10: "After the Evangelical Vatican," KRCC Radio Journalism production, December 4, 2015, Colorado Springs, http://www.krcc.org/post/wish-we-were-here-episode-10-after-evangelical-vatican.

159. See https://switchbackroasters.com/pages/our-story.

160. Interview with Brandon DelGrosso, owner, Switchback Roaster and Café, Colorado Springs, May 8, 2019.

161. Interview with Tyler Hill, co-owner, Loyal Coffee, Colorado Springs, June 3, 2019.

162. Eric Gorski, "Dallas Vies with Springs as Leading Evangelical City," *Colorado Springs Gazette*, May 11, 2002, A-1.

163. Terwilliger, "Finances Get Blurry."

164. Paul Asay, "Figures of Faith," *Colorado Springs Gazette*, January 8, 2005, Life-1.

165. Association of Statisticians of American Religious Bodies, 2010 U.S. Religion Census: Religious Congregations and Membership Study, distributed by the *Association of Religion Data Archives*: accessed March 3, 2019, https://www.thearda.com/Archive/Files/Descriptions/RCMSCY10.asp.

166. Dunn, "Paradoxes"; Dunn, "Who Governs in God's City?"

167. Nate Stein, "It's Happening—Again," *Colorado Springs Independent*, February 24–March 1, 2016, 16.

168. Mark McVay, "New Lawmaker Has His Demons," *Denver Post*, November 12, 2014, 25-A.

169. Pam Zubeck, "This Could Leave a Mark," *Colorado Springs Independent*, September 3–9, 2014, 12.

170. Zubeck, "This Could Leave a Mark."

171. John Hazlehurst, "Living in These Christian Times," *Colorado Springs Independent*, August 21–27, 2003, 8.

172. The Civilians, *This Beautiful City*, 2008; soundtrack for the play downloaded January 3, 2010, www.krcc.org.

CHAPTER 10: PLACE

1. Charles Mulford Robinson, "1905 Report," reprinted in *A City Beautiful Dream: The 1912 Vision for Colorado Springs* (Colorado Springs: Pikes Peak Library District, 2012 [1905]), 16.

2. Ian Convery, Gerard Corsane, and Peter Davis, "Making Sense of Place," in *Making Sense of Place: Multidisciplinary Perspectives*, ed. Ian Convery, Gerard Corsane, and Peter Davis (Woodbridge, UK: Boydell Press, 2012), 1–8.

3. Edward Soja, *Postmodern Geographies: The Reassertion of Space in Critical Social Theory* (London: Verso, 1989).

4. Ian Thompson, "Gardens, Parks, and Sense of Place," in Ian Convery et al., *Making Sense of Place*, 159–167.

5. John Brinckerhoff Jackson, *A Sense of Place, A Sense of Time* (New Haven, CT: Yale University Press, 1994).

6. Jackson, *A Sense of Place*, 160.

7. Doreen Massey, *For Space* (London: Sage, 2005), 141.

8. Eric Schlosser, *Fast Food Nation: The Dark Side of the All-American Meal* (Boston: Houghton Mifflin, 2001).

9. Ed Quillen, "Perhaps It's Time to Pretend That General Palmer Never Existed," *Denver Post*, May 11, 1999, 7B.

10. Accessed June 25, 2019, coloradospringschamberedc.com; "Colorado Springs, Fort Collins Lead State in Growth," *Denver Post*, February 8, 2019, 12A; "Looking for a Job? Colorado Springs Is the Place to Be," *Denver Post*, January 4, 2019, 9A.

11. State of Downtown Colorado Springs 2019 (Colorado Springs: Downtown Partnership, 2019); see https://downtowncs.com/do-business/reports/.

12. Jeff Speck, *Walkable City: How Downtown Can Save America, One Step at a Time* (New York: Northpoint Press, 2012), 259.

13. Speck, *Walkable City*.

14. Charles Montgomery, *Happy City: Transforming Our Lives through Urban Design* (New York: Farrar, Straus and Giroux, 2013).

15. Speck, *Walkable City*, 105.

16. This comment was made by the emcee from the *Gazette* as he introduced panelists for a public forum on bike lanes held February 25, 2019, at the Pikes Peak Center Studio Bee in Colorado Springs.

17. David Ramsey, "VFW Members Want to Dance Away from Colorado Springs Bike Lanes," *Colorado Springs Gazette*, February 23, 2019, https://gazette.com/news/vfw-members-want-to-dance-away-from-colorado-springs-bike/article_13ed0e6c-3776-11e9-bf02-6b18cd0a9633.html.

18. Robinson, "1905 Report," 117.

19. Peter Calthorpe, *Urbanism in the Age of Climate Change* (Washington, DC: Island Press, 2011).

20. Chris Nicholl, "Dr. Caroline Spencer and Colorado Springs' Radicals for Reform," in *Extraordinary Women of the Rocky Mountain West*, ed. Tim Blevins, Dennis Daily, Chris Nicholl, Calvin P. Otto, and Katherine Scott Sturdevant (Colorado Springs: Pikes Peak Library District, 2010), 254.

21. Nicholl, "Dr. Caroline Spencer and Colorado Springs' Radicals for Reform," 278.

22. Jakob Rodgers, "Colorado Springs a Sea of Prosperity—Except for Southeast," *Colorado Springs Gazette*, November 26, 2017, quote is from the digital edition, http://gazette.com; see also Pam Zubeck, "Forging Ahead," *Colorado Springs Independent*, August 1–7, 2018. Note that not all feel safe and accepted, however, as tensions reached high levels when an African American teenager, De'Von Bailey, was shot in the back and killed by police in August 2019.

23. Zubeck, "Forging Ahead," 15.

24. UCCS Economic Forum, *2016/2017 Quality of Life Indicators* (Colorado Springs: Pikes Peak United Way, 2018).

25. UCCS Economic Forum, *2016/2017 Quality of Life Indicators.*

26. Lance Benzel and Kaitlin Durbin, "Some Neighborhoods Safe, Secure; Others Have Residents on Edge," *Colorado Springs Gazette*, November 28, 2017, digital edition, accessed December 11, 2017, http://gazette.com.

27. Rich Laden, "Boosters Cite Potential, but Large Employers Look Elsewhere," *Colorado Springs Gazette*, November 29, 2017, digital edition, accessed December 11, 2017, http://gazette.com.

28. Rodgers, "Colorado Springs a Sea of Prosperity."

29. Laden, "Boosters Cite Potential."

30. Joshua Dunn, "The Paradoxes of Politics in Colorado Springs," *Forum* 12, no. 2 (2014): 329–342, quote is from 333.

31. "Time to De-Bruce," *Colorado Springs Independent*, May 8–14, 2019, 5.

32. Lyn Peterson, "Giving in Colorado Springs Then and Now" (MA thesis, University of Colorado Colorado Springs, 1996).

33. Donna Strom, "Ignoring the People's Voice," *Colorado Springs Independent*, June 12–18, 2019, 6.

34. Pam Zubeck, "Power of One," *Colorado Springs Independent*, April 27–May 3, 2016, 16.

35. The pioneer who first used business names to map vernacular culture regions was geographer Wilbur Zelinsky. See his classic Wilbur Zelinsky, "North America's Vernacular Regions," *Annals of the Association of American Geographers* 70, no. 1 (1980): 1–16. These data were accessed July 1, 2019, whitepages.com. Themes searched were "mountain," "peak," "alpine," "summit," "rampart," "Front Range," "sierra," "high country," and "high altitude." The total number of businesses listed at coloradospring.zoomprospector.com is 22,836.

36. Kevin S. Blake, "Peaks of Identity in Colorado's San Juan Mountains," *Journal of Cultural Geography* 18, no. 2 (1999): 29–55.

37. Kevin S. Blake, "Colorado Fourteeners and the Nature of Place Identity," *Geographical Review* 92, no. 2 (2002): 155–179.

Index